JESUS AND BRIAN

JESUS AND BRIAN

Exploring the Historical Jesus and his Times via *Monty Python's Life of Brian*

Edited by
Joan E. Taylor

Bloomsbury T&T Clark
An imprint of Bloomsbury Publishing Plc

B L O O M S B U R Y
LONDON · OXFORD · NEW YORK · NEW DELHI · SYDNEY

Bloomsbury T&T Clark

An imprint of Bloomsbury Publishing Plc

Imprint previously known as T&T Clark

50 Bedford Square	1385 Broadway
London	New York
WC1B 3DP	NY 10018
UK	USA

www.bloomsbury.com

BLOOMSBURY, T&T CLARK and the Diana logo are trademarks of Bloomsbury Publishing Plc

First published 2015
Reprinted by Bloomsbury Academic 2015, 2016

British Library Cataloguing-in-Publication Data
A catalogue record for this book is available from the British Library.

ISBN:	HB:	978-0-56765-832-6
	PB:	978-0-56765-831-9
	ePDF:	978-0-56765-830-2
	ePub:	978-0-56765-829-6

Library of Congress Cataloging-in-Publication Data
Jesus and Brian : exploring the historical Jesus and his times via
Monty Python's Life of Brian / edited by Joan E. Taylor.
pages cm
" ... a conference held by the Department of Theology and Religious Studies, King's College London, in June 2014, with sponsorship from the School of Arts and Humanities, and support too from T&T Clark Bloomsbury. This conference was titled, Jesus and Brian or: What have the Pythons done for us?"—Introduction.
ISBN 978-0-567-65832-6 (hardback) — ISBN 978-0-567-65831-9 (paperback)
1. Life of Brian (Motion picture)   2. Jesus Christ—Historicity.
I. Taylor, Joan E., 1937– editor.
PN1997.L575J47 2015
791.43'72--dc23
2015018731

Typeset by RefineCatch Limited, Bungay, Suffolk
Printed and bound in Great Britain

CONTENTS

List of Illustrations   vii
List of Contributors   ix
Abbreviations   xiii
Preface   xv
Foreword   xvii
Introduction   xxi

Part I
THE FILM IN ITS CINEMATIC CONTEXT, ITS
RECEPTION AND ITS CHALLENGES

1. *MONTY PYTHON'S LIFE OF BRIAN* AND THE JESUS FILM
   William R. Telford   3

2. THE CHURCH OF ENGLAND'S *LIFE OF PYTHON* – OR
   'WHAT THE BISHOP SAW'
   Richard A. Burridge   19

3. WHEN BRIAN MET MOSES: *LIFE OF BRIAN* (1979), *WHOLLY
   MOSES* (1980) AND THE 'FAILURE' OF BIBLICAL PARODY
   David Shepherd   43

4. 'BLASPHEMY!' ON FREE SPEECH THEN AND NOW
   David Tollerton   55

5. THE MEANING OF MONTY PYTHON'S JESUS
   James G. Crossley   69

6. THE GOSPEL OF BRIAN
   Philip R. Davies   83

Part II
HISTORY AND INTERPRETATION VIA *MONTY
PYTHON'S LIFE OF BRIAN*

7. THE HISTORICAL BRIAN: RECEPTION EXEGESIS IN PRACTICE
   Joan E. Taylor   93

8. 'ROMANI ITE DOMUM' – EXPRESSIONS OF IDENTITY AND
    RESISTANCE IN JUDAEA
    Guy D. Stiebel   107

9. 'YOU'LL PROBABLY GET AWAY WITH CRUCIFIXION':
    LAUGHING AT THE CROSS IN BRIAN AND THE ANCIENT WORLD
    Helen K. Bond   113

10. BRIAN AS A TEACHER OF RIGHTEOUSNESS
    George J. Brooke   127

11. BRIAN AND THE APOCALYPTIC JESUS: PARODY AS A
    HISTORICAL METHOD
    Bart D. Ehrman   141

12. 'ARE YOU A VIRGIN?': BIBLICAL EXEGESIS AND THE
    INVENTION OF TRADITION
    Paula Fredriksen   151

13. BEARDS FOR SALE: THE UNCUT VERSION OF BRIAN,
    GENDER AND SEXUALITY
    Amy-Jill Levine   167

14. 'WHAT HAVE THE ROMANS EVER DONE FOR US?'
    BRIAN AND JOSEPHUS ON ANTI-ROMAN SENTIMENT
    Steve Mason   185

15. HOOK-NOSED HEEBIES: BRIAN, JESUS AND JEWISH IDENTITY
    Adele Reinhartz   207

16. 'THE SHOE IS THE SIGN!' COSTUMING BRIAN AND
    DRESSING THE FIRST CENTURY
    Katie Turner   221

Composite Bibliography   239
Index of Ancient Sources   259
General Index   263

ILLUSTRATIONS

Plate section

1. Terry Jones, John Cleese and Richard Burridge discuss Jesus and Brian at the conference held at King's College London in June 2014.
2. *Sica* and sheath, En Gedi (Courtesy of Gideon Hadas; Photo by Guy Stiebel; after Stiebel, '*Armis et litteris*,' Vol. III, Pl. I.8, no. 2).
3. Ownership tag (*nota*) of L. Magus of the century of Gallus, Gamala (Photo by and courtesy of Danny Syon).
4. Wooden phallus pendant, Camp F, Masada (Courtesy of Benjamin Arubas and Haim Goldfus; Photo by Guy Stiebel; after Stiebel, '*Armis et litteris*,' Vol. III, Pl. III.20E, no. 1).
5. Walter Plunkett's frothy, voluminous dresses created for *Gone with the Wind* epitomize the successful amalgamation of historical knowledge, contemporary fashion, and emotive appeal. Ann Rutherford, Vivien Leigh and Evelyn Keyes in *Gone with the Wind* (1939).
   Credit: Selznick/MGM/The Kobal Collection.
6. Bronze Statue of a Man (Greek, mid 2nd–1st century BCE). 'The himation is kept in place in part by the tasselled weight thrown over his left shoulder, which hangs at his calf . . . Several horizontal bands . . . decorate the fabric.'
   Credit: Metropolitan Museum of Art, Gift of Renée E. and Robert A. Belfer, 2001.
7. A red tunic decorated with black bands (*clavi*) from the Cave of Letters, Nahal Hever.
   Credit: Photo Clara Amit; Courtesy of the Israel Antiquities Authority.
8. Moses and the burning bush. Moses wears a white tunic with wide, purple *clavi*. Wing Panel 1, Dura-Europos synagogue.
   Credit: Yale University Art Gallery, Dura-Europos Collection.
9. An orange mantle decorated with purple Gamma-shaped design. Cave of Letters, Nahal Hever.
   Credit: Photo Clara Amit; Courtesy of the Israel Antiquities Authority.
10. Samuel anointing David. David dressed as a king (in purple) with attendants in gold and red, provides an exception to the pale colours typical on male garments. Notched bands can be seen on the edges of the men's mantels. Dam-393, Dura-Europos Synagogue.
    Credit: Yale University Art Gallery, Dura-Europos Collection.

Main chapters

0.1   John Cleese, Joan Taylor, Richard Burridge and Terry Jones
      in King's College London, at the *Jesus and Brian* conference,
      June 2014.   xxiii
0.2   Terry Jones and John Cleese at the *Jesus and Brian* conference.   xxiv
2.1   Michael Palin and Richard Burridge in the BBC news studio
      (photo: courtesy of the BBC).   29
3.1   *Wholly Moses*. The infant Moses giving his rival Herschel's basket
      a gentle shove down the Nile.   45
3.2   *Wholly Moses*. Herschel tries to extinguish the 'burning bush'.   47
3.3   *Wholly Moses*. Herschel 'heals' a beggar pretending to be blind by
      poking him vigorously in the eyes.   50
7.1   Capernaum (photo © Joan E. Taylor).   102
8.1   Vladimir Putin (photo: premier.gov.ru. Creative Commons
      Attribution 3.0 Unported Licence).   111
10.1 Dead Sea Scrolls exhibition in Drents Museum, Assen
      (9 July 2013–5 January 2014) (photo © Drents Museum;
      photograph: JAV Studios Assen).   132
10.2 Dead Sea Scrolls exhibition in Drents Museum (photo © Thijs
      Wolzak; exhibition design: Kossmann.dejong).   133
14.1 Palestine in the time of Jesus.   190
16.1 A crowd has come to worship Brian.   234
16.2 Brian at the Sermon on the Mount with others.   236

Images from the movie *Monty Pythons' Life of Brian* are reproduced here courtesy of John Goldstone, Producer and are © 1979 Python (Monty) Pictures Limited. All Rights Reserved.

The editor and publisher gratefully acknowledge the permission granted to reproduce the copyrighted material in this book.

The third party copyrighted material displayed in the pages of this book are done so on the basis of 'fair dealing for the purposes of criticism and review' or 'fair use for the purposes of teaching, criticism, scholarship or research' only in accordance with international copyright laws, and is not intended to infringe upon the ownership rights of the original owners.

CONTRIBUTORS

Helen K. Bond is Professor of Christian Origins at the University of Edinburgh and Director of the University's Centre for the Study of Christian Origins. Her publications include *Pontius Pilate in History and Interpretation* (1998), *Caiaphas: Friend of Rome and Judge of Jesus?* (2004) and *The Historical Jesus: A Guide for the Perplexed* (2012).

Richard A. Burridge has been the Dean of King's College London since 1994 and received a personal chair as Professor of Biblical Interpretation in 2008. Before coming to King's, he was Lazenby Chaplain at the University of Exeter, where he also taught New Testament and Ethics. He was originally a classicist and schoolmaster before being ordained in 1985. Richard Burridge is a member of the Church of England's General Synod and chaired their Validation Panel for ordination training and theological education (1996–2004). He is a member of the Academic Board of Saint Mellitus College and the Chairman of the Christian Evidence Society. He is also Canon Theologian of Salisbury Cathedral. He is author of *What are the Gospels? A Comparison with Graeco Roman Biography* (1992, revised ed. 2004) and *Imitating Jesus: An Inclusive Approach to New Testament Ethics* (2007), which was shortlisted for the Michael Ramsey Prize, 2009, among other works. In 2013 he was awarded the Ratzinger Prize by Pope Francis in the Vatican, the first non-Roman Catholic to be so honoured.

George J. Brooke is Rylands Professor of Biblical Criticism and Exegesis in the University of Manchester. Since 1992 he has been a member of the Israel Antiquities Authority's international team of editors of the *Dead Sea Scrolls*. He was a founding editor of the journal *Dead Sea Discoveries* and is an editor of the *Journal of Semitic Studies*. Amongst his many publications are several directly connected with Qumran and the scrolls, including *The Complete World of the Dead Sea Scrolls* (2002, 2nd ed. 2011), *Qumran and the Jewish Jesus* (2005) and *The Dead Sea Scrolls and the New Testament* (London: SPCK/Minneapolis: Fortress Press, 2005).

James G. Crossley is Professor of Bible and Society, St. Mary's University, London. He has published various books and articles on Christian origins and more contemporary receptions of the Bible, including: *Why Christianity Happened: A Socio-historical Account of Christian Origins 26–50 CE* (2006); *Jesus in an Age of Terror* (2008) and *Jesus in an Age of Neoliberalism* (2012). His most recent book, on the use of the Bible in English political debates over the past forty years, is entitled *The Bible in English Politics and Culture: A Reception History* (2014), and it includes further analysis of the *Life of Brian*.

Philip R. Davies is the author of the first scholarly article on the film: '*Life of Brian* Research' (1998). He has written six books on the Dead Sea Scrolls, though most of his work has been on the Hebrew Bible and biblical history, including *In Search of Ancient Israel* (1992), *The Canonization of the Hebrew Scriptures* (1998) and *Memories of Ancient Israel* (2008). He is currently Professor Emeritus at the University of Sheffield.

Bart D. Ehrman is the James A. Gray Distinguished Professor at the University of North Carolina, Chapel Hill. He has published extensively in the fields of New Testament and Early Christianity, having written or edited twenty-four books. Among his most recent books are a Greek–English edition of the Apostolic Fathers for the Loeb Classical Library (2003), an assessment of the newly discovered Gospel of Judas (2006) and four *New York Times* Bestsellers: *Jesus Interrupted* (2010), *God's Problem* (an assessment of the biblical views of suffering), *Misquoting Jesus* (2007) and *Forged* (2011). His books have been translated into twenty-seven languages.

Paula Fredriksen is the Aurelio Professor of Scripture emerita at Boston University and Distinguished Visiting Professor of Comparative Religion at the Hebrew University, Jerusalem. She has published widely on the social and intellectual history of ancient Christianity, and on pagan-Jewish-Christian relations in the Graeco-Roman world. The author of the award-winning *From Jesus to Christ* (Yale Governors' Award for Best Book, 1988; 2000), she has also published *Jesus of Nazareth, King of the Jews* (1999), which won a 1999 National Jewish Book Award. Together with Adele Reinhartz, she contributed to and edited *Jesus, Judaism, and Christian Anti-Judaism: Reading the New Testament after the Holocaust* (2002), and has also edited and contributed to a collection of essays about Mel Gibson's controversial film, *The Passion of the Christ* (2005).

Amy-Jill Levine is University Professor of New Testament and Jewish Studies, E. Rhodes and Leona B. Carpenter Professor of New Testament Studies, and Professor of Jewish Studies at Vanderbilt University Divinity School and College of Arts and Science in Nashville, Tennessee; she is also Affiliated Professor, Centre for the Study of Jewish-Christian Relations, Cambridge, UK. Her recent books include *The New Testament, Methods and Meanings* (2013) and *Short Stories by Jesus: The Enigmatic Parables of a Controversial Rabbi* (2014). With Marc Brettler she edited the *Jewish Annotated New Testament* (2011) and is series editor for the *Feminist Companion to the New Testament and Early Christian Writings* (T&T Clark Bloomsbury).

Steve Mason has recently been appointed Distinguished Professor of Ancient Mediterranean Religions and Cultures in the University of Groningen, the Netherlands. Prior positions were in the University of Aberdeen, Scotland (Kirby Laing Chair in New Testament), Toronto's York University (Canada Research Chair in Greco-Roman Cultural Interaction), and the Pennsylvania State University (Head of Classics and Ancient Mediterranean Studies). He edits the multi-volume series *Flavius Josephus: Translation and Commentary* (Brill: 2000–present), to which he has also contributed two volumes (*Life of Josephus, War 2*). His other books include *Flavius Josephus on the Pharisees* (1991), *Josephus and the New Testament* (2004), and *Josephus, Judea, and Christian Origins* (2009). Now in press is *A History of the Jewish War, 66–74* (2015).

Adele Reinhartz is Professor in the Department of Classics and Religious Studies at the University of Ottawa, in Canada. Her main areas of research are New Testament, early Jewish-Christian relations and the Bible and film. She is the author of numerous articles and books, including *Befriending the Beloved Disciple: A Jewish Reading of the Gospel of John* (2001), *Scripture on the Silver Screen* (2003), *Jesus of Hollywood* (2007) and *Bible and Cinema: An Introduction* (2013). She was inducted into the Royal Society of Canada in 2005.

David Shepherd is Assistant Professor of Hebrew Bible/Old Testament at Trinity College Dublin and co-chairs the Bible and Moving Image programme unit of the International Meeting of the Society of Biblical Literature. He is the editor of *Images of the Word: Hollywood's Bible and Beyond* (2008) and the author of *The Bible on Silent Film: Spectacle, Story and Scripture in the Early Cinema* (2013).

Guy D. Stiebel is Senior Lecturer, Department of Archaeology and Ancient Near Eastern Cultures at Tel-Aviv University, and he has co-directed the Masada Archaeological Project since 1994. He was a post-doctoral researcher at the Orion Center, Hebrew University, 2007–2010. His research areas include the archaeology of *Eretz-Israel* in the Hellenistic, Roman and Byzantine Periods (Classical Archaeology) and land conflict archaeology and history.

Joan E. Taylor is Professor of Christian Origins and Second Temple Judaism at King's College London. She was formerly at the University of Waikato, New Zealand, in the departments of both Religious Studies and History. In 1995 she won an Irene Levi-Sala Award in Israel's archaeology, for *Christians and the Holy Places* (1993, revised ed. 2003). Among her other books, she has written *The Immerser: John the Baptist within Second Temple Judaism* (1997) and *The Essenes, the Scrolls and the Dead Sea* (2012).

William R. Telford is recently retired from a position as Senior Lecturer in Durham's Department of Theology and Religion, and is currently Visiting Fellow at St John's College, Durham. His research interests include the historical Jesus, the Gospels, especially the Gospel of Mark, methods of biblical interpretation, and the Bible in literature and film, and he has published on these subjects in a number of books, journals and edited works, such as *The Theology of the Gospel of Mark* (1998) and *Writing on the Gospel of Mark* (2009).

David Tollerton is Lecturer in Jewish Studies and Contemporary Biblical Cultures at the University of Exeter. His publications include works on post-Holocaust reception of the Bible and the representation of Judaism on stage and screen.

David was previously involved with an Arts and Humanities Research Council project on issues of freedom of expression in contemporary Britain and his current research interests include interfaces between the Bible, violence and blasphemy.

Katie Turner is undertaking doctoral research at King's College London, supervised by Professor Joan Taylor, studying the cultural impact of Passion plays: specifically, how they present and have created misconceptions of first-century Judaea. She has previously completed a BA in History at Stony Brook University, New York, an MA in History at Royal Holloway, University of London, and an MA in Biblical Studies, also at King's.

ABBREVIATIONS

BFI	British Film Institute
IEJ	*Israel Exploration Journal*
JBL	*Journal of Biblical Literature*
JSHJ	*Journal for the Study of the Historical Jesus*
JRS	*Journal of Roman Studies*
JSNT	*Journal for the Study of the New Testament*
JSOT	*Journal for the Study of the Old Testament*
JTS	*Journal of Theological Studies*
NRSV	New Revised Standard Version (of the Bible)
NT	*Novum Testamentum*
NTS	*New Testament Studies*
RSV	Revised Standard Version (of the Bible)
STDJ	Studies on the Texts of the Desert of Judah
WUNT	Wissenschaftliche Untersuchungen zum Neuen Testament

PREFACE

First of all I'd like to thank Joan Taylor for getting the *Jesus and Brian* conference together. It really is astonishing to think the *Life of Brian* is a subject that can make academics assemble to discuss it in all seriousness.

Many academics in this volume of essays refer to the notorious interview between John Cleese, Michael Palin, Mervyn Stockwood (the Bishop of Southwark) and Malcolm Muggeridge. As a matter of fact Muggeridge and Stockwood had turned up late for the showing of the *Life of Brian*. And they missed the beginning, where it makes it clear that Brian is born in the next stable along from Christ. The Wise Men go back to Mandy, retrieve their presents, and give them to Jesus. Jesus and Brian are two distinct people. But Muggeridge and Stockwood were resting on their laurels, and were convinced we were making fun of Christ.

In this volume William Telford asks whether the *Life of Brian* is a Jesus film or an anti-Jesus film. Richard Burridge considers how the Bishop of Southwark and Malcolm Muggeridge wasted an opportunity to talk with Michael Palin and John Cleese about serious problems. David Shepherd looks comparatively at a different film. David Tollerton focuses on blasphemy, and considers free speech now and then. James Crossley considers Brian in comparison to Jesus. Philip Davies asks, 'Was Jesus a Brian?' Joan Taylor goes on to examine the 'Historical Brian' and she finds in him a kind of 'historical person lost from history'. Guy Stiebel delves in to archaeology and reveals the weapons the Judaean people used, concluding that the Romans had the better. Helen Bond discovers how people looked at crucifixion and made fun of it. George Brooke tries to find out how Brian can aid our understanding of the Teacher of Righteousness (from the Dead Sea Scrolls) and notes that Brian represents Jesus' humanity in an encrypted form. Bart Ehrman concentrates on parody and the crucifixion. Paula Fredriksen compares what Paul said in his letters, questions 'Why use "Christ" for Jesus at all?' and asserts that Jesus never claimed to be the Messiah. Amy-Jill Levine considers that the *Life of Brian* is an opportunity missed vis-à-vis gender and sexual stereotyping, yet she allows that the *Life of Brian* does, helpfully, open the conversation on what constituted masculinity in antiquity. Steve Mason confronts the way the Judaean people hated the Romans – or did they? Adele Reinhartz focuses on one aspect of Brian and Jesus' identity: their Jewishness. And Katie Turner concentrates on the costuming in the *Life of Brian* – for which I am forever grateful.

Taken as a whole, the essays form a complete analytical deconstruction of the *Life of Brian*, and very interesting they are too! They take various angles and look at the film from not just a filmic one but from a historical point of view, and read many things I had not noticed at the time. The comparisons are always illuminating, and the commentaries always right on the nose.

Terry Jones, November 2014

FOREWORD

Gone are the days when 'reception history' could be dismissed as 'Biblical Studies on holiday'. Reception historians have worked hard to establish the credentials of their discipline and, so far as Biblical Studies is concerned, to persuade the guild that 'what people believe [the Bible] means and how they actually use it – in everyday situations, in the liturgy, in preaching, in the media, in literature, in art, in music, in film – can be studied with the same degree of scientific sensitivity and rigor as the original'.[1]

The value and scholarly integrity of reception studies are increasingly recognized. It is vital that biblical scholars should not define their work too narrowly and refuse to step outside the circle of their expertise, strictly defined. Interdisciplinary work requires that those who engage in it make themselves vulnerable in this way, ready to venture into territory where connections are made between Biblical Studies, film studies, cultural criticism, intellectual history and much besides, even though no one individual can be expert in all of these fields.

The Department of Theology and Religious Studies at King's College London – one of the University of London family of institutions – has a long and influential history of contributing to innovative approaches in Biblical Studies.[2] So I am delighted as current Head of Department that King's should have hosted a highly successful international conference exploring the historical Jesus and his times, via *Monty Python's Life of Brian*. Tribute is due to Professor Joan Taylor for her indomitable determination to see this come to fruition, as well as her tireless conference assistants Michelle Fletcher and Katie Turner. And warm thanks are due to John Cleese and to Terry Jones, the director of the film, for their wholehearted commitment to the enterprise.

Reception history as a sub-discipline of Biblical Studies is still evolving, and it is clear from recent discussions that its various exponents have diverse views of what it entails. There is still, in my view, all too often a tendency, even among those committed to reception studies, to polarize historical-critical study of the Bible and reception studies.

The insights of reception studies in fact shed light on the whole story of the Bible from the time of its own formation until now. It is important to recognize the

---

1. John F. A. Sawyer, 'Ezekiel in the History of Christianity', in Andrew Mein and Paul M. Joyce (eds), *After Ezekiel: Essays on the Reception of a Difficult Prophet* (Library of Hebrew Bible/Old Testament Studies, 535; New York and London: T&T Clark/Continuum, 2011), pp. 1–10, at p. 2.

2. Paul M. Joyce, 'King's College London, Samuel Davidson, and the Scope of Biblical Studies,' *JTS* (2014), pp. 1–16. New Series, 65/2 (2014), pp. 407–24.

broad range of what may be described as 'reception'. Thus, for example, it makes sense to regard what scholars generally refer to as 'redaction', the elaboration of the biblical text in ancient times before the canonical closure of a final form of scripture, as a stage – the first stage – of reception. Thus it is not just a matter of the Bible being received by later generations; reception takes place even within the Bible itself. And then, turning to modern times, even many reception historians tend to exclude academic biblical scholarship proper from reception history, distinguishing sharply between readers whose aim is to elucidate the biblical text, usually in its ancient context, and readers who, although they may well illuminate the Bible, are motivated by other interests. But it is important to recognize that historical-critical study of the Bible is not an enterprise quite separate from the reception history of the Bible. Historical-critical study, not least in its modernist quest for detached objectivity and in its employment of evolutionary models, is to be seen as historically and culturally located. Thus we should not think of exegesis, the quest for the probable original meaning of biblical texts, as being a totally distinct and *prior* activity, the neutral prelude to the study of reception history. The historical-critical study of the Bible does not stand above the tide of history and culture; it is better understood as a relatively recent phase in the long story of the reception of the Bible, rather than as a kind of foundation on which reception history might be built as a second-stage superstructure.

It is in keeping with this refusal to allow a crude polarization that the contributors to the present volume not only explore the many ways in which the *Life of Brian* uses, adapts and is influenced by the Gospels, but also frequently engage in what has been called 'reception exegesis', which is driven by the insight that how the Bible has been received may provide invaluable assistance in the exegetical task.

The point is that biblical scholars bent on interpretation of the Bible in traditional scholarly ways do not have a monopoly on explicating the ancient text. Illumination can also be derived from textual and other media that are better characterized as responding to or using the biblical text, rather than exegeting it. Use of the Bible in later times can thus shine a spotlight on biblical verses that have been dulled by familiarity; it can foreground biblical concepts and concerns that have faded over time into the background; and it can even give rise to new readings of difficult Hebrew, Aramaic and Greek terms.

This does not mean, of course, that examples of reception history that do not enrich our understanding of the core biblical text are less valuable than those that do. In other words, the legitimacy of reception history as an enterprise by no means depends upon its having to 'pay its way' by yielding exegetical fruit; it is valuable in its own right in multiple ways. That it sometimes, indeed often – as in the present volume – yields new insights that can be shared at the exegetical table is a serendipitous bonus, which offers an additional dimension to reception history as usually understood.

This is an approach that features prominently in teaching within the King's Department in the work of Edward Adams and Joan Taylor on the Gospels and in a commentary on Lamentations I recently produced with our former colleague

Diana Lipton, in which the idea of 'reception exegesis' is given prominent emphasis.[3]

Related straws in the wind may be seen in the work of John Sawyer, who writes '[Reception history] also involves collecting and analyzing the many meanings that each text has had in different contexts, in a way that often gives us new insights into the language and imagery of the Bible'.[4] There is common ground also with the notion of 'reception criticism', favoured by Cheryl Exum over 'reception history' because it signals that the enterprise involves not merely cataloguing cases of reception but also critical analysis.[5] And reference should also be made here to the work of Larry Kreitzer and David Tollerton.[6]

Jesus and Brian has gone from conference to book, and it constitutes an important landmark in the development of reception studies of the Bible. I commend it enthusiastically, with grateful thanks to Dominic Mattos and Miriam Cantwell of T&T Clark Bloomsbury for their support of the conference and their work on this volume.

Paul M. Joyce
Samuel Davidson Professor of
Old Testament/Hebrew Bible
Head of the Department of
Theology and Religious Studies
King's College London
November 2014

3. Paul M. Joyce and Diana Lipton, *Lamentations through the Centuries* (Wiley-Blackwell Bible Commentary; Oxford: Wiley-Blackwell, 2013); cf. John Riches, 'Reception Exegesis of Lamentations', *Expository Times* (4 March 2014), pp. 383–7.

4. John F. A. Sawyer, *A Concise Dictionary of the Bible and its Reception* (Louisville, KY: Westminster John Knox, 2009), p. ix.

5. J. Cheryl Exum, 'Toward a Genuine Dialogue between the Bible and Art', in M. Nissinen (ed.), *Congress Volume Helsinki 2010* (VTSupp, 148; Leiden: Brill, 2012), pp. 473–503.

6. Larry J. Kreitzer, *The New Testament in Fiction and Film: On Reversing the Hermeneutical Flow* (Sheffield: Sheffield Academic Press/London: Continuum, 1993); id. *The Old Testament in Fiction and Film: On Reversing the Hermeneutical Flow* (Sheffield: Sheffield Academic Press, 1994); David C. Tollerton, 'Two Jewish-American Interpretations of the Book of Job in the Aftermath of the Holocaust: A Short Discussion of the Relationship between Job's Modern Reception and Its Ancient Production', in Lidia D. Matassa and Jason M. Silverman (eds), *Text, Theology and Trowel: New Investigations in the Biblical World* (Eugene, OR: Pickwick, 2011), pp. 59–74.

INTRODUCTION

JESUS AND BRIAN: THE CONFERENCE AND THE BOOK

Joan E. Taylor

Monty Python's Life of Brian provoked a furious response in some quarters when the film first appeared in 1979, even leading to cries of 'blasphemy'. However, many students and teachers of biblical literature were quietly, or even loudly, amused. *Life of Brian* in fact contains numerous references to what was then the cutting edge of biblical scholarship, Jewish Studies and Life of Jesus research, founded on the recognition of the historical Jesus as a Jew who needs to be understood within the context of his time. Implicitly, in setting 'Brian' within the tumultuous social and political background of his age, *Life of Brian* sets Jesus within it also. It assumes the audience has some knowledge of the Gospel accounts, which directly inform the comedy.

It is therefore very appropriate for scholars to engage with the film. This book follows on from a conference held by the Department of Theology and Religious Studies, King's College London, in June 2014, with sponsorship from the School of Arts and Humanities, and support too from T&T Clark Bloomsbury. This conference was titled, *Jesus and Brian or: What have the Pythons done for us?*, a title that indicated at the outset that there was a different way of seeing, or interpreting, than what you might expect, and for this see below.

Terry Jones and John Cleese were clearly key to the conference's great success, and I greatly thank Philip Davies for giving me Terry Jones' email when I initially thought of this conference. Philip Davies was the first 'Brianologist', with his article '*Life of Brian* Research', published in 1998, and he planted the seed for what would grow to a great tree of academic interest. Terry Jones, who directed the film, as well as playing the part of Brian's mother Mandy, was immediately enthusiastic about the event, and I am deeply grateful.

Terry Jones very kindly passed on my email to all the other Pythons. Then one Sunday afternoon I received a phone call from John Cleese giving me his support and promising his involvement, and I almost fell off my chair, just as Mandy did when the Three Wise Men arrive in the opening scene of the film. What followed was a conversation that set everything in motion, with practical matters worked out with John Cleese's characteristic efficiency.

The timing of the conference was planned carefully, since John informed me that the Pythons would be putting on their massive farewell shows at the O2 Stadium, so we organized it ahead of this, with a promise from him that he would appear. Both Terry and John agreed to be interviewed, though it was not something to be advertised, in order to keep the conference outside the realm of show business. This would be a surprise for those who registered for the conference in order to study the film, though 'mystery guests' were announced.

It made a huge difference to have both Terry Jones and John Cleese very much involved. Michael Palin was also supportive, though unable to attend, and much to my surprise he sent me an invitation to appear on the BBC Radio 4 *Today* news programme, which he was guest-editing, after Christmas 2013. Reflecting on what they needed for this, given the initial hostile reception to the film from certain church circles, I felt they really required a high-flying Anglican priest rather than an academic pure and simple like me. I was then very glad to be able to send them Rev. Canon Professor Richard Burridge, the Dean of King's College London,[1] who agreed to do the interview. This allowed the conference to be mentioned, and Richard also did a great job in uttering something controversial about the film, namely, the words: 'I think it is an extraordinary tribute to the life and work and teaching of Jesus.' These words then echoed around the world in a huge number of newspapers, blogs, websites and emails. As they say, no publicity is bad publicity.

I invited scholars I knew to be cutting-edge in the field, not only locally within the United Kingdom and Ireland, but also internationally, and only wish I could have invited more, since once word of the event got out I was written to by many who supported the project. My aim was to have a range of voices, from different perspectives, with different views on Jesus and on religion overall, whether the scholars concerned be Christians, Jews, agnostics, atheists or seekers. I was not looking for any one theological perspective. The key points of attraction to me were their stellar scholarship and interest in the film, and how they could answer the question: what have the Pythons done for us? 'Us' here means 'scholars of Jesus and his times', primarily. Whatever could be engaged with in the film was open for use.

Then there was the enormous job of organizing the conference, in which I was helped by two brilliant conference assistants: two of the department's best doctoral candidates, Michelle Fletcher and Katie Turner. I am also heartily grateful to Professor Paul Joyce, Head of the Department of Theology and Religious Studies, and to the Dean of the Faculty of Arts and Humanities, Professor Russell Goulbourne. In addition, administrative staff were on the case: for guidance, publicity, arrangements, and a hundred details. I am very much indebted to all who helped. The Master of Temple Church (and King's colleague), Rev. Dr Robin Griffith-Jones, stepped in to support a conference dinner in the magnificent surroundings of Inner Temple, near King's College, and John Cleese agreed to be

---

1. The Dean of King's College London is an ordained minister of the Church of England responsible for the spiritual development of staff and students, including overseeing the College Chaplaincy team and the Associateship of King's College London (AKC) programme.

the mystery after-dinner speaker: a duty he fulfilled by providing hilarious, witty and insightful responses to questions from the conference dinner guests, which I happily recorded on my phone for my Mum and consider a treasure.

During the three days of the conference, there were papers ranging from the historical to the filmic, considering reception, art, and what the Romans did for Judaeans or not. Top scholars in the study of Jesus and his times employed the film as a tool to reflect on the past. Specialists in the Bible and film considered its contribution and its reception. There was tremendous diversity, and much provocation, but all the papers are linked with a serious wish to engage with a film that has so many bizarrely relevant things for us, even after all these years. Scholars were asked to view *Life of Brian*, and use it as a means of exploring all manner of things related to Jesus and history.

So, there gathered in London an illustrious group of scholars, seasoned with Pythons. The academics were all foremost in their fields, spanning a range of disciplines and they all had in common an interest in utilizing the *Life of Brian* productively as a tool for analysis. In addition, as agreed, Terry Jones and John Cleese gave their valuable time during the O2 rehearsals to speak candidly about the film in an hour-long interview. I asked Richard Burridge – supportive throughout and highly effective at publicity – to interview them on the initial reception of the film and what the Pythons were trying to do. That interview was filmed officially, and is available on the King's College London YouTube channel, in the 'Jesus and Brian' playlist at http://www.youtube.com/watch?v=CspatcnNWSg.

Figure 0.1 John Cleese, Joan Taylor, Richard Burridge and Terry Jones in King's College London, at the *Jesus and Brian* conference, June 2014 (© Department of Theology and Religious Studies, King's College London).

Among the many jewels of their memories and reflections, at ten minutes and thirty-five seconds into the recording, comes this exchange:

> RB: Thank you for sparing the time in the middle of all the preparations [for the O2].
> JC: I'd just like to say how good it is of us to give up our time.
> RB: You've been reading my script . . . [audience laughter]. Why have you given up your time?
> JC: Because it's interesting . . .
> RB: I mean, why do you think? I mean, if you'd been told 35 years ago that some of the world's top biblical scholars and experts on the historical Jesus would fly around the world to come to discuss your work, what would you have said?
> JC: Well, it's just as silly as everything else [audience laughter and applause]. But, I mean I'm delighted. I mean I think if people . . . I think it was somebody who said you were going to say, 'What was the most interesting part that came out of Pythons?' and as far as I'm concerned it's this conference.
> TJ: Yeah, this conference. Absolutely.

It was remarkable to discover just how interested the Pythons were, and I was also able to invite Julian Doyle, the editor of the film, to attend the conference, and he kindly agreed to be interviewed by me on the last day. This interview is also available in the 'Jesus and Brian' playlist, under 'Session 9': http://www.youtube. com/watch?v=treiQnvTH8U. These interviews have not been transcribed for this

Figure 0.2 Terry Jones and John Cleese at the *Jesus and Brian* conference (© Department of Theology and Religious Studies, King's College London).

volume, but I thank Terry Jones, John Cleese and Julian Doyle for their extraordinary contributions and their great generosity.

What does appear in this volume is almost everything else (though sadly Aaron Rosen's astonishing paper is being published elsewhere), and I am enormously grateful to all the contributors. I will not do what is customary and summarize each one here, as Terry Jones has done such a beautifully succint job in the Preface. I do thank especially Bill Telford for providing such a thorough bibliography of the *Life of Brian*, including a large number of web resources. All bibliographic materials are combined in the pages at the end of this book.

I am deeply grateful to Dominic Mattos and Miriam Cantwell of T&T Clark Bloomsbury for all their editorial work and their enthusiasm for the project, and for making this a really nice book with a great cover. I am grateful to Lisa Carden for her fine copy-editing. I thank Ildi Clarke for her index, and John Goldstone for very kindly supplying the wonderful stills from the *Life of Brian* that accompany each chapter. I thank also Michelle and Tom Fletcher for screen-capture shots.

+

People have sometimes asked me where on earth I got the idea for *Jesus and Brian*. I have to reflect back, and say I was a fervent Pythonist during my youth, but when *Life of Brian* was revealed to the world I did not 'answer the call' to follow and instead I let my friends 'enter the narrow gate' ahead of me, since I was concerned it might ridicule Jesus. I was actually pushed into seeing a re-screening of the movie in 1985 by a bunch of seminarians with whom I was a student at Otago University, New Zealand, and we all laughed ourselves to exhaustion. The film is a wonderful parody of the biblical epic yet, in the best tradition of parodies, it works on different levels. It opens up not only elements of movies today and of religious institutions but also offers sharp glimpses into key aspects of Jesus and his times, of all those popular fronts for the liberation of Judaea, and the characters of the age. Within it, there is a clear challenge in terms of the historical Jesus, asking viewers to reflect on him. Have we managed to 'hear' him correctly? Did people of his own time even manage that? They were just as stupid as everyone else, after all.

I am with James Crossley and Philip Davies on this: the *Life of Brian* is a subversive film,[2] and – in my view – we need this subversion. The description of life as 'a bit of shit' in the closing sequence of the film always stings me, for some reason, yet it seems to me to fit Jesus' recognition that suffering of many kinds, especially from being maligned, is a part of this (corrupted) world for those who

---

2. James G. Crossley, 'Life of Brian or Life of Jesus? Uses of Critical Biblical Scholarship and Non-Orthodox Views of Jesus in Monty Python's *Life of Brian*', in *Relegere: Studies in Religion and Reception* 1 (2011), pp. 93–114; Philip R. Davies, '*Life of Brian* Research', in J. Cheryl Exum and Stephen D. Moore (eds), *Biblical Studies/Cultural Studies: The Third Sheffield Colloquium* (London: Continuum Books, 1998), pp. 400–14, and in Philip Davies, *Whose Bible is it Anyway?* 2nd ed. (London: T&T Clark International, 2004), pp. 142–55.

follow him (Mark 13.9–13 and par.). I think it stings though because I see life as a special gift that we need to try to respond to in mindfulness, humility and compassion, no matter what happens. I have my beliefs, but I am one who feels herself to be a seeker travelling on an open-thinking and creative journey rather than remaining in a place with all the answers.

What I like here is that sense that this 'sting' enables me to reflect on what I value. I relish the way the *Life of Brian* challenges. I love the way it fuses Judaism and Christianity for humour, so that Jews too feel the same sting of its parodies, and it was – after all – condemned by both Christian and Jewish groups on its release: quite a good example of cross-religious dialogue and unity!

The very concept of blasphemy is, however, totally alien to me, and I think it is a very problematic accusation in our society. The fact that Jesus himself was apparently accused of being a blasphemer by people in authority who simply did not understand what he was trying to do (e.g. Mark 14.63–64 and par.; John 10.30–33), should make anyone who looks to Jesus for authority be very wary indeed of using such a category of condemnation. In the tradition of the Gospels, Jesus himself only accepted one offence that was unforgiveable, which was to say that the Holy Spirit was essentially Satan (Mark 3.22–30 and parallels). This was an accusation that undermined his entire healing mission, since he trusted that the healings he performed were achieved by means of the miraculously restorative power of the Holy Spirit abiding within him. But such an accusation placed him in league with the Devil, as an arch-magician, for whom the only proper sentence by law was death (Deut. 18.11–12; Exod. 22.18). Likewise, on the basis of this accusation, all his disciples who also healed (Mark 6.7 and parallels) in his name would be placed in the same category of heinous criminality. To accuse someone of something that would make them subject to the death penalty is indeed very serious, and not what most people understand now by 'blasphemy'.

In general, being offended can be a good thing. It makes us squirm with recognition, and asks us to reflect on ourselves. It can show us our boundaries, and what we care about deeply, bringing a consciousness of what we love and value in the face of something that would devalue it. But if it hurts us deeply, then we have created a 'thing' out of our feelings, as if that 'thing' can be smashed or corrupted. I honestly do not think God (or what I would call 'God') gets insulted. God's quite a bit bigger than that. So a bunch of little humans on planet Earth really don't need to be insulted on God's behalf.

In terms of how to use the film productively, I have been intrigued by a new way of using movies, art, literature and drama in terms of engaging with biblical texts that moves beyond what is normally called 'reception history' in the field of biblical studies. In reception history the biblical text is 'received', and it can then be viewed within new contexts. We can trace the ways in which the biblical texts have been used over the centuries, whether in scholarly exegesis, literature, art, drama, music or film. The study is essentially linear: the biblical text is written, and then it is encountered on and on, and we explore the whys and wherefores of that. However, a new way of looking at 'reception' is currently emerging. This has been apparent already in Larry Kreitzer's notion of 'reversing the hermeneutical flow,[3] thinking about how hermeneutics, the science of interpretation, can be turned around, so that it is not just a case of a linear progression through time looking at how the biblical texts are received and interpreted, but rather we can use its 'reception' points as tools to analyse biblical texts. They ask us to turn back and look again.

In the recent work of my colleague Paul Joyce, with my former colleague Diana Lipton, in their study of Lamentations, they talk about 'reception exegesis'.[4] They ask how the various items of 'reception' can make us think and ask questions of the biblical texts under review. This is exactly what I have been doing in an MA module I teach at King's, on the basis of what my colleague Edward Adams pioneered, the module being *The Passion: History, Text and Representation*. Students are asked to pick a creative work of some kind and use it to reflect on a chosen biblical passage concerned with the Passion narratives of the New Testament. It was within this module that I found myself most intrigued by how students used the *Life of Brian* in innovative and insightful ways.

So, in the conference and for this book, I asked eminent scholars to reflect on the film's reception, and to use the *Life of Brian* as a hermeneutical tool, a means of reflecting not only on our texts but on the Jesus of history and on his context in first-century Judaea. What have the Pythons done for us?

Presented here then are the results of these scholarly endeavours, divided up into two main sections. In the first, scholars consider the film as it stands within the genre of biblical movies, and also consider its reception and the question of its alleged blasphemy. In the second part, the focus is backwards: to the Gospels, to Jesus, and to Roman Judaea.

It may seem surprising to some that this very funny film is engaged with as a subject of serious scholarship, in both the conference and this book. However, ever since Philip Davies first wrote on the film, other scholars too have turned their gaze to consider exactly what *Life of Brian* does in regard to Jesus scholarship, and have increasingly delved into its curious corners to reflect on what it says both about the tumultuous times of Jesus and also contemporary scholarly discussions. Biblical scholarship has moved on greatly in the past thirty-five years, and various aspects of *Life of Brian* correlate with themes now intensely explored.

In short, this collection, following from the papers given at the conference, opens up *Life of Brian* to renewed investigation, using the film in an innovative way to sharpen our view. Essays by some of the world's most eminent biblical scholars and historians discuss the film's relevance to history, Biblical Studies and Life of Jesus research. The aim is to use the film to reflect on history, interpretation and meaning, employing it as a tool that can help us consider our assumptions and the historical evidence: a 'reception exegesis' approach. This is also a celebration of a British movie masterpiece.

3. Larry J. Kreitzer, *The New Testament in Fiction and Film: On Reversing the Hermeneutical Flow* (London: Continuum, 1993).

4. Paul Joyce and Diana Lipton, *Lamentations through the Centuries* (Wiley-Blackwell Bible Commentaries; Oxford: Wiley-Blackwell, 2013).

Part I

THE FILM IN ITS CINEMATIC CONTEXT, ITS RECEPTION AND ITS CHALLENGES

Chapter 1

MONTY PYTHON'S LIFE OF BRIAN
AND THE JESUS FILM

William R. Telford

Half a lifetime ago (on 9 November 1979, to be precise), amidst a storm of controversy, two of the team that produced *Monty Python's Life of Brian*, John Cleese and Michael Palin, defended their film on national television. Appearing on BBC2's 'Friday Night, Saturday Morning', the intrepid duo were pitted against the Christian broadcaster and fellow-satirist, Malcolm Muggeridge, and the Anglican bishop, Mervyn Stockwood. I was a young man in my early thirties, just about to take up a post in Christian Origins and the New Testament at the University of Newcastle, and I remember the programme well. Early on in the debate, Muggeridge voiced the opinion: 'And if anybody in the future, who might dredge up this miserable little film, and it is quite possible they might as a piece of social history, they would certainly not wish to relate it to ... Chartres Cathedral, which is built to the glory of Christ.' After Cleese's rejoinder, 'Not a funny building, actually,' Muggeridge went on to say: 'There is nothing in this squalid little number that could possibly affect anybody ..', and then repeated, 'there is nothing in this film that could possibly destroy anybody's genuine faith, that I grant you absolutely, because it's much too tenth-rate for that."[1]

This 'miserable little film' was, nevertheless, a huge box-office success, making some $60,277 in its first five days.[2] 210,532 movie-goers on the Internet Movie Database have given this 'tenth-rate' film an 8.2/10 rating.[3] On its re-release date on 30 April 2004, timed to coincide with Mel Gibson's *The Passion of the Christ*, it gained a 75 per cent rating from critics and an 8.4/10 rating from users on the reviews website metacritic.com.[4] It is now widely regarded as a cult comedy classic,[5] if not one of the funniest films ever made. It is one of the films listed in Steven Jay Schneider's *1001 Movies You Must See before You Die* (2013).[6] Its soundtrack was produced as a successful album.[7] Commissioned for the Luminato Arts Festival in 2007, an oratorio, based on the film and entitled *Not the Messiah (He's a Very Naughty Boy)*, was written and scored by Eric Idle and John Du Prez, and re-performed at the Royal Albert Hall in 2009.[8] The Monty Python team has gone on to international success as directors, actors and screenwriters.[9] Their fans can now have 'Python bytes' on their iPhones, or 'The Holy Book of Days', based on

1. For the 'Friday Night, Saturday Morning' TV debate on *Monty Python's Life of Brian*, see the following websites, accessed 4 September 2014: <http://en.wikipedia.org/wiki/Friday_Night,_Saturday_Morning>; <https://www.youtube.com/watch?v=tl8acXl3qVs>; <https://www.youtube.com/watch?v=1ni559bHXDg>; <http://www.bbc.co.uk/news/entertainment-arts-25464820>; <http://dangerousminds.net/comments/monty_python_vs._god1> <http://www.atheistmedia.com/2012/05/life-of-brian-debate-1979.html>.

2. Richard C. Stern, Clayton N. Jefford and Guerric DeBona, *Savior on the Silver Screen* (New York and Mahwah, NJ: Paulist Press, 1999), p. 254.

3. See <http://www.imdb.com/title/tt0079470/?ref_=nv_sr_1> [accessed 4 September 2014].

4. See <http://www.metacritic.com/movie/life-of-brian> [accessed 4 September 2014].

5. See Sarah Rainey, '*Life of Brian*: Facts and Figures', *The Telegraph*, 11 October 2011 <http://www.telegraph.co.uk/culture/8818328/Life-of-Brian-facts-and-figures.html> [accessed 4 September 2014].

6. Stephen Jay Schneider, *1001 Movies You Must See before You Die* (London: Quintessence, 2013).

7. See *Wikipedia*, 'Monty Python's Life of Brian (Album)' <http://en.wikipedia.org/wiki/Monty_Python's_Life_of_Brian_(album)> [accessed 4 September 2014].

8. See *Wikipedia*, 'Not the Messiah (He's a Very Naughty Boy)' <http://en.wikipedia.org/wiki/Not_the_Messiah_(He's_a_Very_Naughty_Boy)> [accessed 4 September 2014] and YouTube, 'Not the Messiah (He's a Very Naughty Boy)' <https://www.youtube.com/watch?v=LhGqsqW_Wtg> [accessed 4 September 2014].

9. Ephraim Katz (ed.), *The Macmillan International Film Encyclopedia*, 2nd ed. (London: HarperCollins, 1994), p. 963.

Monty Python and the Holy Grail, on their iPads.[10] If you are a Python fanatic, you can even purchase a relic, a senitype, a limited edition of an actual frame of the original motion picture negative. It comes with the Collector's Edition of the movie.[11] A reunion of the five surviving Pythons took place, in a live stage show, 'Monty Python Live (mostly)', at the O2 arena in London on 1 July 2014 (and due to overwhelming popular demand, five further shows were staged on July 15, 16, 18, 19, 20, with live feeds to cinemas throughout the world on the final night).[12] And, as for that TV debate, on BBC2, on 'Friday Night, Saturday Morning', some thirty-five years before, a dramatized version of it, written by Tony Roche, and entitled 'Holy Flying Circus' was aired on BBC4 in 19 October 2011, thereby raising its issues afresh.[13]

Thirty-five years later, too, academics, scholars and experts in Christian origins, first-century Judaism, film studies and other fields, gathered in King's College London (20–22 June 2014), to consider this 'squalid little number', and this book is the outcome of their deliberations. One of their number, Rev. Canon Professor Richard Burridge, recently decorated by Pope Francis, has even declared it 'an extraordinary tribute to Jesus'.[14] So much, then, for Malcolm Muggeridge's judgment on *Life of Brian*!

10. See *Python Bytes 1: Monty Python Series 1* (Heuristic Media, 2014) and 'Monty Python stars reunite to launch app', *The Telegraph*, 4 May 2012 <http://www.telegraph.co.uk/culture/culturenews/9246736/Monty-Python-stars-reunite-to-launch-app.html> [accessed 4 September 2014].

11. See Terry Jones (dir.), *Monty Python's Life of Brian* (Collector's Edition, Amazon, 1979) <http://www.amazon.co.uk/COLLECTORS-including-screenplay-paperback-postcards/dp/B00DS5JWLW> [accessed 4 September 2014].

12. See *Wikipedia*, 'Monty Python' <http://en.wikipedia.org/wiki/Monty_Python> [accessed 4 September 2014].

13. For the dramatized version of the TV debate, 'Holy Flying Circus' and reactions to it, not least the Pythons', see the following websites: <http://dangerousminds.net/comments/monty_python_vs._god1> [accessed 4 September 2014]; <http://www.theguardian.com/media/2011/jun/21/bbc-monty-python-life-of-brian> [accessed 4 September 2014]; <http://www.telegraph.co.uk/culture/tvandradio/8833320/The-Life-of-Brian-When-Monty-Python-took-on-God.html> [accessed 4 September 2014]; <http://www.independent.co.uk/arts-entertainment/tv/news/pythons-annoyed-by-inaccurate-portrayal-of-debate-in-bbc-drama-2368104.html> [accessed 4 September 2014]; <http://www.theguardian.com/film/2011/aug/13/monty-python-life-brian-bbc> [accessed 4 September 2014]; <http://www.dailymail.co.uk/femail/article-2046493/Monty-Pythons-Life-Of-Brian-caused-uproar-release-BBC-drama-reveals.html> [accessed 4 September 2014].

14. See John Bingham, '*Monty Python's Life of Brian* "Extraordinary Tribute to Jesus"', Says Theologian Decorated by Pope Francis', *The Telegraph*, 31 December 2013 <http://www.telegraph.co.uk/news/religion/10543149/Monty-Pythons-Life-of-Brian-extraordinary-tribute-to-Jesus-says-theologian-decorated-by-Pope-Francis.html> [accessed 4 September 2014].

This chapter will examine *Life of Brian* in relation to the biblical epic in general, and the Jesus film in particular. It is frequently maintained that the film is a send-up of old-style biblical epics, or that it is a parody of the classic Christ film, mocking its conventions and satirizing the religious piety with which it is suffused.[15] Is this the whole story? In the first part of the chapter, I shall make a general comparison of *Life of Brian* with the Hollywood epics and the Jesus films. How do they compare with each other, in terms of content, structure, sources and style, with respect to aims, message and ideology, and with regard to audience, social context and reception? What is *Life of Brian's* place within the history of the genre? In the second part of the chapter, I shall address the generic question more directly. To what extent can *Life of Brian* be considered a 'Jesus' film, or an 'anti *Jesus-film*', or even an *anti-Jesus* film? What are its real targets? How should we describe the Python Jesus, in relation to the genre? What are we to make of the Python Brian, and what is the relationship between them? Should Brian be considered a Christ-figure, a counter-Christ figure or even an anti-Christ figure?

Monty Python's Life of Brian *and the Jesus Film Compared*

Content, structure, sources and style

Let me begin with a general comparison of *Life of Brian* and the Hollywood epics and Jesus films. After the success of *Monty Python and the Holy Grail* in 1975, and its demolition of the Arthurian legends, the Pythons contemplated their next cinematic enterprise. With a side glance towards Franklin J. Schaffner's 1970 epic, *Patton: Lust for Glory*, the original tongue-in-cheek title for what eventually became *Monty Python's Life of Brian* was *Jesus Christ: Lust for Glory*, and this is not only an indication of the nature of their next project, but also of how the Pythons intended to treat it.[16] In creating a first-century Jewish everyman figure, Brian

---

15. Compare, for example, this judgment from *The Monthly Film Bulletin*, cited in Roy Kinnard and Tim Davis, *Divine Images: A History of Jesus on the Screen* (New York: Citadel Press, 1992), p. 195: 'The film might also be taken seriously as an attempt to demystify Christ and religious fanaticism, while it unsuccessfully sends up the kind of reverent, choir-laden, star-studded Gospel dramatizations habitually perpetrated by the cinema industry on behalf of God and Mammon.'

16. See Johnny Dee, 'Monty Python, Everything You Need to Know – Infographic', *The Guardian*, 8 February 2013. <http://www.theguardian.com/culture/interactive/2013/feb/08/monty-python-infographic> [accessed 4 September 2014] for an image of a poster bearing this original title along with the marketing slogan for *The Life of Brian* in Sweden ('So funny it was banned in Norway'); the original title is normally attributed to a facetious suggestion from Eric Idle – see, for example, Schneider, *1001 Movies*, p. 657, or *Wikipedia*, 'Monty Python's Life of Brian', <http://en.wikipedia.org/wiki/Monty_Python#Monty_Python.27s_Life_of_Brian_.281979.29> [accessed 4 September 2014]; according to Rainey,

Cohen, in having his life run parallel to that of Jesus, and in making him an awkward, unconfident and very reluctant Messiah, the Pythons were obviously pitching their tent in the biblical epic or Jesus movie field. The trope of parallel or intersecting lives is a not uncommon one in these movies, as, for example, in the traditional *Ben-Hur* (1959)[17] or the more subversive *Jesus of Montreal* (1989), and the reluctant Messiah is, of course, the leitmotif of Scorsese's *The Last Temptation of Christ* (1988).

Where characters are concerned, biblical characters predominate in biblical epics but fictional characters are also created to augment and enhance both plot and *dramatis personae*. By contrast, in *Life of Brian*, there is only one named New Testament character, other than Jesus, namely, Pontius Pilate, and the rest are fictional.[18] In Judith, however, we are invited to think of both Mary Magdalene, whom the Jesus films bring into close relationship with Jesus, and Judas (the masculine form of her name), who betrayed him, as she herself does in the film, albeit with all the innocence of the revolutionary devotee.[19] Closer to the bone is the invited comparison between Mandy, the mother of Brian, and Mary, the mother of Jesus. Otherwise, *Life of Brian* is peopled by the same generic types as are found in the biblical epics and Jesus films, viz. the crowd, the Romans, Jewish prophets and revolutionaries and the Messiah's followers. *Life of Brian* places emphasis on the revolutionary movements, the People's Front of Judaea, the Judaean People's Front, the Popular Front of Judaea (all one of him), but this emphasis is also seen in such films as Ray's *King of Kings* (1961), where Judas and Barabbas play central roles as political revolutionaries. One feature, too, of biblical epics is the employment of celebrities in cameo roles (as, for example, John Wayne, in *The Greatest Story Ever Told,* 1965), and one delight in *Life of Brian* is the brief

---

'Life of Brian', *Telegraph*, the idea for the film arose on a promotional trip to Paris, when both Eric Idle and Terry Gilliam decided that their next film would be entitled *Jesus Christ: Lust for Glory*, this working title being enthusiastically taken up by the other Pythons. Richard Walsh comments on the appropriateness of the original title: 'The troupe's comic title for their film during production, *Jesus Christ: Lust for Glory*, summarizes the point about the Jesus/Gospel tradition succinctly. That no glory attends Brian exposes the desire for glory in the Gospel tradition that obscures Judaism and the Jewish Jesus with spiritual, glorious *Christ*ianity. The film's comedy lays bare the semiotic incongruity between a Jewish nobody and the glorious "Christ".' '*Monty Python's Life of Brian* (1979)' in Adele Reinhartz (ed.), *Bible and Cinema: Fifty Key Films* (London and New York: Routledge, 2013), p. 189.

17. See William R. Telford, 'Jesus Christ Movie-Star: The Depiction of Jesus in the Cinema', in Clive Marsh and Gaye Ortiz (eds), *Explorations in Theology and Film: Movies and Meaning* (Oxford: Blackwell, 1997), p. 131.

18. W. Barnes Tatum, *Jesus at the Movies: A Guide to the First Hundred Years*, 3rd ed. (Santa Rosa, CA: Polebridge, 2013), p. 162.

19. See Adele Reinhartz, *Jesus of Hollywood* (Oxford: Oxford University Press, 2007), p. 168, and Walsh, '*Monty Python's Life of Brian* (1979)', p. 188.

appearance in the film of the fellow comedian and arch-absurdist, Spike Milligan, as himself, as well as George Harrison, the ex-Beatle, who rescued the film when EMI withdrew its funding, and who plays Mr Papadopoulis, the owner of the Mount (scene 19).[20]

The structure of *Life of Brian* has been described as 'essentially a collection of surreal, violent, and very funny sketches held together with a loose narrative thread',[21] an account that, minus the surrealism, violence and humour, makes me think, as a New Testament scholar, of the Gospel of Mark. Being parasitic on the Gospel story as well as on the Hollywood epics and the Jesus films, the coherence of the narrative element is stronger in *Life of Brian* than in other examples of their work. There are some disjunctions, however; the excised scenes with Otto, the Neo-Nazi Nazarene, for example, are present, one notes, in the Methuen edition of the script (scenes 19 and 25),[22] but absent from the online Multi-Media MontyPython.net version,[23] creating aporias in the narrative flow.

Most Jesus films include classic scenes, such as the nativity (as in *The Greatest Story Ever Told*), the Sermon on the Mount (as in *King of Kings*), a stoning (as in *The Last Temptation of Christ*) and, of course, the crucifixion. *Life of Brian* also includes these key scenes, although it gives them a subversive twist. In their infamous version of the Sermon on the Mount (scene 2), for example, the Matthean Jesus' 'blessed are the peacemakers' (Matt. 5.9) is misheard as 'blessed are the cheesemakers'. In David Jasper's words, '[t]he hermeneutical problems of "hearing" a discourse across the temporal abyss of two thousand years of history are parodied in the device of using the spatial problem of listeners at the back of the crowd who are simply too far away from the speaker to catch his words clearly'.[24] Everyone

---

20. See Rainey, 'Life of Brian', *Telegraph*; Tony Roche, 'The Life of Brian: When Monty Python Took on God', *The Telegraph*, 19 October 2011. <http://www.telegraph.co.uk/culture/tvandradio/8833320/The-Life-of-Brian-When-Monty-Python-took-on-God.html> [accessed 4 September 2014]; Robert Sellers, 'Welease Bwian', *The Guardian*, 28 March 2003. <http://www.theguardian.com/culture/2003/mar/28/artsfeatures1> [accessed 4 September 2014].

21. Schneider, *1001 Movies*, p. 657. David Jasper, too, describes the structure as 'little more than a series of satirical sketches', *Readings in the Canon of Scripture: Written for Our Learning* (Studies in Literature and Religion; New York: St Martin's, 1995), p. 92.

22. See, for example, Monty Python, *The Life of Brian Screenplay* (promotional edn; London: Methuen, 2004), pp. 74–7, 89.

23. MontyPython.net, 'Monty Python's "Life of Brian" Script Part 2' <http://www.montypython.net/brianmm2.php> [accessed 4 September 2014] and MontyPython.net, 'Monty Python's "Life of Brian" Script Part 3' <http://www.montypython.net/brianmm3.php> [accessed 4 September 2014].

24. Jasper, *Readings*, p. 92. Cf. also Martin Scorsese's interesting comment on this scene when describing the shooting of *The Last Temptation of Christ* (1988): 'take the case of the Sermon on the Mount, which is usually presented as a man standing on a hill, surrounded by 3,000 people. There's that wonderful scene in *The Life of Brian*, when nobody can hear at

is familiar with the film's notorious 'Always Look on the Bright Side of Life' in the closing scene, but the enormity of Rome's brutal form of execution is subverted, too, through the character of Ben, an ancient, mad, right-wing prisoner who, echoing the famous 'What have the Romans ever done for us?' episode (scene 9) claims that crucifixion is the 'best thing the Romans ever did for us' (scene 11). As Richard Walsh observes: 'The absurdity – along with the claim that the crucified are lucky bastards and that crucifixion is a dawdle that gets one out in the open air – expresses a comic ambivalence toward empire, law and order ideologies, and "revolutionaries".'[25]

Two principal but not exclusive sources employed in Hollywood epics, or Jesus films, are the Gospels, on the one hand, and past exemplars of the genre, on the other. Apart from the aforementioned key scenes, *Life of Brian's* borrowings from the Gospels are less direct. The words of Brian's sermon (scene 16) echo Jesus' Sermon on the Mount (cf. Matt. 7.1–2=Luke 6.37–38; Matt. 6.25–33= Luke 12.22–31; Matt. 25.14–30= Luke 19.12–27)[26] and those of the blood and thunder, false and boring apocalyptic prophets (scene 14) sound like a garbled version of the Apocalyptic Discourse (Mark 13 and par.). Indeed Jesus' words in Mark 13.5–6, 21 par. ('Take heed that no one leads you astray. Many will come in my name, saying, "I am he!" and they will lead many astray ... And then if any one says to you, "Look, here is the Christ!" or "Look, there he is!" do not believe it') might even be taken as the leitmotif of the film.[27] Other Gospel passages or characters suggest themselves to the discerning viewer. Behind the consumption of Simon the Holy Man's juniper berries (scene 18), for example, the feeding stories in the wilderness (Mark 6.34–52; 8.1–9 par.) may be detected. In the prisoner release scenes in the film (scenes 23 and 27), the Barabbas passages in the Gospels (Mark 15.6–14 par.) are clearly in evidence. The 'Saintly Passerby' who offers to shoulder Alfonso's cross only to find him left with it himself (scene 27) brings to mind the biblical Simon of Cyrene (Mark 15.21 par.).

Borrowings from the Hollywood epics or Jesus films can also be observed. The Children's Matinee at the Roman amphitheatre (scene 7) evokes the

---

the back— it sounds like "Blessed are the cheesemakers" — they say, "I guess he said, 'Blessed are the cheesemakers', how very nice of him!" Well, if you hang out in North Africa long enough, you discover that in these villages where we shot the film, where there's no electricity and only a few donkeys, the number of people to gather would be, at most, twenty-five or thirty. That why we used a small crowd, so that Jesus could really speak to each person, go inside the crowd and talk to them individually, making them understand this new philosophy and sharing His soul with them', Ian Christie and David Thompson (eds), *Scorsese on Scorsese* (London: Faber & Faber, 1989), p. 128.

25. Walsh, '*Monty Python's Life of Brian* (1979)', p. 190.

26. Tatum, *Jesus at the Movies*, p. 167.

27. See Jeffrey L. Staley, and Richard Walsh, *Jesus, the Gospels, and Cinematic Imagination. A Handbook to Jesus on DVD* (Louisville and London: Westminster John Knox, 2007), p. 103.

Roman-Christian epics and especially *Ben-Hur* (1959). The 'I am Brian' acclamations before the crucifixion (scene 30) are straight from *Spartacus* (1960). Some have seen allusions to the opening scenes of Ray's *King of Kings* (1961) or Stevens' *The Greatest Story Ever Told* (1965) in the skeletons on crosses seen by Brian and Mandy on the way back to Jerusalem (scene 3).[28] The Pythons' debt to medieval tradition has also been commented upon. Early Jesus films were based on the medieval passion plays, and David Jasper claims that '[t]he essential comedy of the [*Life of Brian*] film draws directly upon the medieval tradition of literature which lampoons corrupt ecclesiastical practices, with stock comic figures drawn from contemporary life'.[29] Commentators on the *Life of Brian* have thus lauded the Pythons' background preparation, and in his now classic essay, '*Life of Brian* Research',[30] Philip Davies has demonstrated convincingly the 'abundant evidence of historical and biblical research reflected in the script of this film'. 'The evidence', he claims, 'is sufficiently extensive to exclude the possibility of happy coincidence, forcing the conclusion that Monty Python, whether real or implied film-maker, is a biblical scholar, however temporarily'.[31]

The style of *Life of Brian*, at least initially, also evokes the biblical epic or Jesus film, as do its settings (not surprisingly since it was filmed in Tunisia using Franco Zeffirelli's sets for *Jesus of Nazareth*, 1977). The opening scene of the Three Wise Men and the star, with its choral background and trumpet fanfare, evoke the rousing and elegiac themes of Miklós Rósza or Alfred Newman, the creators of the music that epitomizes the Hollywood epic.[32] The credits, however, with their animation sequences and their James Bond/Shirley Bassey-style music show that we are in very different territory. The Jesus film, of course, has used animation (cf. e.g. Sokolov's *The Miracle Maker*, 1999) but not in this anarchic fashion. The spaceship scene (scene 13) in the middle of the film takes us into a different cosmos, evoking the successor to the biblical epic, the *Star Wars* (1977) epic.[33] The 'Always Look on the Bright Side of Life' finale, with its voiceover reminding the audience that the record is available in the foyer, has invited comparisons with the Jesus musicals of the 1970s (*Jesus Christ Superstar*, 1973,

28. See, for example, Staley and Walsh, *Cinematic Imagination*, p. 101 and Walsh, '*Monty Python's Life of Brian* (1979)', p. 187.

29. Jasper, *Readings*, p. 92.

30. Philip R. Davies, '*Life of Brian* Research', in J. Cheryl Exum and Stephen D. Moore (eds), *Biblical Studies/Cultural Studies: The Third Sheffield Colloquium* (Sheffield: Sheffield Academic Press, 1998), pp. 400–14.

31. Ibid., pp. 400–1. Cf. also Reinhartz, *Jesus of Hollywood*, p. 18: 'Despite the fictional premise of the spoof, *Life of Brian* is meticulously researched and gleefully intelligent.'

32. See Telford, 'Jesus Christ Movie-Star', pp. 127, 135.

33. Cf. Walsh, '*Monty Python's Life of Brian* (1979)', p. 191: 'That the alien UFO replaces the Gospel's authorizing divine voice is a transformation that befits a culture in which epics like *Star Wars* have replaced biblical epics in "popularity".'

Godspell, 1973).[34] The working-class British accents of the characters are a departure from the clipped, upper-class accents of the traditional Hollywood epics or Jesus films, but Scorsese's *The Last Temptation of Christ* had a similar innovation in acting style. A major stylistic difference, of course, in *Life of Brian,* is the reckless abandonment of what Diane Apostolos-Cappadona has called the traditional 'gravitas and respectability' that is the hallmark of the Hollywood epics and Jesus films.[35]

Aims, message and ideology

If comparisons such as these can be made between *Life of Brian* and the Hollywood epics and Jesus films, the differences are much more striking. The Pythons' aims, it seems, are very different in this film. I say, 'it seems', because Python rationalizations for their project have been ambiguous. Directors of biblical epics and Jesus films have usually offered religiously acceptable motivations for their products. Even as controversial a director as Martin Scorsese, in filming *The Last Temptation of Christ* (1988) claimed that he 'wanted to make the life of Jesus immediate and accessible to people who haven't really thought about God in a long time'.[36] John Cleese seems to fall in with this traditional avowal by claiming that while the Python team were 'clearly making fun of the way people follow religion', they were not making fun 'of religion itself', and that he 'would defend *Life of Brian* as being a perfectly *religious* film'.[37]

When you examine the ideology of the film, however, its underlying values are strikingly different from the traditional Hollywood epic or Jesus film. Combining social criticism with comedic ambiguity, evincing a postmodern and counter-hegemonic perspective, frequently politically incorrect, and seeing absurdity in life and finality in death, it espouses individualism and anti-authoritarianism to a marked degree. In the film's final sequence, Brian tells his crucifixion squad (scene 31), 'You don't have to take orders', and this line, according to Geoffrey Staley and Richard Walsh, 'works well as an underlying theme of the film as a whole'.[38]

34. 'In a final irreverence, the crucified sing "Always Look on the Bright Side of Life (Death)", and a voiceover advertizes the sale of the record in the foyer (compare the successful music of *Jesus Christ Superstar* [1973] and *Godspell* [1973]', Walsh, ibid., p. 189.

35. Diane Apostolos-Cappadona, 'Iconography', in John Lyden (ed.), *The Routledge Companion to Religion and Film* (London and New York: Routledge, 2011), p. 449.

36. Christie and Thompson, *Scorsese on Scorsese*, p. 124.

37. Carl Dyke, 'Learning from *The Life of Brian:* Saviors for Seminars', in George Aichele and Richard Walsh (eds), *Screening Scripture. Intertextual Connections between Scripture and Film* (Harrisburg, PA: Trinity Press International, 2002), p. 239, citing David Morgan, *Monty Python Speaks!* (New York: Spike/Avon, 1999), pp. 247–8.

38. Staley and Walsh, *Cinematic Imagination*, p. 104.

Audience, social context and reception

Where audience is concerned, this might explain why *Monty Python's Life of Brian* has always attracted the younger generation, and, according to Peter Hasenberg, is 'perhaps the only "religious" film with a cult following among young audiences'.[39] The Hollywood biblical epics were conservative in orientation, and invited an older, middle-class spectatorship.[40] They were aimed, moreover, at a mass market. Terry Jones, the director of *Life of Brian*, has admitted, however, that the Pythons 'never had a mass audience', and that they have been accepted by 'an intelligent, articulate minority', including students, academics and intellectuals, one of whom, Carl Dyke, wrote a prominent defence of the film.[41]

A major way of reading Hollywood epics and Jesus films, as with the Gospels, is to interpret them in light of the social context in which they were produced, and which they address, and the Pythons' small, discerning audience has been well positioned to recognize what is really going in their work. In contrast to Cleese, Terry Gilliam is on record as saying that '*Life of Brian* had nothing at all to do with religion but was an "allegory about suburban England" ',[42] and sophisticated viewers will recognize the digs that are made against the class system, the public school, bureaucracy, the trade unions, nationalism, imperialism, and the many other institutions that are the targets of the film. It is not surprising, then, that the film's reception was characterized by outrage, offence and controversy, particularly from Catholic, Protestant and Jewish leaders, and especially in North America, where it was seen as a 'mockery of Christ's life'[43] and a deliberate exploitation of 'much that is sacred to Christian and Jewish religious tradition'.[44]

---

39. Peter Hasenberg, 'The "Religious" in Film: From *King of Kings* to *The Fisher King*', in J. R. May (ed.), *New Image of Religious Film* (Kansas City, MO: Sheed & Ward, 1997), pp. 41–56, at p. 47.

40. See Richard C. Stern, Clayton N. Jefford and Guerric DeBona, *Savior on the Silver Screen* (New York and Mahwah, NJ: Paulist, 1999), p. 263.

41. Dyke, 'Learning from *The Life of Brian*', pp. 229–50. Quotations, p. 239, citing Morgan, *Monty Python Speaks!*, p. 248.

42. See Stern, Jefford and DeBona, *Silver Screen*, p. 254, citing an interview by Jones for *Playboy* (November, 1979). In this excellent chapter, Stern, Jefford and DeBona go on to place *Life of Brian* in its British context. They describe the new Britain that emerged in the 1960s and 1970s, commenting on the weakening of the class system, the rise of the working class and of the trade unions, the attack on imperialism, nationalism and monarchy, the development of social criticism and the influence of programmes like *That Was The Week That Was*. They note, too, the return to conservatism and individualism in the Margaret Thatcher years. Events and reactions in America are also commented on, including Vietnam, Watergate and the Reagan years.

43. Ibid., p. 254.

44. Peter Malone, 'The Roman Catholic Church and Cinema (1967 to the Present)', in Lyden (ed.), *Routledge Companion*, p. 64.

Is Monty Python's Life of Brian *a Jesus Film?*

Genre and targets

Was this perception a valid one? To what extent can *Life of Brian* be considered an *anti-Jesus* film? To what extent can it be considered an 'anti *Jesus-film*'? Or is there a case for placing it, in fact, within the category of the 'Jesus film'? This brings me to the second part of my discussion in which I wish to consider more fully the genric dimension of *Life of Brian*.

Through its title sequence, *Life of Brian* introduces itself to its viewers as a comedy, and through its opening nativity scene as a 'satirical comedy',[45] 'comedic satire'[46] or 'satirical comedy revue'.[47] According to Lloyd Baugh, it 'has the dubious privilege of being the only Jesus-film in the key of satirical comedy'.[48] It is not the only example of biblical comedic satire, however. One needs only to think of Mel Brooks' *History of the World—Part 1* (1981), whose 'Moses & the Ten Commandments' and 'Last Supper' sequences have truly Pythonesque qualities.[49] The terms 'black comedy',[50] 'spoof',[51] 'romp'[52] and 'parody'[53] have also been applied to *Life of Brian*. In encouraging critical reflection on the legendary and mythical aspects of the dominant culture, it has even been described, in suitably biblical fashion, as a 'parable'.[54] Where its place within the history of the genre is concerned, it joins a number of films, on the other hand, which, on account of their counter-hegemonic ideology, have been described as the 'scandal films', Jean-Luc Godard's *Hail Mary* (1984), Martin Scorsese's *The Last Temptation of Christ* (1988) and Denis Arcand's *Jesus of Montreal* (1989) being numbered among them.[55]

---

45. Lloyd Baugh, *Imaging the Divine: Jesus and Christ-Figures in Film* (Kansas City, MO: Sheed & Ward, 1997), p. 48.

46. Craig Detweiler, 'Christianity', in Lyden (ed.), *Routledge Companion*, pp.109–30, at p. 112.

47. Jasper, *Readings*, p. 90: 'Each [*Jesus of Montreal* & *Monty Python's Life of Brian*] refuses to offer a "straight" image of Jesus, but rather, exploiting the cinema's art of surrealism and deception, they grant a "voice" to Jesus (like the Gospels) through the textuality of the "play within the play" (*Jesus of Montreal*) and satirical comedy revue (*Life of Brian*)'.

48. Baugh, *Imaging the Divine*, p. 48.

49. See Peter Malone, 'Jesus on Our Screens', in John R. May (ed.), *New Image of Religious Film* (Franklin, WI: Sheed & Ward, 2000), pp. 57–71, at pp. 61–2.

50. Peter Malone, *Movie Christs and Antichrists* (New York: Crossroad, 1990), pp. 89–90.

51. Reinhartz, *Jesus of Hollywood*, p. 18.

52. John Walker (ed.), *Halliwell's Film and Video Guide 2003* (18th edn; London: HarperCollins, 2003), p. 565 ('Controversial middle-eastern romp which left its creators battered but extremely wealthy. In the face of such an onslaught of bad taste, criticism seems irrelevant').

53. Telford, 'Jesus Christ Movie-Star', p. 121.

54. Walsh, '*Monty Python's Life of Brian* (1979)', pp. 189–90; cf. also Staley and Walsh, *Cinematic Imagination*, p. 105.

55. Baugh, *Imaging the Divine*, chap. 4; Hasenberg, 'The "Religious" in Film', pp. 46–7.

It is a satirical comedy, then, but what are its targets? It is undeniable that the first of these is the Hollywood epics and, in particular, the Jesus movies. In her excellent book, *Jesus of Hollywood* (2007), Adele Reinhartz states that '[t]hough it is a "Brian" movie and not a "Jesus" movie, *Life of Brian* both uses and mocks the clichés of the genre',[56] and here she expresses a widely-held view.[57] In *Monty Python's Life of Brian* (1979), in other words, the Pythons have done for the biblical world, as depicted in the epics, what they did for the medieval world in *Monty Python and the Holy Grail* (1977).[58]

Judging by the reaction from the religious establishment, however, their target was even wider. Many critics and reviewers accused it of an attack on institutional or organized religion, the established church and even Christianity itself. The doctrines of the sacraments or the virgin birth were being mocked in, for example, the symbolic artefacts left behind by Brian, the gourd and the sandal/shoe (scenes 16 and 17), and in the questioning of Mandy's virginity (scene 19). Christian factionalism and sectarianism were being lampooned through Brian's Gourdene, Shoe-ite or Sandalite followers,[59] fundamentalism in their rigid adherence to a belief in Brian's messiahship, and heresy in their treatment of Simon the Holy Man's denial of it (scene 18). In its coded jokes about Christian theology and history, it was even seen as tilting against biblical critics or theologians.[60]

But, as we have observed, *Life of Brian* strikes, albeit with comic ambiguity, at even wider targets still, namely, the political establishment, imperialism, the British public-school system, the class system, and at the other end of the spectrum, economic exploitation, the trade unions, and revolutionary movements. Behind the Romans lies the British empire, its benevolent but inept administrators embodied in Nisus Wettus and his mild-mannered 'one-cross each' organization of the crucifees (scene 22). Behind John Cleese's centurion of the yard, with his issuing to Brian of 100 lines for getting the Latin of his 'Romans Go Home' slogan wrong (scene 8) lies the British public-school system. Behind the meeting of the People's Front of Judaea (scene 21) to pass endless motions and resolutions of immediate action to rescue Brian, lie the trade unions.

And, throughout *Life of Brian*, is the prevailing attack on credulity, closed-mindedness and hypocrisy. Ranged, as it is, against these wider and more diffuse targets, then, Monty Python's *Life of Brian* cannot simply be characterized as a movie that aims to parody the conventions of the biblical epic or Jesus film. It is, in that sense, *not merely* an anti Jesus-film.

---

56. Reinhartz, *Jesus of Hollywood*, p. 18.

57. Compare, for example, Bruce Babington and Peter W. Evans, *Biblical Epics: Sacred Narrative in the Hollywood Cinema* (Manchester: Manchester University Press, 1993), p. 100; Staley and Walsh, *Cinematic Imagination*, p. 104; Malone, 'Jesus on Our Screens', p. 62.

58. See Stern, Jefford and DeBona, *Silver Screen*, p. 253.

59. Tatum, *Jesus at the Movies*, p. 167.

60. See Jasper, *Readings*, p. 92; Dyke, 'Learning from *The Life of Brian*', p. 248.

Monty Python's Jesus

But is it an *anti-Jesus* film? Here the Pythons and commentators are virtually unanimous. The Python Jesus is a traditional one, and is not here under attack. The Jesus of the Christian tradition makes three appearances in the film, the first of which is in a manger, in the opening nativity scene, after the three wise men have discovered the right stable. In this scene, the three wise men acclaim him with familiar New Testament Christological titles, 'Son of God', 'Messiah', 'King of the Jews', and they worship him appropriately. He appears again, as a teacher, seen from a distance (cf. *Ben-Hur*, 1959), when giving the Sermon on the Mount (scene 2). His activity as a miracle-worker is also brought up, when he is referred to, by name, by the ex-leper in scene 5, who complains that, by curing him, Jesus has robbed him of his livelihood as a beggar. Apart from this last example, with its facetious criticism, and the dismissive comments of the People's Front of Judaea on his sermon (Francis: 'Well, Blessed is just about everyone with a vested interest in the status quo, as far as I can tell, Reg'; Reg: 'What Jesus blatantly fails to appreciate is that it is the meek who are the problem'), there is little to indicate that the orthodox Jesus of Christian faith is being attacked.[61] The Python Jesus is essentially the same Jesus that we encounter in Jesus films such as Ray's *King of Kings* (1961), Stevens' *The Greatest Story Ever Told* (1965) and Zeffirelli's *Jesus of Nazareth* (1977).[62]

Monty Python's Brian

But, finally, we have Jesus' possible alter ego to consider. Brian's life is shown parallel to that of his divine counterpart, and it invites us throughout to make comparisons. The Python Brian is a first-century Jew, with revolutionary aspirations. The Python Brian is born in a manger (scene 1). He is the product of dubious parentage, a Roman soldier's bastard (scene 6), as the alternative Jesus ben Panthera tradition predicates of Jesus (cf. Babylonian Talmud, Sanhedrin 104b; 67b; Origen, *Contra Celsum*, 1.69).[63] He has a mother whose virginity is questioned (scene 19). He has

---

61. See Dyke, 'Learning from *The Life of Brian*', pp. 237–8: 'With respect to Jesus, who makes three brief tangential appearances, the movie is downright orthodox. In each case, the message is not that Jesus is wrong, or even that worshipping Jesus is wrong, but that fallible humans find all sorts of creative ways to get worshipping Jesus wrong … The Pythons' Jesus … is divine … The unwise wise men show that men are fallible in their worship, but the object of that worship is left unquestioned (237) … While these episodes [Nativity; Sermon on the Mount; Ex-Leper] are certainly twists on the human reception of Jesus' saving words and miraculous works, those words, works, and their divine source are taken as givens. In terms of core Christian beliefs, the movie is reverent and unquestioning'; compare also Tatum, *Jesus at the Movies*, p. 166: '[T]he portrayal of Jesus in the Python film can best be described as that of a Christian icon'.

62. See Stern, Jefford and DeBona, *Silver Screen*, p. 238.

63. See Walsh, '*Monty Python's Life of Brian* (1979)', p. 188.

a female companion, Judith, the masculine form of whose name, as has already been said, is Judas, and who plays a role, however inadvertent, in his eventual crucifixion. He is lifted up into the heavens in a supernatural journey (scene 13) that has drawn comparison with the Gospel temptation, transfiguration or resurrection narratives.[64] He preaches his own sermon, in the marketplace, with words, as we have seen, that echo Jesus' Sermon on the Mount (scene 16), and that, incidentally, place him in the category, according to W. Barnes Tatum, of wise man rather than apocalyptic prophet.[65] He is considered to be a miracle-worker (scenes 5 and 18). Like the Markan Jesus, he is pursued by crowds wishing to learn his 'messianic secret' and reluctant to accept the role thrust upon him.[66] He is arrested and brought before Pontius Pilate (scenes 11 and 20). He is crucified!

Conclusion

To conclude: is *Monty Python's Life of Brian* a 'Jesus film', therefore? Scholarship on the Jesus films has been divided. In the comprehensive checklist of *The Bible on Film*, compiled by Richard H. Campbell and Michael R. Pitts and published in 1981,[67] the film is missing. In Roy Kinnard and Tim Davis' *Divine Images: A History of Jesus on the Screen* (1992), it is given an entry.[68] In the first edition of W. Barnes Tatum's *Jesus at the Movies: A Guide to the First Hundred Years* (1997), it is omitted, while in the second edition of 2004, it is included, with a note by the author stating that he had now been convinced that 'the *Monty Python* "spoof" was indeed a Jesus

---

64. Compare, for example, Walsh, 'Monty Python's Life of Brian (1979)', p. 191: 'The UFO parodies the Gospel *deus ex machina* pattern and Gospel exaltation of Jesus in the transfiguration (Matt. 17.1–9; Mark 9.2–10; Luke 9.23–27) and resurrection narratives (Matt. 28; Mark 16; Luke 20; John 20–21) and in the Johannine passion (John 18–19). By contrast, Brian is always falling down or out of something – a spaceship, a balcony. Nonetheless, along with Brian's marketplace acclamation, this "lifting up" inaugurates the "messianic" phase of Brian's career.'

65. See Walsh, 'Monty Python's Life of Brian (1979)', p. 188 and Tatum, *Jesus at the Movies*, pp. 167, 168: '[T]he Monty Python troupe, by placing these words of Jesus on Brian's lips and by placing the garbled apocalyptic statements on the lips of the other holy men, has aligned Brian not with the prophets of doom and gloom, but with sages who offer advice about life here and now.'

66. See Staley and Walsh, *Cinematic Imagination*, pp. 102, 103; Walsh, 'Monty Python's Life of Brian (1979)', p. 188: 'A crowd decides Brian is the messiah because he denies it; this may allude to the "messianic secret", a concept developed by scholars to explain Mark's Jesus' avoidance of public messianic acclamations (e.g. Mark 1.44)'.

67. Richard H. Campbell and Michael R. Pitts, *The Bible on Film: A Checklist, 1897–1980* (Metuchen, NJ: Scarecrow, 1981).

68. Kinnard and Davis, *Divine Images*, pp. 192–5.

film'.[69] So what is Brian therefore? Is he a Christ-figure, a counter-Christ figure or an anti-Christ figure? Scholars are divided.[70] He is hardly an anti-Christ figure except, perhaps, in that he, and the other prophets, teachers and crucified characters in the film, challenge the uniqueness of Jesus. The answer, I think, lies in the first of these designations, the Christ-figure. *Monty Python's Life of Brian*, this satirical comedy, lies, I think, within that special category of Jesus films, the Christ-figure films. While definitions of the Christ-figure in film can vary, the essential idea of the Christ-figure film is that it presents a story in which the plot, the characters and the content bring to mind, or resemble, the story of Jesus, and which, accordingly, invite the spectator, in light of it, to reflect on the Jesus tradition in new and potentially different ways. Since this was the theme of our *Jesus and Brian* conference at King's College London, the choice of *Monty Python's Life of Brian* was an appropriate one. Brian, in other words, is 'revelatory', to speak within a Christian or 'religious' discourse. He throws light, however facetiously, on the process whereby we construct our Christs, even although he himself is an everyman figure.[71] While it may be surprising to think of the figure of Brian in the movie as a Christ-figure, it is important to remember that Christ-figures in the movies come in a wide variety of forms. While they can appear as saints, priests or holy men, they also appear as clowns, fools, madmen, outlaws, children, women, or even

---

69. '[Of the 2nd ed., 2004] In addition to adding a concluding chapter on the Gibson film [*The Passion of the Christ*], I also added a chapter featuring *Monty Python's Life of Brian* (1979). A forum featuring the first edition of this book at the annual meeting of the Society of Biblical Literature (SBL) at the Opryland Hotel in Nashville, in November, 2000, had convinced me that the *Monty Python* "spoof" was indeed a Jesus film and should be included', Tatum, *Jesus at the Movies* (2013), p. viii. Cf. also the deliberations of Stern, Jefford and DeBona, *Silver Screen*, p. 234: 'There was some question about whether to include *Life of Brian* in this collection. Because of the widespread perception of this movie as a life of Jesus and because of its positioning in relationship to the genre of films about Jesus' life, it seemed important to include it in our discussion of the Savior on the silver screen'.

70. Compare and contrast the view, for example, of David Jasper, *Readings*, p. 92 ('Brian, the central character, is continually mistaken for the Jesus of the Gospels, and in a curious way, is very similar to the Christs of the medieval passion plays. He plays his part beautifully, and finally almost silently, and is the object of continual misreadings. The point in the end is that Brian *is* Christ precisely in so far as he is misunderstood and his identity mistaken') with that of Stern, Jefford and DeBona, *Silver Screen*, pp. 238–9 ('*Life of Brian* is actually the presentation of two heroes or twin subjects. The first is Jesus of Nazareth himself . . . (238) . . . Our second protagonist . . . is Brian of Nazareth or Brian Cohen. He stands as a sort of common man of the street, rational in thought with the typical concerns of any struggling first-century Jew in Roman-ruled Palestine . . . Brian stands as a type of "counter-christ" figure but certainly not an antichrist (239)'.

71. Cf. George Brooke's chapter in this volume, which throws interesting parallel light on the construction of the Teacher of Righteousness prototype in the Dead Sea Scrolls.

popular adventure heroes.[72] A recent trend in the analysis of Christ-figure movies is the discernment of more ambiguity in our cinematic 'Christ-figures'. As Chris Deacy has pointed out, they are no longer models of Nicean divinity or perfection, as the epics portray him, even though their redemptive struggle is real.[73] *Life of Brian*, I would maintain, then, is a Christ-figure movie and Brian a Christ-figure. But then, I am sure he would reject this!

---

72. Cf. Baugh, *Imaging the Divine, passim*; Adele Reinhartz, 'Jesus and Christ-Figures', in Lyden (ed.), *Routledge Companion*, pp. 420-39; William R. Telford, 'Appendix 2: Christ-Figures in Film', in Eric Christianson, Peter Francis and William R. Telford (eds), *Cinéma Divinité: Religion, Theology and the Bible in Film* (London: SCM-Canterbury, 2005), pp. 351–3.

73. Christopher Deacy, *Screen Christologies: Redemption and the Medium of Film* (Religion, Culture and Society; Cardiff: University of Wales Press, 2001). Travis Bickle in *Taxi Driver* (Martin Scorsese, 1976), Jake La Motta in *Raging Bull* (Martin Scorsese, 1980) and Max Cady in *Cape Fear* (Martin Scorsese, 1991) are three examples cited by Deacy.

Chapter 2

THE CHURCH OF ENGLAND'S *LIFE OF PYTHON* – OR 'WHAT THE BISHOP SAW'

Richard A. Burridge

In this chapter I want to reflect on the *Jesus and Brian* conference as a whole, held at King's College London in June 2014. I will also make particular reference to several discussions about the film, *Life of Brian*, which took place on T V and radio and in the press, both at its first appearance thirty-five years ago, and also more recently. We will look particularly at the reactions from religious groups and the Church and examine the reasons why it was quickly assumed that Christians found the film offensive, or wanted it banned. The particular criticisms which were levelled at the film and at the Pythons themselves will be discussed, and we will attempt to examine what was the real purpose and intention behind the making of the *Life of Brian*. Finally, the question must be faced of whether the Church and the academy missed a golden opportunity in 1979 to debate the life and work of Jesus of Nazareth in wider society.

The Film, the Church and the Media

Shortly after the London premiere of *Life of Brian*, John Cleese and Michael Palin appeared on Tim Rice's BBC show *Friday Night, Saturday Morning*. Two other guests had been invited to review the film: the literary critic and former editor of *Punch*, Malcolm Muggeridge, and the then Bishop of Southwark, Mervyn Stockwood. This interview has gone down in movie history, not least because of the full-frontal assault made on the film by Muggeridge and Stockwood. Even thirty-five years later, there are various versions of the programme freely available on YouTube, which have been watched by hundreds of thousands of people, if not millions.[1] Undoubtedly, part of the reason for this is the inflammatory effect it all had upon the normally placid Michael Palin, who was renowned for getting angry only once before with the rest of the Pythons, after 'being made to crawl through mud for the ninth take on the 1975 film Monty Python and the Holy Grail'.[2] However, on that night, as a result of the lack of real engagement by Stockwood and Muggeridge with the movie and his concerns, he was what John Cleese described recently as 'quite shirty by normal Palin standards'![3]

Significantly, when Michael Palin was the guest editor on the *Today* programme on Radio 4 on 30 December 2013, this was one of the four items from his life which he chose to revisit (along with his boyhood in Sheffield, a visit to India, and finding out what happens to the recycling in the green box outside his home!). Professor Joan Taylor had already been in touch with him about our *Jesus and Brian* conference, and so Palin wrote an email to her: 'I'm guest editing one of the Radio 4 *Today* programmes in the week after Christmas. One of the things I'm doing is John C and myself re-collecting the Muggeridge–Bishop of Southwark interview about *Life Of Brian*. I suggested to my producer that it might be good, after our recollections are finished, to ask what the churches think of *Life Of Brian* now.'[4] Although he invited Joan to come to do the interview on the *Today*

---

1. See for example, https://www.youtube.com/watch?v=CeKWVuye1YE, which has the whole programme, including the later musical item and another interview; another version can be found at https://www.youtube.com/watch?v=1ni559bHXDg, which has most of the programme in several clips; https://www.youtube.com/watch?v=tl8acXl3qVs has an extract, while a ten-minute compilation of clips with a commentary is at https://www.youtube.com/watch?v=oM46jRJnHM. Please note that all the YouTube and other web references and URLs which follow throughout this chapter were accessed and functioning during the first week of September 2014, although, of course, that cannot be guaranteed forever.

2. http://www.telegraph.co.uk/culture/tvandradio/10532357/Michael-Palin-My-wife-keeps-me-grounded.html; see also Michael Palin, *Diaries 1969–1979: The Python Years* (London: Phoenix/Orion, 2007), 13 May 1974, pp. 195–6.

3. In the Radio 4 interview on 31 December 2013; https://www.youtube.com/watch?v=Od2ni3okcww

4. Personal email from Michael Palin to Joan Taylor, dated 11 November 2013, used with his permission.

programme, she kindly asked me if I would be willing to do it instead, seeing it as a great opportunity for someone from both the Church and from King's College London to comment – for which I was very grateful.

So Michael Palin and John Cleese sat down together to watch the original interview and discussed the content as it progressed. Their comments were recorded and then condensed to about six minutes which was broadcast on the *Today* programme, followed by an interview with myself as Dean of King's College London and representing the Church of England.[5]

What was particularly interesting was the ensuing press reaction, despite the fact that the original story about the Church's negative reaction to the film was more than three decades old. The *Daily Telegraph* printed a more in-depth interview with me the next day about why the Church had reacted in that way to the *Life of Brian*.[6] Much of this material was then repeated by *The Sun* (on Page Three, next to the inevitable topless model!) and in the *Daily Mail*.[7]

This juxtaposition of my comments as a 'senior churchman' and the first non-Roman Catholic to receive the Ratzinger Prize from the Pope with the original negative reactions from the Church to the film attracted so much media interest that the story went viral, being regurgitated in newspapers and media websites around the world from Norway to New Zealand. The original interviews and the ensuing media reactions were also picked up and discussed by James Crossley on his Sheffield Biblical Studies blog.[8]

The other TV show which is relevant to all of this is the famous parody of the Muggeridge and Stockwood debate with Cleese and Palin which was broadcast also on the BBC in the *Not the Nine O'Clock News* comedy series a short time after the original *Friday Night, Saturday Morning* show. Here the roles are reversed, with a clip supposedly taken from a spoof film made and released by the Church of England under the title of *The Life of Python*. In this mock discussion, Rowan Atkinson plays the part of the bishop responsible for making the film, while Pamela Stephenson as the chat show host tries to mediate between him and Mel Smith as Alexander Walker, a leading 'Pythonist', who has been offended and outraged by the film, appalled that it could be shown in what is still 'ostensibly a Python-worshipping country'. Walker/Smith's criticisms of the film are almost verbally identical with those made about the *Life of Brian* by Muggeridge and Stockwood, while Atkinson, as the bishop playing with the chain around his neck in exactly the same way that

---

5. An audio recording with clips of both the film of *Life of Brian* and the Muggeridge-Stockwood interview is available to view at https://www.youtube.com/watch?v=Od2ni3okcww

6. http://www.telegraph.co.uk/news/religion/10543149/Monty-Pythons-Life-of-Brian-extraordinary-tribute-to-Jesus-says-theologian-decorated-by-Pope-Francis.html

7. http://www.dailymail.co.uk/news/article-2532171/A-U-turn-Biblical-proportions-34-years-release-senior-churchman-calls-Life-Brian-extraordinary-tribute-Jesus.html

8. http://sheffieldbiblicalstudies.wordpress.com/2014/01/05/life-of-brian-richard-burridge-and-the-media/

Mervyn Stockwood had done, tries hilariously to defend himself against these charges. Once again, despite the passing of many years, this sketch is a firm favourite with various versions on *YouTube* having received over half a million viewings.[9]

Thus the criticisms made by Muggeridge and Stockwood and the original debate with Cleese and Palin remain very current today and so are well worth revisiting, in order to explore the Church's reaction to the *Life of Brian* and to answer the question, 'what *did* the bishop see?'!

Blasphemy: the Reactions and the Backlash

However, before considering these criticisms in detail, we must consider that the launch of the film and the result of the Pythons' interview with Muggeridge and Stockwood created a backlash, which was precisely what Michael Palin and the other Pythons had been hoping to avoid. It must be remembered that while the Pythons were writing the script for *Life of Brian*, there had been a recent – and successful – prosecution for blasphemous libel, the first since the 1920s. Mary Whitehouse brought this case against *Gay News* regarding the publication (in its 16 June 1976 issue) of 'The Love that Dares to Speak its Name'. This was an erotic poem by James Kirkup which is narrated from the perspective of the centurion guarding Jesus on the cross (Mark 15. 39 and par.). The editor of *Gay News*, Denis Lemon, was fined and given a suspended prison sentence, which was quashed on appeal, even though the original verdict was upheld.[10] Significantly, Graham Chapman, who plays Brian in the film, was himself homosexual and one of the co-founders and financial backers of *Gay News*, so the Pythons would have been all too aware of the potential for litigation arising from their film.

It is also quite clear from Michael Palin's *Diaries*, written at the time, that the Pythons were conscious of the possibilities of a blasphemy charge. Therefore, they took legal advice all the way through the production process. Palin recounts a small viewing of *Brian* at the Bijou Theatre on 14 June 1979, with all the Pythons, except Graham Chapman, and with Oscar Beuselinck and John Mortimer present to 'represent the law'. As well as being a barrister, Mortimer was a playwright and novelist, the creator of *Rumpole of the Bailey*. Palin notes that he is: 'clearly chuffed to be amongst such humorous company. He loves the film and reckons we are quite safe. The chances of a jury convicting Python of blasphemy on the basis of this film are very remote, he believes – but not impossible.'[11] Indeed, some months earlier in the process, legal advice about the script was sought by Barry Spikings, who worked for Bernard Delfont at EMI who were, at that point, backing the film financially; the letter from the lawyers on 15 February 1979 advised that

9. https://www.youtube.com/watch?v=asUyK6JWt9U; https://www.youtube.com/watch?v=Ku9lt_TvR1k

10. See the discussion in George Perry, *The Life of Python* (London: BCA Pavilion, 1994), p. 158.

11. Palin, *Diaries*, 14 June 1979, p. 619.

the only possible area of concern were words used by Michael Palin as the 'ex-leper' who had been cured by Jesus to describe him.[12]

Another related group which the Pythons were concerned about all the way through the production process was the Christian organization, the Nationwide Festival of Light, who were promoting a moral 'clean-up' of society. Michael Palin notes as early as 29 December 1978 in his *Diaries* that their protests about the planning of the film were concerning his mother; some months later, in his entries for 4 and 12 April 1979, he writes that the Festival of Light 'are almost daily ringing the censor's office' and 'will try and use the blasphemy law (upheld in the *Gay News* case) to try and stop the film'.[13] However, by 7 November, shortly before the film is released, Palin notes that he has been able to reassure his mother that 'the Festival of Light are now taking a much saner view of the movie' and have realized that it is 'extremely unlikely that the film would sustain a successful prosecution in English law'.[14]

Therefore it is not perhaps surprising that Tim Rice and the BBC invited Raymond Johnston, the Director of the Festival of Light, to attend the recording of the debate between Cleese and Palin with Stockwood and Muggeridge. Palin gives an account of meeting him afterwards in his diaries:

> In the hospitality room we were surrounded like heroes returning from a war. I was introduced to Raymond Johnston of the Festival of Light – always our most arch enemies. Instead I found myself confronted with a thin, rather nervous man, a committed Christian who had been embarrassed at the display of the Bishop. He (Johnston) *had* seen the film. He found it quite clear that Brian and Jesus were separate people. He had many differences of opinion with us, but he thought the film not malicious, not harmful and, furthermore, he saw and appreciated that we were making very valid points about the organised religions which told you what to think, in the same way that Stockwood tonight had used the cheapest and most dishonest methods to tell people what to think. Later I watched it [the TV debate] go out and fortunately the Bishop's 'performance' came over as badly on air as it did in the studio.[15]

It is interesting to read Palin's reaction to this encounter with Raymond Johnston written at the time. Significantly, the Festival of Light had tried to ban the film in advance and yet, once Johnston had seen it, he appreciated the difference between the figures of Brian and Jesus.

Nonetheless, while there was no prosecution for blasphemy, the original tactics of the Festival of Light to lobby local authorities to ban the film in their area were

---

12. For a facsimile of the lawyers' letter, see The Pythons with Bob McCabe, *Autobiography* (London: Orion, 2003), p. 284.

13. Palin, *Diaries*, pp. 575, 604, 606.

14. Palin, *Diaries*, 7 November 1979, p. 657.

15. Palin, *Diaries*, 9 November 1979, pp. 659–60.

successful. In many areas it was banned altogether, while in others the official
BBFC rating of an AA-certificate (open for 14 year-olds and over) was upgraded
to an X-certificate (for adults over 18 only).[16] Speaking personally, I was a young
school teacher at the time, teaching Latin and Greek and Classical Civilization.
Our local curate, who is now a diocesan bishop (and who shall be nameless),
insisted from the pulpit that we were not allowed to go and see the film at our local
cinema. As a devoted Python fan, and a Classics teacher, this did not stop me from
going to see it!

However, there was great debate about *Brian* receiving bans across the United
States, in Britain, and beyond. It is often said that it was banned in Aberystwyth
until Sue Jones-Davies, the actress who plays the character of Brian's girlfriend,
Judith, became the mayor in 2009 and held a screening, attended by Terry Jones
and Michael Palin, to celebrate; however, others have stated that it was actually
shown in Aberystwyth before then. Similarly, the film was banned in Norway for
many years, causing it to be advertised in Sweden as 'a film so funny that they had
to ban it in Norway'. This might help to explain why the *Today* interview with
Michael Palin and myself at New Year even made it into *Dagbladet*, the Norwegian
tabloid newspaper.[17] Clearly, therefore, the sorts of criticisms made about the *Life
of Brian* by the Bishop of Southwark and Malcolm Muggeridge not only had their
effect at the time but have also continued to do so.

The Main Criticisms

We now need to consider the main criticisms made by Stockwood and Muggeridge
in the original debate, which are then also picked up and debated by Cleese and
Palin in their discussion for the *Today* programme on Radio 4.[18] They fall into
several main categories.

The first criticism made by the Bishop of Southwark early on concerns the
quality of the film, namely that it is cheap and tawdry, or 'tenth-rate' according to
Muggeridge. In contrast to it being 'cheap', the Bishop's final criticism was that the
film was produced for financial gain: Stockwood's parting shot at the close of the
interview was, 'You'll get your thirty pieces of silver'. In between these two criticisms,
the bulk of the discussion centred around some form or another of blasphemy,
that the *Life of Brian* is mocking Jesus, and nothing Cleese or Palin could say
persuaded them otherwise. Malcolm Muggeridge's constant complaint is that a
fourteen-year-old going into the film (an allusion to its AA-Certificate) would fail
to realize 'the significance of the incarnation'. As part of this overall objection, the
final scene of the mass crucifixion was also particularly criticized, although since
Cleese himself recognized that he had a 'tiny quibble' about this right at the start

16. See Perry, *The Life of Python*, p. 164.
17. http://www.dagbladet.no/2014/01/03/kultur/komedie/monty_python/life_of_
brian/religion/31094614/
18. https://www.youtube.com/watch?v=Od2ni3okcww

of the programme before Muggeridge and the Bishop came on stage to join them, perhaps this should be considered as a fourth area. We shall consider them each in turn.

1 'Tawdry . . . tenth-rate . . . squalid little number'? The question of quality

Mervyn Stockwood began the debate with a long and sometimes rambling speech, in which he made it clear that he was 'not the least bit horrified' by the film, but rather he thought that it was extremely poor quality. As a former vicar of the University Church in Cambridge he was 'familiar with undergraduate humour', and he described *Brian* as 'the sort of thing at Cambridge that the Footlights did on a damp Tuesday afternoon or the Lower Fourth when I was a schoolmaster'. Muggeridge was similarly dismissive, describing the film as 'this squalid little number' and 'extremely cheap and tenth-rate'. He stressed how the 'story of the incarnation' built 'our civilization', and 'inspired every great artist, every great writer, every great composer, every great builder, every great architect'; instead the Pythons 'had succeeded in reducing something which has inspired the greatest art . . . in terms of the lowest art'. If anybody were to 'dredge up this miserable little film' in the future, they would never relate it to something like 'Chartres Cathedral, which was built to the glory of Christ'. John Cleese immediately noted that Chartres Cathedral is 'not a funny building – and not even intended to be a funny building'. Michael Palin's response also referred to their intention: 'we don't want to influence people, we are trying to make them laugh, make them happy'.

The Pythons were surely correct to seek to defend themselves against these accusations by referring back to their intention not to create great art or influence people, but to make a comedy film, and to entertain their audience. However, these accusations that the film is of poor quality with no possibility of doing anything in the future are extremely embarrassing to watch today in the light of the artistic success of the *Life of Brian*.[19] For years and years the film has featured at the top of various lists of popularity and ratings. For example, the film is listed in Stephen Schneider's very influential list, *1001 Films You Must See Before You Die*.[20] It features at number 28 in the British Film Institute's '100 best British films of the century', as voted for by one thousand leading figures of the movie industry'.[21] This world-wide appreciation of *Life of Brian* as perhaps the best-ever British comedy has surely disproved beyond any shadow of doubt Muggeridge and Stockwood's accusations that it was 'squalid', 'cheap' or 'tenth rate' – and certainly it is far above what the Cambridge 'Footlights did on a damp Tuesday afternoon or the Lower Fourth'. For most devotees and critics of British humour, the *Life of Brian* is easily the most successful and artistically satisfying work of the Monty Python team.

19. See William Telford in this volume, Chapter 1.

20. Stephen Jay Schneider, *1001 Films You Must See Before You Die* (London: Quintessence, 2013).

21. http://news.bbc.co.uk/1/hi/entertainment/455170.stm; http://www.imdb.com/list/ls000050201/

2 'You'll get your thirty pieces of silver.' The question of finance

The second accusation made in this debate was that the Pythons had produced the film simply for financial gain. The bishop was clearly determined to get his final Parthian shot in just as Tim Rice was trying to wrap things up by saying not once, but twice, 'You'll get your thirty pieces of silver'. In one edited version of the debate on YouTube, the commentator's laborious voice-over explains 'for those of you who did not attend Sunday School, this is a biblical quote, and refers to the money that Judas was paid to betray Jesus Christ'![22]

Although EMI had originally agreed to fund the film, the money was withdrawn just as members of the Python team were about to travel to North Africa to begin filming. Michael Palin's diaries record that 'Lord Delfont stopped the EMI/Python deal because he was so outraged by the script' on 1 March 1978 and that they all convened to discuss the next steps on 13 March.[23] At this point George Harrison, a friend of Eric Idle, intervened and offered to put up the money, setting up the company HandMade Films with his manager Denis O'Brien; both men even put their homes and offices as collateral. Harrison said simply, 'Ah, you know, I want to see it', a decision which Eric Idle describes as 'the most anybody's ever paid for a cinema ticket in history. God bless him'.[24]

The investment paid off handsomely: HandMade Films went on to become a major independent British film production company, while the *Life of Brian* grossed $20 million overall; it was the highest-grossing British film in the United States in 1979, and the fourth-highest-grossing film of any sort in Britain in 1979. I do not know what the exchange rate for 'thirty pieces of silver' is in 1979 figures, but these sums of money are not a bad return. If you listen carefully to the final credits, as 'Always Look on the Bright Side of Life' fades out and Eric Idle remarks that viewers can buy copies of the song in the foyer, his last line is, 'I said to him, "Bernie, they'll never make their money back on this one"'. The 'Bernie' he is referring to is, of course, Bernard (Lord) Delfont, so the very last line of the film is a dig at EMI for having withdrawn their financial support.

This was not to be the last time that the Pythons needed to raise money. John Cleese's divorce from Alyce Faye Eichelberger, an American psychotherapist who was his wife from 1992 to 2008, cost him a settlement of $20 million, prompting him to launch his so-called 'Alimony Tour' in 2011, starting out in his old haunts in Cambridge and ending up on DVD, to raise the money.[25] More recently, the reunion shows of the Pythons at the O2 came about, at least in part, for financial

22. https://www.youtube.com/watch?v=oM46jRJnHM; listen to the final comment at the end of 10 minutes.

23. Palin, *Diaries*, pp. 493–6.

24. Pythons, *Autobiography*, pp. 284–5; see also Perry, *The Life of Python*, p. 160.

25. For DVD, see http://www.amazon.co.uk/John-Cleese-Live-Alimony-Tour/dp/B005GDULLY; reviews of the live show are available at http://www.telegraph.co.uk/culture/comedy/8494687/John-Cleese-The-Alimony-Tour-Corn-Exchange-Cambridge-review.html; http://www.theguardian.com/stage/2011/may/06/john-cleese-review

reasons. In a candid interview with the *Daily Telegraph*, Michael Palin said: 'The cupboard was a bit bare, and we went to a guy called Jim Beach [the manager of Queen and a film producer] and he suggested, "Why don't you do the O2? Might clear your debts in a couple of days"'. These debts were a result of the Pythons' involvement in a major court case over the royalties for the musical show *Spamalot*, based upon their previous film, *Monty Python and the Holy Grail*.[26] Given that the original one-night show sold out in around 43 seconds, it was not surprising that they eventually ended up with a run of ten nights filling the O2, which helped refill the coffers. While some newspaper reports suggested that as well as the £20,000 raised for charities from those who bid for a walk-on cameo each night,[27] they received over £2 million each, Terry Jones says this is a huge exaggeration.[28]

Thus we might conclude that, even if the Pythons' motivation to make the *Life of Brian* was to make people laugh rather than for financial reward, the Bishop of Southwark's final comment has come true, whatever the exchange rate for 'thirty pieces of silver' is in today's money.

3 'You say, "Brian isn't Jesus", but that's just rubbish.' The question of mockery

Clearly, the main substance of the interview turned on whether the film is mocking Jesus or not. This was the principal criticism cited by Muggeridge and Stockwood throughout the programme despite Palin and Cleese's regular denials. About four minutes into Stockwood's opening speech, he says 'I know you are going to say that "Brian isn't Jesus", but, I mean, that's just rubbish'. Both Muggeridge and the bishop accuse the Pythons several times of 'lampooning' Jesus, and especially his death on the cross. After nearly ten minutes of almost uninterrupted assault from Stockwood and Muggeridge, Tim Rice has to break in as host and chair to ask for some space for John Cleese to answer the long list of criticisms which are 'building up'. Cleese's immediate reaction is to say, 'the problem that we have got is that you think that we are ridiculing Jesus, and we say, sincerely and truthfully, that that is certainly not what we intended to do, and I believe that we are *not*', emphasizing the point with his hand gestures. Having asserted this, he argues that the best way to answer this is to explain their actual intention, which is to encourage people to take a critical view and think for themselves.

So this raises the important question about what is the source of this idea that the Pythons' aim was to mock Jesus. We have already referred to the famous *Not the Nine O'clock News* parody about the Church of England's *Life of Python*. What is interesting here is how Rowan Atkinson and Mel Smith very carefully and deliberately parody both Stockwood and Muggeridge, rather than Palin and Cleese – despite the fact that they are supposed to be on opposite sides of the spoof debate. Thus Rowan Atkinson

26. http://www.telegraph.co.uk/culture/tvandradio/10532357/Michael-Palin-My-wife-keeps-me-grounded.html

27. http://www.heraldscotland.com/news/home-news/monty-python-reunion-shows-raise-more-than-20000-for-charities.1405592109

28. Terry Jones, personal email to Joan Taylor (10 November 2014).

plays the part of the bishop who made the film, but does so impersonating Stockwood, resplendent in purple and fingering a camera lens on an ornate chain around his neck in exactly the same way that the Bishop of Southwark played with his pectoral cross throughout the original interview. Meanwhile, Mel Smith as Alexander Walker, a leading 'Pythonist', rehearses many of Muggeridge's complaints, including his disgust that 'a fourteen-year-old child can get into see this film', describing it as 'highly distasteful' and 'tenth-rate'. However, his main objection is that 'the leading figure in this film – what is his name? Jesus Christ? – is quite clearly a lampoon of the comic messiah himself, our Lord John Cleese. I mean, come on, even the initials "JC" are exactly the same'.[29] The visual effect of Atkinson's use of the pectoral camera lens and the verbal echoes of 'fourteen-year-old', 'tenth-rate' and 'lampoon' are clearly designed to remind the audience of both Stockwood and Muggeridge.

In response, 'Bishop' Atkinson's arguments in defence are more ridiculous, and played, rightly, for laughs: 'I must explain, the Christ figure is not Cleese; he's just an ordinary man who happens to be born in Weston-super-Mare at the same time as Mr Cleese, who is mistaken for the Comic Messiah by vast crowds of people who follow him about, doing silly walks, shouting "no, no, not the comfy chair!" and other slogans from the Good Box'. Finally, Mel Smith/Alexander Walker complains about the final scene: 'Here we have the ultimate blasphemy. It is set in a hotel in Torquay and literally hundreds of Spanish waiters are being clipped about the ear by this Jesus Christ bloke. It is clearly a lampoon of the Comic Messiah's greatest half hour'. It is a hilarious scene, and deserves all the views it gets on YouTube.[30]

However, I want to argue that this parody is in some sense responsible for the idea that the Church of England was generally against *Brian*. Significantly, when Dr Rowan Williams became Archbishop of Canterbury, it was not unusual for him to be referred to 'Archbishop Rowan Atkinson' in a Freudian slip of the tongue! I think this also explains the extraordinary press interest in my discussion with Michael Palin on Radio 4 – not least because I was pictured with Palin on the Radio 4 website wearing a clerical ('dog') collar.

Significantly, all the reactions from listeners were positive, with various letters and emails being sent to me, saying that they were glad that someone in the church had finally come out and said something positive about the *Life of Brian*.[31] Even

---

29. Funnily enough, I once went to a seminar at the Annual Meeting of the Society of Biblical Literature in the USA where a paper on 'inter-textual hermeneutics' argued that Jim Carrey movies should be interpreted like this because the actor's initials, JC, were the same as Jesus Christ.

30. https://www.youtube.com/watch?v=asUyK6JWt9U; https://www.youtube.com/watch?v=Ku9lt_TvR1k

31. I even had a very nice email from Sally Muggeridge, Malcolm's niece, saying, 'Well said about "Life of Brian". Watched the interview again with John Cleese and Michael Palin. Couldn't help thinking that Malcolm, always with a sharp impish sense of humour, might have secretly enjoyed the satire of the film but was somewhat "required" to pompously criticise it by the set-up of the panel' – reprinted with her permission.

Figure 2.1 Michael Palin and Richard Burridge in the BBC news studio
(photo: courtesy of the BBC).

the *Church Times* asked me to write an opinion piece assessing the criticisms made
of the film by Muggeridge and Stockwood thirty-five years later, which eventually
was published on 13 June 2014 in order to anticipate the *Jesus and Brian* conference
and for the O2 reunion.[32]

However, as noted above, in the original Tim Rice BBC show, both Cleese
and Palin attempt several times to argue that Brian is not meant to be Jesus.
Jesus is clearly differentiated from Brian in the film. It is worth noting that, due
to a mix-up over timings, Muggeridge and Stockwood arrived late for the showing
of the film and missed the opening scenes for the first fifteen minutes or so. This
early part of the film includes, of course, the scene of the three kings going to a
stable and worshipping the infant Brian with Mandy his mother (played by Terry
Jones), giving him the traditional gifts of frankincense, myrrh and gold. They then
leave the stable and suddenly see an angel by the real stable and go to worship the
real Jesus instead, but only after reclaiming the gifts from a bemused, and
disappointed, Mandy.

After the titles, the film cuts straight to the Sermon on the Mount in which Ken
Colley, the well-known actor whom the Pythons chose to play Jesus, is clearly
differentiated from Brian. The camera shot begins with a close-up on Jesus
delivering the Sermon on the Mount, and then it pans back to focus on Brian at the
back of the crowd with Jesus still visible in the far distance, but not properly

32. *Church Times*, 13 June 2014, p. 13.

audible. This gives rise to one of the most quoted lines from the film, 'blessed are the cheesemakers' (which, of course, is funny only if one knows Jesus' original saying, 'blessed are the peacemakers', Matt. 5.9).

There then follows a wonderful parody of the work undertaken in biblical interpretation as a rather supercilious bystander remarks that it is 'clearly not meant to be taken literally' but applies 'to all makers of dairy products'.

However, even if Muggeridge and Stockwood missed these two opening scenes, later on in the film Palin appears as an 'ex-leper' whose livelihood as a poor beggar has been taken away because he has been cured by Jesus. Palin's character thus complains about Jesus to Brian as he seeks alms from him.[33]

Therefore there are at least these three instances where Jesus is clearly differentiated from Brian in the film – which is not the case in the Church of England's *Life of Python*. As Terry Gilliam noted, 'we were being very cautious about not being blasphemous ... My mother, an avid church-goer, saw it, but she didn't have a problem because it wasn't about Jesus'.[34]

However, it may well have been that the original intention for the film was to be as blasphemous and as mocking of Jesus as possible. The often-related story of the film's genesis is set at a premiere of *Monty Python and the Holy Grail*, where a journalist asked Eric Idle what the next film would be; Idle, noting the title of the movie *Patton: Lust for Glory*, which was also being screened in the next-door cinema, quipped, 'I don't know; how about *Jesus Christ: Lust for Glory*?'! In my extended interview with John Cleese and Michael Palin on the Friday night of the *Jesus and Brian* conference (20 June 2014), I asked these two Pythons where this incident took place, and the two of them could not agree.[35] In fact, each of the Pythons, while agreeing on the original title of *Jesus Christ: Lust for Glory*, remembers a different location where this idea was conceived (ranging from Canada, to New York, to Soho, to Amsterdam).[36]

As a side-note, it is really interesting for us as biblical scholars that eye-witnesses involved in this incident cannot now remember or agree on where or how it happened, some 35 years later, which is about the same period as between the ministry of the historical Jesus (c. 28–30 CE and the first writing of it down in Mark's Gospel in the mid-60s). However, in terms of historical likelihood, or what might sound like *ipsissima verba*, the original title actually 'sounds like' the 'authentic voice' of Eric Idle: certainly, it fits in with Idle's nihilism as seen elsewhere, as in his closing song for the film *The Meaning of Life*, where after describing just how insignificant our little planet is in terms of all the statistics about the size of our galaxy, the universe and the speed of light, he concludes by singing as the climax of the song and that movie as a whole:

33. See the facsimile of the lawyers' letter, Pythons, *Autobiography*, p. 284.

34. Pythons, *Autobiography*, p. 279.

35. The whole interview is available on YouTube at https://www.youtube.com/watch?v=CspatcnNWSg

36. Pythons, *Autobiography*, pp. 276–9; see also Perry, *The Life of Python*, p. 156.

So remember when you're feeling very small and insecure,
how amazingly unlikely is your birth,
and pray that there's intelligent life somewhere out in space,
'cos there's bugger all down here on earth.

Whatever was the original Pythons' intention, what is clear is that they started to undertake a substantial amount of historical research into Jesus and the Gospels. David Sherlock, Graham Chapman's partner, who also contributed towards the Python *Autobiography*, states, for example, 'What fascinates me, or did at the time, is the amount of background reading they were prepared to do.'[37] Eric Idle himself also makes it clear: 'We all went off and read the Bible, and I read the Dead Sea Scrolls and books on the Bible. Then we met again ... and we realized we couldn't make a film about Jesus Christ because he's not particularly funny, what he's saying isn't mockable, it's very decent stuff, you can't take the piss out of it.' Terry Jones agrees: 'It quickly became obvious that it wasn't going to be the life of Christ because that wasn't where the humour lay.' As in the debate with Muggeridge and Stockwood, John Cleese again directs attention away from mocking Jesus to their intention to pillory mindless followers: 'Quite genuinely I don't know how you could try to be funny about Jesus' life, there would be no point in it. What is absurd is not the teachings of founders of religion, it's what followers subsequently make of it.'[38]

Despite these denials by the Pythons that Brian is not meant to be Jesus, both Philip Davies and James Crossley have pointed out the various parallels between what Brian says and does, and the life and ministry of Jesus.[39] These include the similarities of being born in a stable, being known by their home-town 'Jesus/Brian of Nazareth', being proclaimed Messiah by their followers and asked for 'a sign', as well as the parallels with Jesus' teachings which Brian makes up when posing as a wayside prophet to avoid the Romans, with both of them ending up being 'crucified as revolutionary threats'.[40] From all these parallels, Davies concludes that 'Brian both *is* and is clearly *not* Jesus'.[41] However, Crossley then develops a more detailed comparison of Brian with various aspects of historical Jesus research,

37. David Sherlock in Pythons, *Autobiography*, p. 279.

38. All quoted in Pythons, *Autobiography*, p. 279.

39. See Philip R. Davies and James Crossley, Chapters 5 and 6 in this volume and also, Philip R. Davies, '*Life of Brian* Research', in *Whose Bible is it Anyway?* 2nd ed. (London: T&T Clark International, 2004), pp. 142–55; James Crossley, 'Life of Brian or Life of Jesus? Uses of Critical Biblical Scholarship and Non-orthodox Views of Jesus in Monty Python's *Life of Brian*', *Relegere: Studies in Religion and Reception* 1, no. 1 (2011), pp. 93–114; much of the latter is reworked and amplified in James G. Crossley, *Harnessing Chaos: The Bible in English Political Discourse since 1968* (London: T&T Clark Bloomsbury, 2014), pp. 129–52.

40. Davies, 'Research', p. 147–8; Crossley, 'Life of Brian', pp. 96–7; *Harnessing Chaos*, p. 134.

41. Davies, 'Research', p. 148.

including links to Jewish revolutionary groups, his mother's virginity, being acclaimed as Messiah, Jewish identity, and sexual relationships with Judith or Mary Magdalene to conclude that 'certain opponents of the film are in one sense right: Jesus sort of is Brian'.[42]

In this way, Crossley argues that, despite the Pythons' denials of blasphemy and claims that Jesus and Brian are different, the parallels are none-the-less designed to mock and offend at least some reconstructions of Jesus: 'the physical Jesus in the film may be the Christ of faith who is never *directly* challenged but this Christ of faith is undermined by the portrayal of Brian who is, in effect, the historical Jesus of more mildly subversive imaginations'.[43] One is reminded of the way the parallels are brilliantly parodied by 'Bishop' Rowan Atkinson's attempt to deny that 'JC' is not the same as John Cleese in the *Not the Nine O'Clock News* sketch.

However, such parallels do not necessarily mean that things are being equated. When biblical scholars undertake parallel criticism in synopses of the Gospels, it is *not* so that we can equate the sayings, but to enable us to see the difference between the different versions, and better understand what is being said. In his paper at the *Jesus and Brian* conference on films about Moses and Jesus, David Shepherd invoked the useful concept of 'parodic inversion'. I would prefer to argue that the parallels between Brian and Jesus do not mean that Brian becomes simply a cipher for Jesus. As Gospel scholars do when we look at the synoptic parallels, such comparisons help us to see the *difference* between Brian and Jesus. Brian does go around doing very similar things to Jesus, as indeed so did many other historical figures in the first century who were leaders of various messianic or restorationist movements, who were also crucified or otherwise dealt with by the Romans. What is significant is that such executions were the end of their story. What makes Jesus different from all the other historical parallels – and, indeed, from Brian – is that only in his case was this not the end, but he is still followed and worshipped two millennia later.

4 'Why lampoon death?' The crucifixion

Part-way through his five-minute opening speech, after attacking the Pythons for producing 'undergraduate humour' or being reminiscent of 'the Lower Fourth', Bishop Stockwood's first substantial point concerns the final scene of the mass crucifixion at the end of the film: 'Why lampoon death? This is the thing that really worried me. I don't think one would make a farce about Auschwitz, or of death. Whatever we think about Jesus – we may think he's the Son of God, we may think he's a mistaken fanatic – but it was a pretty shattering thing, what happened, the crucifixion.'

Interestingly, at the start of the programme, before the Bishop and Muggeridge came on stage, Tim Rice asked John Cleese and Michael Palin if there was 'anything which could offend you, on screen?', to which Cleese confessed 'I have one tiny

---

42. Crossley, 'Life of Brian', p. 97; *Harnessing Chaos*, p. 134.
43. Crossley, 'Life of Brian', p. 114.

'quibble' about the crucifixion scene. He was worried about a couple of close-up shots of 'one or two people registering pain'; he thought it was 'possible to be relatively cheery about death', but not pain. However, when they joined them, Muggeridge and Stockwood complained that they had not been able to hear the opening conversation in the Green Room, so they will have missed this, as well as the opening scenes of the film itself. In addition to Stockwood's opening comment about 'lampooning' death, Muggeridge also criticized the final scene, 'of people on crosses, singing a sort of ... musical' and also complained again towards the end about their 'lampooning' of Jesus' death (note that word again).

This final scene has a whole chapter in this book devoted to it (see Chapter 9), based on Dr Helen Bond's paper at the conference, a paper which looked in great detail at the historical accuracy of the Pythons' depiction of crucifixion.[44] However, in the context of this discussion, we need to consider Muggeridge and Stockwood's charge that the film is mocking the death of Jesus on the cross.

It is probably fair to say that for many Christians (and for that matter people not particularly Christian at all) who may have enjoyed the rest of the film, the most difficult scene has always been the mass crucifixion, with many of the various characters being roped to lots of crosses, in a scene highly reminiscent of multiple crucifixions at the end of the film *Spartacus*. This allusion is made explicit when John Cleese arrives as a Roman centurion with a pardon for Brian, obtained when Judith inspired the crowd to ask Pilate to 'Welease Bwian!' Brian is too busy complaining to hear his name at first, and, following Eric Idle's character volunteering 'I'm Brian', everybody else joins in, even with 'I'm Brian, and so's my wife!', in a parody of Spartacus' followers all claiming 'I'm Spartacus' to prevent the Romans from identifying their slave revolutionary leader (played by Kirk Douglas). There is plenty of humour in things like the argument about whether Jews and Samaritans should be executed in strictly segregated areas, and in Reg and the rest of the People's Front of Judaea coming to read an oration in praise of Brian on this 'your martyrdom' and, after the inevitable vote, a (brief) rendition of 'For He's a Jolly Good Fellow'.

The other scenes at the foot of the cross follow the classic crucifixion episodes not only from the paintings of the Gospel scenes by the Great Masters, but also in all Hollywood epic movie versions of the life of Christ; thus, Brian's mother, Mandy, comes to talk to him in her pain, grief and anger while, in a reprise of so many depictions of Mary Magdalene, Judith appears to say goodbye to Brian. This then leads into Eric Idle's cheeky cockney character (Mr Frisbee in the script) saying, 'Cheer up, Brian' and leading them all in the mass chorus of 'Always Look on the Bright Side of Life', including even dance movements on the cross for those whose legs are not tied down – with which the final credits eventually start to roll.[45]

This is not only a parody of the heart of the Christian faith, which, as Muggeridge pointed out, has inspired some of the world's greatest art, but I have to admit that

44. See Helen Bond, Chapter 9 in this volume.

45. It was, of course, entirely predictable that the Pythons '(Mostly) Live' shows at the O2 should end with the entire ensemble leading the audience in a mass sing-along of this song!

I found this scene difficult myself, both originally, and for many years subsequently. Like Muggeridge and Stockwood, I found the apparent mocking of a grisly form of execution at the least in bad taste, and it came the closest to anything in the film offending me, as someone who believes that the Cross is God's way of dealing with human sin and evil. However, the more I have reflected on the lyrics of 'Always Look on the Bright Side of Life', the more I have recognized its resonances with the funeral service. Idle's cockney character asks Brian, 'What have you got to lose? You know, you come from nothing and you're going back to nothing! What have you lost? Nothing! Nothing will come from nothing.' This clearly echoes the funeral liturgy, which is realistically adamant that we are born into the world with nothing and we leave it with nothing: 'we brought nothing into the world, so that we can take nothing out of it' (1 Tim. 6.7); 'the Lord gave, and the Lord has taken away; blessed be the name of the Lord' (Job 1.21).

It does seem to me that this attitude and stress on 'nothing' accords closely with Idle's nihilism (that is, the belief in 'nothing', *nihil* in Latin) which we also noticed in the song at the end of the *Meaning of Life*. There is something existentialist about looking into the face of death and whistling at it when you think everything is all utterly meaningless and that there is no kind of afterlife. It is significant that in my interview with the Pythons at the Conference, John Cleese stated that 'there is only one question that really matters: and that is – is there an afterlife?'[46] If you do think that there is nothing after this brief life on earth, then you can almost make meaning out of meaninglessness, by saying 'I am going to look on the bright side of life' and whistling defiantly in the face of death. I am sure I cannot be the only priest who has been surprised by the number of times mourners have requested this song at the funeral of their loved ones. There is also the famous story that the crew of *HMS Sheffield*, having been attacked by an Argentine missile during the Falklands War, killing twenty of the crew and leading to the loss of the first British ship to be sunk since World War II, responded by lining up on deck to sing, 'Always Look on the Bright Side of Life'.[47] Therefore, more recently I have come to change my view of this song, seeing it more as an atheistic-nihilist attempt to draw 'the sting of death' by refusing to be cowed by it, and insisting on whistling in its face. Crossley, as a non-believer, also comes to a similar conclusion: 'Brian's stark fate is finally and conclusively underscored by Eric Idle's famous song, "Always Look on the Bright Side of Life", where a full embrace of the joys of this life is the only challenge to the inevitability of an eternity in the dust.'[48]

There is one other scene during the final crucifixion sequence which needs some discussion, which is the trumpet call and sudden appearance of a group of people wearing rather odd bamboo uniforms, vaguely reminiscent of Japanese warriors.

46. Available on YouTube at https://www.youtube.com/watch?v=CspatcnNWSg

47. http://www.bbc.co.uk/dna/place-london/plain/A13074662; https://uk.news.yahoo.com/on-this-day--hms-sheffield-destroyed-by-argentina-during-falklands-war-130409123.html#JkaiPxL

48. Crossley, 'Life of Brian', p. 105; *Harnessing Chaos*, p. 140.

Their leader, another Eric Idle character, instructs them all to commit suicide instead of saving the prisoners, dying with the words, 'well, that showed them'– which all seems rather pointless, given that the Roman guards had already run away in terror when they came over the hill. No wonder Brian says 'You silly sods!'

In the past, I interpreted the scene solely as a spoof of a Samurai-type movie, without really knowing why it was included. Interestingly, Philip Davies also suggests that it is a superficial parody of Japanese suicide squads, while James Crossley compares it to Masada.[49]

It is only now that the original versions of various deleted scenes are available in newer DVDs and on YouTube that it makes sense.[50] Earlier in the film, just after his night with Judith, Brian had previously met this group, and its leader, Otto, played by Eric Idle sporting a small moustache reminiscent of Hitler. He acclaims Brian not as Messiah, but as 'Hail, Leader!' with an outstretched arm salute. Otto is impatient, waiting for the 'Leader who will save Israel by ridding it of the scum of non-Jewish people, making it pure! No foreigners; no riff-raff; no gypsies.'[51] Their helmets are also decorated with a star of David with side bars, reminiscent of a swastika, designed by Terry Gilliam, which can still be seen in the retained scene at the crucifixion.

As the writer of this scene, Eric Idle describes it as 'a pretty savage attack on rabid Zionism, suggesting it's rather akin to Nazism, which is a bit strong to take, but certainly a point of view'.[52] Julian Doyle, the editor of the film, who wanted to keep it in, relates that there was 'a long, painful discussion, but in the end the Pythons have a rule that if someone doesn't like their stuff they can take it out. So Eric took it out'. Doyle wonders whether if they had retained the scene, it might have helped 'liberal forces in Israel' and led to 'a better relationship between Jews and Palestinians'.[53] Terry Gilliam is more pragmatic: 'Eric, I think, got cold feet because he was now living in Hollywood and he felt the Jewish producers of Hollywood would take great offence at it. I said, "Listen, we've alienated the Christians, let's get the Jews now".'[54]

However, Otto and his group could not be completely excised because both Mandy and Judith have to step across their bodies for their final conversations with Brian at the foot of the cross – and the squad's corpses even join in moving their feet in time to 'Always Look on the Bright Side of Life'!

---

49. Davies, 'Research', p. 144; Crossley, 'Life of Brian', p. 105; *Harnessing Chaos*, p. 139–40.

50. See https://www.youtube.com/watch?v=wthHB3iTC7M

51. For the Otto scene, see https://www.youtube.com/watch?v=h1dZ0YddG7w. Interestingly, in the fuller version of the script included by the film's editor, Julian Doyle, it says it is 'time we Jews racially purified ourselves' and, when Brian asks about the Samaritans, Otto suggests, 'we'll put them in little camps', which could be taken as a reference either to the experience of Jews in concentration camps under Hitler, or Palestinians in refugee camps today. Julian Doyle, *The Life of Brian/Jesus* (Leicester: Troubador, 2011), p. 191.

52. Pythons, *Autobiography*, p. 299.

53. Julian Doyle, *The Life of Brian/Jesus* (Leicester: Troubador, 2011), pp. 190–4.

54. Pythons, *Autobiography*, pp. 298–9.

Therefore, they had to shoot a brief close-up cameo of Terry Jones later in London to insert just before the squad's arrival to explain who they are. In this discussion of Muggeridge and Stockwood being offended by the film in general and the crucifixion scene in particular, it is interesting to reflect on whether the Pythons were willing to mock Christians but not Jews, so I am glad that Adele Reinhartz also raised this issue in her paper at the Conference.[55]

Thus we have examined the several criticisms made by Muggeridge and Stockwood, concerning the film's alleged poor quality, its being made for financial gain, and the main issue about whether they are mocking Jesus through Brian, particularly with regard to the crucifixion. In response to all these criticisms, Cleese and Palin consistently tried to steer the debate back to their original intention in making the film and the real target of their satire.

'Take a critical view'; 'you're all individuals' – the Pythons' Real Target

When Cleese is first permitted to get a word of reply to the criticisms 'building up' over Muggeridge and Stockwood's ten minutes of diatribe, he answers the Bishop's question of what they were 'trying to do' as 'make up your own mind, don't let other people tell you ... take a critical view, find out about it, don't just believe because somebody tells you to, somebody in a pulpit ... question it and work it for yourself'. Both he and Palin attempt to make this point several times in the debate.

This is made clear in the film where there is the wonderful scene where Brian shouts, 'Look, you've got it all wrong! You do not *need* to follow me. You do not *need* to follow *anybody*! You've got to think for yourselves! You're *all* individuals!' Everyone in the crowd all chorus back together, 'Yes! We're all individuals!' (Except, of course, for the one 'individual' who says, 'I'm not'.).

Throughout the film, it is repeatedly made clear that the real target is the crowds of mindless followers, who want to find a messiah figure, even if, as with Brian, he himself does not want to be their 'Leader'. As another of Cleese's characters puts it, 'but I say you are the Messiah, and I should know – I've followed a few!' Furthermore, they quickly split into groups over trivia like whether he has given them the gourd or the sandal as his sign.

Sadly, the Christian church has all too frequently exhibited such schisms rather than following Jesus himself. This satire of political and religious groups' tendency to split into factions, fight each other, and miss the entire point of their founder is also brilliantly depicted in the various 'popular fronts' for the liberation of Judaea, who hate each other more than the Romans – especially the group Brian joins, the People's Front of Judaea, led by Reg (another typical Cleese character), caricaturing 1970s trade-union meetings and resolutions.[56]

---

55. See Adele Reinhartz, Chapter 15 in this volume.

56. See Crossley, *Harnessing Chaos*, pp. 141–4, for a fuller discussion of both the first-century Jewish factions and of 1970s trades unions.

In our discussion on Radio 4's *Today* programme, Michael Palin noted that they had prepared very carefully for the discussion with Muggeridge and Stockwood and he had looked forward to a proper debate to find out what the church really thought. This is confirmed in Palin's diary from that very day, Friday 9 November 1979, which makes the same point *before* he sets off for the studio: 'I go for a run across the heath. Tonight is our confrontation with Muggeridge and the Bishop of Southwark, and, as I squelch through the now leafless beech-woods around West Meadow with Kenwood House, a glittering white symbol of order and reason in the background, I sort out my thoughts about *Brian* and the points that the movie tried to make seem to be all to do with power – its use and abuse by an establishment.'

Reflecting on this, Palin continues: 'As I work in the afternoon on committing to paper some of my morning's thoughts, I find myself just about to close on the knotty question of whether or not I believe in God. In fact, I am about to type "I do not believe in God" when the sky goes black as ink, there is a thunderclap and a huge crash of thunder, and a downpour of epic proportions. I never do complete the sentence. Look for the last time at my notes and drive down through Aldwych, and across Waterloo Bridge to the Greenwood Theatre.'[57]

We have already noted the later entry for that day, where Palin describes his meeting at the reception afterwards with Raymond Johnston from the Festival of Light where they agreed that, 'Stockwood used cheapest and most dishonest methods to tell people what to think', exactly what the movie was intended to protest about.[58] It is perhaps the ultimate irony that Michael Palin wanted to talk about the 'use and abuse of power' by an establishment – and instead of discussing it, the editor of *Punch* and the doyen of the previous generation of satirists and the Lord Bishop of Southwark displayed precisely that, the 'use and abuse of power' by their establishment in patronizing and dismissing Cleese and Palin as the younger generation, rather than engaging with what they really wanted to talk about – encouraging people to think critically for themselves.

A Missed Opportunity?

In conclusion, I want to suggest that Muggeridge and Stockwood – in failing to discuss the *Life of Brian* properly with Michael Palin and John Cleese – missed an enormous opportunity.

57. Palin, *Diaries*, 9 November 1979, p. 658; ironically, the Greenwood Theatre, which was then a major TV studio used for such programmes, is now within King's College London's Guy's Campus at London Bridge and it is used as our major medical lecture theatre, while the conference took place on our Strand campus adjacent to the Aldwych, both referenced in this entry.

58. Palin, *Diaries*, 9 November 1979, pp. 659–60.

During the *Jesus and Brian* conference, we discussed at various points whether the *Life of Brian* could be made today, tending towards a negative answer. There are several possible reasons for this. The first concerns the fact that there was much more of a shared literary and educational culture in Britain of the 1970s. For example, I find Cleese hilarious as the Roman centurion giving Brian a Latin lesson for his grammatically incorrect graffito, *Romanes eunt domus* (translated by Cleese's centurion as '"People called the Romanes they go the 'ouse?", boy!') because not only was I was taught Latin like that at school myself, but in 1979 I was a young schoolmaster teaching twelve- or thirteen-year-olds Latin grammar about imperatives and how *domus* uses the locative case – something which many fewer viewers would understand today.[59] Equally, the debate between Reg and the People's Front about 'what have the Romans ever done for us?' requires some knowledge about the benefits brought by the Roman empire regarding sanitation, medicine, education, wine, roads, public order, irrigation, water supply, public health, peace and so forth, as discussed at the conference, especially in Steve Mason's paper.[60] It is arguable that this shared culture of classical education is absent in today's society.

There is also a similar issue about the extent to which biblical literacy and knowledge of the Christian scriptures are shared today. We have already noted above that the famous line, 'Blessed are the cheesemakers', only works if you know the Beatitudes in Matthew 5, since as viewers we never actually hear the original words, 'Blessed are the peace-makers', knowledge of which is assumed in order to appreciate the parody. Equally, after the opening titles, we see lots of people in biblical costumes behind the words, 'Judaea AD 33'. Again, this is sufficient in the shared culture of 1979 to indicate that we are about to enter some scene from the ministry of Jesus, while the addition of the subtitle, 'about tea-time', merely adds to the humour. Whether such knowledge can be assumed today is quite another matter. As biblical scholars, we need to ask questions about the extent to which biblical literacy is shared in our society and in our educational system today.

It is against such a shared background of biblical literacy in 1979, that I think Muggeridge and the Bishop of Southwark missed the real opportunity which probably could not happen in today's culture. I gave the sub-title of this paper 'The Church of England's *Life of Python*' as 'What the Bishop Saw', in a parody of the British sea-side humour, 'What the butler saw'. But this is a vital question to consider in conclusion: what *did* the Bishop see – and what did he miss? Of course, the first thing he did not see was the first fifteen minutes of the film where he missed the clear distinction between Brian and Jesus. But more significantly, I think he, and for that matter, Malcolm Muggeridge, saw what they wanted to see. It is well known that Mervyn Stockwood was a great showman who loved nothing better than controversy and playing to the media and the public crowd.[61] As Palin

59. See Guy Stiebel, Chapter 8 in this volume.

60. See Steve Mason, Chapter 14 in this volume.

61. He enjoys describing his various controversies throughout his book, Mervyn Stockwood, *Chanctonbury Ring: An Autobiography* (London: Hodder & Stoughton, 1982).

mentions in the *Today* programme interview, when they went off air Stockwood turned to him and said, 'I think that went rather well, don't you?' It is ironic that the Bishop had completely missed just how angry he had made Michael Palin; we have already noted John Cleese's description in our Radio 4 interview that he was 'quite shirty by normal Palin standards'. I suspect that Stockwood would be amazed that thirty five years later, Palin, by now 'a national treasure', would still be wanting to revisit the debate and have the constructive discussion he had wanted and prepared for all those years ago.

More importantly, Mervyn Stockwood also had no idea of the controversy he stirred up that night. He was, after all, no stranger to controversy: he was banned from pulpits as a young man in 1938 when he changed his political views and left the Conservative Party, partly over Chamberlain's appeasement policies, and the final chapter of his autobiography details several controversies of his later years, including his criticism of the Archbishop of Canterbury's 'Call to the Nation' in the *Morning Star*.[62] But significantly, he states that 'my final controversy as Bishop of Southwark, though that is too strong a word, was prior to the General Election in 1979', when he hit the headlines about his loss of faith in politicians.[63] While this 'final controversy' was in 1979, the year of the *Life of Brian*, the event to which he refers was in May 1979, when Mrs Thatcher won her first election. This was a full six months before Stockwood announced his long-planned resignation in November 1979, shortly after his TV debate with Cleese and Palin. Yet the latter is the 'controversy' for which he is now most remembered and viewed by millions on YouTube, but which is completely absent from his recollections in his autobiography.

Another thing which may have changed since 1979 is greater sensitivity to giving religious offence. We have already noted that Terry Gilliam was quite happy to offend Jews over his swastika-Star of David design for Otto, but that Eric Idle withdrew the scene, according to Gilliam more out of concern for his relationships with Jewish film-makers than to avoid general offence.[64] In the light of the complaints of anti-Semitism levelled at Mel Gibson over the depiction of Jews and Jewish religious leaders in his *Passion of the Christ*, something similar might have been said about Brian if it were made today. Even in the 1979 TV debate, Muggeridge suggested that 'if you had made that film about Mahomet [*sic*, his version of Mohammed], there would have been an absolute hullabaloo in this country'. And yet it does seem perfectly possible to continue to mock Jesus and Christians, even if we have argued that the Pythons' target in Brian was the latter, rather than the former.

However, given the greater shared classical and biblically literate culture in Britain in 1979, Muggeridge and the Bishop of Southwark missed a significant opportunity to debate the real difference between Jesus and Brian. As I have shown above, the Pythons individually and collectively came to the view after careful

---

62. Stockwood, *Chanctonbury Ring*, see pp. 33–6 and 205 on 1938 and pp. 183–90 about Archbishop Coggan.

63. Stockwood, *Chanctonbury Ring*, p. 191.

64. Pythons, *Autobiography*, pp. 298–9.

study of the Gospels and related literature that they could not make fun of Jesus of Nazareth himself – and so they had to create Brian as someone who attempts to do many things like Jesus but gets it wrong all the time, and in doing so, is actually very funny. Surely it was hugely significant that well educated and intelligent, but not necessarily religious people, like the Pythons who undertook some study, who did go and read the Bible and the Dead Sea Scrolls, ended up being fascinated by the teaching and person of Jesus rather than wanting to mock him?

Twice in the TV debate, John Cleese seemed quite angry that he had not been taught more fully about Jesus and the Gospels. In his first main response, he asks, 'Does one accept every word in the Bible? The Sermon on the Mount – did they get it all right, when Mark wrote it down thirty years later?' – even if, of course, he has not attributed the Sermon to the correct Gospel writer (Matthew). Later he is even more agitated:

> I went to an English preparatory school and an English public school ... and I was given ten years of a form of Christianity which I grew to despise and dislike, largely because it insulted my intelligence; the sermons ... insulted my intelligence. When I got into writing this film – and we all had exactly the same reaction – we started to discover a lot of stuff about Christianity and I started to get angry because I started to think, why was I given this rubbish, this 'tenth-rate' series of platitudes, when there are interesting things to have discussed ... nobody ever told me that they don't know what language the Gospels were written in, they don't even know who wrote them and they are not even sure what cities they were written in.

The extraordinary thing is that the person, life and ministry, teachings and activities of Jesus of Nazareth, and why he was executed and what, if anything, happened afterwards to convince his followers that he was still alive – these questions still fascinate millions, despite the often appalling behaviour of believers over the last 2,000 years, as so tellingly satirized in the film. Furthermore, this was still the same challenge that John Cleese put to us as biblical scholars in our interview on the Friday evening:

> What I find so fascinating about the work that you guys are doing is that there is nothing in the world that is more important than what you are doing, and you could hardly raise a paragraph in the *Daily Mail*, you know, because society now is so insane, so trivial and stupid, and the values are so crap, that nothing of any importance seems to get paid attention to ... there is only one question that really matters: and that is, is there an afterlife? ... That's what I think, that's the question that interests me – and what do you hear about *that* on television?

Finally, therefore, let us return to the subtitle to the conference: *What have the Pythons done for us?* In 1979, they gave both biblical scholarship and the Christian church an extraordinary opportunity to discuss in public life with a shared biblically literate culture the real question of what made Jesus different from ordinary people like Brian, and why religious and political individuals and groups fail to think for themselves and form factions to fight each other, rather than putting things like Jesus' teachings and example into practice. And instead of seizing this opportunity to discuss the real significance of Jesus, Malcolm Muggeridge and the Bishop of Southwark indulged in precisely the abuse of power by the establishment that Michael Palin wanted to debate.

Who is Jesus, why does he matter, and why is he so different from all the rest of us who, like Brian, just fall over ourselves most of the time and get it wrong? That challenge is what the Pythons really did for us and 'we', both in the church and the academy, missed the opportunity. I wonder whether, through the resurgence of interest in the re-issue of the film, as the conference demonstrates, we will do any better this time?

Chapter 3

WHEN BRIAN MET MOSES: *LIFE OF BRIAN* (1979), *WHOLLY MOSES* (1980) AND THE 'FAILURE' OF BIBLICAL PARODY

David Shepherd

The vantage point from which the following chapter will explore Monty Python's *Life of Brian* is that of the biblical film, a genre which includes but stretches well beyond the 'Jesus' film, whose diversity and relationship to *Life of Brian* is discussed elsewhere in this volume.[1] Indeed, just as Brian's epic cinematic precursors paved the way for his appearance, so too *Life of Brian*'s own send-up of epic and other expressions of the biblical film prepared the way for *Wholly Moses* (Columbia, 1980), a film which was very much inspired by it. Indeed, *Life of Brian*'s unexpected success[2] augured well for a happy and profitable run for *Wholly Moses*, when the

1. See William Telford, Chapter 1 in this volume.
2. The American domestic box office gross for *Life of Brian* was approximately US$20 million. (http://www.boxofficemojo.com/movies/?page=weekend&id=montypythonslifeof brian.htm)

film opened in June of 1980.[3] The director Gary Weis had been impressing with his work on Saturday Night Live and had worked with Python Eric Idle on *The Rutles*, a mockumentary precursor to *This is Spinal Tap*, and one which had appeared on both American and British television in Spring 1978.[4] Moreover, the Rutles' formula of including multiple cameo appearances of the biggest and best names in comedy was employed again in *Wholly Moses,* with Dom Deluise, James Coco, John Houseman, Madeleine Kahn and John Ritter all appearing along with Richard Pryor as Pharaoh. While the cameo cast was primarily American, the lead role was given to Englishman Dudley Moore, fresh from his breakout role alongside Bo Derek in Blake Edwards' *Ten* – a film which had grossed more than $74 million on a budget of just $7 million in 1979, when *Life of Brian* also appeared.[5] Second only to Christ in terms of previous cinematic exposure,[6] Moses must have seemed a very likely biblical figure for lampooning – prominent enough to mildly offend adherents of all three Western religions, but not sufficiently sacred to incite the sort of serious opprobrium which attended the release of *Life of Brian*.[7]

Despite its apparent promise, it is safe to say that *Wholly Moses* was not wholly successful. Indeed, those who have not seen the film are in good company. Judging from the disappointing box office returns,[8] not many did see it, and judging from the reviews, it seems likely that many of those who did see it wished they hadn't.[9] While our analysis may well suggest incidentally some reasons for the film's critical

3. The film was released in America on 13 June, 1980 and internationally in the months that followed.

4. The film was broadcast in March 1978 on BBC2 in the UK, having been broadcast already in America on the 22nd of that month on NBC, where it received mixed reviews (http://www.rutlemania.org/reviews.html).

5. For precise details of gross box office and budget see http://www.boxofficemojo.com/movies/?id=10.htm

6. For Moses' prominence as a subject in the early cinema, see David Shepherd, *The Bible on Silent Film: Spectacle, Story and Scripture in the Early Cinema* (Cambridge: Cambridge University Press, 2013).

7. For a brief discussion of efforts to ban the film in America see, Kendall R. Phillips, *Controversial Cinema: The Films That Outraged America* (Westport, CT: Greenwood, 2008), p. 143. In Britain, eleven local councils banned the film outright (http://www.telegraph.co.uk/news/3073308/Monty-Pythons-The-Life-Of-Brian-film-ban-lifted-after-28-years.html).

8. US domestic box office gross was US$14,155,617 on a budget of approximately US$12 million. (http://boxofficemojo.com/movies/?id=whollymoses.htm)

9. The reviewer for the *New York Times*, Janet Maslin, was underwhelmed, concluding that: '*Wholly Moses* is gently amusing, but it isn't as funny or audacious as its premise makes it sound.' (*NYT* Friday 13 June 1980, C10.) Roger Ebert (*Chicago Sun-Times*, 16 June 1980) was less gentle: 'The movie's not funny on its own, and since movie audiences are scarcely going to be shocked by its mild but relentlessly repetitive irreverence, it all boils down to a very old joke.'

and commercial 'failure', our primary concern in what follows is to parse *Wholly Moses'* modus operandi as parody, as a means of reflecting on the parodic 'success' of *Life of Brian* (1979), the more famous film it sought to emulate.

That *Wholly Moses* really did seek to emulate Python's *Life of Brian* released the previous summer is immediately clear from its premise and the narrative use of the doppelganger. Like Python's 'Brian Cohen', whose life is contemporary with the life of Christ, the career of *Wholly Moses'* protagonist, Herschel son of Hyssop, runs parallel to and intersects with the biblical Moses. Like *Life of Brian*, whose 'Life of' reiterates its target genre and subverts it with 'Brian', so too *Wholly Moses*, signals its target, 'Moses', but also ironically subverts it by constructing a film which is not 'Wholly Moses' at all, but only barely so and focused instead on his 'double', Herschel. Herschel's status as doppelganger is established near the outset by the film's version of the 'Finding of Moses' or 'Moses saved from the waters' – a scene which appeared frequently in the earliest filmic depictions of Moses thanks to its prominence in the pictorial traditions of Western art.[10] Like *Life of Brian*, whose parody of the nativity begins with a serious reiteration of the Kings' journey and arrival at the manger, so too *Wholly Moses* begins with Jokeved placing Moses in the famed basket (Exodus 2.3), which the camera then follows down the Nile where it passes Herschel being launched in his own basket by his father Hyssop. As they both float toward the bank occupied by Pharaoh's daughter and her maidservants, Herschel's basket sails past thanks to the rather oversized hand of the infant Moses which appears to give Herschel's basket a gentle shove (Fig. 3.1).

Figure 3.1 *Wholly Moses*. The infant Moses giving his rival Herschel's basket a gentle shove down the Nile.

10. For more on the representation of Moses in the early cinema and its dependence on antecedent traditions in the performing and visual arts, see Shepherd, *The Bible on Silent Film*.

Discovering on his arrival at the royal float that it is Moses not Herschel who has been plucked from the water, Hyssop asks if the princess has seen another 'ark' bearing '… the same kind of kid …'. Instead of it being found by the princess, Hyssop discovers that his son's basket has been found by a family of idol-makers, Senmut and Sons. In terms of parodic taxonomy, the initially straight reiteration of the 'biblical' nativity traditions (the launching of the infant Moses on to the Nile and the arrival of the Magi at the [wrong] manger) sets up and facilitates the parodic inversion which in both *Wholly Moses* and *Life of Brian* involves the doppelganger's initially promising nativity being eventually disclosed as inferior in various ways to the canonical nativities of the biblical figures, Moses and Jesus.[11] If Moses giving Herschel's basket a shove down the Nile is an impiety, it is a gentle one indeed, blunted by the fact that Moses is still but a babe. After their close encounter on the Nile, Herschel has not much more to do with Moses than Brian does with Jesus. In the case of both doppelgangers, their anticlimactic nativities anticipate careers which predictably fall rather short of their illustrious biblical counterparts. In the Python film, Brian's struggles with his (Roman/Jewish) identity propel him toward political resistance before he literally falls into the role of reluctant – indeed unwilling – Messiah. In *Wholly Moses*, Herschel's own conflicted identity (as Hebrew and Egyptian) is overshadowed by the moment of his vocation in Midian. Having fled there from Egypt and married Jethro's 'other daughter' Zerelda (Laraine Newman), Herschel is saddled with looking after the 'stragglers' of the flock on the slopes of Sinai, while his brother-in-law Moses tends the main flock. There on Sinai, a booming bass voice and King Jamesian paraphrase convince Herschel that he has been called by God to deliver the Hebrews from Egypt, before the camera trucks left to reveal on the other side of the boulder, the real recipient of the divine commission, Moses, on his knees before the burning bush.

With Moses already departed, Herschel's eventual response to the 'bush which is not consumed' is comic rather than reverential – trying as he does without success to put out the flames (Fig. 3.2), before rushing off to tell his wife the good news. Thus the scene again begins with straight reiteration of the epic tone before the ironic inversion where we discover that Herschel has got the wrong end of the stick, or rather 'staff'. The main target of the parody is, however, the means of revelation and authentication of the divine message as becomes clear when Moses returns to share the news with his wife and father-in-law. As Jethro puts it: 'How did you know it was God and not some practical joker?' Unlike Moses, who recognizes the burning bush and treats it reverentially, Herschel merely smells the smoke and eventually tries to put out the fire. The fact that Herschel recognizes God by the sound of his voice signals the parodying of this scene in Cecil B. DeMille's 1956 *Ten Commandments* where the voice of God, composed of multiple voices including those of DeMille and Charlton Heston, booms forth in stentorian tones. When Herschel's attempted impression of the divine voice fails to persuade

11. See Dan Harries, *Film Parody* (London: British Film Institute, 2000) for examples and discussion of 'reiteration' (pp. 43–54) and 'inversion' (pp. 55–61) in cinematic parody.

Figure 3.2 *Wholly Moses*. Herschel tries to extinguish the 'burning bush'.

even the family of Jethro, it may be a gentle mocking of the biblical tradition of Moses' own initial failure to persuade his people (Exodus 3–4) but the more likely parodic target is surely the stereotypical cinematic (and specifically DeMillean) representation of the divine voice.

There can be little doubt that whatever else the *Life of Brian* sends up, it too regularly has in its sights biblical films in the epic register and especially the cinematic lives of Christ released in the 1960s and 70s. For instance, the set of the Pythons' 'Sermon on the Mount' parodies the epic scale of the same scene in Nicholas Ray's *King of Kings* (1961) where the size of the crowd and the volume of Jesus' voice preclude the possibility of the crowd actually hearing the sermon clearly.[12] The well-known scene from Spartacus where those loyal to him seek to thwart his execution by all claiming 'I am Spartacus' is comically inverted when those being crucified seek to escape the cross by all claiming 'I am Brian'. To these may be added the examples included in William Telford's chapter in this volume, and for good measure, the Terry Gilliam-orchestrated homage to *Star Wars* (1979), a film which makes no pretense of being a biblical film per se but is hardly short of biblical themes or narrative resonances.[13]

Following Herschel's accidental epiphany at Sinai, *Wholly Moses'* regular mocking of DeMille's *Ten Commandments* (1956) is increasingly supplemented

12. The Pythons' allusion to Ray's film is noted in passing by Richard Walsh, '*Monty Python's Life of Brian* (1979)', in Adele Reinhartz (ed.), *Bible and Cinema: Fifty Key Films* (London and New York: Routledge, 2013), pp. 187–92, at p.187. The title visuals of *Life of Brian* are also an aping of those of Ray's film.

13. See, for instance, John C. Meldrum, '*Star Wars*' Saving Return', *Journal of Religion and Film* 13 (1) (2009) http://www.unomaha.edu/jrf/vol13.no1/StarWars.htm for a discussion of the 'christology' of the franchise as a whole.

by a range of cinematic intertexts. Henry King's *David and Bathsheba* (1951) prompts Herschel's encounter with a giant 9 cubits in height, in which Herschel's unheroic use of a Davidic sling succeeds only in inflicting a head wound on himself and a low blow on the giant. Herschel's middle-eastern meandering next takes him to 'New Sodom, more sinful than ever' – a tipping of the hat to Robert Aldrich's 1962 *The Last Days of Sodom and Gomorrah*, which furnishes *Wholly Moses* with not only an epic battle scene and the inevitable biblical orgy/feasting to mock,[14] but also allows Herschel's wife Zerelda to be turned into a pillar of salt *à la* Lot's wife.[15]

Perhaps more interesting than *Wholly Moses'* aping of the epics is the way in which the film alludes even to the biblical/Jesus film in non-epic mode. Filmed some six years earlier, the cinematic version of the stage musical, *Jesus Christ Superstar* (1973) begins with a long camera pan across the desert accompanied by stereotypically 'Middle Eastern' music as the camera finally settles on ancient ruins. The inversion of this reiteration of the ancient setting of the epic is then signaled first by the camera coming to rest on modern scaffolding, then by the musical transition to the strains of the electric guitar and finally and most definitively by the appearance out of the desert of a battered school bus bearing the cast of the Passion play about to be performed.

Wholly Moses too opens with a long pan across a desert-scape with appropriate musical accompaniment. That this film too will puncture the ancient orientalizing atmosphere of the epic, just as *Superstar* does, becomes more clear when the pan across the desert lasts far too long – manifesting a typical trope of cinematic parody: exaggeration.[16] That *Wholly Moses'* parodic target here is specifically *Jesus Christ Superstar* becomes perfectly clear when the panning camera comes finally to rest on, inevitably, a battered school bus. Instead of disgorging its young and energetic cast as in *Superstar*, however, this bus in *Wholly Moses* is being boarded by an unpromising group of American tourists foolish enough to sign up for a self-proclaimed 'no frills' tour of the Holy Land. While offering a modern frame story in which the biblical story of Herschel will be set,[17] the film also evidently pokes fun at the musical manifestation of the filmic Jesus by replacing *Superstar's* energetic interpreters with underwhelmed tourists. Given *Wholly Moses'* similarity to *Life of Brian* in terms of

---

14. For more on the motif of feasting/orgiastic indulgence in the biblical film of the silent period, see Shepherd, *The Bible on Silent Film*, pp. 217–26.

15. For a useful discussion of Aldrich's film in the context of his other directorial work, see Tony Williams, *Body and Soul: The Cinematic Work of Robert Aldrich* (Lanham: Scarecrow Press, 2004), pp. 335–47. The notorious cities of Genesis had already appeared in *Sodom und Gomorrah* (1922), an epic biblical film made in Vienna by Michael Curtiz before the Warner brothers lured him to Hollywood. See Shepherd, *The Bible on Silent Film*, pp. 217–26.

16. For examples of parodic exaggeration see Harries, *Film Parody*, pp. 83–92.

17. The situating of the biblical/ancient sequence alongside or framed within a contemporary story was a well-established feature of biblical films from Griffith's *Intolerance* (1916) until the end of the silent era; see Shepherd, *The Bible on Silent Film*.

parodic spirit and the narrative structure of the doppelganger, it is perhaps unsurprising that its indebtedness may be seen even in specific scenes.

Perhaps the best example appears when Herschel and Zerelda make their way from Midian to Egypt.[18] Spotting them as they approach the village, a man pretending to be blind and lame (David Lander) takes up a position on the road and asks them for alms. Emboldened by his apparent theophany and prophetic vocation, Moses insists on healing the man of his 'infirmities'. Having nothing to be healed of but fearing the loss of income such a 'healing' would entail, the beggar urges Herschel to use his healing powers instead 'at a leper colony, not three leagues from here . . .'. Undeterred, Herschel proclaims 'Thou shalt see' and pokes the man forcefully in both eyes (Fig. 3.3) prompting the man's indignant response, 'What are you trying to do, blind me?' even as both the crowd and Herschel himself proclaim a miracle.

The crowd's blind credulity and the false attribution of miracles to the doppelganger is of course drawn directly from *Life of Brian*. Moreover, the reluctance of the able-bodied and fully-sighted beggar to be healed of his 'blindness' and 'lameness' in *Wholly Moses* must also be borrowed from Michael Palin's equally able-bodied ex-leper in *Life of Brian* who, as he begs for alms from Brian and Mandy, complains that Jesus' healing of him ('bloody miracle') has robbed him of his livelihood such that he contemplates asking Jesus to make him 'a bit lame in one leg during the middle of the week . . .'. The reference to a leper colony three leagues down the road removes all doubt that Weis has attempted to pilfer and elaborate on the comedic premise of the Python scene, even if he fails to extract a similar wit or humour from his own version.

Figure 3.3 *Wholly Moses.* Herschel 'heals' a beggar pretending to be blind by poking him vigorously in the eyes.

18. Perhaps unsurprisingly, the enigmatic 'bridegroom of blood' episode (Exodus 4) has never, to the author's knowledge, featured in a filmic representation of the life of Moses.

Of course such borrowings hint at parody on the cusp of pastiche, at least according to the definitions of Gerard Genette and others who contrast parody's transformation with pastiche's mere imitation.[19] More to the point, if pastiche is often seen as drawing from a wider range of intertexts than simple parody then, by this measure at least, *Wholly Moses* may well be more pastiche than parody, especially when one considers that its borrowings from the biblical film tradition are so frequent – indeed, pervasive – and so narratively substantial.[20] In comparison, *Life of Brian*'s appropriation of cinematic intertexts is more limited, less extended, and – following Rick Altman's approach to genre analysis – more at the level of the lexical than the syntactical.[21] The shoe of pastiche fits *Wholly Moses* all the better if, as Fredric Jameson suggests, 'pastiche is, like parody, the imitation of a particular mask . . . but a neutral practice of such mimicry'.[22] Indeed, in *Wholly Moses* there is much imitation, but arguably little transformation and one might well wonder whether the film's sending up of the biblical film in non-epic mode – in the shape of *Jesus Christ Superstar* and especially *Life of Brian* – was perhaps seen to be simply too derivative and insufficiently innovative. It is also unlikely that *Wholly Moses* was helped by the fact that by 1980, most of the film's epic Old Testament/ Hebrew Bible cinematic targets (filmed in the late fifties and early sixties) may not have been sufficiently familiar to audiences to activate the parodic impulse.

Yet if *Wholly Moses* appears to veer toward pastiche, it nevertheless shares with *Life of Brian* another feature of the contemporary parodic impulse, finding humour in the incongruous interpolation of the contemporary into the ancient biblical setting. As has been widely observed, *Life of Brian* takes great delight in extracting laughs by situating instances of typically British culture and convention within its parody of the ancient *Life of Brian/Jesus*.[23] Amongst many examples, one thinks of

19. See Gerard Genette, *Palimpsestes* (Paris: Seuil, 1982), p. 34, followed by Linda Hutcheon, *A Theory of Parody: The Teachings of Twentieth Century Art Forms* (New York and London: Methuen, 1985), p. 38.

20. For a discussion of 'biblical parody' with a rather different focus, see Richard Walsh, 'Barabbas Rewrites the Cross: Parody or Parable?', in David Shepherd (ed.), *Images of the Word: Hollywood's Bible and Beyond* (Atlanta: Society of Biblical Literature, 2008), pp. 113–29.

21. Rick Altman, *Film/Genre* (London: British Film Institute, 1999) and *idem*, 'The Semantic/Syntactic Approach to Film Genre', in Barry Grant (ed.), *Film Genre Reader* (Austin: University of Texas Press, 1986).

22. Frederic Jameson, 'Postmodernism, or the Cultural Logic of Late Capitalism', *New Left Review* 146 (1984), p. 65.

23. See, for instance, Philip Davies, '*Life of Brian* Research', in J. Cheryl Exum and Stephen D. Moore (eds), *Biblical Studies/Cultural Studies: The Third Sheffield Colloquium* (Sheffield: Sheffield Academic Press, 1998), p. 411 and especially Carl Dyke, 'Learning from *The Life of Brian*: Saviors for Seminars', in George Aichele and Richard Walsh. *Screening Scripture: Intertextual Connections between Scripture and Film* (Harrisburg, PA: Trinity Press International, 2002), p. 241, though the latter's insistence that it is class struggle which is the target of these scenes rather than ethnocentrism seems difficult to sustain.

Cleese's centurion interrupting Brian's seditious graffiti with a Latin lesson intended to be typical of that found in countless English public schools of the time. The verbal – and eventual physical – exchange between 'Big Nose' and his tormentor during *Life of Brian's* 'Sermon on the Mount' offers another example, as does Brian's amusing 'British' aversion for haggling, the cultural incongruity of which in Middle Eastern contexts is likewise lampooned in the film. *Wholly Moses* too regularly mocks mostly American mannerisms – Zerelda's insistence on asking if Moses said 'hi to God from her' being one of countless examples. Another has Herschel pause in his windblown desert wanderings to exchange pleasantries with another desert wanderer in the shape of old acquaintance Dom Deluise, resuming their parched staggering across the desert after rapidly running out of things to say and insisting that they 'must have lunch'.

Contemporary consumerism and marketing is another regular subject for lampoon in both films, as for example in *Life of Brian*, when the carnage of the coliseum becomes the 'Children's Matinee' and Brian is employed as a vendor of suitably exotic snacks such as 'wren's livers', 'jaguar's earlobes' and the especially appetizing 'wolf nipple chips' ('get 'em while they're hot, they're lovely'). So too in *Wholly Moses*, where 'Senmut and Sons', Herschel's idol-making employers not only boast that they '... stock what you worship ...', but will also gift wrap an idol for 'that someone special' or for those looking for a God 'that won't clash with your tent'.

Notwithstanding the tendency toward pastiche in *Wholly Moses*, in light of the above, there can be little doubting the intentions if not necessarily the achievements of both *Wholly Moses* and *Life of Brian* as filmic parody. At the same time, such an observation invites reflection on the relationship of parody to satire, with which it is often confused and conflated. If as is often alleged, satire's targets are extra-literary, or in our case 'extra-cinematic', norms (including religious norms, as well as philosophical, moral and social ones)[24] then *Wholly Moses* is hard-pressed to qualify as satire for as we have seen, its parodic sights are rarely trained on targets beyond the epic biblical films at which it seeks to poke fun. While *Wholly Moses* may well be more than merely pastiche, tightly defined, it nevertheless appears, like pastiche, to lack in Jameson's words 'ulterior motives' and thus to be 'amputated of satiric impulse'.[25] Indeed even when *Wholly Moses* lampoons the contemporary, it largely limits itself to manners and mannerisms and does so with great restraint or perhaps simply a lack of conviction. It is of course at precisely this point that *Life of Brian* reveals itself to be quite a different creature, for not only does it show little restraint in dissecting contemporary manners, contemporary mores are also lacerated with great satirical conviction. So while *Life of Brian* happily foregrounds ancient factionalism (including resentment of Sadducees and Samaritans), its persistent

24. Bertel Pederson, 'The Theory and Practice of Parody in the Modern Novel: Mann, Joyce and Nabokov', unpublished PhD dissertation, University of Illinois, Urbana-Champaign, 1972, p. 21. See also Hutcheon, *Theory of Parody*, p. 25.

25. Jameson, 'Postmodernism', p. 65.

lampooning of the preposterous People's Front of Judaea and its rivals serves to puncture the inconsistencies and absurdities of modern sectarianism especially but not only in its Middle Eastern varieties. So too while *Life of Brian* displays an amused interest in gender roles in antiquity (in for example the scene of the stoning of the blasphemer), the rather sharper edge of its satirical sword is shown to then contemporary feminist movements, especially in the PFJ's discussion of Loretta's transgender aspirations and his/her desire to bear a child.[26]

Messianic movements and those who populate them are increasingly lampooned as Brian's followers not only proclaim him as the messiah against his wishes and disagree vehemently about how to follow the messiah, but also interpret every word and gesture in messianic terms and then persecute someone perceived to be a heretic. Finally, the general tendency to follow, to conform and to allow others to think for oneself are all subject to general ridicule in Brian's memorable 'window scene'. While the satirical target here may well be broader than merely a conventional Christian notion of discipleship, this is of course the bull's eye at which the *Life of Brian* takes aim and succeeds in hitting quite squarely. As it happens, the film's suggestion that Christ's healing of a leper might legitimately prompt something other than gratitude does resonate with the Gospel account of the lepers who did not return (Luke 17), but it is hardly surprising that the reporting of Jesus' response as 'Some people are never happy' would lead some viewers to take umbrage, as would the film's suggestion that the teachings of Jesus/Brian might be impenetrable in part because they are simply being made up as he goes along.

Such a notion offers a final vantage point from which to reflect on Brian's status as parody and/or satire. The film's training of its comic sights however obliquely on the *ipsissima verba* of Jesus highlights *Life of Brian*'s status as parody by foregrounding its fundamental narrative dependence on the Life of Jesus/Christ as articulated in the Christian Gospels and mediated by the cinematic tradition. That the film's target is an intertextual one – as its name suggests, 'a Life' – confirms its generic status as parody: that is, a genre whose aim is to lampoon another literary or in our case cinematic text. The fact that *Brian's* target text was no ordinary text – not even merely canonical in the literary sense – but in fact considered sacred to some degree within many of the receiving cultures in which it was viewed explains why the *Life of Brian* was and remains no ordinary parody. Indeed, the parody of sacred texts and their interpretive traditions offers the clearest possible illustration of the point that the textual norms transgressed by parody may not always be 'merely' textual norms, but may entail social and political consequences, not least when the textual norms are ones which have shaped social and political cultures like those of the Christian canon have.

---

26. This allows Dyke, 'Learning from *The Life of Brian*', pp. 240–1, to accuse the film of being 'frustratingly uncritical' from a feminist perspective and even 'functionally' hegemonic in this and other ways.

Yet if this suggests that the very act of parodying the Gospel (however innocently) is controversial in any culture which prizes the Gospel at some level, what makes *Life of Brian*'s parody extraordinary compared to *Wholly Moses* and most parodies since is that the Pythons were not content to parody the *Life of Christ*, but to liberally season their already parodic pot with a brand of satire which took aim at not only contemporary feminism and sectarianism but also the messianism which forms the bedrock of the Christian tradition.

The Pythons were far from the first to combine biblical parody and satire in this way. To take but one example, almost exactly forty years earlier, the playwright Bertolt Brecht was putting the finishing touches on the *Rise and Fall of the City of Mahagonny*, further operatic fruit of his collaboration with the composer Kurt Weill. While Brecht never finished the play *David* that he had begun in his early twenties, its fragments offer tantalizing hints of what a 'biblical drama' from the pen of the more mature (and more Marxist) Brecht might have looked like.[27] Yet, it is worth remembering that a sixteen-year-old Brecht's earliest dramatic effort was entitled nothing less than *The Bible*, a playlet whose exploration of biblical themes and resonances in a 'modern' setting would presage the influence of the Christian canon on his later output, including *Mahagonny*.[28]

As its title would suggest, the opera relates the story of the rise and fall of Mahagonny, a city founded ostensibly in the Californian desert, and the setting for Brecht's satirical exploration of what Nietzsche's discovery that 'God is dead' means for individuals and society as a whole.[29] What animates and complicates the satire of *Mahagonny* is Brecht's decision to tell the story by parodying a variety of biblical traditions. The city's founder, Trinity Moses, leads his band of travellers in their flight from the police across the desert in search of a city which cannot be found and is therefore 'founded' by them. The belated arrival in the city of Jimmy Mahoney, an Alaskan lumberjack, begins the messianic phase of the story, although like Brian, Jimmy is a Messiah who is reluctant and clearly imperfect. Unlike the Christ who preaches self-denial, Jimmy's initial Gospel is one of self-indulgence, but like Christ he too is tried and executed. Writing forty years earlier, Brecht's satirical targets are obviously not identical to the Pythons', but their cultural enchantments and disenchantments might well be compared. Here, however, we must content ourselves with a concluding

27. For a wonderfully informed discussion see David Jobling, '"David on the Brain": Bertolt Brecht's Projected Play "David"', in Tod Linafelt, Claudia V. Camp and Timothy Beal (eds) *The Fate of King David: The Past and Present of a Biblical Icon* (LHBOTS, 500; London: T&T Clark, 2010), pp. 229–40.

28. For a full and helpfully nuanced discussion of the function of the Bible in Brecht's work, see Ronald Murphy, *Brecht and the Bible: A Study of Religious Nihilism and Human Weakness in Brecht's Drama* Mortality and the City (Chapel Hill, NC: University of North Carolina Press, 1980).

29. See Ronald Speirs, *Brecht's Early Plays* (London and Basingstoke: Macmillan Press, 1982), pp. 162–9 for a brief but useful analysis of the biblical resonances in *Mahagonny*.

comment on the dramatic admixture of biblical parody and satire in Brecht and *Brian*. In *Mahagonny*, Brecht chose to infuse the genre of the 'satirical opera' with sustained biblical parody. By contrast, the Pythons chose rather to season their 'biblical parody' with an all-too-knowing satire of Christian Britain and its cultural trappings. The fact that Brecht's opera caused very nearly as much controversy in 1929 as the Python's film did four decades on suggests that it matters little whether one deals in satirical parody or parodic satire: when canonical traditions are the target someone will inevitably be offended.[30]

30. Amongst the host of reservations raised by reviewers of the play following its Leipzig premiere in 1930, religious objections were prominent, especially to the so-called 'God in Mahagonny' elements. For the critical response to the perceived blasphemy of the production, see the reviews cited and discussed in Steve Giles' introduction to *Rise and Fall of the City of Mahagonny* (London: Methuen Drama, 2007), pp. 103, 108–9.

Chapter 4

'BLASPHEMY!' ON FREE SPEECH THEN AND NOW

David Tollerton

We all know the scene. Brian and his mother watch on as a group of beard-wearing women champ at the bit for the opportunity to begin stoning Matthias Son of Deuteronomy of Gath for the crime of uttering the name 'Jehovah'. But the formality of proceedings rapidly disintegrates as Matthias starts to question the judgement and the gathered crowd prove to be an unruly and ill-disciplined collection of over-enthusiastic executioners. At the culmination of the scene it is not Matthias but rather the priest who lies dead for speaking the name of God amidst his futile attempts to maintain order.

It is a scene that parodies Jewish blasphemy laws of first-century Judaea but also anticipates the very critics of *Life of Brian* who in 1979 themselves cried 'blasphemy!' in response to Monty Python's creation.[1] It is therefore a useful place from which to consider the relationship between the film and ideas of blasphemy across distinct historical periods. But rather than keeping to a dual focus on first-century

1. For an overview of the early opposition to *Life of Brian*, see Robert Hewison, *Monty Python: The Case Against* (London: Eyre Methuen, 1981), pp. 78–93.

Judaea and the late 1970s, I will also consider perceptions of blasphemy in contemporary Britain, that is, over three and a half decades since *Life of Brian*'s cinematic release. For as I hope to show in the later parts of this chapter, both the cultural place of Monty Python's film and the nature of blasphemy have shifted so considerably in recent years that the relationship between the two has now become one that many readers will likely find strangely counterintuitive.

More broadly, however, in this chapter I wish to highlight the contested and fluid character of blasphemy across a variety of time periods. The focus is wide-ranging, and certainly much more could be said about each era, but despite the limitations I hope to introduce the manner in which *Life of Brian* usefully opens a window into discussion of the repeatedly blurry lines that mark the limits of tolerable first-, twentieth- and twenty-first-century expression.

First-century Judaea

As many scholars down the years have observed, Monty Python were notably diligent in reading up on the historical context of first-century Judaea.[2] But we should be wary of celebrating this fact too uncritically because the precise nature of blasphemy as understood in the Jewish society of Judaea at that time is actually a little hard to pin down.

It is worth starting with the crime specifically parodied in the stoning scene: uttering the name of the Lord. The roots of this censure can be found in Leviticus 24.16: 'One who blasphemes the name of the Lord shall be put to death; the whole congregation shall stone the blasphemer.' Attestations to this understanding of blasphemy appear in several later texts, two notable examples being in the Community Rule of the Dead Sea Scrolls and in Tractate Sanhedrin of the Mishnah.[3] The latter indeed specifically stipulates that ' "The blasphemer" is not culpable unless he pronounces the Name itself'.[4]

---

2. Philip Davies, '*Life of Brian* Research', in Cheryl Exum and Stephen D. Moore (eds), *Biblical Studies/Cultural Studies: The Third Sheffield Colloquium* (Sheffield: Sheffield Academic Press, 1998), pp. 400–6; James G. Crossley, 'Life of Brian or Life of Jesus? Uses of Critical Biblical Scholarship and Non-orthodox Views of Jesus in Monty Python's *Life of Brian*', *Relegere: Studies in Religion and Reception*, 1, 1 (2011), pp. 93–114; Hans Wiersma, 'Redeeming *Life of Brian*: How Monty Python (Ironically) Proclaims Christ Sub Contrario', *Word and World*, 32 (2012), pp. 166–77, at p. 169; Graham Chapman et al., *The Pythons Autobiography by The Pythons* (London: Orion, 2003), pp. 354–5.

3. The Community Rule 6.27–7.2 reads: 'If any man has uttered the Venerable Name even though frivolously, or as a result of shock or for any reason whatever, while reading the Book or the blessing, he shall be dismissed and shall return to the Council of the Community no more'. Geza Vermes (trans.), *The Complete Dead Sea Scrolls in English* (London: Penguin, 1997), p. 107.

4. Tractate Sanhedrin 7.5. Herbert Danby (trans.), *The Mishnah* (Oxford: Oxford University Press, 1933), p. 392.

Although none of these sources precisely informs us about blasphemy at the time of Jesus/Brian, it seems reasonable to assume that this understanding of the crime existed within the spectrum of Jewish thought during this era. Geza Vermes has recently taken such a view, suggesting that the detailed rabbinic descriptions of stoning in Tractate Sanhedrin do reveal customs present during the Second Temple period.[5] The stoning scene from *Life of Brian* can thus reasonably be said to have *some* foundation in history.

But the situation of blasphemy in first-century Judaea is nonetheless a bit tricky to decipher. The picture begins to be complicated by what would later turn out to be the most famous blasphemy trial of the age: that of Jesus of Nazareth. In the accounts of Mark and Matthew's Gospels, the crime for which Jesus is convicted is specifically described as being blasphemy.[6] The problem is that, unlike Matthias Son of Deuteronomy of Gath, Jesus never actually says 'Jehovah'. Scholars have responded to this in varying ways. In his broad history of the offence of blasphemy, Leonard Levy simply cites this as evidence that the Gospel accounts of Jesus' trial are faulty.[7] Adela Yarbro Collins has instead proposed that there were varying standards of blasphemy at play during this period and perhaps the Sadducees and high priest who controlled Jesus' trial had a broader understanding of blasphemy – one that extended *beyond* merely uttering the divine name.[8]

One way to support such a broader understanding is to draw upon the more general command of Exodus 22.28 that 'You shall not revile God'. This rather looser configuration allows for a more expansive understanding of what constitutes blasphemy. And by simply translating God (in the singular) as gods (plural), as indeed happens in the Greek of the Septuagint, you are able to command that people should not even speak out of turn against the gods of *any* tradition. Two notable first-century Jewish commentators, Josephus and Philo, each allude to such a tradition, the latter justifying it on the grounds that if you avoid blaspheming against other gods you are more likely to steer well clear of reviling the God of Israel.[9] And there are other modes by which blasphemy may have been expanded among the various religious groupings of Second Temple Judaism. Another apparent example is found in Josephus' description of capital punishment among the Essenes, whom he suggests would execute those committing blasphemy not only against the name of God, but also the name of Moses.[10]

So the exact extent of what did or did not constitute blasphemous speech in first-century Judaea was not quite as clear cut as the *Life of Brian* stoning scene might

5. Geza Vermes, 'Was Crucifixion a Jewish Penalty?', *Standpoint*, April 2013, pp. 66–9.

6. Mark 14.64 and Matt. 26.65.

7. Leonard W. Levy, *Treason Against God: A History of the Offense of Blasphemy* (New York: Schocken, 1981), pp. 29–62.

8. Adela Yarbro Collins, 'The Charge of Blasphemy in Mark 14.64', *JSNT* 26 (2004), pp. 379–401.

9. See ibid., p. 392 and p. 389.

10. See Joan E. Taylor, *The Essenes, the Scrolls, and the Dead Sea* (Oxford: Oxford University Press, 2012), pp. 78–9.

initially imply. At one point Matthias begins to query the justice of his sentence, protesting 'Look, I don't think it ought to be blasphemy, just saying Jehovah'. Were he thrown back into the reality of ancient Judaea, he might do the same in the knowledge that there *was* seemingly a glimmer of legal ambiguity on the topic. Amidst the 'remarkably broad range of Jewish religious tendencies' that characterized late Second Temple Judaism, this ambiguity makes sense, as in such a situation of ideological flux the boundaries of correct speech may well have been a disputed issue.[11]

Late-1970s Britain

The stoning scene is, however, not just a parody of criminal law in first-century Judaea, but also deals with concerns faced by Monty Python within their own time. And again, it is an era of both ideological division and debate concerning the meaning of blasphemy.

But before focusing on late-1970s Britain, a little historical contextualization is required. The modern British blasphemy law can be traced back to the Restoration period of the seventeenth century and was largely founded on the idea that to undermine Christianity is equivalent to undermining the state.[12] However, despite the evolving configuration of the blasphemy law and its application, by the middle decades of the twentieth century there was a widespread view that such legislation had had its day. In 1949 the prominent judge Lord Alfred Denning remarked:

> We have attained to as high, if not a higher degree of religious freedom than any other country . . . The reason for this law was because it was thought that a denial of Christianity was liable to shake the fabric of society, which was itself founded on the Christian religion. There is no such danger to society now and the offence of blasphemy is a dead letter.[13]

This sense of a gradual move away from enforcing blasphemy legislation was, however, disrupted by a trial in 1977 during which Mary Whitehouse was able to bring a successful prosecution for blasphemy against the editor of *Gay News* for publishing James Kirkup's erotic poem 'The Love that Dares to Speak Its Name'.[14] The backdrop of the trial was a decade in which Mary Whitehouse and the Christian grassroots organization the Nationwide Festival of Light had sought to battle against what they perceived to be the moral permissiveness stemming from

11. Robert M. Seltzer, *Jewish People, Jewish Thought: The Jewish Experience of History* (London and New York: Macmillan, 1980), p. 197.

12. St John A. Robilliard, *Religion and the Law: Religious Liberty in Modern English Law* (Manchester: Manchester University Press, 1984), p. 25.

13. Cited in Geoffrey Robertson, *Obscene: An Account of Censorship Laws and their Enforcement in England and Wales* (London: Weidenfeld and Nicolson, 1979), p. 239.

14. See Mary Whitehouse, *Quite Contrary: An Autobiography* (London, Sydney and Auckland: Pan Books, 1993), pp. 47–60.

social changes of the 1960s.[15] This was essentially a battle for the centre ground of British culture in which Whitehouse and the Festival of Light fought against what they saw as the erosion of traditional Christian morals. As hinted at in relation to first-century Judaea, we again have inner tensions within society and dispute regarding blasphemy. In this instance the debate centred on whether it was an anachronistic and unnecessary law, or a valuable tool in the fight to preserve Britain's Christian heritage.

Monty Python were well aware of the *Gay News* trial and in fact even helped fund the defence of *Gay News* against prosecution.[16] It therefore seems reasonable, returning to the stoning scene, to regard the crowd of bearded women as a group of crazed pseudo-Mary Whitehouses, frenzied and uncontrollable in their desperate desire to be morally offended. The scene, in other words, should be understood as a parody of blasphemy laws in both first-century Judaea and twentieth-century Britain.

But consideration of how *Life of Brian* relates to the British blasphemy law is ultimately more complicated than this. Most specifically, the question of whether *Life of Brian* was in fact partially self-censored is not entirely straightforward to answer. On the one hand, there is plenty of evidence that Monty Python were strongly opposed to altering the film in the face of legal action. In his diary entry for 3 June 1979, Michael Palin describes a group conversation as follows:

> We discuss our attitude to censorship, on which there is total agreement within the group that we do not and will not change anything because we're told to, unless we happen to agree that it isn't funny anyway. We're all happy to go to court in defence of the movie.[17]

This does fit with the fact that what might at first-glance appear to have been the group's greatest moment of self-censorship – namely the shift of focus during its early development from Jesus to Brian – actually took place well before Whitehouse announced her plans to take *Gay News* to court.[18] So in other words, it seems unfair to conclude that the original vision of *Jesus Christ: Lust for Glory* was altered simply out of fear of prosecution.

But there are nonetheless complicating factors. It is clear that by the time of the film's release, Monty Python *were* genuinely concerned by the possibility of prosecution and actively sought legal advice on the matter.[19] And at one point in

---

15. See Amy C. Whipple, 'Speaking for Whom? The 1971 Festival of Light and the Search for the "Silent Majority"', *Contemporary British History*, 24, 3 (2010), pp. 319–39.

16. Hewison, *Monty Python*, p. 62.

17. Michael Palin, *Diaries 1969–1979: The Python Years* (London: Phoenix, 2006), p. 616.

18. According to Palin's diary, the group began moving toward a focus on Brian rather than Jesus in April 1976, *Diaries 1969–1979*, p. 345. Mary Whitehouse did not read 'The Love That Dares to Speak Its Name' until November of the same year, *Quite Contrary*, p. 47.

19. Hewison, *Monty Python*, p. 62, pp. 67–9; Palin, *Diaries 1969–1979*, p. 606.

his diary Palin complains that Eric Idle is trying to censor the content of interviews by strongly discouraging any mention of the *Gay News* case in association with *Life of Brian*.[20] Then there is the contentious example of Otto, a kind of crazed Jewish Nazi, cut from the film at a relatively late stage. From some of the interviews and diaries it is suggested that Otto was removed for reasons of pacing, but Terry Gilliam has made it clear that he, in contrast, felt that Otto's removal was ultimately a disappointing act of self-censorship.[21]

What are we to make of all these pieces of evidence? In his 2007 book *Blasphemy in the Christian World,* David Nash repeatedly suggests that the film *should* be understood as self-censored.[22] He reflects that this self-censorship highlighted a key weakness in the blasphemy law: if you were simply canny enough you could get your point across without prosecution.[23] My own point of view is rather that we should just be careful about expecting *total* ideological coherence from both Monty Python and their film. In their interviews they occasionally make conflicting remarks, and indeed when watching the film with a source-critical hat on it can seem quite fragmentary, essentially a sequence of semi-autonomous sketches written by different individuals and pairings that have then been melded together.[24] In that particular regard *Life of Brian* is reminiscent of many a biblical text, and the Gospel of Brian, it turns out, has got just as many fissures running across it as the canonical synoptic ones. Compared to Monty Python's more obviously disjointed cinematic outings *Life of Brian* does admittedly hang together far more effectively, but Gilliam mischievously remarks that it was 'just a more clever version of disguising the fact that they're a bunch of sketches than the others [i.e. the other films] have been'.[25]

We should, in sum, be wary of thinking of *Life of Brian* as a *completely* unified film. And getting into focus its precise relationship with the blasphemy law and issues of self-censorship is, I have suggested, just that bit harder than it may first appear.

20. Palin, *Diaries 1969–1979*, pp. 638–9.

21. Palin, *Diaries 1969–1979*, p. 606; Chapman et al., *The Pythons Autobiography*, pp. 381–2. For Gilliam's remarks see ibid., p. 381.

22. David Nash, *Blasphemy in the Christian World: A History* (Oxford: Oxford University Press, 2007), pp. 214–15, 218.

23. Ibid., p. 218.

24. One particularly apposite example of disagreement in interviews concerns whether *Life of Brian* may be understood as 'heretical'. See Chapman et al., *The Pythons Autobiography*, p. 359.

25. David Morgan (ed.), *Monty Python Speaks!* (London: Ted Smart, 1999), p. 184. Regarding the disjointed nature of Monty Python's other films: (i) *And Now for Something Completely Different* (1971) was an anthology of sketches; (ii) on the uneven nature of *Monty Python and the Holy Grail* (1975) see Idle's comments in Chapman et al., *The Pythons Autobiography*, pp. 318–19; (iii) the difficulties of creating a coherent storyline for *Meaning of Life* (1983) are well-documented – see Palin, *Diaries 1969–1979*, p. 662; Michael Palin, *Diaries 1980–1988: Halfway to Hollywood* (London: Phoenix, 2009), pp. 148, 150, 153; Chapman et al., *The Pythons Autobiography*, pp. 394–9; Morgan, *Monty Python Speaks!*, pp. 211–13.

Contemporary Britain

In this final section I will think about *Life of Brian* and blasphemy from our current perspective midway through the second decade of the 21st century, because, although it is only a few decades since its release, the situations of both the film and blasphemy law have radically altered.

The situation of blasphemy has altered because, quite simply, in the UK the blasphemy law no longer exists. In a sequence of developments that themselves had a suitably Pythonesque absurdity, after several hundred years' existence, this law was finally shelved via a mixture of Jerry Springer and a Sudanese teddy bear. In 2007 the organization Christian Voice unsuccessfully attempted to bring a prosecution for blasphemy against both the producer of *Jerry Springer: The Opera* and the BBC Director General (for broadcasting the opera in 2005).[26] Also in 2007, a British schoolteacher, Gillian Gibbons, was briefly imprisoned in Sudan for allowing her class to name a teddy bear Muhammad.[27] Both events had the effect of highlighting the extent to which the ongoing existence of a blasphemy law appeared out of step with public opinion. After petitioning from leading public figures, including even former Archbishop of Canterbury George Carey, in May 2008 parliament voted to repeal the blasphemy law, an act celebrated by the actor and activist Ian McKellen publically reading Kirkup's 'The Love that Dares to Speaks Its Name', the poem prosecuted for blasphemy back in 1977.[28]

This may, however, ultimately seem irrelevant if we take the view that the passing of the controversial Racial and Religious Hatred Act had, in 2006, already effectively replaced the blasphemy law. But this is not a tenable interpretation of the Act. Despite concerns publically voiced by several comedians that the Act would outlaw satire of religion, in reality the way it is framed makes it extremely unlikely that any such prosecution would ever take place.[29] If anything, the 2006

26. See Ivan Hare, 'Blasphemy and Incitement to Religious Hatred: Free Speech Dogma and Doctrine', in Ivan Hare and James Weinstein (eds), *Extreme Speech and Democracy* (Oxford: Oxford University Press, 2009), pp. 289–310, at pp. 297–300.

27. The BBC, 'UK teacher jailed over teddy row', 30 November 2007, http://news.bbc.co.uk/1/hi/world/africa/7119399.stm [accessed 10 August 2014].

28. Philip Pullman, Rt Rev. Lord Harries of Pentregarth, Ricky Gervais, Nicholas Hytner, Shami Chakrabarti, Professor Richard Dawkins, Rt Rev. Lord Carey of Clifton, Professor A. C. Grayling, Sir Jonathan Miller, David Starkey, Lord Lester of Herne Hill, Stewart Lee, Michael Cashman, Joan Smith, Lady D'Souza, Peter Tatchell, Lisa Appignanesi, Hanif Kureishi, Lord Desai, Roger Smith and Hari Kunzru, 'Repeal the Blasphemy Laws', *The Telegraph*, 8 January 2008, http://www.telegraph.co.uk/comment/letters/3553469/Letters-to-the-Telegraph.html [accessed 10 August 2014]. See also Martin Beckford, 'Blasphemy Laws are Lifted', *The Telegraph*, 10 May 2008, http://www.telegraph.co.uk/news/1942668/Blasphemy-laws-are-lifted.html [accessed 10 August 2014].

29. See, for example, BBC, 'Atkinson's Religious Hate Worry', 7 December 2004, http://news.bbc.co.uk/1/hi/uk_politics/4073997.stm [accessed 10 August 2014].

Act actually enshrines the right to satirize religion, declaring at one point that it should not be 'read or given effect in a way which prohibits or restricts discussion, criticism or expressions of antipathy, dislike, ridicule, insult or abuse of particular religions or the beliefs or practices of their adherents'.[30] It would seem that makers of a film like *Life of Brian* are now well and truly protected by the law.

This mirrors the way in which the situation of *Life of Brian* has also changed. Where it was once an edgy and controversial challenge to tradition, it is now quoted at Prime Minister's Questions and 'Always Look on the Bright Side of Life' is sung at the Olympic closing ceremony.[31] As Gilliam recently remarked in a newspaper interview, 'we've become the Establishment we took the piss out of'.[32]

So what has become of blasphemy? Do we now live in some kind of enlightened blasphemy-free age? The answer, I wish to suggest, is 'no' on several grounds, some of which ultimately invert the way we have tended to think of the relationship between *Life of Brian* and issues of blasphemy.

The first point to recognize is that we do of course still live in an age in which religious minorities are willing to loudly voice their objection to what they see as the denigration of their tradition. Two well-known examples involving the Islamic community are the 2006 images of Muhammed published in the Danish newspaper *Jyllands-Posten* and the *Innocence of Muslims* film uploaded to YouTube in 2012.[33]

Yet perceptions of blasphemy can be more subtle than this. One curiosity about the *Innocence of Muslims* controversy was that during the very same month it was

30. UK Government, 'Racial and Religious Hatred Act 2006', http://www.legislation.gov.uk/ukpga/2006/1/pdfs/ukpga_20060001_en.pdf [accessed 10 August 2014].

31. Prime Minister's Questions, 3 May 2006, http://www.publications.parliament.uk/pa/cm200506/cmhansrd/vo060503/debtext/60503-03.htm#60503-03_spmin17 [accessed 10 August 2014]; Ian Garland, 'Feeling sad about the end of the Games? Eric Idle leads 80,000 crowd in rendition of Always Look on the Bright Side of Life', *The Daily Mail*, 12 August 2012, http://www.dailymail.co.uk/news/article-2187413/London-2012-Closing-Ceremony-Eric-Idle-leads-crowd-rendition-Always-Look-Bright-Side-Life.html [accessed 10 August 2014].

32. Brian Logan, 'Was Terry Gilliam right to call the Monty Python reunion "depressing"?', *The Guardian*, 16 May 2014, http://www.theguardian.com/stage/2014/may/16/terry-gilliam-calls-monty-python-reunion-depressing [accessed 10 August 2014].

33. For an overview of Islamic reactions to the Danish cartoons see Jytte Klausen, *The Cartoons That Shook the World* (New Haven: Yale University Press, 2009). For details of British protests against the *Innocence of Muslims* see BBC, 'Protesters gather at Birmingham Bullring centre', 21 September 2012, http://www.bbc.co.uk/news/uk-england-birmingham-19681547 [accessed 10 August 2014]; BBC, 'Muslims protest in Cardiff over Innocence of Muslims film', 22 September 2012, http://www.bbc.co.uk/news/uk-wales-19687030 [accessed 10 August 2014]; *The Telegraph*, 'Protesters burn flags outside US embassy in London', 14 September 2012, http://www.telegraph.co.uk/news/uknews/9544579/Protesters-burn-flags-outside-US-embassy-in-London.html [accessed 10 August 2014].

provoking upset within the Islamic community another news story about desecration gripped British newspapers. This was the outrage of sections of the media at the publication of topless photos of the Duchess of Cambridge.[34] Is it the case that, in some curious sense, the former Kate Middleton has become in the eyes of some British people a sacrosanct figure, whose very image can be profaned and desecrated? Certainly I would not be the first person to suggest that her portrayal in parts of the media has become tinged with an aura of the sacred. In 2013, for example, the street artist Pegasus commented on this phenomenon shortly after the birth of Prince George by representing her as a religious icon in the style of the Virgin Mary.[35] '[S]he is worshipped in her own way', he remarked in one newspaper interview on the piece.[36]

I will leave readers to weigh up the issues surrounding this particular example, but there is a broader point that comes out of the Middleton photos controversy, one that relates to the very idea of blasphemy: if you leave aside the legal issues, blasphemy is essentially about the nature of the sacred. If you can figure out what it is for a community that is sacred, what is holy and set apart, you will also know how to commit blasphemy. But in contemporary Britain what actually *is* sacred for society at large?

I doubt that there is any simple, comprehensive answer, but one idea I will consider here can be traced back to the late 19th century and the writings of the sociologist of religion Emile Durkheim. He proposed that in his time there was a growing sense of sacredness surrounding the freedom and authority of the individual. The importance of individual autonomy is, he was even willing to write, 'a religion in which man is at once the worshiper and the god'.[37] Running the clock

---

34. See, for example, the editorial 'The Duchess and the Irony of Privacy Laws', *The Daily Mail*, 14 September 2012, http://www.dailymail.co.uk/debate/article-2203465/ Kate-Middleton-topless-photos-Duchess-Cambridge-irony-privacy-laws.html [accessed 10 August 2014]; Ann Gripper, 'Be ashamed! Twitter reaction to French Closer over Kate sunbathing photos', *The Mirror*, 14 September 2012, http://www.mirror.co.uk/news/uk-news/kate-middleton-topless-pictures-french-1323799#.U-eFqPldU8w [accessed 10 August 2014]; Russell Myers, ' "I'm profoundly dismayed at what my paper published": Media Baron Richard Desmond's fury at Irish Daily Star's decision to print topless pictures of Kate', *The Daily Mail*, 15 September 2012, http://www.dailymail.co.uk/news/article-2203868/Kate-Middleton-topless-photos-Richard-Desmonds-fury-Irish-Daily-Stars-decision-print-pictures.html [accessed 10 August 2014].

35. Pegasus, 'Kate and George', http://www.pegasusartist.co.uk/#!Kate-and-George/zoom/c1g3o/image1bss [accessed 10 August 2014].

36. 'Duchess and her newborn prince get the biblical look in graffiti art inspired by the Virgin Mary', *The Mail on Sunday*, 10 August 2013, http://www.dailymail.co.uk/femail/article-2389082/Duchess-newborn-prince-biblical-look-graffiti-art-inspired-Virgin-Mary.html [accessed 10 August 2014].

37. Emile Durkheim, *On Morality and Society*, Robert Bellah (ed.) (London and Chicago: University of Chicago Press, 1973), p. 46.

forward through the twentieth century and into the twenty-first, those proposing that individualism has become central to the values we consider most important are able to point toward a variety of phenomena: the language of individual human rights, the normalization of democracy, the consumerism that structures our economics, and the focus on the self that shapes both New Age religiosity and many contemporary articulations of older religious traditions. In his 1999 book *The Empowered Self*, the lawyer and academic Thomas Franck stated that for the individualist 'we have entered a new era – engineered by modern technology and legitimated by new social attitudes and laws – that empowers each of us to ask who we are and then challenges us to make the answering of that question a central enterprise of our lives'.[38] It is, in other words, an outlook that declares, 'You've got it all wrong. You don't need to follow me. You don't need to follow anybody! You've got to think for yourselves! You're all individuals! We're all different! We've got to work it out for ourselves!' This message, proclaimed by Brian to a group of adoring followers, uncannily sums up the prevailing individualism of our current age.

Readers might protest that this takes the scene a little too seriously, but there are grounds for viewing this speech as more than simply dialogue created for comic effect. The following reflection by Palin on the overall philosophy of the film and its makers is especially illuminating:

> There's a real feeling that we'd moved up a notch with *Life of Brian*. It was taking on something that could be difficult and controversial, but essentially dealt with all sorts of things that were right at the basis of what Python comedy was all about, which is really resisting people telling you how to behave and how not to behave. It was the freedom of the individual, a very Sixties thing, the independence which was part of the way Python had been formed, the way Python had gone on.[39]

Brian's individualism can be reasonably interpreted as reflecting a serious message that Monty Python wished to convey.[40] Responding in particular to Palin's reference to the 1960s, I agree with Kevin Schilbrack that emphasis upon the autonomy of the individual should not be seen simply as a peculiarly 1960s phenomenon, but as a cultural shift with deeper roots within modernity.[41] The social changes of the 1960s may have marked a vivid moment of change, but the rumblings of individualism were felt by Durkheim and others much earlier, and it has increasingly moved to the centre of Western consciousness.

38. Thomas M. Franck, *The Empowered Self: Law and Society in an Age of Individualism* (Oxford: Oxford University Press, 1999), p. 3.

39. Chapman et al., *The Pythons Autobiography*, pp. 386–7.

40. Graham Chapman similarly commented, 'That movie, if it said anything at all, said think for yourselves, don't blindly follow, which I think isn't a bad message,' in ibid., p. 370.

41. Kevin Schilbrack, '"Life's a Piece of Shit": Heresy, Humanism, and Heroism in Monty Python's *Life of Brian*', in Gary L. Hardcastle and George A. Reisch (eds), *Monty Python and Philosophy: Nudge Nudge, Think Think!* (New York: Open Court, 2006), pp. 13–24, at p. 17.

Brian's speech is, in other words, a kind of Sermon on the Mount for individualists, and it has remarkable resonance with what some suggest is driving the evolution of religiosity in contemporary Britain. In their 2005 book *The Spiritual Revolution*, two of the UK's leading sociologists of religion, Paul Heelas and Linda Woodhead, propose that if you want to understand belief and practice in our present age, you need to recognize that '[t]he subjectivities of each individual [have] become a, if not the, unique source of significance, meaning and authority [...] The goal is not to defer to higher authority, but to have the courage to become one's own authority'.[42] Brian's individualistic values have become mainstream, mirroring the authority of self that frames our contemporary attitude toward spirituality, society, politics and consumption.[43]

But if the self has become a sacred authority, what now amounts to blasphemy? It is an issue that Durkheim saw coming. In his 1898 essay he remarks that for the individualist it is personal freedom that 'is considered sacred', and '[w]hoever makes an attempt on a man's life, on a man's liberty, on a man's honor, inspires in us a feeling of horror analogous in every way to that which the believer experiences when he sees his idol profaned'.[44] In this particular situation blasphemy is anything that violates the sanctity of individual freedoms. And with specific regard to the focus of this chapter, blasphemy now includes censorship itself, for censorship is the suppression of an individual's right to make up their own mind. It involves a ruling body declaring that the autonomy and authority of the individuals under its control should be suppressed for the greater good. So if, as various commentators suggest, ours is now an age dominated by an underlying individualism, to blaspheme you do so not by screening or praising *Life of Brian*, but by banning it.

Though not directly concerned with Monty Python's film, in his 2012 book *The Future of Blasphemy*, the American philosopher Austin Dacey reaches a similar conclusion about the taboos of contemporary society.[45] Yet his final suggestion is not, naturally enough, for us to actually enact such desecration by routinely suppressing the freedom of individuals. What he does propose is vigilance, in order that the dominant values do not become so fixed, unscrutinized and inflexible that they lack a meaningful basis.[46] With regard to *Life of Brian* the risk is that

42. Paul Heelas and Linda Woodhead, *The Spiritual Revolution: Why Religion is Giving Way to Spirituality* (Oxford: Blackwell, 2005), pp. 3–4.

43. For a recent consideration of the individualist philosophy of *Life of Brian* in relation to the rise of Thatcherism, see James Crossley, *Harnessing Chaos: The Bible in English Political Discourse Since 1968* (London: T&T Clark Bloomsbury, 2014), pp. 129–52, at pp. 151–2.

44. Durkheim, *On Morality and Society*, p. 46.

45. He writes that when you consider that 'sacred things are important, inviolable, and incommensurable values, the modern liberal paradigm of the sacred – the dignity of the individual human person – emerges as a species of the genus'. Austin Dacey, *The Future of Blasphemy: Speaking of the Sacred in an Age of Human Rights* (London: Continuum, 2012), p. 116.

46. Ibid., p. 129.

individualism becomes an empty mantra. Just as most of the crowd who listen to Brian repeat back to him his language of individual freedom without actually thinking it through at all, so perhaps should we be wary that our own engagement with such values does not become simply ritualized speech, which when challenged provokes only the outrage of a believer whose idol has been desecrated.[47]

Conclusion

This is a very wide-ranging chapter and certainly to give each time period full justice would require a much lengthier treatment. My hope, however, is to have given an introductory view of how *Life of Brian* may lead us into thinking about the changing perception of blasphemy across three distinct social contexts.

But, before bringing together the various strands of this discussion, it is worth addressing briefly how this consideration of *Life of Brian* and blasphemy fits into the rest of the volume. It is a chapter that departs a little from the mode of 'reception exegesis' championed by the organizers of the *Jesus and Brian* conference upon which this volume is based. Described as a method that aims 'to use the film [...] as a tool that can help us consider our assumptions and the historical evidence', reception exegesis has an orientation that self-consciously uses post-biblical material to look *back* into the ancient world.[48] This book's very subtitle – 'Exploring the Historical Jesus and his Times, via *Monty Python's Life of Brian*' – explicitly reflects this direction of travel and in so doing bears resemblances to Larry Kreitzer's 'reversing the hermeneutic flow' project of over twenty years ago.[49] However, 'reception exegesis' is a term coined only very recently and so the parameters of its method are especially open to debate.[50] It appears to me that

47. In terms of the crowd's reaction, the obvious counter-example is the man who ironically declares that he is not an individual. See Stephen Benko, 'Ironic Faith in Monty Python's *Life of Brian*', *Journal of Religion and Film [digital]*, 16, 1 (2012), Article 6, available at http://digitalcommons.unomaha.edu/jrf/vol16/iss1/6, pp. 9–10.

48. 'About the Conference', http://www.kcl.ac.uk/artshums/depts/trs/events/jandb/about.aspx, *Kings College London* [accessed 10 August 2014].

49. Larry Kreitzer states that his 'aim is to reverse the flow of influence within the hermeneutical process and examine select NT passages or themes in the light of some of the enduring expressions of our own culture' in *The New Testament in Fiction and Film: On Reversing the Hermeneutical Flow* (Sheffield: Sheffield Academic Press, 1993), p. 19. See also Larry Kreitzer, *The Old Testament in Fiction and Film: On Reversing the Hermeneutical Flow* (Sheffield: Sheffield Academic Press, 1994). I am indebted to Jon Morgan for pointing me toward these works.

50. At the close of their recent commentary on the Book of Lamentations Paul Joyce and Diana Lipton write, 'we found that material from the history of reception sensitized our reading of Lamentations and generated insights that provided fresh options for understanding the ancient text. This was the process that we termed "reception exegesis"', *Lamentations through the Centuries* (Oxford: Wiley-Blackwell, 2013), p. 193.

despite its merits, a fundamental risk reception exegesis must guard against is treating post-biblical material superficially. The most meaningful interaction between *Life of Brian* and study of the ancient world, it is hoped, engages with the reality that Monty Python's film is in so many ways a rich and complex cultural artefact in its own right. *Life of Brian*, in other words, deserves not to be used as simply an entertaining pit stop on the way to antiquity.

In this chapter I have endeavoured to avoid this, but in doing so perhaps ultimately ended up breaking away from the primary ambitions of reception exegesis. I have not consciously tried to interpret the ancient via the modern, nor indeed the modern via the ancient. Rather, each subsection of this chapter might be taken to stand as its own relatively free-standing temporal unit. But if we do momentarily attempt to set our gaze across all three at once we can nonetheless draw some tentative conclusions. Most notably it appears to be the case that spanning these varying situations is blasphemy's status as a socially contested category. The particulars of the debate are vividly different in first-century Judaea, late-1970s Britain and contemporary Britain, but one point of continuity is the difficulty we find in pinning down an agreed view of what is and is not blasphemous. In each context blasphemy is likely disputed because of the way in which the borders of a society's moral order become particularly fuzzy during periods of change. Only in a situation of cultural stability can everyone agree on the exact borders of free speech, and such stability is lacking in first-century Judaea as well as in late-1970s and twenty-first-century Britain. Change means re-evaluation, competing social forces, and a blurring of the lines that must not be crossed. As the culmination of the stoning scene from *Life of Brian* shows, at the end of the day the person who actually ends up being found to be the most reprehensible blasphemer might not be the one you were expecting.

Plate 1. Terry Jones, John Cleese and Richard Burridge discuss Jesus and Brian at the conference held at King's College London in June 2014.

Plate 2. *Sica* and sheath, En Gedi (Courtesy of Gideon Hadas; Photo by Guy Stiebel; after Stiebel, '*Armis et litteris*,' Vol. III, Pl. I.8, no. 2).

Plate 3. Ownership tag (*nota*) of L. Magus of the century of Gallus, Gamala (Photo by and courtesy of Danny Syon).

Plate 4. Wooden phallus pendant, Camp F, Masada (Courtesy of Benjamin Arubas and Haim Goldfus; Photo by Guy Stiebel; after Stiebel, '*Armis et litteris*,' Vol. III, Pl. III.20E, no. 1).

Plate 5. Walter Plunkett's frothy, voluminous dresses created for *Gone with the Wind* epitomize the successful amalgamation of historical knowledge, contemporary fashion, and emotive appeal. Ann Rutherford, Vivien Leigh and Evelyn Keyes in *Gone with the Wind* (1939).

Credit: Selznick/MGM/The Kobal Collection.

Plate 6. Bronze Statue of a Man (Greek, mid 2nd–1st century BCE). 'The himation is kept in place in part by the tasselled weight thrown over his left shoulder, which hangs at his calf . . . Several horizontal bands . . . decorate the fabric.'

Credit: Metropolitan Museum of Art, Gift of Renée E. and Robert A. Belfer, 2001.

Plate 7. A red tunic decorated with black bands (*clavi*) from the Cave of Letters, Nahal Hever.

Credit: Photo Clara Amit; Courtesy of the Israeli Antiquities Authority.

Plate 8. Moses and the burning bush. Moses wears a white tunic with wide, purple *clavi*. Wing Panel 1, Dura-Europos synagogue.

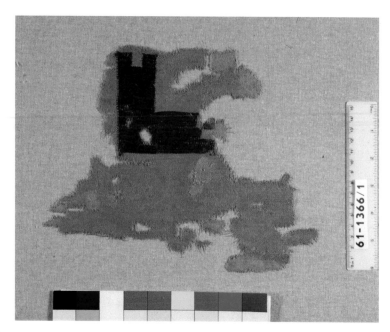

Plate 9. An orange mantle decorated with purple Gamma-shaped design. Cave of Letters, Nahal Hever.

Credit: Photo Clara Amit, Courtesy of the Israeli Antiquities Authority.

Plate 10. Samuel anointing David. David dressed as a king (in purple) with attendants in gold and red, provides an exception to the pale colours typical on male garments. Notched bands can be seen on the edges of the men's mantels. Dam-393, Dura-Europos Synagogue.

Credit: Yale University Art Gallery, Dura-Europos Collection.

Chapter 5

THE MEANING OF MONTY PYTHON'S JESUS

James G. Crossley

It has become something of a truism in certain circles that historical Jesus scholars will invariably see their reflection at the bottom of the deep well. While not entirely disputing this, we would get a fuller picture of what is being projected on to Jesus should we think more broadly and include the backdrop, thereby including a wider range of often unconscious cultural values. And in this respect we might include Monty Python's *Life of Brian* which, it will be suggested, might also be categorized as part of the quest for the historical Jesus. I want to look at the kinds of cultural values their Jesus (/Brian) embodied, how their Jesus (/Brian) stands in a tradition of anti-ecclesiastical Jesuses, and how their own critique of dogma and church interpretations might actually be turned on Jesus and Jesus scholarship, both of which are largely treated with a far higher degree of seriousness than others by Monty Python. To explore this issue, we first need to look at the ways in which Monty Python constructed a Jesus through the character of Brian because it is this connection which is crucial to understanding their presentation of the quest for the historical Jesus and the cultural values their Jesus and the quest can reveal.

The Historical Brian/Jesus

Once we peel away the ideas attributed to Brian in the film and get back to the ordinary, everyday Brian, this Brian of History might, by analogy, be a problem for those believers confronted with an ordinary, everyday Jesus. This Brian is *not* the Messiah, he is *not* a martyr, he is *not* resurrected, and the crucifixion is *not* significant, yet all of these are attributed to Brian by his deluded followers. Blasphemy and offence are, of course, in the eye of the beholder, but the film's potential for offence underpins some attempts to rehabilitate the *Life of Brian* as a relatively unthreatening film which, so the argument goes, attacks the excesses of religious behaviour rather than the core of the religion itself. Richard Burridge, who had previously sparked off a media controversy for his reading of *Life of Brian*,[1] recently put forward a more informed version of this common view.[2] He comments:

> Sadly, the Christian Church has all too frequently exhibited such schisms rather than following Jesus himself … This satire of political and religious groups' tendency to split into factions, fight each other, and miss the entire point of their founder is also brilliantly depicted in the various 'popular fronts' for the liberation

---

1. Burridge made his praise of *Life of Brian* on BBC Radio 4 which was then reported (faithfully) in the *Telegraph*. See John Bingham, 'Monty Python's *Life of Brian* "extraordinary tribute to Jesus", says theologian decorated by Pope Francis,' *Telegraph* (31 December, 2013), available at http://www.telegraph.co.uk/news/religion/10543149/Monty-Pythons-Life-of-Brian-extraordinary-tribute-to-Jesus-says-theologian-decorated-by-Pope-Francis.html [accessed 2 September 2014]. In *Life of Brian*-style, media reporting then misconstrued the *Telegraph* piece and came up with alternative readings of Burridge, made particularly clear in the headlines, such as the following from the *Irish Independent* which effectively presented the *Telegraph* piece: ' "*Life of Brian*" was true, theologian swears on Bible,' *Irish Independent* (December 31, 2013) http://www.independent.ie/world-news/life-of-brian-was-true-theologian-swears-on-bible-29876229.html [accessed 6 September 2014]. The *Sun*, which also presented the 'controversy' on Page Three (which, for those not familiar with British culture, is the home to photographs of topless models), also had a piece by Jeremy Clarkson, 'Cheese's Christ, what a miracle!,' *Sun* (January 4, 2014), available behind the paywall at http://www.thesun.co.uk/sol/homepage/suncolumnists/jeremyclarkson/5356133/more-iron-man-films-and-explosions-suit-jeremy-clarkson.html [accessed 6 September 2014]. Clarkson suggests that the presentation of the character Jesus in *Life of Brian* is not even positive: 'the Rev. Prof Richard Burridge has stepped forward to say that the condemnation was wrong because the film, in fact, is a remarkable tribute to the life of Jesus. No it isn't. Jesus only appears once, as a muttering Yorkshireman whose incoherent speech about blessing the cheesemakers starts a fight. Not really much of a tribute, is it?'

2. 'Common' is, of course, vague and anecdotal. But the 'non-offensive' reading of *Life of Brian* is almost always the initial reading given by students when I have taught about the film (typically to class sizes of more than fifty) since 2005.

of Judaea ... Amazingly, his person, teaching, and life still fascinate millions, despite the appalling behaviour of his followers over 2,000 years ...[3]

But can we not extend the critique of 'miss[ing] the entire point of their founder' to the Gospel writers and the earliest followers of Jesus in *Life of Brian*? I have discussed the overlaps between Brian and scholarly constructions of the *historical* Jesus in detail elsewhere,[4] but such overlaps remain important because it is clear that the historical Brian (/the historical Jesus) is someone who is:

- born out of wedlock, with a Roman soldier as a father who raped Mandy (read: Mary) 'at first', and with high Mandiology/Mariology attributed to her by deluded followers
- emphatically not the Messiah with Messiahship misattributed to him by deluded followers, including one who knows because he has followed a few
- a Jew loyal to Jews and Judaism with no intention of starting any new movement in his name (quite the opposite)
- an anti-Roman insurrectionist
- happy to enjoying non-marital sex with Judith (read: Mary Magdalene)
- going to die with death being the end and with no resurrection
- keen to suggest that we are all individuals who should not let anyone tell us what to do and that should think for ourselves

As I argued, this might be the sort of historical Jesus that was certainly 'in the air' as Monty Python were researching *Life of Brian*, and it should not be difficult to see Brian as telling us something about Monty Python's Jesus (or vice versa).

Related points may be added which would suggest that the film is trying to provoke Christians, or at least a certain sort of Christian view of Jesus. Biblical and parabolic language (including that language attributed to Jesus in the Gospels) is clearly mocked in the proclamations by Brian and other prophets, not least as being silly and potentially confusing:

Consider the lilies ... Well the birds then. ... Have they got jobs? ... They [the birds] eat but they don't grow anything, do they? ... OK. And you're more important than they are, right? Well there you are then. What are you *worrying* about ... (cf. Matt. 6.25–34)

Look, there was this man and he had two servants ... And he gave them some talents ... there were these two servants ... or wait a moment were there three?

---

3. Richard Burridge, 'Is he more than a "naughty boy"?' *Church Times* (13 June 2004), available at http://www.churchtimes.co.uk/articles/2014/13-june/comment/opinion/is-he-more-than-a-naughty-boy.

4. James G. Crossley, 'Life of Brian or Life of Jesus? Uses of Critical Biblical Scholarship and Non-Orthodox Views of Jesus in Monty Python's *Life of Brian*', *Relegere: Studies in Religion and Reception* (2011), pp. 93–114.

... Three ... well *stewards* actually ... (cf. Matt. 18.23-3–5; 21.28–32; 25.14–30; Luke 16.1–8; 19.11–27)

Er hear this! Er ... Blessed are they ... who convert their neighbour's ox ... for they shall inhibit their girth ... and to them only shall be given ... (cf. Matt. 5.1–12; Luke 6.20–26. See also Exod. 20.17; Deut. 5.21)[5]

The crowd look for the absurdities in these sayings such as the incredulous exclamation by one member of the crowd: 'Do the birds have jobs?!' Jesus may not be present to defend himself but his sayings do not come away unscathed from this scene and there is the clear implication that the sayings are only loosely connected to the teller; certainly no serious degree of profundity was supposed to have been suggested by all the talk of birds and talents.

But if Jesus is lightly (and rarely directly) mocked, is there not a stronger case that the Gospel writers, the apostles, the Twelve, and the earliest followers are much clearer targets for the humour? Who, after all, are supposed to have attributed martyrdom, messiahship, resurrection, and so on, to Jesus/Brian? This, in turn, raises the problems for the cultured defenders of *Life of Brian* and its apparent lack of offence: would they be happy with the suggestion that Gospel themes and theology are effectively deemed to be deluded or even just silly? It is imaginable that there are Christians of a certain liberal stripe – perhaps those who appreciate the Jesus Seminar, Westar Institute, John Dominic Crossan or Marcus Borg – who could accept the mocking of theological themes found in the Gospels and see this as a legitimate part of understanding who the historical Jesus was behind these themes. But if we read *Life of Brian* as an attack on the creation of Gospel theology then there are obviously Christians who would not. This sort of argument is implicit in Burridge's article in that it makes clear what *Life of Brian* is *not* attacking:

Muggeridge and Stockwood repeatedly charged the Pythons with blasphemy and mocking Jesus. They had, however, arrived late to see the film, and missed the opening scenes. It begins with the Wise Men visiting a stable, worshipping the infant Brian, and giving his mother, Mandy, the traditional gold, frankincense, and myrrh – although she is interested only in the gold ... Their real target is those who seek to follow Brian and turn him into the Messiah, which he frequently denies ... Many Christians find the mass crucifixion at the end of the film difficult, but it accurately reflects its frequent, brutal use by the Romans. Eric Idle's song 'Always Look on the Bright Side of Life' may grate, but it confronts us with the meaninglessness of life and death without God ...

But might Monty Python not be turning these criticisms back on the stories about Jesus? Who would be so odd as to bring a gift as offbeat as myrrh? Who else might be deluded in telling stories about Messiahs? What if crucifixion is so frequent that it is casually (and consistently) deemed little more than a

---

5. Monty Python, *The Life of Brian Screenplay* (London: Methuen, 2004), pp. 54–5.

doddle?[6] And what if death is the end and a familiar story ended *without* resurrection? And what if life really is just meaningless and without a God? As Richard Walsh put it: 'One may remember that messianic acclamations are wrong more often than not, if not always. At least one laughs at the incongruity of an ordinary, Jewish, bastard, Messiah. Of course (wink wink) this is not the Gospel Jesus.'[7] Yet might the acceptance of *Life of Brian* as something positive for Christianity in fact suggest that the more deliberately provocative elements of the film have now been domesticated?

The Meaning of the Good Man Jesus

I think the answer based on the above argument shows that *Life of Brian* clearly has been domesticated in this respect. Another reason for this domestication is that Jesus himself – whether through the cipher Brian or the actual Jesus in the film – is not typically mocked and is presented relatively seriously. Brian (/historical Jesus) and the Jesus of the film (effectively the Christ of faith in the guise of the cinematic Christ[8]) are presented seriously so as to provide a foil or straight guy for all the comedic others, from the Jewish revolutionaries to the ex-leper. But if deluded interpreters provide much of the comedy, why is Brian then so straight? Comic reasons are no doubt present, particularly in presenting 'one like us' in absurdist world. But there are, I think, other reasons, particularly surrounding the admiration for a Jesus behind the deluded interpretation. This has been suggested by two of the Pythons. Terry Gilliam's recollection of the genesis of Brian after the completion of *Monty Python and the Holy Grail* (1974) is telling: 'very quickly we came around to the feeling that Jesus was OK we weren't going to take the piss out of him, he was genuinely OK, so that's where Brian got created, he was a parallel.'[9] Graham Chapman similarly commented: 'That movie, if it said anything at all, said think for yourselves, don't blindly follow, which I think isn't a bad message and I'm sure Mr Christ would have agreed.'[10]

This 'rescuing' Jesus from Christianity, religion, Gospel writers, or deluded ecclesiastical interpreters has a long history, particularly since the Enlightenment

6. On crucifixion and *Life of Brian*, see Hans Wiersma, 'Redeeming *Life of Brian*: How Monty Python (Ironically) Proclaims Christ *Sub Contrario*', *Word and World* 32 (2012), pp. 166–77.

7. Richard Walsh, 'Monty Python's *Life of Brian* (1979),' in Adele Reinhartz (ed.), *Bible and Cinema: Fifty Key Films* (London and New York: Routledge, 2013), pp. 187–92, at p. 191.

8. Philip R. Davies, '*Life of Brian* Research' in Philip R. Davies, *Whose Bible Is It Anyway?* (London & New York: T&T Clark/Continuum, 2004), pp. 142–55. This essay was first printed in J. Cheryl Exum and Stephen Moore (eds) *Biblical Studies/Cultural Studies: The Third Sheffield Colloquium* (Sheffield: Sheffield Academic Press, 1998), pp. 400–14.

9. The Pythons, with Bob McCabe, *The Pythons: Autobiography* (London: Orion, 2003), p. 353.

10. Pythons, *Autobiography*, p. 370.

and in competing understandings of Church and State, and popular among those who would identify as secular, agnostic or atheist (or, indeed, comedians). This serious treatment of a sensible Jesus contrasted with the lampooning of the Church has proved a means to keep Jesus as a weapon against what might be classified as, or assumed to be, 'organized religion'. This Jesus also has a long politicized history among those identifying as radical or liberal and used to uphold ideas of peace, justice, freedom, tolerance or even revolution. This sort of Jesus can be found among diverse figures such as Pierre-Joseph Proudhon, Oscar Wilde, Alexander Berkman, H. G. Wells, John Lennon, Douglas Adams, Bill Hicks and Philip Pullman, and might be compared to vague popular receptions of (equally marketable) figures like Ghandi, Malcolm X, Martin Luther King or Che Guevara.[11] Around the same time as *Life of Brian*, the openly atheist Douglas Adams published *The Hitchhiker's Guide to the Galaxy* which talked about a girl in a cafe in Rickmansworth who realized how the world could be a decent place, echoing the views of a man not unlike Brian who was nailed to a tree nearly 2,000 years earlier for suggesting that it would be nice for people to be pleasant to each other for once. Once again we have the theme of the sane 'one of us' ruined by idiocy and absurdity.

There is an implied reinterpretation of Jesus going on in these sorts of traditions which projects its own ideological interests onto Jesus and cannot quite let go of the major 'religious' figure in European heritage, even if God and religion may disappear in a puff of logic. Instead of reinterpreting Jesus to fit the needs of the ancient world and ancient beliefs, this radical, liberal, non-ecclesiastical historical Jesus undergoes a new reinterpretation to make sure he fits the beliefs of our time, perhaps an interpretative move as absurd as those made by the deluded followers of Brian/Jesus given the massive historical and cultural differences between then and now. Jesus/Brian *must*, it seems, share our values to some extent, or at least be recognizable to some extent, and these values are kept pure, so to speak, by the seriousness of the understanding of Jesus and Brian. Precisely what 'our values' are can, of course, be quite complicated, not least due to the amount of unconscious and cultural baggage we carry, but a Brian who tells us to think for ourselves, that we are all individuals, not to take orders blindly, and enjoy a bit of casual sex, is someone that would hardly be out of place today, not even among historical Jesus scholars. Moreover, some of the more precise contemporary targets of satire are fairly transparent, most notably trade unions and leftist groups. Yet, in another way, Brian and *Life of Brian* were not the only ones in 1979 proclaiming the importance of individuals while challenging received authority, collectivist bureaucracy of the trade unions and leftist groups. For 1979 was also the year that heralded the electoral triumph of Margaret Thatcher as what we now label 'Thatcherism' was gathering momentum.[12] Indeed, a comparison between Brian/Jesus and Thatcher

11. James G. Crossley, *Harnessing Chaos: The Bible in English Political Discourse since 1968* (London: T&T Clark Bloomsbury, 2014), pp. 29–32, 268–9.

12. Crossley, *Harnessing Chaos*, pp. 129–52.

should not be underestimated. Even Terry Jones could still make a loose comical connection between (the more serious) Jesus and Thatcher: 'My feelings towards Christ are that he was a bloody good bloke, even though he wasn't as funny as Margaret Thatcher.'[13] In a curious twist, we might rethink the past and suggest that perhaps the leftists and liberals of the 1970s and 1980s missed a trick as they too should have joined Mervyn Stockwood, Malcolm Muggeridge, Mary Whitehouse, Harrogate, Swansea, parts of Surrey, East Devon, Cornwall, Ireland, Norway and Italy in protesting against Monty Python and *Life of Brian* for (unintentionally) giving Thatcherism an assist. Perhaps they too might have shaken their heads and spoke as Brian did on the cross: 'You stupid bastards!'

Of course, Thatcherism was hardly the fault of Monty Python. Nevertheless, we can see how Brian becomes a projection of 'our values' by the end of the 1970s by looking at important cultural contexts for *Life of Brian*. As David Harvey has shown, the emerging Thatcherite form of neoliberal capitalism was picking up on a range of challenges to establishment authority from Right and Left in light of the social and cultural upheavals of the 1960s, including the rhetoric of freedom, liberty and individualism constructed over against 'the stifling bureaucratic ineptitude of the state apparatus and oppressive trade union power'.[14] As the Thatcherite push for radical economic change involved challenging and reconfiguring traditional upper-class dominance and consensual politics, youth movements, pop culture and political satirists had been mocking politicians, the upper-classes, the British class system and union bureaucracy. In Britain, the so-called 'Satire Boom' of the early 1960s generated some of the most prominent anti-establishment comedy of the century, including that of Peter Cook, Dudley Moore, Jonathan Miller, Alan Bennett, David Frost, John Bird, John Fortune, *That Was the Week That Was*, *Private Eye* and, of course, Monty Python. And those challenges ended up in ways plenty of people – including most, if not all, the Pythons – probably did not entirely like. But put another way, the sub-cultural capital of Monty Python and *Life of Brian*—which politicians rarely have—became one important carrier of cultural change in the embedding of values which became associated with Thatcherism.[15]

The Jewishness of Jesus; or, On Not Taking Scholarship Too Seriously

What we can now start to see is the ideological significance of Monty Python's take on what Philip Pullman would later call 'the Good Man Jesus', that is this figure of Jesus 'rescued' from ecclesiastical or Gospel dogma.[16] It is striking that Brian's

---

13. Quoted in Robert Sellers, *Always Look on the Bright Side of Life: The Inside Story of HandMade Films* (London: John Blake, 2003), p. 5.

14. David Harvey, *A Brief History of Neoliberalism* (Oxford: Oxford University Press, 2005), p. 57.

15. Crossley, *Harnessing Chaos*, pp. 129–31, 151–4.

16. Philip Pullman, *The Good Man Jesus and the Scoundrel Christ* (Edinburgh: Canongate, 2010).

views on individualism and thinking for yourself are treated seriously (and with
no small amount of exasperation) in the midst of the deluded silliness of the
crowd. This Brian (/Jesus) and his values reflects a more serious attitude towards
the apparently serious world of the scholarship Monty Python were reading. And
one thing is certainly clear (and particularly so in the debate with Muggeridge and
Stockwood): ideas, learning, study, scholarship and 'critical thinking' were to be
taken very seriously, even to the extent of their absence in the Muggeridge and
Stockwood debate angering the usually placid Michael Palin.[17] The contrast
between comedy and the seriousness of scholarly thinking is clear in other
comments by Palin and John Cleese:

> ... it was a very academic approach. We read books about the Bible story and
> that period, the Dead Sea Scrolls and various new interpretations of the Gospels,
> that sort of thing, just because we all felt, well, we can't just do silly jokes about
> people being knocked off donkeys, there's got to be a kind of philosophical
> approach as well. (Palin)[18]

> I don't know about the miracles, I mean a lot of the healing, the faith healing, I
> would imagine was absolutely sensible. I mean anyone who is suffering
> from the symptoms of something that's basically got a hysterical foundation
> then that could easily happen. I would have thought that just as much as faith
> healing is a fact of life. It all makes sense to me. Water into wine I would be very
> dubious about, frankly Brian [*laugh*]. Over the moon if it happened but ...
> (Cleese)[19]

Yet perhaps Monty Python missed another trick here: scholarly reconstructions of
the historical Jesus might not be as serious, or even as sensible or worthy of respect,
as might have been implied in both their statements and presentation of Brian/
Jesus. In turn, we might suggest that, on Monty Python's logic, such scholarship
might equally deserve the satirical treatment of the other targets in *Life of Brian*.
For a start, do not the plethora of scholarly Jesuses (already growing when *Life of
Brian* was released) suggest that something like the confused behaviour of Brian's
first followers could be applied as much to scholarship as to the early Christians or
deluded religious interpreters?

We can again see how much historical Jesus scholarship, from around the time
of the film to the present, acts in ways not widely removed from the followers of
Brian: reinterpreting Jesus means what the cultural context wants him to mean – a
bit liberal and certainly not too alien or weird. Let us take a more precise example,
prominent both in scholarship and in *Life of Brian*: the 'Jewishness' of Jesus/Brian.
Despite Mr Cohen not being Brian's real father, Brian's emphasis on his Jewishness
is clear enough. He wears a skullcap and his surname 'Cohen' is as recognizably

17. Sellers, *HandMade Films*, pp. 18–19, 21–2.
18. Quoted in Sellers, *HandMade Films*, p. 4.
19. *The Pythons – A Documentary* (BBC/Python [Monty] Pictures, 1979).

Jewish as can be imagined. When stunned about the news of his father being a Roman, Brian throws an adolescent tantrum, proclaiming, 'I'm not a Roman, Mum, and never will be! I'm a kike! A yid! A hebe! A hook-nose! I'm kosher, Mum. I'm a Red Sea pedestrian and proud of it!' This Jewish Brian was paralleling what was starting to happen in historical Jesus studies. Since Geza Vermes' book in 1973, *Jesus the Jew* (a possible influence on *Life of Brian*),[20] historical Jesus scholars have gone out of their way to tell us how 'Jewish' their Jesus is, whether in book titles, rhetoric or arguments.[21] So far, so serious; indeed, in the case of historical Jesus scholarship, Jesus' Jewishness should not be underestimated given that it was preceded by some explicitly anti-Jewish, anti-Semitic and even Nazi understandings of Jesus and Judaism.

But what happened next is where scholarship takes a curious turn. Vermes' Jesus did not do anything unknown to Judaism but the process of reinterpreting Vermes' Jesus gets, we might say, Pythonesque. Jesus, we are repeatedly told by scholars, is 'very Jewish' or 'thoroughly Jewish' or 'robustly Jewish'.[22] But what, exactly, is a 'very Jewish' Jesus? What is a not-very-Jewish Jesus? What is a partially Jewish Jesus? What is a moderately Jewish Jesus? James Charlesworth has even claimed that 'Jesus . . . is perhaps the most Jewish Jew of the first century'.[23] But how is it possible for scholarship to 'measure' such things? If Jesus was perhaps the most Jewish Jew, would it then be possible to say who was the second, fifth or least 'Jewish Jew' of the first century?

Michael Bird has attempted to measure the 'Jewishness' of Jesus in a different way. As an aside, Bird is also an interesting figure here because he is one of the few New Testament scholars who have attempted to use (and has been praised for using) comedy as part of their scholarly rhetoric, whether in his 'Comic Belief' sections in his systematic theology,[24] his recent YouTube parody of 'hipster' readers of the Bible[25] or his elaborate analogies in response to people like Bart Ehrman which provoked a negative response from J. R. Daniel Kirk for being 'clownish'

---

20. Geza Vermes, *Jesus the Jew: A Historian's Reading of the Gospels* (London: SCM, 1973). On Monty Python engaging with critical scholarship see e.g. Crossley, 'Life of Brian or Life of Jesus?'

21. William Arnal, *The Symbolic Jesus: Historical Scholarship, Judaism and the Construction of Contemporary Identity* (London & Oakville: Equinox, 2005); James G. Crossley, *Jesus in an Age of Terror: Projects for a New American Century* (London & Oakville: Equinox, 2008).

22. On what follows see James G. Crossley, *Jesus in an Age of Neoliberalism: Quests, Scholarship and Ideology* (Durham: Acumen, 2012) and James G. Crossley, 'A "Very Jewish" Jesus: Perpetuating the Myth of Superiority,' *JSHJ* 11 (2013), pp. 109–29.

23. James H. Charlesworth, 'The Historical Jesus in the Fourth Gospel: A Paradigm Shift?' *JSHJ* 8 (2010), pp. 3–46, at p. 45.

24. Michael F. Bird, *Evangelical Theology: A Biblical and Systematic Introduction* (Grand Rapids: Zondervan, 2013).

25. Michael F. Bird, 'Biblica Hipsteria,' http://www.youtube.com/watch?v=6K9N3vYM4vc

rather than 'serious'.[26] Yet, in his serious 'Jewish Jesus' he collects together some dominant scholarly assumptions about 'Jewishness' and its interpretation which are ripe for satire. For instance, Bird published an article on the Jewishness of Jesus and how to avoid the 'peril' of modernizing Jesus.[27] The central example of an anachronistic 'de-judaizing' of Jesus is, for Bird, casting him as a Cynic or Hellenized figure which, he claims, is also analogous to Nazi New Testament scholarship.[28] To help us appreciate his concept of 'de-judaizing', and its apparent distinction from 'un-Jewish', Bird turns to a rarely developed analogy in discussions of Jewish identity: 'De-alcoholized wine still retains a small measure of alcohol, but not enough to impact the drinker. Thus by "de-Judaizing"[29] I mean the act of moving Jesus' Jewishness to the periphery or else negating its effects by blanketing it with a Hellenistic overlay'.[30] For Bird, high levels of Jewishness – or, by analogy, sizeable alcohol content – is 'the fail safe' to stop us modernizing Jesus. More specifically, this 'Jewishness' must mean that Jesus was 'in conversation and confrontation with his times rather than ours', including 'intra-Jewish disputes about halakhah, the status of Samaritans, paying imperial taxes, and maintenance of purity stipulations' which are 'more likely to feature as topics of Jesus' interest than feminism, globalization, or church growth strategies'.[31]

Not unlike the crowds gathered to see the prophets and the unintentional prophet Brian in *Life of Brian*, we might ask some slightly absurdist questions of this approach to Jesus. What if someone was identified as Jewish but was not interested in intra-Jewish disputes concerning halakhah, the status of Samaritans, paying imperial taxes and maintenance of purity stipulations? What about those Jews in the ancient world who may never have met a Samaritan or those who did not think too much about Samaritans? Could not someone who identified as a Jew, pay taxes, and think indifferently that one master was as good or bad as another? What happens if we play the game on Bird's terms? Is Bird's Jesus a 13 per cent vol. Jew if a Cynic Jesus is low alcohol? Were there moments when Jesus did not think

26. Michael F. Bird et al., *How God Became Jesus: The Real Origins of Belief in Jesus' Divine Nature – A Response to Bart Ehrman* (Grand Rapids: Zondervan, 2014); J. R. Daniel Kirk, 'How God Became Jesus: Part 1, In Review of the Evangelical Response to Ehrman', *Storied Theology* (24 April 2014), http://www.jrdkirk.com/2014/04/24/god-became-jesus-part-1-review-evangelical-response-ehrman/. Kirk claims that Bird needs to be set on 'a trajectory of learning the appropriate time for entertainment versus the appropriate time for serious mental exertion', that it is 'difficult to describe Bird's work as anything other than clownish', and that 'the buffoonery that plagues the chapters displaces what needs to be a critical argument'.

27. Michael F. Bird, 'The Peril of Modernizing Jesus and the Crisis of Not Contemporizing the Christ', *Evangelical Quarterly* 78 (2006), pp. 291–312.

28. Bird, 'The Peril of Modernizing Jesus', p. 296.

29. Bird uses lower and upper case for 'Judaizing'.

30. Bird, 'The Peril of Modernizing Jesus', p. 297, n. 29.

31. Bird, 'The Peril of Modernizing Jesus', p. 310.

about Samaritans, legal issues or taxes? If so, did his alcoholic content vary from time to time, and place to place? Or, what if someone who identified as a Jew thought a lot about taxes and a fair bit about Hellenistic philosophy but little about Samaritans or halakhah? Was such a person a 'one-third Jewish' or, perhaps, a white wine spritzer of a Jew? What would we make of the work of N. T. Wright, whose scholarship on Jesus has had a significant influence on Bird and whom Bird would cite as presenting a particularly Jewish Jesus? Wright's Jesus has some of Bird's key aspects rendered 'redundant' and opens up the promises to Jews beyond Samaritans.[32] What percentage of alcohol is this? Is this too a low-alcohol Jesus? Or because this Jesus engages in such relevant questions (which is how Bird phrases it), does this Jesus reach 13 per cent? Or does the intensification of Jewishness by this Jesus mean that he is now a fortified wine like port? And if Wright or Bird both agree with the ideas of their presentation of a 'Jewish' Jesus in their faith, does that make them both . . . Jewish?

What playing around with scholarly absurdities shows clearly is that such statements work with the assumption of a seemingly fixed, measureable Jewish identity, as well as revealing – contrary to Bird's expectations – contemporary ideological tendencies at work in scholarship. Like Brian and the Good Man Jesus tradition, such Jewish Jesuses tell us something else about the interpreter and contemporary understandings about Judaism. For a start, how many times over the past forty years have we heard of scholars telling us how 'Jewish . . . but not *that* Jewish' their historical Jesus is? How often does the scholarly Jesus 'transcend' or 'intensify' the Judaism scholarship conveniently constructs? For E. P. Sanders, one of the scholars of the past four decades who has tried to take Judaism seriously, the historical Jesus may have done lots of 'Jewish' things but this Jesus provocatively did not want 'the wicked' to engage with certain other 'Jewish' things such as the Temple system of forgiveness and was challenging anything known in Judaism in the saying 'let the dead bury their dead' (Matt. 8.21–22; Luke 9.59–60).[33] John Meier's subtitle in his Jesus series – *A Marginal Jew* – is striking, and Meier has his Jewish Jesus be different from Jews on oaths.[34] Ben Witherington picks up a common theme that Jesus was nicer to women than a block of illiberal Jews and illiberal Judaism.[35] We could go on and reference any number of implicitly or explicitly radical Jesuses constructed over against (a constructed) Judaism on purity, family, forgiveness, Temple, Sabbath, gender, eschatology, politics and so on.

32. N. T. Wright, *Jesus and the Victory of God* (London: SPCK, 1996).

33. E. P. Sanders, *Jesus and Judaism* (London: SCM, 1985), pp. 252–4.

34. John P. Meier, 'Did the Historical Jesus Prohibit All Oaths? Part 1' *JSHJ* 5 (2007), pp. 175–204; John P. Meier, 'Did the Historical Jesus Prohibit All Oaths? Part 2', *JSHJ* 6 (2008), pp. 3–24.

35. Ben Witherington, *Women in the Ministry of Jesus: A Study of Jesus' Attitude to Women and Their Roles as Reflected in His Earthly Life* (Cambridge: Cambridge University Press, 1984), p. 117.

As Wright put it, this Jesus is 'a very Jewish Jesus who was nevertheless opposed to some high-profile features of first-century Judaism'.[36]

More precisely, this 'Jewish ... but not that Jewish' Jesus (perhaps exemplified in the name 'Brian Cohen') tells us something significant about the cultural contexts of, for instance, Anglo-American scholarship.[37] The 1967 Six Day War brought about major shifts in Anglo-American understandings of Israel and Judaism in popular, political, religious and intellectual culture, from indifference to a dominant discourse of staunch support, support which nevertheless has included attitudes of cultural and religious superiority in relation to Jews, Judaism and Israel. A crucial post-1967 cultural shift included a new widespread interest in the Holocaust, at least in America (e.g. Holocaust memorials, museums, changes in Jewish assimilation and identity politics). Such trends played a crucial role in bringing forward the emphasis on the 'Jewishness' of Jesus, including the tensions about how to evaluate 'Judaism'. These sorts of tensions, incidentally, played themselves out in what was to be done with the 'Zionist' character of Otto in *Life of Brian*.[38]

Such contemporary constructions of Jesus are also tied in with the increasing dominance of neoliberal capitalism which emphasizes, among other things, the power of the individual, image, free trade, the private sector, and freedom.[39] As Fredric Jameson and David Harvey in particular have shown, the general connections between late capitalism/neoliberalism and the cultural 'condition' of postmodernity – with its emphasis on eclecticism, multiple identities, indeterminacy, depthlessness, scepticism towards grand narratives and so on – are clear enough.[40] In this context, we might begin by thinking of the rhetorical and actual marketplace of multiple, sometimes competing, Jesuses (eschatological prophet, sage, Cynic-like social critic, wisdom teacher, Mediterranean Jewish peasant, apocalyptic eschatological wisdom teacher etc.). One dominant (neo-)liberal form of multiculturalism that has emerged over the past forty years involves and embrace of others while ensuring that anything problematic is removed; or, as Slavoj Žižek defined this discourse of contemporary multiculturalism, the Other is welcomed but without the Otherness in this liberal

---

36. Wright, *Victory*, p. 93.

37. For full discussion, with bibliography, see Crossley, *Jesus in an Age of Terror*; Crossley, *Jesus in an Age of Neoliberalism*; Crossley, 'A "Very Jewish" Jesus'. In addition to the bibliography cited there, see now Robert J. Myles, *The Homeless Jesus in the Gospel of Matthew* (Sheffield: Sheffield Phoenix Press, 2014) and Michael J. Sandford, *Poverty, Wealth, and Empire: Jesus and Postcolonial Criticism* (Sheffield: Sheffield Phoenix Press, 2014).

38. Sellers, *HandMade*, p. 14.

39. Harvey, *Neoliberalism*; Dieter Plehwe, Bernhard J. A. Walpen and Gisela Neunhoffer (eds), *Neoliberal Hegemony: A Global Critique* (London: Routledge, 2007); Philip Mirowski and Dieter Plehwe (eds), *The Road from Mont Pelerin: The Making of the Neoliberal Thought Collective* (Cambridge, MA: Harvard University Press, 2009).

40. David Harvey, *The Condition of Postmodernity* (Oxford: Blackwell, 1989); Fredric Jameson, *Postmodernism, or, The Cultural Logic of Late Capitalism* (London and New York: Verso 1991).

democratic embrace.[41] This multicultural acceptance of the Other deprived of Otherness is precisely what we see with dominant views on Jesus the Jew: scholarship regularly embraces this 'very Jewish' Jesus but the stranger bits of, say, Law observance or Temple worship now 'transcended' or made 'redundant', to use another phrase from Wright.[42]

Concluding Remarks

If we want to mock the historical Jesus scholar as an interpreter along the lines of those deluded-but-pious interpreters in *Life of Brian*, then this poses problems for constructing Jesus and Brian in our image. Monty Python created a Jesus that should still be more offensive than its reception presently suggests but maybe Monty Python should have gone one step further and really gone for Jesus (and more than just sayings about birds, stewards and oxen) as well as his interpreters because if we can recover the historical Jesus then he really is going to be a figure alien to us and with minimal contemporary relevance. Perhaps, then, the historical Jesus himself was sillier (to us) than we sometimes think. Perhaps he was not a 'bloody good bloke' by our standards. After all, can we not say that the earliest tradition in his name has Jesus predicting imminent end times, claims that he conversed with demons, suggestions that he practised something like 'magic', proclamations that he would play a major role in judging people and peoples in the end times, polemical attacks on money and wealth, and a portrait of someone wandering around the Galilean countryside, possibly with nowhere to lay his head? Such Gospel traditions have as good a chance as any Gospel traditions of reflecting the earliest material. And are these ideas not as odd to some of us as any of the claims crazed prophets, deluded followers, right wing prisoners, or women bearding up to enjoy the pleasures of stoning in *Life of Brian*? It may not have made for a better film or for better satire, but taking Monty Python's approach one stage further in the quest for a weirder, crazier and more comical Brian may have made for a more likely historical Jesus.

---

41. Among various publications see e.g. Slavoj Žižek, 'Multiculturalism, or, the Cultural Logic of Multinational Capitalism,' *New Left Review* (1997), pp. 28–51; id. *The Puppet and the Dwarf: The Perverse Core of Christianity* (Boston: MIT Press, 2003); id. *Welcome to the Desert of the Real! Five Essays on September 11 and Related Dates* (London & New York: Verso, 2002); id. 'Liberal Multiculturalism Masks an Old Barbarism with a Human Face,' *Guardian* (3 October 2010), http://www.theguardian.com/commentisfree/2010/oct/03/immigration-policy-roma-rightwing-europe; id. *Living in the End Times* (revised edition; London & New York: Verso, 2011). For broader discussions of 'race' multiculturalism and neoliberalism with more detailed analysis see e.g. David T. Goldberg, *The Threat of Race: Reflections on Racial Neoliberalism* (Oxford: Wiley-Blackwell, 2009) and Alana Lentin and Gavin Titley, *The Crises of Multiculturalism: Racism in a Neoliberal Age* (London: Zed Books, 2011).

42. Wright, *Victory*, pp. 399–402.

Chapter 6

THE GOSPEL OF BRIAN

Philip R. Davies

A scholarly emanation of a famous comic film brings together an irresistible force and an immovable object. On the one hand is a film that takes every opportunity to extract humour from, or impose humour on, all aspects of life (not just religion); on the other hand, scholarship aiming to imbue any and every aspect of human life with deep seriousness. Who will emerge the victor in this confrontation? Will scholars succeed in reducing the *Life of Brian* to a cultural artefact lying, as it were, on the mortician's slab, extracting and examining every organ? Or will the humour and its comic vision of life subvert such an aim by making instead us laugh at our own scholarship? What I am going to try here is, instead of looking at the film from the direction of scholarship, to look at scholarship from the direction of the film. From one point of view, that *is* of course taking it very seriously, as a pretext for self-criticism, metacriticism or whatever.

The *Life of Brian* does not engage biblical scholarship overtly, except perhaps in the guise of the learned exegesis that interprets cheesemakers as the dairy industry (to be really serious and scholarly here I should characterize this exegesis as a case of the rabbinic *middah kelal u-ferat u-ferat u-kelal*,[1] the rule that applies the general to particular and vice-versa) with a clever allusion to the Tyropoean valley, the 'Valley of the Cheese-makers'.[2] Its major target is rather religion, and it is generally recognized, including by the makers, as an outright attack, if not on religion itself, then at least on a certain kind of religiosity.

The film's notoriety is partly due to the way in which it illustrates how a strong religious sensibility induces a less than average receptivity to humour. Whether or not this is indeed the case, immediate reaction to the film certainly seemed to supply confirmation. A more scientific demonstration has in fact been undertaken by Vassilis Saroglou, Director of the Center for the Psychology of Religion at the Catholic University of Louvain-la-Neuve in Belgium. He asked eighty-five students to spontaneously produce a humorous response to some hypothetical daily hassles. Some of these students were first exposed to a religious video, some to a humorous one, and others to no stimulus at all. The outcome of this experiment suggested that seeing a religious video inhibited a subsequent humorous response, while seeing a humorous video promoted it.

This of course only proves that humour can provoke humour. So Saroglou went further, distinguishing *kinds* of religious attitude. In an article entitled 'Religiousness, Religious Fundamentalism, and Quest as Predictors of Humor Creation',[3] he reported comparing people with a fundamentalist belief and those with what he calls a 'quest religiosity' – a more open, perhaps what we may call 'consumerist', attitude towards religion – and found that the former had a lower response to humour compared with the latter.

Here, surely, is a parade example of scholarship taking humour very seriously as a psychological disposition that a certain kind of religiosity can inhibit. But we can also describe this from the point of view of humour itself and conclude that however many people know something to be true, however blindingly obvious it is, there will always be researchers and research programmes ready to prove it (and, I must add, in the modern climate of academic research: funding bodies to throw money at it). I don't want to impugn this particular research project or Saroglou himself, but it is surely true that most people already know that a strict religious mentality struggles to express humour as freely as other mentalities. Umberto Eco, to take a well-known example, illustrated this thesis in *The Name of the Rose*; Malcolm Muggeridge and Mervyn Stockwood did the same in that famous TV interview on the *Life of Brian*. Proving the

---

1. This is the sixth of thirteen rules scribed to R. Ishmael: for elaboration see http://www.jewishvirtuallibrary.org/jsource/judaica/ejud_0002_0009_0_08805.html.

2. For this name designating the central ravine running through the city, see Josephus, *War* 5.40.

3. *International Journal for the Psychology of Religion* 12, 177–88. 'Quest' religion describes an open-ended path towards spirituality, on the assumption that there is more than one way to take. See further C. D. Batson and W. L. Ventis, *The Religious Experience: A Social-Psychological Perspective* (New York: Oxford University Press, 1982).

obvious does not always appear funny to the academic researchers who do it, nor to those who fund it, but anyone who listens to the radio or reads newspapers regularly will have their attention drawn now and then to a study proving something such as cats like milk or that pigs really do not have the ability to fly.

I merely make the point that scholarship itself sometimes deserves to be laughed at for its quasi-religious devotion to seriousness. Indeed, in this respect religion and scholarship are really quite similar. So how often do we encounter humour in the articles or reviews of academic journals? And in the case of New Testament scholarship, which in this instance is the most relevant discipline, can anyone deny that religion and scholarship have long been, and mostly still are, in cahoots?

I'd like to probe this link between New Testament scholarship and religion a bit further. The challenge of the *Life of Brian* is to that kind of religious belief that creates its own object of veneration. The film is (mostly) about people mistaking the hero for what he is and imposing on him some other identity: a revolutionary, a preacher, a martyr or a messiah. We know that the Monty Python team went to a bit of trouble to get elements of the historical setting authentic. But there is a more insidious authenticity in its portrayal of how a certain kind of religiosity creates holy people, whether messiahs or saints. In our own time we can observe how the interval shortens between the death of a pope and his (should I follow a rule sometimes applied in scholarly debate and add 'or her'?) automatic canonization on his death, as their predecessors, the Roman emperors, came to be deified? Against this kind of behaviour, Monty Python's film suggests that beneath all the pious legends and icons lie ordinary persons to whom, if extraordinary things happen, they occur mostly by accident. Brian's career is a lesson about the ultimate frailty and futility of human life, a life in which humour provides the best consolation. The viewer is obviously invited to contrast this philosophy with the purposeful trajectory towards the redemption of humanity by a holy figure via a meaningful death and a resurrection. We are left to ponder whether the heroic saviour of the Christian Gospels is likewise the creation of people chasing after a sign of a shoe or a gourd. And here, although I hate to say this, the mildly comic Bishop of Southwark, Mervyn Stockwood, was right: Brian is *undoubtedly* meant as a Jesus doppelgänger. To suggest that he clearly is *not* Jesus is to miss a crucial point: what Jesus *are* we talking about? The historical one or the figure(s) of the Gospels? No, he is not the latter. But what about the former? The question is not whether Brian 'is' really Jesus or not, but: *was Jesus a Brian?*

We should bear in mind, too, that the creation of the holy figure of Jesus is not entirely the result of his gullible contemporaries. New Testament scholarship, at least that large part of it that concentrates on the life of Jesus, embellishes the iconopoeic (yes, that is a real word) religiosity that the *Life of Brian* lampoons by retroverting the icon created by centuries of pious tradition into a 'Jesus of History', but without anything concrete but the icon itself to go on. Such scholarship therefore includes itself within the film's target.

I would like to illustrate my claim about the power of tradition to turn itself into history by way of my own earlier essay on the film, where I fell into a trap. What I wrote was this:[4]

> Its main flaw, in my own view, is revealed in the final scene. Hanging on a cross, singing 'Always look on the bright side of life' is funny so long as the viewer forgets what crucifixion was actually like. The scene just does not work with nails and blood as it does with rope ... Is there ultimately a deep flaw in the anthropology of *Brian*?

My first ambition for this essay was to demonstrate a way round this flaw, somehow. My first attempt was to say that it did not matter, because the *Life of Brian* is a tragedy while the *Life of Jesus* is a comedy: that is, Brian's death is the end of a pointless life, while Jesus' is the prelude to a resurrection and an eternal reign in heaven, offering the promise of a meaningful and blessed resolution to every individual's existence. So, I concluded, who needs nails? Of course Christians have always liked to dwell on the pain and suffering of their Messiah, but the nails don't really have any theological significance whatever, nor does the crucifixion, despite Paul's playing around with Deuteronomy 21.22–23[5] in Galatians 3.13. Any kind of premature death could have served the purpose of human redemption (if that *was* the purpose), so long as it could be attributed to God and followed by a resurrection. A crucifixion of a few hours is, after all, better than what was said to have happened to Herod the Great.[6] And quite a few Christians, as well as non-Christians, have over the course of history, suffered worse things.

But I abandoned this line of argument, at least for the time being, and I am only summarizing it here because while pursuing it I stumbled over another take on the problem. *Why did I say that Jesus was nailed?* The Romans did not always nail such victims – our evidence is still rather too patchy – and none of the biblical descriptions of the event thought it relevant to say whether Jesus was nailed or not. The only mention of a nail is in the fourth Gospel (John 20.24–29), where Thomas wants to 'see the mark of the nails in his hands, and put my finger in the mark of the nails and my hand in his side'. There are plenty of New Testament scholars of

4. Philip R. Davies, '*Life of Brian* Research', in J. Cheryl Exum and Stephen D. Moore (eds), *Biblical Studies, Cultural Studies: The Third Sheffield Colloquium* (Sheffield: Sheffield Academic Press, 1998), pp. 400-14; quotation from p. 414.

5. 'When someone is convicted of a crime punishable by death and is executed, and you hang him on a tree. His corpse must not remain all night upon the tree; you shall bury him that same day, for anyone hung on a tree is under God's curse.'

6. According to Jan Hirschmann at the Clinical Pathologic Conference (CPC) in the US on 25 January 2002 in Baltimore, Herod the Great expired from chronic kidney disease probably complicated by Fournier's gangrene: 'The texts we depend on for a close description of Herod's last days list several major features of the disease that caused his death—among them, intense itching, painful intestinal problems, breathlessness, convulsions in every limb and gangrene of the genitalia.' See http://news.bbc.co.uk/1/hi/health/1782739.stm.

the view that the wound, and the entire incident with Thomas, are the writer's invention; and, if so, it follows that then nailing is also either an invention or an assumption. Moreover, it seems that this author was under the impression that victims were nailed though the palms of the hands, which, as far as we know, was not the practice. So much for the evidence; and so I must thank Monty Python for helping me to realize just how what we might reverently call 'tradition' can so easily make up what comes to be not only a major component of the entire Passion legend, but also something accepted (even by me until recently) as a historical fact. I searched for the combination of 'Jesus' and 'nailed' on the internet and came up only with the question whether he was nailed through hands or wrists: not one site raised the query whether he *was* nailed, or the flimsy basis on which this tradition has grown. I did learn from this trawl, however, that there is still disagreement over whether the arms of the one Jewish crucifixion victim unearthed to date were in fact nailed, or only the feet.[7]

This little detail (*kelal upherat*, etc., from particular to general, and especially after watching the *Life of Brian*) leads me to ask whether *any* details of the traditions of Jesus of Nazareth are historically true – bearing in mind that traditions are all that we have. I'll give another example: the reason for Jesus' arrest, trial and execution. The traditional explanations are manifold: blame the Jews, the priests, the Romans, God or even Jesus' own ambitions of martyrdom. Monty Python's answer is: there is no explanation and no need. This is what Romans did, especially in politically unstable times and places. They were not particularly scrupulous about the judicial niceties, and there is no prescription in Roman law for the ceremony of washing the hands before passing sentence. Jesus was, quite probably, not in the right place at the right time, but, like Brian, in the wrong place at the wrong time. There can be a dispute about the theological reasons for his arrest, but these do not need to be translated into historical ones. I once argued (in a very friendly way) for two hours about this with the rightly respected New Testament scholar Ed Sanders, who was seeking a pretext for Jesus' death in his table-turning at the Temple; and we did not convince each other. I still think Monty Python's implied explanation as good as any. Neither the Romans nor anyone else cared much for the legal basis of yet another 'nailing-up'. The figure of Judas is a nice element in this story, but the entire betrayal process is somewhat implausible, not to say theatrical. Isn't this, again, dear old tradition finding a way to personify the theological claim that the Jewish Messiah was betrayed by his own people?

The modern scholarly Jesus biographer tries to convert traditions like these into historical facts, and theological explanations into historical ones. The outcome is instructive: a plurality of Jesuses, among whom are a charismatic holy man (Vermes), deluded prophet (Schweitzer), Cynic (Crossan), revolutionary (Brandon), incarnate deity (any number, including N. T. Wright). In making these

7. For further information and discussion, see http://www.biblicalarchaeology.org/daily/biblical-topics/crucifixion/roman-crucifixion-methods-reveal-the-history-of-crucifixion/, and the articles cited there.

reconstructions the biographer also has to decide whether, as in the case of Q (if there was a Q), anything but the words ascribed to Jesus mattered or, as with Paul, it was really only his death (and you can't get much more different than that!). The plurality of ancient and modern Jesuses gives Christian believers more choice than they probably want, but in this age of consumer choice we should not expect too much complaint.

As I see it, then, New Testament scholarship represents a third phase in the development of religious tradition. First comes the hypothetical ordinary historical personage or event; then the conversion of that into tradition, namely the creation of the holy man, the sacred story. Then the story gets converted into history. New Testament scholarship has access to the range of classical texts with which we can compare ancient lives of Jesus, and additionally sophisticated tools such as form criticism, redaction criticism and tradition history. But can these resources really suffice to reverse the work of tradition and reveal the ordinary, the everyday, a life such as that of Brian? Indeed, since so much New Testament criticism is the work of religious believers and a religious agenda, does it really *want* to confront the possibility that behind the tradition stood a Brian-like figure who is just a little bit too uncomfortably human in a too uncomfortably human world?

We may reflect on this state of affairs for a moment and ask, 'why do University courses and student textbooks not start with the question: how can we be sure that there *was* a Jesus?' Or, less sceptically, how can we know anything certain about him? The reason why we cannot begin a course or a textbook this way is rather straightforward, of course: we can't go anywhere beyond it except by answering one way only. The entire 'Life of Jesus' industry is based on an assumption that the traditions actually let us get behind them to historical reality.

Let me close by underlining my argument in showing how the *Life of Brian* offers us three interlocking figures. One is Brian himself, an ordinary man, gullible but also a bit defiant, conforming to a set of social conventions that reflect pretty closely our own. If you like, he *is* just a naughty boy. He is of course fictional but also quite credible historically. We all know people like that. Aren't most of us in fact actually like Brian in so many ways? He and most of the other people in his world (Pontius Pilate excepted) talk in normal speech, and exhibit familiar human characteristics, emotions and opinions including gullibility, mass hysteria, cheek, mischief, cynicism, resignation and, of course, humour, often of the gallows variety. This portrayal takes incarnation all the way. You don't get more like us than Brian does.

Then we have the second figure, Brian the Messiah, the figure he is being made into by the religious zealots, the man with the sign and the virgin mother. We see how he is being transformed by them even during his life, but what do we imagine happens after his death? If Brian is at all aware of this inevitable process being perpetuated, the bright side of his life is that he can, like Vespasian, feel himself becoming a god, even as he sings that life away. The film illustrates and (more gently than it deserves) mocks the process of transition from a human being to a figure of holy tradition, just as resignation to a humdrum and rather meaningless life and death is transmogrified into a belief in the myth of humanity's redemption, the conquest of death, the overthrow of worldly powers and direct rule from heaven, answering the unspoken question: 'What has God ever done for us?'

Then there is the third messiah, the one who remains offstage. The Monty Python crew can say, in concert with some learned commentators too, that the whole point of the film is that Brian is NOT Jesus, because the real Jesus is also there; but this is a 'real' Jesus, of course, in the sense of being the *recognizable* Jesus. This figure is a creation of tradition, an amalgam of traditions, in fact, and no more historically real than Brian. But he occupies two contradictory positions. He is of course the foil to Brian: the person that Brian is definitely *not*. But he *is* also Brian, the Brian of the future, the fully finished and polished product of that process that transformed an ordinary Brian into a Messiah. A few more centuries will create the icon of the Christian religion. From the birth of Brian to the Nativity of Jesus in the opening shots of the film is a short camel-ride; but between them also lie centuries of piety. The absence of the Jesus figure from the screen does of course enhance his dignity but at the expense of removing him from the real world that the film claims to portray. He belongs not to the time of the film but to much later.

It is centuries of pious reflection, elaboration and invention that take us from a world of a Palestinian Jew to one blessed by the florid garb of popes, cardinals and bishops, by ceremonies of blessing ships and guns, by the waiting for the alien abduction that is called the Rapture. Or even, so as to be even-handed, from the Palestinian Jew to the black-suited, black-hatted, orthodox observer of elaborate codes. Religion can make the absurd appear normal like nothing else: New Testament scholars can write about the 'victory of God' (now there is a rigged contest if ever there was!) and seriously argue for the resurrection of Jesus as a *historical* event. This kind of attitude must entail a belief not just in miracles but in evil spirits – because Jesus actually removed them – and, I suppose, in the ascension too, which leaves the question of where the body is now and indeed where heaven is if you actually have to take a lift to get there. Goodbye to the world of Monty Python, and hello to another . . .

In conclusion, I now take off my Python spectacles, through which I have been looking at religion, Christian tradition and New Testament scholarship, and ask myself, does the world look any better, clearer or more attractive without these glasses? Am I now feeling more serious about life, and about scholarship, or less? In the battle between scholarship and humour for the soul of Brian, who is ultimately the winner?

Part II

HISTORY AND INTERPRETATION VIA *MONTY PYTHON'S LIFE OF BRIAN*

Chapter 7

THE HISTORICAL BRIAN: RECEPTION EXEGESIS IN PRACTICE

Joan E. Taylor

In this chapter, I would like to reflect a little on reception exegesis as a method, and to explore how it can work. David Tollerton has raised an interesting point in Chapter 4, by stating that it should not be superficial or 'an entertaining pit stop on the way to antiquity'.[1] I hope to show here how in fact reception exegesis means being particularly conscious of what really does appear in a creative work, allowing it to take us and turn us in a particular direction. It requires reflection on matters that perhaps have not been given due attention. In fact, it seems to me that in 'reception exegesis' both the artefact of cultural reception and the primary text can come closer to being equalized, since the reception artefact is not considered purely derivative, but a conversation partner. As we listen to one, we are asked to listen again to the other, very attentively, without any assumption that we are arriving at a conclusive interpretation of either.

---

1. David Tollerton, above, p. 67.

A critical dimension here is point of view. In terms of reception history, the point of view travels from the primary text on through time, moving forward to new points of reception. In reception exegesis, one is situated in the present, moving backwards to both the point of reception and on to the original primary text. It does not mean that the reception artefact is a *mere* tool; it is a closely observed and appreciated tool. The reception artefact is one that can act dynamically as a kind of sat-nav directing the observer's view towards the primary text, so that it becomes a tool to guide observation and direction. Overall, once the reception artefact is in the past rather than in the present, there are three temporal points.

We are embedded in a cultural context in the same way that both the primary text and the reception artefact are embedded in a context. What starts off as our own context, as in the case of *Life of Brian* when it was first released, is now a historical one, nearer to us than the primary text and yet still removed from the present. I am reminded of that in terms of the curious film sequence of Brian's abduction by monstrous aliens, who rescue him from falling off a tower in Jerusalem, fly him into space, fight a battle, and crash land on earth just near where Brian was taken up, leaving him still pursued by those who wish to hail him as Messiah.

When I first saw this sequence, in 1985, I encountered it at a time that was not far on from the 1970s, and I found it very funny not because of any *Star Wars* references that might be more obvious today, but because of a film called *Chariots of the Gods*. The impact of *Chariots of the Gods* is not that well known at the present time. It was a German documentary, *Erinnerungen an die Zukunft*, directed by Harald Reinl, based on a book by Erich von Dänekin, released in 1968 in English, following a German version: a book which became a massive bestseller.[2] Remarkably for something so far-fetched and foreign, the film had a very widespread distribution, grossing $25,948,300; it was even nominated for an academy award as best documentary feature, in 1970.[3] In 1973 the film was given an English narration and was very widely shown in cinemas, including in New Zealand, where I saw it with a school friend, probably sometime in 1974. In Dänekin's view, Earth has been repeatedly visited by aliens, who have left traces in many of the world's ancient civilizations and literature, including in the Bible. Stories of heavenly ascents are therefore just as likely to be trips into space.

Therefore, when I saw the alien sequence I laughed with recognition, because in the world of Brian clearly there were aliens messing about with Earth just as in the *Chariots of the Gods*. The message seemed clear: if aliens could abscond with Brian, then they could just as well have done so with Jesus. Jesus' ascension (when he is

---

2. Erich von Dänekin, *Erinnerungen an die Zukunft: Ungelöste Rätsel der Vergangenheit* (Düsseldorf: Econ Verlag, 1968); *Chariots of the Gods: Unsolved Mysteries of the Past* (New York: Putnam, 1970).

3. http://www.worldwideboxoffice.com/movie.cgi?title=Erinnerungen%20an%20die% 20Zukunft&year=1970 [accessed 15 September 2014]. The film can be viewed on YouTube at http://www.youtube.com/watch?v=OtBfBGCaABU [accessed 15 September 2014].

taken up into the clouds following his resurrection in Mark 16.19; Luke 24.50–53 and Acts 1.9-11) is the kind of mythic moment that is just perfect for Dänekin's hypothesis. But, in the *Life of Brian*, this 'ascension' happens to poor old Brian, just a regular guy, who has no idea what is going on, and he does nothing with it to indicate he is in any way special, sanctified, chosen or enlightened. Abduction by terrifying aliens is just another absurd thing in his absurd life.

The film version of *Chariots of the Gods* did not have to be specifically referenced here, or even known to the Pythons, because talk of visiting aliens was simply 'in the air' in the 70s as a silly thing that could be used in comedy. What happens now, then, is that the cultural reference points of the 1970s are not known fully. Those of a newer generation will see different things, and make different connections, about a film that uses biblical source material as a primary text. As such, the *Life of Brian* itself becomes a historical text that needs to be unpacked and discerned.

If we were to use a reception exegesis approach to the alien abduction scene in the *Life of Brian*, it would require a careful unpacking of both the scene itself, the cultural context in which the reception artefact takes place, and then a reflection on the ascension as found in the Gospels and Acts. The aim would not be to determine whether the Pythons got anything right, but how the scene asks us (now) to reflect on the biblical texts. How do we feel now about the ascension, given our knowledge of the world being a planet in space, a space in which there may well be other life forms? How does that make us think about meaning when the ascension cannot be historically/scientifically true, on the basis of what is actually real according to meteorology and empirical observation? Surely, we have to suspend our knowledge in order to embrace the knowledge of the authors and audience of the Gospels, in order to define its claim about the nature of Jesus' transformation to the Divine realm. In Jesus' time, no one flew up to where God was supposed to dwell; today, we do it all the time, and God is not there. The point is not whether the scene is historically true, but why it was *necessary*. Flying (ascension) then, for Brian in the scene in the film, can be a motif explored in the biblical text, subjecting it to re-analysis, with potentially illuminating results.

Reception exegesis can make us ask surprising questions. To develop what I stated in the Introduction, the concept of 'reception history' derives from Gadamer's concept of *Wirkungsgeschichte*, 'the history of effects', in which the effects of texts on recipients through time was recognized as an important element in interpretation.[4] New ground was broken already in Larry Kreitzer's notion of 'reversing the hermeneutical flow',[5] in using aspects of literature and film to reflect

---

4. Hans-Georg Gadamer, *Truth and Method*, trans. Joel Weinsheimer and Donald G. Marshall of *Wahrheit und Methode,* 2nd ed. (New York: Crossroad, 1992); for an overview see Mark Knight, '*Wirkungsgeschichte*, Reception History, Reception Theory,' *JSNT* 33 (2010), pp. 137–46.

5. Larry J. Kreitzer, *The New Testament in Fiction and Film: On Reversing the Hermeneutical Flow* (London: Continuum, 1993), and see the interesting review article by John Riches, 'Reception Exegesis of Lamentations,' *Expository Times* (4 March 2014), pp. 383–7.

on biblical meanings. Stefan Klint has devised a more dynamic engagement with the historical past via reception criticism.[6] Paul Joyce and Diana Lipton, in their study of Lamentations, defined the hermeneutic of 'reception exegesis', by reference to Jewish midrash: '[r]eception exegesis can shine a spotlight on biblical verses that have been dulled by familiarity; it can foreground biblical concepts and concerns that have faded over time into the background; and it can even give rise to radical new readings'.[7]

If we let this process work in terms of *Monty Python's Life of Brian,* one of the most obvious features of the film itself is the portrayal of an ordinary man as the central figure. My proposition here is that the presentation of an ordinary man as the 'hero', and the presentation of a world as seen through his eyes, destabilizes not only the presentation of Jesus as it was generally seen in films at the time, but the presentation of the ordinary person and, by doing this, the *Life of Brian* points us to the ordinary people of the Gospels at whom Jesus' teaching is aimed, as well as asking us to imagine how these ordinary people understood Jesus.

Jesus of the Movies

Let us first consider the Jesus we see in films of this time. When *Monty Python's Life of Brian* arrived in cinemas in 1979, audiences were quite familiar with biblical epics that purported to tell the story of the life of Christ. As a teenager on a class trip, I remember weeping in a rescreening of *Ben-Hur.* Such epics were invariably productions that aimed to elicit emotion, and to ensure that Jesus was presented in a way that would be entirely acceptable to Christians. As such, there was absolutely no indication that there had been any long history of scholarly discussion about how the Jesus of history, the man, needed to be separated from the Christ of faith, if we were to see him as he really was in his time. The 'Jesus' of the biblical epics is not really a historical figure; he is a Hollywood Christ, loaded with 2,000 years of theology and all the weight of the Nicene Creed.

The *Life of Brian,* in preserving intact the Christ of Faith, creates a dissonance with the 'reality' it portrays of the comedic 'historical' times. The perfect presentation of the Hollywood Christ is itself a form of parody. One need only look at the 1961 movie *King of Kings* to recognize the template, the conventions that it would portray so brilliantly. The films of Jesus were so extremely non-historical, non-scholarly, as if biblical exegesis and historical enquiry never happened. Choirs like singing bands of angels accompanied the soundtrack. Cinema audiences were expected to be encouraged in piety. We were required to gaze in wonder. We were all to be deeply moved.

---

6. Klint, Stefan, 'After Story – A Return to History: Introducing Reception Criticism as an Exegetical Approach', *Studia Theologica* 54/2 (2000), pp. 87–106.

7. Paul Joyce and Diana Lipton, *Lamentations through the Centuries* (Wiley-Blackwell Bible Commentaries; Oxford: Wiley-Blackwell, 2013), p. 18.

The movie poster advertising the *Life of Brian* exactly copies the cut-in-stone towering edifice of the *King of Kings'* title words.[8] The film opens with the choirs of angels and soundtrack reminiscent of epics: the scene of the Three Wise Men on camels is exactly as we know it from Christmas cards. But the awe and emotion inherent in this Hollywood Christ of Faith epic is punctured. We go not to the infant Jesus but to the infant Brian, another boy entirely; the radiant manger scene is down the road. So what it did was appeal to us as ordinary people, as ourselves, going to a movie, rather than transforming us into a virtual church of people sitting in pews, waiting for sacred mysteries to unfold, waiting to hear a sermon played out in film. We experience the humour born of the dissonance between the epic and the comedy, and it overtly points to the difference between the Hollywood Christ of Faith and the Jesus of history.

In the movie *King of Kings* there is the scene in which Christ stands on the Mount of Beatitudes delivering the lines of Matthew's Gospel (Matt. 5.1–10) with all the wooden dignity every actor who played Jesus had to muster, and in the *Life of Brian* we have much the same Christ delivering the same lines. But what is different in the *Life of Brian* is an explicit zooming in on the guy at the very back of the scene. This is important, because the audience of the Sermon on the Mount in movies has been presented as 'us', the audience in the cinemas: the virtual church. The audience are to be in continuity with 2,000 years of Christians hearing the teaching of Jesus. The Christ of Faith of course always exists in relationship to the faithful: he exists insofar as they do. For one, a typifying feature is glory, for the other piety.

The *Life of Brian* shows us a 'historical' reality that breaks this simple relationship: while the people standing in silent, polite and attentive poses at a respectful distance from Jesus would indeed have been able to hear him quite well, the people at the back probably couldn't. Shouting very loudly would have broken the perfect composure of the Hollywood Christ; he speaks in a normal voice. Right at the back, as we all know, they couldn't quite catch, 'Blessed are the peacemakers' (Matt. 5.9).

Yet this is actually quite biblical: it has to be said that the Gospels themselves are quite clear about the distinction between the 'glorified' Christ and a more ordinary Jesus. The sense of the ordinariness of Jesus is – paradoxically – nowhere clearer than in the scene of the Transfiguration (Mark 9.2–8 and par.). In this sequence, we are told that Jesus' clothing was changed to become 'glistening, intensely white, as no fuller on earth could bleach them' (Mark 9.3). He is thus transformed into wearing heavenly attire, and God's voice endorses him as he converses with Moses and Elijah. Since both Moses and Elijah were considered to have been 'assumed' into Heaven,[9] Jesus here ascends to converse with fellow prophets who represent

---

8. King of Kings: http://www.imdb.com/title/tt0055047/; Life of Brian http://www.imdb.com/media/rm1617927936/tt0079470?ref_=ttmi_mi_all_prd_34.

9. For Elijah, see 2 Kings 2.1–18; for Moses, see the Assumption/Testament of Moses: J. Priest, 'Testament of Moses,' in James H. Charlesworth (ed.), *The Old Testament Pseudepigrapha* (London: Darton, Longman and Todd, 1983), 919–34.

the sacred writings: the Law and the Prophets. They are all on the same page, as it were. In the synoptic Gospels' understanding, Jesus, 'a prophet mighty in deed and word', would be assumed into 'his glory' in the heavenly sphere in due course (Luke 24.19; 26.44–53); his glory would be in the future, not in the present (Mark 8.38; 10.37; 13.26–27; 14.62 and parallels). In the Hollywood Christ, pre-Brian, there is no *biblical* disjunction between the ordinary and the transfigured: Jesus often wears very white clothing in such films, just as he wears such clothing in Victorian art, often clad also in a sky-blue robe. Yet, from Mark 9 one has to say that Jesus is presented as an ordinary man, wearing ordinary clothes, in this case apparently undyed wool that could be significantly brightened by bleaching, but wasn't.

Thus, in the *Life of Brian*, while it faithfully presents the usual Hollywood Christ, ultimately this Christ looks peculiarly out of place in the context of the comedic 'history' that is the filmic reality; he might as well have been put there by the aliens we meet when Brian is abducted in a spaceship. As James Crossley has explored, the film does then make us consider also a possibility of a very different Jesus to the Hollywood Christ, which is why the film is subversive: 'It subtly but clearly takes up some of the more challenging reconstructions of the historical Jesus from popular and scholarly thought and applies them to Brian.'[10] If the Hollywood Christ of Faith sits uncomfortably in the world of Brian, does the Church's Christ of Faith sit comfortably in the world of Jesus?

That point is noted, but what interests me here is the fact that the film is definitively about *Brian*, the ordinary man who is not a pious believer but a marginal and confused loner, trying to find a place in an apparently mad world. His life weirdly parallels the life of Jesus, but he is not Jesus. The *Life of Brian* scene of the Sermon on the Mount is important for more than the comedy of the misheard line and its subsequent 'superior' exegesis that inclusively embraces all manufacturers of dairy products; it gives us ordinary people rather than pious believers, and thus the fundamental relationship between the audience and the presentation of the Hollywood Christ is broken. In giving us ordinary Brian, with whom we identify, beside a Jesus in the *Life of Brian* just as dignified and un-human as in the *King of Kings*, it challenges us to recognize a man missed from history. This is actually the man at the back of the crowd: the 'historical' Brian.

The Historical Brian

In the *Life of Brian* we take the perspective of a man at the bottom of society's strata. Brian is the ordinary man that has been left out of the pages of history, one of the *ochlos*, the crowd, a man who would never be king, never great, never

10. James G. Crossley, 'Life of Brian or Life of Jesus? Uses of Critical Biblical Scholarship and Non-Orthodox Views of Jesus in Monty Python's *Life of Brian*', in *Relegere: Studies in Religion and Reception* 1 (2011), pp. 93–114, at p. 114.

one to change the course of history. We have here exactly the kind of man Josephus would find despicable, as one of the common crowd,[11] one of that populace of Judaea, who can run off – deluded – after false prophets, revolt (e.g. *War* 2.258), get massacred by irate Roman governors, die in famines, protest, and generally prove troublesome in one way or another: Brian of Nazareth, Brian Cohen. The 'historical Brians' almost never actually have a voice in history; they are described by men who do have the voices as being masses and multitudes prone to be stupid. They are almost never defined as individuals unless they lead rebellions and die horrible deaths.

The identification of the elite point of view of our historical texts is increasingly common in historiography today, influenced by subaltern and Marxist studies in which attempts are made to view history 'from below' rather than from the perspective of elites. For example, in Sara Forsdyke's groundbreaking study of 'popular' (= ordinary) culture in ancient Greece, she asks how we can 'recover the culture of the ordinary people of the past' when there is so little evidence, and proposes strategies of identification via the elite texts by focusing on reading them for disjunctions, for the excavation of metaphors from non-elites, with employment of comparative models for analysis.[12]

Thus, I am going to use *Life of Brian* as a jumping-off point for imagining an ordinary man of first-century Galilee. I am going to take my cue from Elisabeth Schüssler Fiorenza's hermeneutic of imaginative identification,[13] and do with Brian's name as we can do with the name of Jesus, which in Aramaic is *Yeshua*, from which we get in Greek *Iesous*, from which we get Latin *Iesus*. The historical Jesus was probably named *Yeshua bar Yosef*, the Aramaic for 'Jesus the son of Joseph'. So I will 'translate' Brian back to an Aramaic name, in this case let us suppose Bar-Hanan. His mother Mandy is named as in Latin Amanda, literally, as Wikipedia will tell you, 'deserving to be loved':[14] really, the perfect nickname for a Roman-friendly prostitute. As Tal Ilan has shown in her list of names, such Latin names for Jews were known in Judaea.[15]

In undertaking this exercise I am engaging in a conscious act of imagination, allowing the reception artefact to conjure up a historical verisimilitude for the 'missing' ordinary people of the past that I can then use to reconsider the biblical text. It is now a question of what precisely the unconventional ordinary people we find here in the film might point to within the biblical texts.

11. See Rebecca Gray, *Prophetic Figures in Late Second Temple Jewish Palestine: The Evidence from Josephus* (Oxford: Oxford University Press, 1993), pp. 134–5.

12. Sara Forsdyke, *Slaves Tell Tales: And Other Episodes in the Politics of Popular Culture in Ancient Greece* (Princeton: Princeton University Press, 2012), pp. 6–18.

13. Elisabeth Schüssler Fiorenza, *But She Said: Feminist Practices of Biblical Interpretation* (Boston: Beacon Press, 1992), pp. 26–8.

14. http://en.wikipedia.org/wiki/Amanda_(given name) [accessed 14 September, 2014].

15. Tal Ilan, *Lexicon of Jewish Names in Late Antiquity, Part 1, 330 BCE–200 CE* (Tübingen: Mohr Siebeck, 2002), pp. 325–45.

The *Life of Brian* then can make us reflect on the Bar-Hanans and Amandas of first-century Galilee, and Judaea as a whole: the ordinary people. The imaginative Brian asks us to consider historical people lost from history. With an imaginative reconstruction of a historical figure built out of elements of Brian, we can 'play' with perspective and destabilize the hegemony of both texts and traditions. With a marginal and downtrodden Bar-Hanan growing up in a poor Nazareth, we can understand precisely why someone like Nathaniel can say, of Jesus (ignorant of Jesus' actual birthplace/identity): 'What good can come from Nazareth?' (John 1.46). In the film, Brian's was a birth that was truly among the poor and meek and lowly, born in a stable, and put in a cattle feeding trough, with only his Mum, Mandy, on her own, not even with a kindly Joseph by her side, let alone a star shining on the roof as for the baby down the road. Thus we imagine a Bar-Hanan in the same situation, with a lone mother.

What of 'Dad', as we might imagine him: Hanan? If we allow our historical yet imaginative Bar-Hanan to have a father who gave him his designation Cohen, meaning 'priest', this might make a fascinating twist, as historically it would put a poor Bar-Hanan into a slightly problematic place in terms of Judaean society, since, according to Leviticus 21.13–15, regarding a priest:

> 'The woman he marries must be a virgin. [14]He must not marry a widow, a divorced woman, or a woman defiled by prostitution, but only a virgin from his own people, [15]so that he will not defile his offspring among his people. I am the LORD, who makes him holy.'
>
> (NJV)

From the *Life of Brian* we can then use the film to imagine a 'Dad' (Hanan) who was never actually married to Mum, and assume that the designation 'Cohen' never really meant to indicate that this Bar-Hanan would be a Cohen as a priest who was called up for Temple duties. As an audience in the film, also, we all know that 'Dad' was really a Roman.

In fact, 'Cohen' in the film functions like the name 'Levi' the tax collector in Mark 2.13–17, a man whose usual friendship group were other 'tax collectors and sinners' (Mark 2.15–16). Levi is a name appropriate for someone in the category of Levites,[16] who were supposed to ensure a high standard of good conduct. It is exactly for this reason that in Jesus' parable of the Good Samaritan he can use the category of a priest and a Levite as upstanding members of society, that should have been linked with the third term of 'Israelite', before he draws on the shocking example of a Samaritan as one who actually shows the compassion God wants (Luke 10.25–37), as

16. See Ilan, p. 182. Shmuel Safrai and Menahem Stern (eds), in co-operation with David Flusser and Willem C. van Unnik, *The Jewish People in the First Century: Historical Geography, Political History, Social, Cultural and Religious Life and Institutions* Vol. 2 (Compendia Rerum Iudaicarum ad Novum Testamentum; Assen: Van Gorcum, 1976): 'Generally, those who bore the name Levi or son of Levi in this period may be assigned to the Levites', p. 599.

Amy-Jill Levine has discussed.[17] Brian Cohen, our 'historical' Bar-Hanan, the Cohen, is then of the same ilk as Levi the tax collector, a man who should be classified within a commendable category of holiness, but is very far from it.

The historical poor and marginal of Galilean society have been illuminated of late by archaeology, a science that has provided evidence of ordinary people's actual houses, their cooking pots, their lost coins. The study of ancient Galilee has revealed a tiny rich elite – much aligned with the Romans and their client ruler Herod Antipas – and a massive poor.[18] Small farmers were squeezed out and land consolidated in large estates of the super-rich.[19] At Capernaum, numerous excavations show how densely packed the houses were, with tiny living spaces and central courtyards shared by several families, with compounds built of rough black basalt rock, roofs being straw and mud. The poor of Capernaum lived in dark and cramped spaces.[20]

Archaeologists and historians have now identified the problems faced by the ordinary people of Galilee, such as over-population and a strain on available arable land to sustain the population density. There was also widespread malaria and other illnesses that severely cut short life expectancy. As Jonathan Reed has stated, summarizing results from analysis of skeletal remains:[21]

> life in first-century Galilee – though not necessarily dissimilar to other parts of the Mediterranean – was substantially different from the modern world and cannot be characterized as stable. Chronic and seasonal disease, especially malaria, cut down significant segments of the population and left even the healthy often quite ill. The age structure was youthful, women bore many children, random death made family and household patterns ephemeral, young men were often mobile, and elderly women especially vulnerable. Survival depended on extended family networks, especially for the most vulnerable: old woman and young children.

This parallels, of course, many parts of the world today. The poor are often stated as being those Jesus specifically addressed; they are the ones who are 'blessed'

17. Amy Jill Levine, 'The Many Faces of the Good Samaritan – Most Wrong', *Biblical Archaeology Review* 38:01, Jan/Feb 2012, id. *Short Stories by Jesus* (New York: Harper Collins, 2014), pp. 71–106.

18. Seán Freyne, *Galilee and Gospel* (Boston: Brill, 2002), pp. 86–113; 266–7.

19. Seth Schwartz, 'Josephus in Galilee: Rural Patronage and Social Breakdown', in edited by Fausto Parente and Joseph Sievers, *Josephus and the History of the Greco-Roman Period: Essays in Memory of Morton Smith* (Studia Post-Biblica 41; Leiden, The Netherlands: Brill, 1994), pp. 290–306.

20. See for an overview of the site Stanislao Loffreda, *Capharnaum, the Town of Jesus* (Jerusalem: Franciscan Printing Press, 1985), and also Vassilios Tzaferis, *Excavations at Capernaum I, 1978–1982* (Winona Lake, IN: Eisenbrauns, 1989).

21. 'Instability in Jesus' Galilee: A Demographic Perspective', *JBL* 129 (2010), pp. 343–65, at p. 345.

Figure 7.1 Capernaum (photo © Joan E. Taylor).

in the Kingdom of God (Luke 6.20 cf. Matt. 5.3[22]). As James Dunn notes, it should not 'be forgotten that the Lord's Prayer, however much it transcends its originating context, is at heart a prayer of the poor'.[23] Jesus' disciples are configured as the poor who pray for their 'daily bread' at a subsistence level (Matt. 6.11; Luke 11.3), trusting in God when they would otherwise be very worried (Matt. 6.25; Luke 12.22). As Forsdyke has observed, the 'culture of peasants' is often characterized by bodily images, especially themes, patterns and motifs from hunger.[24]

The high population density of Galilee and the strain on agricultural resources surely accounts for the many references to hunger and its satisfaction in the transformation of the world coming with the Kingdom of God (e.g. Luke 1.53; 6.21). Scholars usually doubt Josephus' figures in terms of the accuracy of Galilean population density, but even if there are exaggerations, the massive population of Galilee is nevertheless Josephus' theme: there are 204 cities and villages in Galilee (*Life* 235), he states, and not one has fewer than 15,000 inhabitants (*War* 3.43). With archaeological excavations now exposing the extent of some of these towns,

22. Gospel of Thomas 54.

23. James D. G. Dunn, *Christianity in the Making, Vol. 1: Jesus Remembered* (Grand Rapids: Eerdmans, 2003), p. 520.

24. Forsdyke, *Slaves Tell Tales*, p.10.

urban areas can be determined, but actual population estimates remain somewhat speculative; Capernaum, with an area of no more than seventeen hectares, is oddly estimated by archaeologists to have had a population of about 1,700 people.[25] A population density of 100 people per hectare seems rather a benign assumption. In the Old City of Jerusalem today, which in many ways is comparable to ancient walled cities, the population density for residential areas is ninety persons per dunam, i.e. 900 persons per hectare.[26] Using this ratio, Capernaum would have had 15,300 people. The fact is that we cannot know from the structures themselves how many people managed to squeeze into their walls, but nothing datable to the first century in Capernaum looks anything but poor. Given the strain on arable land as a result of this high population, it is no wonder that crop failure produced famine (Acts 11.27–28 and Josephus, *Ant.* 20.49–53, 101).

In the usual Hollywood movie portrayals of the poor and marginal they are inevitably extremely docile and grateful and know their place, ready to receive charity with all humility, and ready to adore Jesus the moment he appears among them. They do not have personality. When we read the Gospel accounts of Jesus eating with tax collectors and 'sinners', were they any more docile, meek and prone to adoration as the cartels of the Brazilian favelas? For the marginalized women who worked as prostitutes in order to survive, the 'Mandys', we might well understand how they would have loved to put on beards, dress as men, and stone some hapless man in public. The destitute of society could be just as mean-minded as the rich and educated. They could, indeed, really be 'sinners', as in wrong-doers, *hamartoloi*.

Mandy and Brian in the film therefore point to the category of the down and out 'prostitutes and wrong-doers' that Jesus himself had parties with, according to the synoptic Gospels. So Mark 2.15–17:

> He reclined at table in his house, and many tax collectors and wrong-doers reclined with Jesus and his disciples, for there were many and they followed him. The scribes of the Pharisees, seeing that he was eating with the wrong-doers and tax collectors, said to his disciples: 'Why does he eat with tax collectors and wrong-doers?'
>
> Hearing this, Jesus said to them, 'The robust ones have no need for a healer, but the sick. I have not come to call righteous people, but wrong-doers.'

So Jesus was 'calling' them, apparently, to change and be healed (literally), but in the meantime he was more than a pious do-gooder. He was having dinner with them, sharing table fellowship, while recognizing they were really not in the category of the righteous. And people talked, of course. According to Matthew 11.19 (= Luke 7.34):

---

25. Jonathan Reed, *Archaeology and the Galilean Jesus: A Re-Examination of the Evidence* (Harrisburg: Trinity Press, 2000), pp. 82–3.

26. http://ipcc-jerusalem.org/Old%20City.pdf, Rassem Khamaisi et al., *Jerusalem: The Old City: Urban Fabric and Geopolitical Implications* (Jerusalem: International Peace and Cooperation Center; Publication XVII, 2009), p. 22.

This man came eating and drinking and they say, 'Look – greedy man and a drinker, a friend of tax collectors and wrong-doers!' But Wisdom is vindicated by her actions.

Or take Luke 15.2 (cf. Luke 18.10–14):

But the Pharisees and the scribes grumbled saying, 'This man welcomes wrong-doers and eats with them'.

To which Jesus could apparently reply (Matt. 21.31):

Amen, I say to you that the tax collectors and prostitutes will go ahead of you into the Kingdom of God.

That Jesus 'welcomes' wrong-doers, as apparently classified, actually indicates that he invites them into his own place of residence; the verb for 'welcomes' (*prosdechetai*) in Luke 15.2 is appropriate to someone acting as a host rather than a guest. Jesus eats a decent meal and drinks wine, reclining in a dining situation with people who have not been at this stage taken from the social category of tax-collectors, prostitutes and wrong-doers but rather remain within that category during dinner. He is their 'friend', concerned about their healing. What is real historically in terms of Jesus' teaching context were these messy parties full of people like our Bar-Hanan and Amanda.

In this environment, it is easy to imagine laughter, though it is hard to imagine Jesus laughing. As John Cleese noted in the interview at the *Jesus and Brian* conference, the Bible tells us on one occasion that Jesus wept (John 11.35), but it never says he laughed.

However, if we ask the imagined historical Bar-Hanan to meet Yeshua, it is not hard also to imagine some absurdist, wry, quip. In making the ordinary man their hero, the Python's *Life of Brian* makes us look through his eyes at a world that is completely absurd, but how could the world have looked any other way for one of our historical Bar-Hanans? Those at the bottom of society do not necessarily invest in it; they simply have to survive in it, whether they are doing the right things or the wrong things. Their rulers, looked at from below, can appear ridiculous. It is fruitful to apply humour studies to the Gospels, since humour is exactly what we might expect given that it is so often a vehicle of resistance among the powerless.[27]

If we search for humour in the available tradition of Jesus' sayings, there may be some food for thought. In looking at those who judged him for the company he kept,

---

27. See for example the rich range of studies collected in Marjolein 't Hart and Dennis Bos (eds), *Humour and Social Protest* (Cambridge: Cambridge University Press, 2007) and Amy-Jill Levine, 'Women's Humor and Other Creative Juices', in Athalya Brenner (ed.), *Are We Amused? Humour About Women in the Biblical Worlds* (London: T&T Clark, 2003), pp. 120–6.

Jesus jibed back in a way that seems to me to have elements of the comic. Humour is, after all, a brilliant weapon for undermining the superior, know-it-all vanity of those who feel they have God on their side, scorning those who obviously don't. Therefore, appropriately, folk humour – which is often obscene – is noted in Forsdyke's study: ridicule of authorities and official power is part of the culture of the poor.[28] Humour can put down the mighty from their thrones. Thus, when Jesus states that the scribes and Pharisees, who criticize him, 'make their phylacteries broad and their fringes long' (Matt. 23.5) what was he trying to do?[29] He was surely painting a caricature, laughing at clothing that was designed to advertise piety: the phylacteries that held Torah texts that would be worn on the forehead and arms of men praying, the fringes or *tzittzit* that were distinctive of Jewish men's mantles (Num. 15.38) are, in the case of the Pharisees, made bigger than anyone else's. Here he was ridiculing the pompous criticisms that come from those who claimed to speak for the righteous. Ironically the same tone of speaking for the pious and righteous was adopted by Malcolm Muggeridge and Mervyn Stockwood, Bishop of Southwark, in addressing the Pythons Michael Palin and John Cleese in that infamous BBC interview. This kind of humour that would make fun of clothing as a way of puncturing the arrogance of the men in question we find precisely in the *Not the Nine O'Clock News* send-up of the interview soon after it screened, in the form of the fingering of Stockwood's giant cross, here transformed into a prop for Rowan Atkinson.[30]

It is the acerbic humour of the poor, then, we find in Jesus' caricature of the Pharisees' self-advertising of piety in their clothing, a humour that is quite sarcastic, not designed to give us a giggle so much as to allow those normally criticized – the wrong-doers themselves – to retaliate against their accusers. It presupposes that there are those who claim authority, to speak for right-thinking people, that should indeed be challenged for their vanity and hypocrisy, and it has a bite that is just as relevant today as in the first century. As Jesus would advise his own disciples, before looking to the speck in the eye of your brother or sister, look to the log in your own eye (Matt. 7.3–5; Luke 6.42). These scribes, who accuse Jesus of greedily eating food with wrong-doers, 'eat up widow's houses' (Mark 12.40), the houses that someone like Mandy – our historical Amanda – lives in.

Conclusions

What the *Life of Brian* does then is provide us with a Bar-Hanan, a 'historical Brian', that Jesus might well have sat down with, and looked to with sympathy as he stared

---

28. Forsdyke, *Slaves Tell Tales*, esp. pp. 91–6.

29. From Josephus, it is apparent that the Pharisees were one of three schools (*haireseis*) of Judaean law and practice, and indeed the most respected school, so that their interpretations held sway in terms of law and practice, even in terms of the Temple operations. For an insightful discussion, see Steve Mason, *Josephus, Judea and Christian Origins: Methods and Categories* (Peabody: Hendrickson, 2009), pp. 185–238.

30. http://www.youtube.com/watch?v=asUyK6JWt9U [accessed 12 September, 2014].

out at an absurd world. Brian in the film has few joys in life (his only real joy was very short lived indeed), and he is permanently anxious and confused by the mad world around him that ultimately puts him on the cross, as it would Jesus. In this world, the Prefect of Judaea is a fool, the priests paranoid about blasphemy, his fellow comrades in the fight to free Judaea of Roman control pathetically war among themselves and stymie their effectiveness by useless 'correct' procedures, and the Romans crucify him for being in the wrong place at the wrong time. Implicitly, this film then asks us also to laugh at this absurdity, and therefore puts us as viewers at the bottom of the social ladder in much the same way as the Gospel stories do. We see the world here from below.

The *Life of Brian* therefore gives us Brian, an ordinary man, and makes us think of the world as seen from those who are at the margins and at the bottom in terms of social hierarchy: the people that Jesus actually lived with. Jesus as presented in the film is yet another version of the Hollywood Christ, but the film makes us think of an alternative historical Jesus who is not permanently transfigured but rather looking for the transformative, as he was eating and drinking with the Bar-Hanans and Amandas of first-century Galilee. In *Life of Brian* we view the world from a Brian perspective, and taking this as a starting point for reception exegesis I have here imaginatively created corresponding historical characters of poor and the marginal of first-century Galilee that have provided a vehicle for considering the actual evidence for real lives found in archaeological and historical materials. In considering them more fully, we can note aspects of the biblical texts themselves in terms of a historical Jesus who literally lay with the poor and the marginal, drinking and eating. We can notice aspects otherwise unseen, for example Jesus' own sense of humour: a humour that – in ridiculing those with respected authority – places him alongside those who would see the elite's deep absurdity.

Chapter 8

'ROMANI ITE DOMUM' – EXPRESSIONS OF IDENTITY AND RESISTANCE IN JUDAEA

Guy D. Stiebel

REG: If you want to join the People's Front of Judaea, you have to really hate the Romans.
BRIAN: I do!
REG: Oh yeah, how much?
BRIAN: A lot!
REG: Right, you're in.

Watching *Life of Brian*, anyone who ever studied Latin cannot avoid the overwhelming wave of sympathy towards Brian Cohen when he is being interrogated and exercised by a Roman *centurion* ably using his *gladius*. But it is the punishment that followed that explains the writing on the wall: the Romans were from Mars and the Jews were from Venus. Nevertheless, they did communicate. This episode accurately encapsulates much of the tension between the two parties, one that intensified towards the second half of the first century CE and erupted in the image of the First Jewish Revolt (66–70 CE). It takes indeed two to tango, and military groups on both sides played major roles in the clash. In the *Life of Brian* we have John Cleese's brilliant portrayal of a Roman centurion, who is keeping a careful eye not only on potential Jewish rebels but also on the governor he serves, as well as the parallel Jewish insurgency leader, Reg. This chapter is devoted to exploring the tentative prototypes of these warriors, and more precisely what we have from archaeology to inform how we see them in the Early Roman period of Judaea, also known as the late Second Temple period.

In recent years, military equipment has become a significant source of information in the study of the identity of institutionalized martial bodies such as the Roman army and local militias.[1] Today we have in our possession a large corpus of data, culled from a wealth of well-dated military equipment from strata in Judaea representing in part the historical conflict.[2] This data will be instrumental for my present discussion of a variety of soldierly identity of both local and Roman forces, as well as the nature of Jewish opposition to Roman military occupation whose attitude was so finely expressed in the words of the Pythons: 'Romani Ite Domum.'

Let us begin with the Judaean People's Front, or should it be the People's Front of Judaea? I pick up with Josephus' reference to the *Sicarii*, a most nationalistic group that is held responsible, in both contemporary ancient sources as well as in later accounts, for the dire results of the revolt:

> And then it was that the *Sicarii*, as they were called, who were robbers, grew numerous. They made use of small swords, not much different in length from the Persian *acinacae*, but somewhat crooked, and like the Roman *sicae*, as they were called; and from these weapons these robbers got their denomination; and with these weapons they slew a great many.
>
> (*Ant.* 20.185–186)

The item that defined this group was a weapon that literally gave it its name. Until recently no metal specimens were known from the Roman world, until a sheathed ferrous item from Ein-Gedi, Israel, that was uncovered in 1961, was finally published.[3] (See plate section, image 2.)

1. M. C. Bishop and J. C. N. Coulston, *Roman Military Equipment, From the Punic Wars to the Fall of Rome*, 2nd ed. (Oxford: Oxbow, 2006); Michel Feugère, *Les armes des Romains, de la République à l'Antiquité tardive* (Paris: Errance, 1993); Thomas Fischer, *Die Armee der Caesaren, Archäologie und Geschichte* (Regensburg: Friedrich Pustet Verlag, 2012); Simon T. James, *The Arms and Armour and other Military Equipment: The Excavations at Dura-Europos conducted by Yale University and the French Academy of Inscriptions and Letters 1928 to 1937, Final Report VII* (London: Oxbow, 2004).

2. Guy D. Stiebel, 'Armis et litteris – The Military Equipment of Early Roman Palestine in Light of the Archaeological and Historical Sources', Ph.D. dissertation submitted and approved at University College London, University of London, 2007.

3. Stiebel, 'Armis et litteris', Vol. I, 112-3; id., 'Dressed to Kill – Military Dress as an Ideological Marker in Roman Palestine', in Shoshana-Rose Marzel and Guy D. Stiebel (eds), *Dress and Ideology: Fashioning Identity from Antiquity to the Present* (London: Bloomsbury, 2014), pp. 153–67.

The *sica*, in this case, functioned not merely as a weapon but at the very same time also formed a status symbol as well as an ideological marker.[4] As such it indicates once more the prominent place of the *militaria* – military artefacts – as markers of status and identity and as social indicators. Today, for films and television documentaries, as also for experimental archaeology and re-enactments, we are capable of dressing up the rebels and reconstructing their arsenals, based first and foremost upon the artefactual record. The panoplies of the Jewish militias may be described as combinations of peasants' equipment, looted and old weapons, as well as locally manufactured weapons. Hence we have clear indications for the use of staves, slings and stones alongside swords, bows, javelins and bucklers.

An intriguing question that stems from this understanding is the origin of the rebels' weapons. Reading Josephus one learns about local manufacture of arms in Jerusalem in the face of the coming siege of 70 CE: 'in every quarter of the city missiles and arms were being forged' (*War* 2.649). Two foci of hearths that were excavated in the Western Palace, Masada (L442, L456), have been interpreted as smithies of the rebels,[5] and presumably had been used for forging of arrowheads. One further reads about the use of 'old weapons' (*War* 2.576) by the rebels.

So we return to the *Life of Brian*'s Roman centurion, with his *gladius*. During the excavations at Masada, a sword of the type *gladius hispaniensis* (145–1510) was uncovered in a context clearly dated to the period of the First Revolt.[6] The fact that this type is commonly dated to the late Republic does suggest in our case a lengthy use of the weapon. One possible explanation may lie in the storerooms of Herod the Great that, according to Josephus, were stocked with weapons intended for 10,000 soldiers (*War* 7.299); this datum is known to form one of the motivations for the *Sicarii* to seize the mountain fort in 66 CE. In addition, no fewer than three such swords were uncovered in Jerusalem, and all derive from First Revolt contexts.

On the other hand, the Roman military force that garrisoned in Judaea during the first half of the first century CE was seemingly based upon the army of Herod the Great. Ruling under Roman auspices (37–4 BCE), Herod established a substantial military force which included mercenary contingents of foreign origins, including Thracian, Galatian (or Gauls?), German and even Babylonian Jewish soldiers, as well as a naval force.[7] His army offered assistance to the Romans

4. Stiebel, 'Dressed to Kill', pp. 157–8.

5. Ehud Netzer, *The Buildings, Stratigraphy and Architecture: Masada III, The Yigael Yadin Excavations 1963–1965, Final Reports* (Jerusalem: Israel Exploration Society and the Hebrew University of Jerusalem, 1991), pp. 250, 285–6; Jodi Magness, 'Masada – Arms and the Man,' *Biblical Archaeology Review* 18 (1992), pp. 58–67, at p. 63.

6. Guy D. Stiebel and Jodi Magness, 'The Military Equipment from Masada', in Joseph Aviram, Gideon Foerster, Ehud Netzer and Guy D. Stiebel (eds), *Masada VIII: The Yigael Yadin Excavations 1963-1965, Final Reports* (Jerusalem: Israel Exploration Society, 2007), pp. 1–65, at pp. 3–4, Pl. 4.

7. Israel Shatzman, *The Armies of the Hasmoneans and Herod: From Hellenistic to Roman Frameworks* (Tübingen: Mohr Siebeck, 1991), pp. 129–309.

on not a few occasions. Examining the equipment uncovered in Herodian contexts, for example at Jericho and Cypros, appears to reveal, among others, clear Roman affinities, such as hobnailed sandals (*caligae*), spearheads (*hastae*), alongside evidence for the use of torsion artillery, such as *ballistae* and *catapult* bolts.[8]

Yet at the end of the day, in addition to supplying the warrior with martial equipment, much weight was given to public relations, which shaped the image of the ideal soldier in the eyes of the public, whether one indeed wanted to be a warrior or just pretended to be one.

Hence, much like today's rulers (compare to Vladimir Putin's public staged appearances, see Figure 8.1), the ancient sovereign wanted to manipulate and shape his image in the eyes of the public, as a great combatant:

> Now Herod had a body suited to his soul, and was ever a most excellent hunter, where he generally had good success, by the means of his great skill in riding horses; for in one day he caught 40 wild beasts ... He was also such a warrior as could not be with stood: many men, therefore, there are who have stood amazed at his readiness in his exercises, when they saw him throw the javelin directly forward, and shoot the arrow upon the mark. And then, besides these performances of his depending on his own strength of mind and body, fortune was also very favourable to him; for he seldom failed to success in his wars ...
>
> (*War* 1.429–430)

If we do wish to reconstruct the image of the Roman army presented in the film, legionaries played, no doubt, an important part. Perhaps the best preserved example that testifies to the appearance of the Roman soldier is to be found in the dramatic discovery in Gutman's excavations at Gamala in 1982, when the entire panoply of a Roman soldier of *Legio V Macedonica* was uncovered.[9] The substantial remains of his helmet, edged weapons (*gladius* and *pugio*), segmental armour (*lorica segmentata*), shield (*scutum*) as well as a 'dog-tag' = ownership tag (*nota*), enabled me to reconstruct not only his equipment and appearance, but also his name – L. Magus of the *centuria* of Gallus (see plate section, image 3).

The decoration motifs discernable on the Roman martial equipment clearly indicate their association to specific units and pride, in particular of being soldiers of Rome or of the legion, most notably in the image of the *aquila* (eagle). Other

8. Guy D. Stiebel, 'Military equipment from the Jericho and Cypros', in Rachel Bar-Nathan and Judit Gärtner (eds), *Hasmonean and Herodian Palaces at Jericho, Volume IV, Final Reports of the 1973–1987 Excavations, The Finds from Jericho and Cypros* (Jerusalem: Israel Exploration Society and the Hebrew University of Jerusalem, 2013), pp. 290–8.

9. Guy D. Stiebel, '"Dust to dust, ashes to ashes" – Military Equipment from Destruction Layers in Palestine', *Carnuntum Jahrbuch* (2005), pp. 99–108; Stiebel, '*Armis et litteris*', pp. 23, 41–2, 93–5, 111, 126, 171, 180, 212, 225; id., '"*Miles Gloriosus*"? – The Image of the Roman Legionary', in Ofra Rimon (ed.), *The Great Revolt in the Galilee* (Haifa: Hecht Museum and the University of Haifa, 2007), pp. 111–18 (Hebrew).

Figure 8.1 Vladimir Putin (photo by premier.gov.ru).

motifs, such as gods and goddesses, demonstrated the Roman self-image as the most pious nation on earth. This is illustrated, for example, by the Isis and Harpocrates pendants from Masada,[10] or by ample equine harness pendants from Gamala and Masada[11] that exhibit clear Bacchic linkage. The latter association also applies to the wooden phallic pendant that was discovered in one of the Roman siege camps at Masada (see plate section, image 4). Such an element apparently hung from the triumphal chariot during the procession to ward off the evil eye (Pliny, *Nat. Hist.* 28.39).

Conclusion

After four years Rome's military superiority, in nearly every possible respect, played its part and the First Jewish Revolt was suppressed. Yet the Jewish flame of resistance, seeds of which are so skilfully narrated in *Life of Brian*, was still burning thereafter. It was only six decades later, under Hadrian, that the Empire struck again, this time putting an end to Jewish national aspirations, at least in the ancient era.

10. Stiebel, '*Armis et litteris*', Vol. III, Pl. III.19: nos. 3–4.
11. Stiebel and Magness, 'The Military Equipment from Masada', pp. 28–30, Pl. 30.

Chapter 9

'YOU'LL PROBABLY GET AWAY WITH CRUCIFIXION': LAUGHING AT THE CROSS IN *BRIAN* AND THE ANCIENT WORLD

Helen K. Bond

There's nothing funny about crucifixion – or is there? Certainly some of the funniest scenes in the *Life of Brian* are when the hero is on the cross. Whether it's the wealthy couple demanding execution in a 'purely Jewish area', the ineffectual efforts of the Suicide Squad, or the film's final rousing chorus, it's difficult (like Pilate's soldiers) to keep an entirely straight face. But it was particularly the fact that the film made fun of crucifixion that so disturbed the Bishop of Southwark in the now infamous *Friday Night, Saturday Morning* discussion. 'Why lampoon death?' the Bishop asked, clearly supposing that all good people must agree with him. But was he right? Is the cross, and the suffering and death associated with it, really above all forms of satire and parody?

The problem, it seems to me, is that the Bishop was too influenced by centuries of Christian spin. As a terrible form of execution, the cross urgently needed rebranding, to turn it into something more acceptable, and we can see this process beginning already in the Gospels. Mark's desolate crucifixion scene, in which Jesus goes to his death rejected and almost alone, is systematically transformed by the later Gospels into something much more palatable. Now we see Jesus supported not only by disciples, but by his mother; no longer calling out in abandonment, but forgiving his enemies and declaring his mission complete. Luke borrows themes from the death of Socrates as he presents Jesus as an innocent martyr; John portrays the cross as Jesus' glorification, his cosmic defeat of Satan. And all of the Gospels transform what was probably a hasty and shameful burial in a shallow grave by Jesus' enemies into a decent interment in a rock-hewn tomb; indeed, John imagines a burial fit for a King (John 19.38–42). What we have here is a completely understandable transformation of an ignominious end into a noble death, worthy of any Roman. Jesus dies as he has lived, with courage, obedience, mastery of his emotions, and concern for those he leaves behind.[1] And most Jesus films, of course, replete with Christian piety, buy into this narrative: we see a serene Jesus, his nakedness covered by a natty little loincloth, an awed crowd, and a natural world that rises up in protest through storms and cosmic portents. It's a moving account of the self-sacrificial death of the Son of God – but is it the only possible way to envisage the crucifixion?

G. K. Chesterton famously argued that the only subjects worth joking about were serious ones – like getting married or being hanged. I don't have much to say about marriage in this essay, but it does seem to me that Chesterton has highlighted something important here.[2] Often it's precisely in the most tragic and heartbreaking of situations that comedy can offer a means of release – a way of dealing, if only temporarily, with our deepest fears and anxieties. There have always been jokes about death, but the gallows, with all its violence and unpredictability, elicits a very specific kind of macabre humour. What I'd like to do in this chapter is to look at ways in which people at the time of Jesus made sense of crucifixion through humour, and how the gruesomely comic enabled them to live with and perhaps even to transcend this most hideous form of execution. Sifting through the references, they seem to me to divide broadly into two categories: (1) those that find humour through parodying or mocking the victim, and (2) those in which the victim himself initiates the humour (I've reserved the term 'gallows humour' only for this latter type). I'll look at both of these in turn, and hope to show why it is that the first of these (mockery of the victim) couldn't work in the *Life of Brian*, while the second (gallows humour) offered a range of comic possibilities.

---

1. On the 'noble Roman death' tradition, see Valerie M. Hope, *Death in Ancient Rome: A Sourcebook* (London/New York: Routledge, 2007), pp. 39–45. See also the Maccabean martyrs of 2 Macc. 6.18–7.42 and 4 Macc. 5.1–18.24.

2. G. K. Chesterton, opening paragraph to 'On Mr McCabe and a Divine Frivolity' (part of his 1905 collection of essays, *Heretics*).

Parody/Mockery of the Victim

It's well known that crucifixion was the most brutal and degrading form of capital punishment, reserved for slaves, brigands, and any who dared show disdain for imperial rule.[3] It was intentionally as barbaric and painful as possible. Stripped of his clothes, the victim was humiliated and shamed as he suffered extreme agony, perhaps for several days, until, overcome by suffocation and exhaustion, the merciful end would come. The cross symbolized the complete destruction not only of the physical body, but also of the person's identity. In most cases, the corpse was left to rot or to be eaten by birds, and the victim's remains were left unburied. So offensive was crucifixion that civilized people preferred not to talk about it, and few Roman writers dwelt on the details.[4]

An important aspect of crucifixion was its public nature. Crosses were meant to be *seen*, not only to act as a deterrent but to provide spectacle and even entertainment to the onlookers. And this is where the element of parody comes in. Martin Hengel notes that 'crucifixion was a punishment in which the caprice and sadism of the executioners were given full reign'.[5] This is amply illustrated by the sources:

- Josephus describes the scene after the fall of Jerusalem in 70 CE: 'So the soldiers, out of the rage and hatred they bore the prisoners, nailed those they caught, in different postures, to the crosses, *by way of jest*, and their number was so great that there was not enough room for the crosses and not enough crosses for the bodies' (*War* 5.51).

These are crucifixions following a long drawn-out battle, when we'd expect the soldier's brutality and sadism to be at its height, but there's ample evidence to suggest that parody was a common feature at other times:

- Seneca notes the different shapes that crosses might take, some impaling the victims' private parts (*Dialogue 6: On the Consolation to Marcia* 20.3).

3. The following paragraphs owe a great deal to the following works: Martin Hengel, *Crucifixion: In the Ancient World and the Folly of the Cross* (London: SCM, 1977); Kathleen M. Coleman, 'Fatale Charades: Roman Executions Staged as Mythological Enactments', *JRS* 80 (1990), pp. 44–73; David W. Chapman, *Perceptions of Crucifixion Among Jews and Christians in the Ancient World* (Tübingen: Mohr Siebeck, 2008); and the following three articles by John G. Cook, 'Roman Crucifixions: From the Second Punic War to Constantine', *ZNW* 104 (2013), pp. 1–32, id. 'Crucifixion as Spectacle in Roman Campania', *NT* 54 (2012), pp. 68–100; and id. 'Envisioning Crucifixion: Light from Several Inscriptions and the Palatine Graffito', *NT* 50 (2008), pp. 262–85.

4. So Cicero, *For Rabirius* 16; more generally, Hengel, *Crucifixion*, pp. 37–8. On the possibility that Jesus may have been buried (albeit in shame), see Helen K. Bond, *Historical Jesus: A Guide for the Perplexed* (London: Bloomsbury, 2012), pp. 162–5.

5. Hengel, *Crucifixion*, p. 25.

- Philo recalls with horror the mass crucifixions of Jewish council leaders in Alexandria who were crucified amidst theatrical shows (*On Flaccus* 73–85).
- Suetonius tells of a man who was given a particularly high, white cross to mock his high social status (*Galba* 9.1).
- It's possible that the well-known young man from Givat ha-Mivtar (the only crucified victim to have made his mark in the archaeological record) might well have been crucified upside down – an apparently common variant.[6]
- An early third-century graffito etched into the wall of the Domus Gelotiana, a training school for imperial pages on the Palatine in Rome, depicts a donkey-headed man on a cross, next to which stands a beardless man (or boy) with his left hand raised as if in prayer. Underneath are the words 'Alexamenos worships God'. Clearly the scene ridicules Alexamenos' Christian beliefs by mocking the monstrous figure on the cross.[7]

The mockery, of course, made the victim an object of ridicule and enhanced his humiliation and shame. In the case of the routine crucifixion of slaves (who could find themselves on the cross for any number of trivial matters), the creativity of the executioners might not be stretched particularly far. There's evidence to suggest that most cities in the Empire had a place outside the walls where funeral contractors operated a torture and execution service for private citizens and public authorities alike.[8] At busy times, it might be enough simply to get the crucifixion done. When the crucified was a brigand or a rebel leader, however, the mockery might be particularly severe, as the soldiers poked fun at his pretensions in a particularly grotesque way.[9]

And people seem to have enjoyed watching the spectacle. Sociologically, it seems to have functioned in the same way as the show in the Roman arena or – closer to home – a good execution in the Middle Ages.[10] What exactly attracted people to this kind of gruesome display is open to debate. What's clear, though, is that public

6. So Yigael Yadin, 'Epigraphy and Crucifixion', *IEJ* 23 (1973), pp. 18–22.

7. See Raymond E. Brown, *The Death of the Messiah: From Gethsemane to the Grave* (London: Geoffrey Chapman, 1994), I: 875; also Cook, 'Envisioning Crucifixion'.

8. See Laurence L. Welborn, *Paul the Fool of Christ: A Study of 1 Corinthians 1–4 in the Comic-Philosophic Tradition*. JSNT Supplement Series 293 (London/New York: T&T Clark, 2005), pp. 131–2. Welborn cites much of the same evidence as I have listed here, though without making the distinction (which I think crucial) between parody and gallows humour, pp. 129–46.

9. On the cross as parody, see Joel Marcus, 'Crucifixion as Parodic Exaltation', *JBL* 125 (2006), pp. 73–8.

10. See Coleman, 'Fatal Charades', pp. 58–9; Hope, *Death in Ancient Rome*, pp. 28–31; and Chris Epplett, 'Spectacular Executions in the Roman World', in Paul Christesen and Donald G. Kyle (eds), *A Companion to Sport and Spectacle in Greek and Roman Antiquity* (Oxford: Wiley-Blackwell, 2013), pp. 520–32.

executions served an important purpose in encouraging onlookers to identify with the upholders of justice. The humiliation of the offender distanced him from the onlookers: the more the crowd laughed and jeered, the greater their own sense of moral superiority, and the more they felt that justice had been seen to be done. The last thing Roman executioners wanted was to encourage a spirit of sympathy amongst the crowd – horror, ridicule and rejection were much more useful emotions – but of course the theatre didn't always work, and sometimes people retained their sympathy for the victim to the end. There's evidence from both Philo and Josephus that people were sometimes filled with horror at the sight, and Josephus tells of his own (undoubtedly exceptional) experience of recognizing three of his friends on crosses after the siege of Jersualem, and tearfully appealing to Titus for them to be cut down from their stakes – successfully as it happens (*Life* 76).

Had the Pythons wanted to draw on this particular type of grim parody they would have found plenty of material in the Gospels themselves, particularly in Mark, our earliest account. Jesus is mocked as a false prophet immediately after the Jewish trial (Mark 14.65), parodied by the soldiers as a mock-Emperor (that is, King of the Jews) after the Roman trial (15.16–20), and lampooned on the cross by onlookers, the chief priests and those crucified with him (15.29–32). The title on the cross – the King of the Jews – also needs to be seen as part of this mockery. The evangelists exploit its ironic potential, but underlying it is a mocking disparagement not only of the ridiculous pretensions of the prisoner but also of his fellow Jews and their futile messianic hopes. On a historical level, it seems highly likely that Jesus *was* mocked in this way – not only because it was common practice, but also because as an apparently failed prophetic leader, Jesus would have seemed utterly contemptible to his executioners. And most Jesus films do retain this element of parody: Jesus wears the crown of thorns and the soldier's cloak, and often we see a jeering crowd.[11] Yet the *Life of Brian* resolutely avoids mocking the hero at this point. There is no attempt to humiliate him (at least, nothing further to the general humiliation of his everyday life), no mockery of his messianic claims (or those of others on his behalf), and no scoffing crowd. In fact, Brian's whole experience of the cross is a far cry from what I've just outlined.

It seems to me that there's a very good reason for this. In order for this type of mocking parody to work, the onlooker has to completely accept the judicial processes and the authority of the perpetrators. For us to derive any kind of humour from the ridicule of the victim, we need to see things through the eyes of Rome. And we don't do this in the *Life of Brian*. Unlike the average Hollywood Jesus film, the Empire receives a mixed report card in *Brian*: Rome has done a

---

11. These features are common to most Jesus films, although Mel Gibson's 2004 *Passion of the Christ* clearly goes further than most in its violent mockery (and its claims to historical accuracy). Importantly, however, mockery of Jesus at this point is a form of emphasizing the tragic, or perhaps the Satanic, in Jesus' death. No film seriously attempts to *laugh* at Jesus in this way – for reasons discussed in the next paragraph.

lot for the Judaeans: the aqueduct, sanitation, roads, etc. etc.[12] Ben the dungeon-dweller admiringly declares that they're 'a terrific race, the Romans'. And even Brian's dad, it turns out, was a Roman soldier (much to Brian's disgust). Throughout the film, Roman centurions and officials are presented as a generally benign presence, a cross between decent civil servants, schoolmasters in a boys' public school, and mild Anglican vicars. They are concerned with maintaining strict grammatical standards, sensitively guiding people to their crosses, ensuring that the crucifixion party march through the city in a good, straight line, and even take a moment to reflect on the senseless waste of life inherent in crucifixion. But if the average Roman soldier is a decent chap, his superiors are satirized relentlessly. Pontius Pilate and his friend Biggus Dickus, with their speech disorders, are objects of unremitting fun. We actually know a lot about Pilate from other sources, and it's pretty clear that he was nothing like this![13] The centurion at Pilate's court (played by John Cleese) has an accurate grasp of the situation and does all he can to keep Pilate from appearing in front of the mob, but to no avail. The Roman prefect is dimly aware that the crowd might be making fun of him (which is more than can be said for Biggus Dickus), but has no real sense that his supposedly superior position is completely undermined by the laughing crowd. Thus the Barabbas scene, which in the Gospels represents the climax of Jewish rejection of Jesus, is transformed in the *Life of Brian* into a big joke at the Romans' expense.

The film plays with the idea of colonizers and the colonized. One of my favourite scenes is where the jailers pretend to be deaf or stupid in front of the Roman centurion, but once alone speak quite normally and intelligently. This is a perfect example of James C. Scott's 'everyday forms of resistance', where the colonized deliberately appear to be dimwitted or ignorant as a means of low-level protest.[14] From the perspective of the colonizers, too, the film shows an astute grasp of the realities of domination. The one thing that the ruling classes can never allow is for the occupied to laugh at them. Once they lose the people's fear, once their careful performance of mastery and command is allowed to disintegrate, they have lost their position as rulers.[15] It's clear from the trial scene in particular that *Brian's* Roman elite have lost all credibility with their Jewish subjects, though the irony is that they don't seem to have noticed. As a strategy to produce humour

12. For a comparison of Rome in the *Life of Brian* with the more typical Hollywood portrayal, see Adele Reinhartz, *Jesus of Hollywood* (Oxford: Oxford University Press, 2007), p. 62.

13. For the view that Pilate was a generally capable administrator (and a discussion of the relevant primary literature), see Helen K. Bond, *Pontius Pilate in History and Interpretation* (Cambridge: Cambridge University Press, 1998).

14. James C. Scott, *Weapons of the Weak: Everyday forms of Peasant Resistance* (New Haven: Yale University Press, 1985); see also his more general *Domination and the Arts of Resistance: Hidden Transcripts* (New Haven: Yale University Press, 1990). Scott specifically mentions stammering as common in the colonized (*Domination*, p. 30).

15. Scott, *Domination*, p. 11.

in the crucifixion scene, then, parody or mockery of Brian simply wouldn't have worked. We don't side with the Romans. Some of them might be quite nice people, but we don't fundamentally see things from their point of view.

Yet the *Life of Brian* is fully aware of the predilection of the Roman world for this type of distraction. Early on, Brian's mother is keen to swap the entertainments of the Sermon on the Mount (which she can hardly hear anyway!) for a good stoning. The film also features a historically improbable amphitheatre, though it has to be said that the ensuing show is generally lacklustre and the audience is minimal (even allowing for a different budget, we're a far cry from Ridley Scott's *Gladiator* here). And of course there's poor old Ben in the prison, upside down and shackled to the wall for five long years. But even in these three cases, we're not sneering at the *victims* of stoning, the arena, or Roman justice, but laughing at the absurdity of the situations as a whole: a stoning in which beard-wearing women end up attacking the religious leader in charge; a gladiator who dies of cardiac arrest rather than from any fighting; and, significantly I think, a victim of prolonged Roman torture who turns out to be the most right wing, pro-Roman character in the whole film!

What's also striking about not only Brian's crucifixion, but also the stoning, the arena and the tortured Ben, is their almost complete lack of blood (the only gory bit involves someone stuffing mutilated body parts into a sack at the Colosseum, presumably because the 'Children's Matinee' is about to begin). The reason for this is presumably good taste: whatever the partiality of an ancient audience, modern viewers would find it impossible to laugh at any of these situations if they seemed in the least bit realistic[16] – and I expect the Bishop would have been even more scandalized than he already was.

If we're not on the side of the Romans, then, whose side are we on? This isn't a simple question to answer – the film urges us to think for ourselves, not to follow unquestioningly. We're to hold up everything, including presumably the film itself, to critical analysis and ridicule. But if there is a hero, it's undoubtedly Brian. He's not your sophisticated James Bond-type (despite the opening theme tune), but he does at least have a normal accent and a reasonably normal walk. While other characters seem unaware of their own ridiculousness, Brian sees the absurd world around him with perfect vision. And we share his gaze. Any humour in Brian's crucifixion, then, is going to come not from the Roman vantage point, but from Brian's own. This brings me to the second way of adding humour to the cross – what's generally referred to as 'gallows humour' – 'grim and ironical humour in a desperate or hopeless situation'.[17]

---

16. So also Philip R. Davies, '*Life of Brian* Research', in J. Cheryl Exum and Stephen D. Moore (eds), *Biblical Studies/Cultural Studies: The Third Sheffield Colloquium* (Sheffield: Sheffield Academic Press, 1998), pp. 400–14, here p. 414.

17. This is the definition given by the Oxford Dictionary (Oxford University Press) at http://www.oxforddictionaries.com/definition/english/gallows-humour.

Gallows Humour

Searching for examples of gallows humour in the context of crucifixion encounters a problem almost straight away. Victims of this penalty were, almost by definition, slaves, whose friends and followers tended not to leave any literary remains. This of course makes it very hard to find an authentic slave voice. The closest thing to what we're looking for comes from the more popular end of the literary scale – for example the plays of Plautus, which feature a number of wily slaves who get the better of their masters. In these plays, the theme of painful retribution is everywhere, slaves frequently call one another 'cross-meat' or 'cross-bird,' or talk of 'cruising for crucifixion' (even though within the play they get away with their bad behaviour).[18] These were of course comedies, deriving their humour from the idea of normal life and conventions being turned upside down, and providing their audience with a temporary escape from reality, but it's possible that they do give an accurate insight into how at least some slaves responded to the ever-present threat of the cross.

Brian draws a great deal on gallows humour. It's seen at a very basic level in the trivializing of the cross all the way through the film, leading to a comic mismatch between what the audience know about this terrible penalty and its filmic presentation. But noticeably it's the *Romans* who stress its horrible nature, while those most likely to experience it are the ones who make light of it. This is particularly clear in the exchange between old Matthias, who keeps the safe-house, and the Roman Centurion. When the Roman notes that crucifixion is nasty, Matthias says, 'Could be worse, you could be stabbed.' 'Crucifixion's worse,' the soldier argues, 'it lasts for hours. It's a slow, horrible death!' 'Well, at least it gets you out in the open air,' Matthias adds. Later the Centurion continues the discussion, 'Have you ever seen anyone crucified?' 'Crucifixion's a doddle,' the old man replies. Ben the dungeon-dweller (played by Michael Palin) is a fan of crucifixion: it's the 'Best thing the Romans ever did for us,' he declares. 'If we didn't have crucifixion, this country would be in a right bloody mess. Nail 'em up I say. Nail some sense into them.' And as he catches sight of the crucifixion party, he calls Brian a 'lucky bastard'.

The prime example of gallows humour is Mr Cheeky, who's almost an embodiment of what it means to laugh in the face of despair. Rather like a character from a Greek Romance, he inhabits a world where crucifixion is a routine hazard, where characters do sometimes escape from their crosses, and people can be saved in the nick of time. He jokes with the Centurion in the crucifixion queue that he's going to be released and put on an island somewhere (and almost gets away

---

18. For a useful discussion of Plautus, see Erich Segal, *Roman Laughter: The Comedy of Plautus* (Cambridge: Harvard University Press, 1968), especially pp. 137–69. Segal gives a number of examples, with Libanius' victorious shout in *Asinaria* (ll. 545–51) and Chrysalus' pun on his name in *Bacchides* (l. 362) being the most instructive. See also Justin Meggitt, 'Laughing and Dreaming at the Foot of the Cross: Context and Reception of a Religious Symbol', *Journal for the Critical Study of Religion, Ethics, and Society* 1 (1996), pp. 9–14.

with it!). He's still calling people 'Big Nose' as he makes his way to the cross, and when threatened by a soldier, he says: 'Oh, dear. You mean I might have to give up being crucified in the afternoons? . . . That would be a blow. Wouldn't it?' Once he's on the cross, he says it's 'Not so bad once you're up,' and looks forward to his randy brother coming to help him get down. The irony is that Mr Cheeky is the only one of the crucifixion party who doesn't end up dying on the cross; he gets released in place of Brian and no one believes him even when he tells them he's only joking. But then that's the trouble with the Romans: they can't take a joke.

Sometimes in ancient literature we do get instances where elite Roman authors allow victims to joke about their imminent execution – though we always have to ask what purpose our author has in recounting it. Josephus relates the story of a prisoner from Jotapata who 'had held out under every variety of torture, and, without betraying to the enemy a word about the state of the town, even under the ordeal of fire, was finally crucified, meeting death with a smile' (*War* 3.321). Jewish valour, even humour, in the face of death is a theme Josephus uses elsewhere, and it's difficult not to see this as a subtle hint at Jewish superiority.[19] Seneca refers to victims of crucifixion who are 'slanderous and witty in heaping insult on others', and even 'spit upon spectators from their own cross' (*On the Happy Life* 19.3). At other times we hear of rebels or gangs of rebels strengthening their compatriots' morale in the face of unspeakable cruelty. Silius Italicus tells of a Spanish slave who, after the most extreme tortures imaginable, like an on-looker despised his suffering and the shortcomings of his Carthaginian assailants, and demanded to be crucified like his master (*Punica* 179–181). Of particular relevance to our present topic is a story from Strabo, relating the behaviour of Spanish prisoners after the Cantabrian wars who continued to sing victory songs, even when nailed to their crosses (*Geography* 3.4.18). Strabo took this as a clear indication of madness, but from the prisoners' point of view, it's easy to see their songs as a final act of defiance, as a way of strengthening morale, and a last laugh in the face of Roman oppression. There's something rather heroic about these wild Cantabrians, unwilling to be snuffed out by Rome, or even to collude in the judicial or military processes that put them on the cross. As Mel Gibson might have said (in a very different context): they may take our lives, but they'll never take . . . our freedom!

Of course, there's nothing heroic about Brian. He might have joined a political liberation movement, he might even have had some initial success as a revolutionary, but his heart's not really in it. He only joined the People's Front of Judaea (PFJ) as a protest, and his continued support seems more down to the attractions of Judith than any great commitment to the cause. Rather than seizing the moment and making it his own, as the Cantabrian rebels did, Brian tries to get out of being crucified, to say it's all been a mistake and that he wants a lawyer. His time on the cross is dominated by what initially appear to be attempts to release him, but which all end in failure: the PFJ, who decide to congratulate him on his martyrdom, the suicide squad who could have been useful (particularly since the

---

19. See also *War* 2.153 (on the Essenes) and 7.418 (on the *Sicarii*).

Roman guards have run away in fear), but who pointlessly take their own lives, and of course the actual offer of release, which Brian misses because he's too busy doing other things.

The film makes fun of the theme of the freedom fighter who goes to his death in defiance of Rome – specifically in its parody of another great swords and sandals film – Stanley Kubrick's *Spartacus*. Unlike the real slave leader, who probably perished in the battle against Crassus in 71 BCE, the film features a justly famous scene where the surviving slaves are offered their lives if they will give up their leader to Rome. Just as Kirk Douglas is ready manfully to accept his fate, his fellow slaves begin to compete with one another in their attempts to take his place, until the valley rings with the shouts of 'I'm Spartacus'. In the *Life of Brian*, the request of the Roman soldier for Brian, after he has been rather belatedly granted his pardon by Pilate, is similarly met with a chorus of 'I'm Brian', including the memorable line 'I'm Brian and so's my wife'. In fact, the very sight of the large number of crosses filling the screen again recalls the 6,000 slaves crucified along the way from Capua to Rome in the aftermath of Spartacus' revolt.[20] But whilst the slaves' shout seals their place on a cross, the characters in Brian are all trying to save their own skins.

The film's message is summed up in the final, jaunty chorus: in the end, nothing can be put on a pedestal. Life is a joke, and the only sane response to the craziness around us is to laugh.[21] It takes a little while for Brian to get this, but by the time he actually joins in with the singing, the camera is no longer focused specifically on him. He and his fellow Judaeans are linked together by their fate, and all they can do is to look on the bright side of life – and death. The song has sometimes been criticized as 'nihilistic', although this is probably too extreme.[22] Ideas of some kind of post-mortem resurrection had come into Judaism two centuries before Brian and, following the lead of the Pharisees, had taken hold amongst the vast majority of the population. Few first-century Jews, then, would have argued that 'death's the final word'. And yet the line in the song which urges that 'you came from nothing – you're going back to nothing' has clear parallels with ideas expressed both in Job 1.21 ('Naked I came from my mother's womb, and naked shall I return') and in 1 Timothy 6.7 ('for we brought nothing into the world, and

---

20. For a discussion of the film, see Larry J. Kreitzer, *The New Testament in Fiction and Film: On Reversing the Hermeneutical Flow* (Sheffield: Sheffield Academic Press, 1993), pp. 21–43.

21. On the film's message, see Richard C. Stern, Clayton N. Jefford and Guerric DeBona, *Savior of the Silver Screen* (New York: Paulist Press, 1999), pp. 233–63 and Jeffrey L. Staley and Richard Walsh, *Jesus, the Gospel and the Cinematic Imagination: A Handbook to Jesus on DVD* (Louisville and London: Westminster John Knox, 2007), pp. 101–8.

22. Hans Wiersma describes it as 'upbeat nihilism', although he detects a final irony in that, as the chorus winds down, nihilism itself is crucified. 'Redeeming *Life of Brian*: How Monty Python (Ironically) Proclaims Christ Sub Contrario', *Word and World* 32 (2012), pp. 66–177, here pp. 176–7.

we cannot take anything out of the world'). Even in the Christian Bible, then, hope and realism can exist side by side. Perhaps this explains why the song has become so popular at funerals, and why it was reputedly sung by the survivors of *HMS Sheffield*, sunk in 1982 during the Falklands War, while awaiting rescue.

Implications for Historical Jesus Research

In keeping with the theme of this volume, what have the Pythons done for us? By 'us', I mean biblical scholars with an interest in how we go about reconstructing the historical Jesus, specifically the events around his crucifixion. At first sight, *Brian* tells us very little. After his two brief cameo roles, Jesus disappears from the scene. We don't see how he behaves on the cross (and if we did, I suspect he'd offer a perfect rendition of the Christian tradition with which I began). But it's well known that Jesus/Brian represent the two sides of Christian orthodoxy. The film's Jesus is of course the Christ of Christian piety, with Brian as support act in the altogether messier human condition (and reflecting a number of debates about the 'historical Jesus', both ancient and modern).[23] Through its artistic and creative presentation, the film forces us to look at the story in a slightly different way, to face up to questions which may not have presented themselves before, and to ask whether the Pythons might have unearthed some things of importance. In our ongoing quest to understand Jesus of Nazareth, then, it seems to me perfectly responsible to draw on whatever insights *Brian* might offer.

And *Brian* does have some important things to say. It's particularly in their analyses of Jesus' death that scholars, particularly those of a Christian persuasion, tend to be at their most docetic[24] – or, if that's too strong a term, at their most pious and least critical. The Gospels give us a surprisingly full account of Jesus' last few hours – they're actually the longest accounts of any crucifixion that we possess – but this is precisely the problem. As biblical scholars, we know that the texts were written several decades after the time of Jesus, that they're intricately intertwined with Scriptural motifs, and that they are now embedded in biographical narratives that aim to encourage belief and discipleship. And yet it's hard to break free from their hold. We actually know far less about Jesus' death than we think, and we should be wary of relying on the Christian images too unreflectively.

23. See, for example, Davies, '*Life of Brian* Research', pp. 406–10; Carl Dyke, 'Learning from *The Life of Brian*: Saviors for Seminars', in George Aichele and Richard G. Walsh (eds), *Screening Scripture: Intertextual Connections between Scripture and Film* (Harrisburg: Trinity Press International, 2002), pp. 229–50, specifically p. 37; James G. Crossley, 'Life of Brian or Life of Jesus? Uses of Critical Biblical Scholarship and Non-Orthodox Views of Jesus in Monty Python's *Life of Brian*', *Relegere: Studies in Religion and Reception* 1 (2011), pp. 93–114, here p. 114.

24. Docetism sees Jesus as only having the appearance of humanity, while actually being fully divine; this heresy was rejected by the early Church.

And this is where *Brian* comes in. At its broadest level, the film refuses to give us the iconic image of the cross that we're expecting. The traditional Christian portrait features three crosses on a hill: a slightly higher central one, its victim nailed, flanked by two smaller crosses on which the victims are tied. The detail that Jesus was between two other rebels (the Greek word here is *lēstai*, or bandits) comes from the Gospels, but there is nothing to suggest that these were the sum total of those crucified that day. (Moreover, the historical material analyzed above suggests that the neat cross formation – that is, rows of victims crucified in a †️ shape – is already a sanitization of a much more gruesome spectacle in which bodies could have been nailed or tied in any posture which appealed to the executioners.) In *Brian*, instead of three crosses on a hill we're confronted by 140. As the camera pans out over the whole skyline, it becomes increasingly difficult to work out which one actually is Brian. Viewers are faced with the potentially troubling fact that there's nothing unique about him.[25] Furthermore, his death achieves absolutely nothing.[26] Admittedly we don't actually see him die, but it's a reasonable assumption that it wouldn't be accompanied by cosmic portents or the angelic choruses so beloved of other Jesus films. Brian's death is as futile as his life. But this is undoubtedly how some of those assembled at Golgotha saw the death of Jesus: as a pointless waste of a man's life, one more victim of state violence. Even some who had at one time been followers would undoubtedly have turned away: a man rejected by the chief priests (characters noticeably absent in *Brian*) and humiliated by Rome, was clearly a dead end.

Brian's fellow political activists are also instructive. Early on in the film they learn the language of martyrdom, talking of the 'glorious deaths' of those who perished in the botched kidnapping. And Brian is barely on the cross before Reg's committee have branded him a martyr too, and have started to interpret his death as part of the continuing struggle against Roman oppression. Judith adds that Brian is dying for them, and she'll never forget him. What's interesting here is just how quickly the process of interpretation begins. Brian's experience reminds us that there never was a neutral, historical narrative of the death of Jesus onto which various interpretations were grafted such that it might be possible to separate one from the other. Rather, interpretative frameworks were necessary as soon as people began even to consider the death of Jesus. And this raises other disturbing questions: how far did Jesus collude, let alone inspire, the myth that quickly surrounded him? To what extent were motifs such as self-sacrifice, obedience, and passivity important to him? And does it matter?

And what of Brian himself? Brian is the only sane figure in a mad world. First-century Jews made sense of life through their belief in God and the scriptures, but there must have been times, particularly in their relations with Rome, when life was hard to fathom, and the decisions of overlords difficult to understand. I would like to argue that we shouldn't underestimate the serious use of humour in daily

---

25. So also Crossley, 'Life of Brian or Life of Jesus?' p. 101.
26. So Wiersma, 'Redeeming *Life of Brian*', pp. 171–2.

life, as a strategy for coping with the capriciousness of existence. The Christian tradition doesn't allow Jesus much laughter: he is allowed to be angry, compassionate, even to cry, but laughter seems to elude him. Perhaps the teacher who enjoyed socializing with those that respectable society deemed to be 'outcasts' did appreciate the funny side of life. And this might be extended to his death too, though I realize that I'm now on rather contentious ground.

When Jesus predicts his death in Mark's Gospel (and those that follow), it's with great solemnity; he talks of being rejected by the Jewish religious leaders, 'handed over' to the Gentiles, and suffering many things (Mark 8.31, 9.31, and 10.33). For Mark, Jesus' death is a ransom for others (10.45), his blood a covenant, poured out for many (14.23). But we need to remember that this whole presentation of Jesus' death is a Markan formulation. The three-fold passion prediction is thoroughly Markan – we might compare the triple sequence in Gethsemane, where Jesus returns to his sleeping disciples three times, and where (as with the second passion prediction), the second repetition is rather cursory and lacking in detail (Mark 14.32–42). Despite the fact that words are put into the mouth of Jesus, this is *Mark's version of events*, encapsulating the way that *Mark* wants his readers to see Jesus approach his imminent death. Not only are theological themes at play here, but the evangelist might well be writing for people who may have experienced some kind of suffering themselves (especially if the Gospel is to be located in Rome shortly after Nero's brutal persecution[27]). Mark is less interested in giving his readers an accurate account of the way in which Jesus met his end than in presenting him as a model for others who might similarly be called upon to 'take up their cross'. Nor is John's Gospel much help here. John's Jesus goes to his death perfectly in control, laying down his life for his friends (John 10.18). In this Gospel, Jesus is 'God striding over the earth', perfectly assured of his earthly vocation and his heavenly home. It is hardly surprising that the Johannine Jesus has no need of a helping Simon of Cyrene, and dies acknowledging that his work is done (John 19.30). Once again, the whole death scene has been overlaid by theological concerns.

On a historical level, it is very likely that Jesus did expect to die. When he entered Jerusalem not on foot (as other pilgrims did), but on the back of a donkey, amidst the excited cries of the crowd, he became a concern for the Jewish and Roman authorities alike (Mark 11.1–10 and parallels). And when he performed a symbolic act in the Temple, quite likely prophesying the destruction of the holy place, his fate was probably sealed (Mark 11.12–18).[28] But we need to realize that we have no way of knowing how he faced that death. Like Brian, Jesus was one of the 'little people', a provincial peasant – someone who, in Rome's eyes, had no worth at all. It would be only too clear to Jesus that his actions were likely to attract the attention of the authorities, and that the likely result would be the cross.

27. The fullest ancient description of this event comes from the early-second-century Roman writer Tacitus, *Annals* 15.44.

28. For my own reconstruction of historical events at this point, see Bond, *Historical Jesus*, pp. 152–62.

Perhaps, like Brian, he sometimes passed by a crucifixion, with the body still attached to the stake, a gruesome reminder of where his path might take him. And might it be possible that he sometimes resorted to humour because it was the only way he could come to terms with the terrible reality of what lay before him?[29]

As Jesus hangs on the cross, Mark allows him to quote the opening line from Psalm 22: 'My God, my God, why have you forsaken me?' (Mark 15.34). Scholars debate whether the evangelist intended to evoke only the first verse (in which case it is a cry of dereliction), or whether we should hear the psalm as a whole (which ends with God hearing the psalmist's cry). On the level of Mark's narrative, I would incline toward the first of these interpretations: Mark presents a bleak picture of Jesus' death where he is abandoned by everyone – disciples, Peter, the crowd, even (apparently) by God himself. But the *Life of Brian* offers us other ways of linking Psalm 22 to Jesus' death. Perhaps, for example, he sang it, and perhaps rather than a cry of dereliction it was an act of solidarity with those crucified with him. Scholars who argue that Jesus set himself against imperial Rome might want to go further. Did Jesus die in a state of *passive obedience*, or rather with a song drawn from the most deeply held memories of his Jewish tradition – a final act of defiance in the face of a corrupt system?

And what of Jesus' disciples, many of whom were also called upon to face martyrdom? These people clearly believed that the death of Jesus achieved a purpose, and that their own martyrdoms would enable them to share his glory. But would they have been human if they hadn't sometimes doubted, or resorted to humour to cover their fear and anxiety? Occasionally martyr texts do allow their heroes to joke in the face of appalling deaths.[30] While these accounts are quite rightly regarded as late and legendary by scholars, it is possible that those who composed them knew something of the power of gallows humour in terrifying situations.

The last few paragraphs are, of course, pure speculation; imaginative reconstructions based on a new set of images provided by the *Life of Brian*. In a similar way, we might allow Martin Scorsese's equally controversial *The Last Temptation of Christ* (1988) to provide us with images of how the dying Jesus might have contemplated an alternative destiny in which he got down from the cross and lived an ordinary family life. In the end, we can't possibly know how Jesus or those that followed him faced their deaths, but it does seem to me that *Brian* raises questions that we shouldn't too quickly dismiss as grotesque and irreligious. The Bishop of Southwark was right – death is a serious matter, and crucifixion is terrible beyond imagining, but it's precisely because of its unfathomable seriousness that people sometimes needed to laugh.

---

29. For a similar suggestion, see David Heim, 'A Joking Matter: And Jesus Laughed', *Christian Century* 120 (2003), pp. 27, 29–30.

30. St Lawrence, for example, a deacon in Rome in the mid-third century, was roasted on a gridiron with coals beneath it. After some time, he is supposed to have said: 'I'm well done. Turn me over.' The story can be found in Ambrose, *On the Duties of the Clergy* 1.41.

Chapter 10

BRIAN AS A TEACHER OF RIGHTEOUSNESS

George J. Brooke

On Monday 23 January 1956, the BBC North of England Home Service broadcast a short talk by John M. Allegro, the second in a series of three. At the end of the talk Allegro conjectured that the Teacher of Righteousness, the leader of the sectarians who had come to settle at Qumran, had been crucified there on the north-west shore of the Dead Sea by the Gentile troops of Alexander Jannaeus.[1] For Allegro, the Wicked Priest who figures in some of the sectarian scriptural commentaries was to be identified as the Jewish king Jannaeus, active at the start of the first century BCE. The following week Allegro introduced the third talk as follows: 'Last week I said that the leader of this monastic community by the Dead Sea was persecuted and probably crucified by Gentiles at the instigation of a wicked priest of the Jews. For most of us, these events will associate themselves automatically

---

1. John M. Allegro, *The Dead Sea Scrolls (2)*, pp. 6–7 (unpublished script for broadcast on the North of England Home Service, 23 January 1956).

with the betrayal and crucifixion of another Master living nearly a century later.'[2]
The point was clear.

Allegro was widely criticized for his conjecture that had combined pieces of
evidence in a particular way to suggest that the Teacher of Righteousness was
some kind of prototype of another Master, Jesus. However, although the particular
details of Allegro's speculation are distinctive and probably incorrect, his idea in
seeing the role of the sectarian Teacher as in some way an anticipation of the role
of Jesus was not new. A few years earlier André Dupont-Sommer had written:
'Everything in the Jewish New Covenant heralds and prepares the way for the
Christian New Covenant. The Galilean Master, as He is presented to us in the
writings of the New Testament, appears in many respects as an astonishing
reincarnation of the Master of Justice.'[3] And the idea has endured.

But how is the relationship between the Teacher and Jesus to be understood? We
cannot know whether Jesus ever visited Qumran or any other sectarian settlement,
but he could well have known about the sectarians and some aspects of their
teachings. There is no clear evidence, however, that Jesus modelled any of his
teaching or actions on those of the Teacher of Righteousness or that the Gospel
writers deliberately took the pattern of the Teacher amongst others as they
configured their various portraits of Jesus. But the Teacher of Righteousness can be
seen as a type of Jewish sectarian leadership and as such he needs to be factored into
how any life of Jesus research might look for contextual clues. As Eric Idle noted:

> We all got together and we talked about it a little bit and said, 'Let's do a couple
> of weeks' research'. So we all went off and read the Bible, and I read the Dead Sea
> Scrolls and books on the Bible. Then we met again and decided what this could
> be about. I think we realized at that point we couldn't make a film about Jesus
> Christ because he's not particularly funny, what he's saying isn't mockable, it's
> very decent stuff, you can't take the piss out of it. But the idea of somebody who
> is mistaken for a Messiah came out and I think that's how that process started.[4]

A similar recollection has been attributed to Michael Palin: 'We read books about
the Bible story and that period, the Dead Sea Scrolls and various new interpretations
of the Gospels.'[5] So this is my purpose here, to think about someone whom some
of that ancient Jewish sectarian movement and also some modern scholars have

---

2. John M. Allegro, *The Dead Sea Scrolls (3)*, p. 1 (unpublished script for broadcast on
the North of England Home Service, 30 January 1956).

3. André Dupont-Sommer, *The Dead Sea Scrolls: A Preliminary Survey* (Oxford: Basil
Blackwell, 1952), p. 99.

4. Graham Chapman, John Cleese, Terry Gilliam, Eric Idle, Terry Jones, Michael Palin,
with Bob McCabe, *The Pythons Autobiography by The Pythons* (London: Orion, 2005),
pp. 355–6.

5. Robert Sellers, *Always Look on the Bright Side of Life: The Inside Story of HandMade
Films* (London: Metro Publishing, 2003), p. 4.

taken or mistaken for an eschatological figure, even a prophet[6] or Messiah,[7] and to wonder whether Brian can assist our thinking.[8] After all, the study of reception history is as much about how later readings might help the better understanding of earlier phenomena as they are about the history of interpretation itself.[9]

The Life of Brian *as a Cultural Marker*

Two matters are worth mentioning briefly concerning the *Life of Brian* as a cultural marker, one larger and more general matter, and one more specific item. First, the history of research on the Teacher of Righteousness reveals that in the first thirty-five years or so, from 1947 until about 1980, there was a dominant concern with trying to identify the Teacher with some historical person, notably as the unnamed high priest of 159–153 BCE, and with recognizing him as the author of some of the sectarian compositions.[10] Those concerns have not gone away, but they now play a minor role when compared with interests in the Teacher since the 1980s. The shift of interest that took place in the 1980s can be seen in the discussion of the authorship of the composition entitled *Miqsat Ma'aśeh Ha-Torah* (*MMT*). As information on this composition began to emerge in the 1980s the proposal was that this epistolary summary of various legal decisions together with some moral exhortation had been penned by the Teacher of Righteousness and sent to his rival outside the sect, probably a Jerusalem leader.[11] This idea was

---

6. As discussed by me in George J. Brooke, 'Was the Teacher of Righteousness Considered to be a Prophet?', in Kristin De Troyer and Armin Lange (eds), *Prophecy after the Prophets? The Contribution of the Dead Sea Scrolls to the Understanding of Biblical and Extra-Biblical Prophecy* (Contributions to Biblical Exegesis 52; Leuven: Peeters, 2009), pp. 77–97.

7. See, e.g., Michael A. Knibb, 'The Teacher of Righteousness – A Messianic Title?' in Philip R. Davies and Richard T. White (eds), *A Tribute to Geza Vermes: Essays on Jewish and Christian Literature and History* (JSOT Supplement 100; Sheffield: JSOT Press, 1990), pp. 51–65.

8. James Crossley has notably discussed Brian in relation to the so-called messianic secret of the Gospel accounts, especially Mark: James G. Crossley, 'Life of Brian or Life of Jesus? Uses of Critical Biblical Scholarship and Non-orthodox Views of Jesus in Monty Python's *Life of Brian*', in *Relegere: Studies in Religion and Reception* 1/1 (2011), pp. 93–114, at pp. 106–9.

9. The methodological remarks of Stefan Klint are helpful in insisting that the reception should not be applied to the historical text by way of allegory, but in the spirit of Gregory the Great so that 'the Holy Scripture grows with all those who read it' (Stefan Klint, 'After Story – A Return to History: Introducing Reception Criticism as an Exegetical Approach', *Studia Theologica – Nordic Journal of Theology* 54 [2000], pp. 87–106, at p. 104); here we are concerned with both scripture and sectarian texts in which similar phenomena of collective memory and identity construction are at work.

10. See most notably Hartmut Stegemann, *Die Entstehung der Qumrangemeinde* (Bonn: Privately published, 1971).

11. See Elisha Qimron and John Strugnell, 'An Unpublished Halakhic Letter from Qumran', *Israel Museum Journal* 4 (1985), pp. 9–15.

challenged[12] and few, if any, would defend the identification now; it is recognized as too historicist, an over-reading of what might be knowable about the composition and its origins. In fact, the authorial voice of *MMT* is the first plural personal pronoun ('we'), not a first singular ('I'), as might be expected if the Teacher were the author.

Two dimensions of the discussion of the Dead Sea Scrolls are indicative of this change in a more positive scholarly fashion. On the one hand, the *Damascus Document*, the major sectarian rule book in which the Teacher figures, was dissected into its parts and layers and the attempt to read the opening Admonition as a naïve historical summary was seen to be problematic.[13] On the other hand, there was reconsideration of the *pesharim*, the sectarian biblical commentaries that are the only other textual source for explicit information about the Teacher. In general they are no longer understood as principally about the early second century BCE history of the sectarian movement, but rather as some kind of quasi-prophetic literary phenomenon of the late first century BCE.[14] This change is attested in another way. So, for example, by the time of the fiftieth anniversary of the 1947 discovery of Cave 1, a collection of studies describing the state of the question, *The Dead Sea Scrolls after Fifty Years: A Comprehensive Assessment*,[15] had no room for an article on the Teacher. The Teacher, whose identity was never very secure in the first place, seemed to be losing his identity altogether. More recently, he has been re-imagined as proto-typical of sectarian identity,[16] and he has been heard rather than seen, as the traditions about him have been discussed in terms of the echoes of his voice rather than his historical persona.[17]

---

12. Not least by Strugnell himself: John Strugnell, 'MMT: Second Thoughts on a Forthcoming Edition', in Eugene Ulrich and James VanderKam (eds), *The Community of the Renewed Covenant: The Notre Dame Symposium on the Dead Sea Scrolls* (Notre Dame: University of Notre Dame Press, 1994), pp. 70–3.

13. See especially the multiple articles of Jerome Murphy-O'Connor, not least as it was summed up in his study, 'The Damascus Document Revisited', *Revue Biblique* 92 (1985), pp. 223–46; see also Philip R. Davies, *The Damascus Covenant: An Interpretation of the 'Damascus Document'* (JSOT Supplement 25; Sheffield: JSOT Press, 1982).

14. See, e.g., George J. Brooke, 'The Pesharim and the Origin of the Dead Sea Scrolls', in in Michael O. Wise, Norman Golb, John J. Collins and Dennis G. Pardee (eds), *Methods of Investigation of the Dead Sea Scrolls and the Khirbet Qumran Site: Present Realities and Future Prospects* (Annals of the New York Academy of Sciences 722; New York: New York Academy of Sciences, 1994), pp. 339–54.

15. James C. VanderKam and Peter W. Flint (eds), *The Dead Sea Scrolls After Fifty Years: A Comprehensive Assessment* (Leiden: Brill, 1998–1999).

16. See Jutta Jokiranta, 'Qumran – The Prototypical Teacher in the Qumran Pesharim: A Social-Identity Approach', in Philip Esler (ed.), *Ancient Israel: The Old Testament in Its Social Context* (London: SCM Press, 2005), pp. 254–63.

17. See Florentino García Martínez, 'Beyond the Sectarian Divide: The "Voice of the Teacher" as an Authority-Conferring Strategy in Some Qumran Texts', in Sarianna Metso, Hindy Najman and Eileen Schuller (eds), *The Dead Sea Scrolls: Transmission of Traditions and Production of Texts* (STDJ 92; Leiden: Brill, 2010), pp. 227–44.

Why mention this history of scholarship and the evolution of thinking about the Teacher? In his recent book on the Bible in silent film, David Shepherd has astutely noted that there is an analogy between what happens to the epic depiction of biblical narratives in the silent era and in that of sound. For Shepherd the 'appearance of Monty Python's *Life of Brian* following a long line of earnest cinematic depictions of Christ in the 1960s and 1970s'[18] was an indication of the exhaustion of the biblical epic that sought to represent matters historically on ever grander scales.[19] While others are better qualified to discuss the *Life of Brian* as marking a moment of cultural change in relation to life of Jesus research, it certainly seems to be the case that the film is a leading indicator of several features of a cultural shift which itself is eventually reflected in scholarship on the Teacher. That shift is a move away from somewhat narrow historicist concerns towards larger questions of textual and other kinds of construal and mis-construal. It is also partly a move away from history as a sequence of grand moments towards narrative as reflecting the everyday. It is also a move away from any attention to the divine in Jesus to the human in Brian, perhaps with Brian representing Jesus' humanity in an encrypted form; in fact on that score the Teacher is a much better quasi-messianic archetype for juxtaposition with Brian than is Jesus, since there was never any claim that the Teacher was divine.[20] By moving beyond historicism with the mood of the moment, Brian puts humanity at the top of the agenda of theological discourse.

The more specific item concerning how the *Life of Brian* has become a cultural marker for Dead Sea Scrolls scholarship concerns a recent exhibition. Mladen Popović of the University of Groningen was the curator of the major exhibition of Dead Sea Scrolls and related artefacts at the Drents Museum in Assen (9 July 2013–5 January 2014). The exhibition, not surprisingly, had no mention of the Teacher of Righteousness in any of its handouts or displays, but did have mention of him in its more technical accompanying catalogue.[21] In addition to some scrolls and various archaeological artefacts from contemporary Judaea, one large room was devoted to the Roman period. On one wall, above and between display cases concerned with Judaea after the revolt of 66–70 CE, was the following vertical list

---

18. David Shepherd, *The Bible on Silent Film: Spectacle, Story and Scripture in the Early Cinema* (Cambridge: Cambridge University Press, 2013), p. 294.

19. Note the similar observations by Philip R. Davies, 'Life of Brian Research', in J. Cheryl Exum and Stephen D. Moore (eds), *Biblical Studies/Cultural Studies: The Third Sheffield Colloquium* (London: Continuum Books, 1998), pp. 400–14, at p. 400.

20. On the divinity-humanity issue in relation to the figures of Jesus and Brian see Davies, 'Life of Brian Research', pp. 406–9, and especially Crossley, 'Life of Brian or Life of Jesus?'

21. The Teacher is not mentioned in the small booklet that was handed out to those attending the Exhibit – Mladen Popović and Adi Ziv-Esudri, *De Dode Zeerollen: De tentoonstelling* (Assen: Drents Museum, 2013) the more technical catalogue is published as Mladen Popović (ed.), *De Dode Zeerollen: Nieuw licht op de schatten van Qumran* (Zwolle: W Books, 2013), pp. 34, 169, 200.

in large letters: 'water system, aqueduct, medicine, roads, irrigation, wine, education, sanitation' – all listed as aspects of Roman construction and establishment.[22]

When showing visitors around, the curator delighted in testing their wider understanding of what the list represented. It was, of course, a representation of the answer to Reg's question, 'What *have* the Romans done for *us*?'[23] He had also set up a wider intertextual reading for the cognoscenti, for in place of also listing 'peace', which features as the climax of the list offered by Xerxes and others in the film, the exhibition displayed on the opposite wall a very threatening and deathly flock of flying arrowheads.

It is now the case quite clearly that the *Life of Brian* is a significant cultural discourse partner, even in the study of the Scrolls and this should not be surprising;

Figure 10.1 Dead Sea Scrolls exhibition in Drents Museum, Assen (9 July 2013–5 January 2014). (© Drents Museum; photograph: JAV Studios Assen.)

22. As Davies ('*Life of Brian* Research', p. 410 n. 16) has noted: 'The rehearsal of Roman benefactions in *Life of Brian* is not actually entirely accurate: irrigation, wine and education were not introduced by the Romans to Judaea.'

23. The order in the film script is: 'aqueduct, sanitation, roads, irrigation, medicine, education, health, wine, public baths, safety in walking the streets.' And in Reg's summary: 'All right ... all right ... but apart from better sanitation and medicine and education, and irrigation and public health and roads and a freshwater system and baths and public order ... what *have* the Romans done for *us* ...?' See Graham Chapman et al., *Monty Python's Life of Brian (of Nazareth)* (London: Methuen, 1979), p. 20.

Figure 10.2 Dead Sea Scrolls exhibition in Drents Museum. (© Thijs Wolzak; exhibition design: Kossmann.dejong)

as I have already noted, at least some of the Pythons had done more than some students of Jesus: they had actually gone away and read the Dead Sea Scrolls.

The Teacher of Righteousness

From the brief history of scholarship mentioned above we have noted that the figure of the Teacher of Righteousness has moved from being an unnamed but identifiable historical figure to being an authoritative voice. What really is known about the Teacher of Righteousness and is there anything there that can be understood better through juxtaposition with Brian? 'The sobriquet Teacher of Righteousness is given in the Dead Sea Scrolls to the individual who is commonly believed to have played the decisive role in the formation and early history of the group, assumed here to be Essene, that lies behind the scrolls.'[24] The sobriquet is widely understood as being a play on the end of the phrase in Joel 2.23, 'for he has

24. Michael A. Knibb, 'Teacher of Righteousness', in Lawrence H. Schiffman and James C. VanderKam (eds), *Encyclopedia of the Dead Sea Scrolls* (New York: Oxford University Press, 2000), pp. 918–21, at p. 918.

given you the early rain for your vindication' (*ha-mōreh li-tsedāqāh*). Like much else in the sectarian compositions, in some way the Teacher's designation is in part at least a fulfilment of prophecy.

References to him are limited to the *Damascus Document* and four of the sectarian scriptural commentaries (the *pesharim*), one each on Habakkuk and Micah, and two on the Psalms.[25] The extant copies of the *pesharim* date to the second half of the first century BCE and the texts themselves were most likely composed at that time. The *Damascus Document* is extant in multiple copies from the Qumran caves and is widely thought to have had a longer pedigree, even going back, at least in part to the second half of the second century BCE. If the designation 'Teacher of Righteousness' in the *Damascus Document* does indeed refer to an historical individual, then the description of him as belonging to the second generation of a Jewish reform movement and becoming the focal point of its formation is not unlikely.

How the Teacher became a prominent leader in the movement is not clear. Was he a mere stooge, a parodic leader as Philip Davies has indicated of Brian?[26] At least, as with Brian, these things just happen when people with various expectations and aspirations transfer them to an individual. But more significantly, in the light of the depiction of Brian's experience, what is transferred is indeed to be recognized as a matter of projection. For Jesus, Brian challenges the viewer to look again at the evidence without all the projected baggage of the churches. For the Teacher of Righteousness, by implication, Brian poses the question as to how much scholars have really understood the character of what is being projected on him by the composers and compilers of the *Damascus Document* and some of the *pesharim*.

Remembering the Teacher

The references to the Teacher of Righteousness in the sectarian scriptural commentaries, the *pesharim*, deserve further consideration. The likely date of the commentaries as composed in the second half of the first century BCE means that it is very unlikely that any founding Teacher from a much earlier period, perhaps even a century before, had any direct part in their composition. The *pesharim* do indeed contain a projection back on to the Teacher of what their composers or compilers considered to have been suitable ways of describing the founding figure of the past. What was it about him that the compilers of these texts thought should be remembered about the Teacher?

In his study of the Teacher of Righteousness remembered, Loren Stuckenbruck has outlined six items that were probably thought significant about the Teacher as his memory was constructed.

---

25. It is possible that the Teacher was the subject of a sentence in 4QpIsa^c frgs 1–2, l. 3.
26. Davies, '*Life of Brian* Research', p. 410.

1. He was identified as a priest in the commentary on Psalm 37.23–24, an identification implying that his 'priestly function underpins the community's cultic understanding of itself'.[27] Something similar can be said based on the interpretation given to Habakkuk 1:5 in *Pesher Habakkuk* where there is mention of the 'mouth of the priest'.

2. The Teacher is described as an interpreter of authoritative scriptures. In particular, according to *Pesher Habakkuk*, the Teacher of Righteousness is the one 'to whom God made known all the mysteries of his servants the prophets' (1QpHab 7.4–5). The Teacher is probably being set up as the role model and authorization for exactly the kind of prophetic interpretation that *Pesher Habakkuk* contains.

3. The Teacher is also remembered as a founding figure. According to *Pesher Psalms* he is the one who built the Congregation. Stuckenbruck has noted that this might be something of an overstatement if the full picture of the *Damascus Document* is taken into account.[28]

4. The Teacher is remembered for his conflict with 'the man of the lie'. It is highly likely that such remembrance reflects a desire for the audience of the commentaries to believe that they are on the side of particular truth claims over against various falsehoods. This is the rhetoric of sectarian rivalry or even inner-sectarian group fighting.

5. The Teacher also opposed 'the wicked priest', a character whose activity is not always linked to the Teacher and so may represent an ongoing contemporary conflict with priests elsewhere, an outsider conflict.

6. The Teacher of Righteousness is remembered as just that; his sobriquet is a marker of instruction that is righteous.

In all six respects the indications are that this is in no small part remembrance as a mechanism for coping with contemporary issues, the projection back on to some earlier leader of all the contemporary anxieties about priestliness, authoritative interpretation, communal fragility, infighting and outfighting, as well as a genuine quest for meaning.

Without overstating the case, the *Life of Brian* highlights several similar issues and forces the reader of the scrolls to recognize at least some of the dynamics through which the sectarian commentaries were created. First, there is the problem of Brian's own lineage. Mandy has to break it to him early on that his father might not be Mr Cohen (that is Mr Priest), but a Roman centurion, a feature of several

---

27. Loren T. Stuckenbruck, 'The Teacher of Righteousness Remembered: From Fragmentary Sources to Collective Memory in the Dead Sea Scrolls', in Stephen C. Barton, Loren T. Stuckenbruck and Benjamin G. Wold (eds), *Memory in the Bible and Antiquity: The Fifth Durham–Tübingen Research Symposium (Durham, September 2004)* (WUNT 212; Tübingen: Mohr Siebeck, 2007), p. 79.

28. Ibid., p. 84.

later Jewish traditions about Jesus.[29] Though obviously crafted with an eye on the identity of Jesus' parents, the discussion between mother and son evokes the question about whether it is enough for the sectarian Teacher simply to be identified as a priest. The Teacher is not explicitly named. Stuckenbruck boldly states: '[n]ot anonymous to the community, he is anonymous to us (who are outsiders) and, more importantly, he remains without a proper name in the world of the texts.'[30] I cannot avoid wondering to what extent the very commonality of the name Brian creates a kind of anonymity, a space onto which it is all the easier for the aspirations of others to be projected. He is a virtual nobody who is constructed by others.

Second, there is no extensive biography of the sectarian Teacher. As the one to establish or confirm a school of thought, sometimes likened to Pythagoras, some further biographical details might be expected. In many instances we know more about founding figures than is the case with the Teacher. What we do seem to know cannot be constructed into a consecutive narrative biography with any certainty. Almost every item in the *Damascus Document* and the sectarian commentaries, the *pesharim*, has now been deconstructed and thought to reflect the concerns and ideological traits of those who wrote such documents. And although the historians of Jesus have undertaken similar deconstructions of their subject, they have forever been tempted to put the story back together, often – as has commonly been pointed out – constructing a Jesus in their own image. With the *Life of Brian* such deconstruction is brought into sharp focus. Both for Jesus – who becomes a misheard figure in the distance and whose healings cause economic setbacks for those healed – and for Brian – who is misunderstood by his mother and by nearly everybody else – the question arises concerning how anything in a potential Teacher's biography might be assembled. Some few scholars keep trying to create the Teacher's biography and a very clearly mapped history of his early community, but they are just the kind of scholars who probably have not been to see the *Life of Brian*.

Third, little or no teaching remains. Unless, as is widely supposed, some significant parts of the *Thanksgiving Hymns* (the *Hodayot*) were composed by this founding figure, then the readers of the *Damascus Document* and the sectarian scriptural commentaries are left with the need to make the jump from what is offered in those texts by way of legal and prophetic interpretation to supposing that it was instigated or certainly was in tune with what the Teacher said. What did Brian actually say or do that resulted in him being pushed forwards into the particular role aspects of which he somewhat reluctantly eventually agrees to play? There is a little teaching that is Brian deliberately pretending to be a prophet to avoid Roman capture; that is clearly imitation of some kind and eventually leads to the audience deciding that he's not saying much of value.[31] At which point a youth

29. As pointed out by Davies, '*Life of Brian* Research', p. 404.
30. Stuckenbruck, 'The Teacher of Righteousness Remembered', p. 91.
31. See Crossley, 'Life of Brian or Life of Jesus?' pp. 96–7.

arrives on the scene as Brian is trying to extricate himself from speaking and wants to know what Brian isn't sharing with his audience: it must be a secret, even the secret of Eternal Life. Then there's a gourd[32] and a sandal. After some further action there is the denial scene in which Brian's denial is taken as proof of his divinity.[33] In a similar way we might wonder about what the Teacher of Righteousness was imitating, perhaps poorly and under duress, and whether the Teacher of the scrolls ever agreed or even hinted at the kinds of things that were later projected back onto him; just where are the continuities and discontinuities in the voice of the Teacher?

Fourth, the Teacher is useful in a time of conflict. Discourse about him helps people not only to take the right side, but also once on the right side to be part of a core group. Perhaps there are ideological conflicts of various kinds so frequently that the concomitant need for such a Teacher of Righteousness is common enough. In the *Life of Brian* the factionalism of the Jewish resistance to Rome is highlighted in the squabbles between the Judaean People's Front and the People's Front of Judaea (and whatever happened to the Popular Front?) and is a reflection of the types of internecine struggle that is only too common amongst resistance movements, especially religious ones. Philip Davies has suggested that the *Life of Brian* is entirely in accord with 'the fragmentation and mutual loathing of Jewish resistance groups' as indicated by Josephus;[34] and Josephus' portrayal of the Jewish fanatics who committed suicide on Masada that lies behind the scene of the resistance fighters doing just that is one such faction.[35] The movement behind the sectarian scrolls seems to have been no exception; there was factionalism within it at some stage or stages, the existence of traitors, as is reflected in the very same texts as present the Teacher to us, and there was antagonism against both those who were resisting Rome and those who were accommodating themselves to Gentile authority.

Fifth, there is an issue not just about right teaching but also about truth claims, what might be better labelled as 'revelation'. It is claimed in *Pesher Habakkuk* that God made known to the Teacher all the mysteries of his servants the prophets. But did the Teacher ever claim that for himself? And if not, how did it come about that his words were understood as in some way inspired, revelatory. Who decides these things? In the *Life of Brian* it is quite clear that it is audiences who assign authority to words and sayings, who hear and don't hear, and who mishear. There is a major question left for any hearer: do I ascribe authority to what I have heard and on what grounds?

---

32. A possible allusion to the gourd of Jonah 4.6–10 might be at play, since the one sign that Jesus gives is the unexplained sign of Jonah (Davies, 'Life of Brian Research', p. 405).

33. It is this matter that provokes the line of discussion undertaken by Giordano Vintaloro, *Non sono il Messia lo giuor su Dio! Messianismo e modernità in* Life of Brian *dei Monty Python* (Trieste: Battello stampatore, 2008).

34. Davies, 'Life of Brian Research', 402.

35. See also the comments by Crossley, 'Life of Brian or Life of Jesus?' pp. 98–101, on 'Jesus and Brian: Revolutionary Comrades'.

Creating Identity through a Prototype

All that has been mentioned based on how the Teacher was remembered is taken a stage further when it comes to the construction of identity. In a neat article on the *pesharim*, Jutta Jokiranta has summarized several aspects of social identity theory and applied them to the Teacher of Righteousness.[36] Jokiranta makes two principal observations, one concerning the Teacher as a persecuted person and one concerning the Teacher as privileged. She argues that these two identity markers are what result in the modern reader being able to identify the similarities between the Teacher and the social in-group responsible for the texts. Social identity theory then supports the claim that the Teacher is constructed as a prototype of the identity of much later groups and individuals.

First, then, persecution. The persecution of the Teacher is a well-recognized feature of the *pesharim*. Jokiranta's point is that this mirrors the experiences of the in-group described in the same texts. As the Teacher is oppressed by the wicked priest, so that in-group is also hard pressed at the hands of the stereotyped wicked outsider. This makes the Teacher's experience prototypical for the identity of the in-group even though such experience might be the construct of those writing the texts. It is intriguing to see how negative experience is turned into a positive identity marker; but, of course, that is a common phenomenon. The lack of the experience of violence, that is of being violated, can lead to a loss of identity; and the same is true the other way round, as violence feeds a particular sense of self, even self-worth.

Second, what of privilege? The claims to elect status of the sectarian movement behind the scrolls have been widely recognized. Jokiranta has suggested that the key matter in this respect concerns the correct interpretation of scripture. Whilst for the prototypical Teacher this is principally constructed around the interpretation of the prophets, for the movement itself it is the right interpretation of the Torah that is of major significance. The discrepancy is only slight since the *Damascus Document* implies that the founding Teacher in some way is responsible for the legal interpretation in the text itself and the *Hodayot* proclaim correct teaching within the covenant against the false teachers whose stereotypical characterization implies that it is matters of halakhah that are involved. Scripture is used to justify deviance from societal norms.

What of Brian? Is he prototypical in any way? Two things come to mind. On the one hand, the sense of confusion in his self-understanding and amongst those who encounter him suggests that the film constructs confusion, rather than persecution, as a major identity marker of messianic movements and those on whom they project their aspirations. The confusion is intricately interwoven with chance circumstances arising out of the Roman occupation and where people happen to be at particular moments. Confusion and accident are significantly those very factors that are usually forgotten both by the groups who write about

---

36. Jokiranta, 'Qumran – The Prototypical Teacher in the Qumran Pesharim', pp. 254–63.

their founding moments for early group members and also by scholars who attempt to reconstruct social movements and their founders, usually from those very texts. Social history should not all be written in terms of neat chains of deliberately intended cause and effect. There are always matters beyond the control of those involved and multiple factors that are never recorded. Only making a film of what could have happened in which the circumstantial and the misunderstood is privileged can an audience perceive the reality of things as far more complex than any single text could ever represent. Brian puts the mess back into messianism, as Mandy explicitly states in a mocking aside.[37]

On the other hand, the prototypical characterization of Brian seems to lie in another direction than that of the constructed Teacher of Righteousness. The Pythons project onto Brian a somewhat convoluted insistence on individualism. In preaching that people should really make up their own minds and live their lives their own way, Brian inadvertently risks subverting himself and creating a movement inspired by such a message – just what he is preaching against. For the sectarian Teacher the construction of identity is not for the sake of individualism – it's intriguing how very few proper names survive amongst the 250 sectarian scrolls from the Qumran caves—but for a group identity of some sort, perhaps the sort through which the marginalized, even including some who could be counted as elite, might justify their group deviance from various social norms.

Conclusion

Where have we got to and what are we left with? I am aware that I have not discussed one matter where there is much intersection between the Dead Sea Scrolls and the *Life of Brian*, namely the matter of sex and sexuality. Such could be the subject of a study on its own,[38] but the thing to note by way of my excuse is that in fact in the scrolls sex and the Teacher are never immediate textual bedfellows. Perhaps the same could be said for Brian, whom I read as a very basic straight guy who stands out against all the noise of transgender, cross-dressing, sexual innuendo and nudity in the film.

Whatever the case might be about his sexuality, the Teacher was not the Messiah, though, as with Brian, some people might have thought that he was. Likewise he

---

37. This must have been in my subconscious when I wrote without proper acknowledgement in a somewhat technical article: 'In many ways over the last fifty years, the Scrolls have put the "mess" into "messianism", making it difficult to be clear what constituted Jewish eschatological expectation at the time of Hillel and Jesus': George J. Brooke, 'Kingship and Messianism in the Dead Sea Scrolls', in John Day (ed.), *King and Messiah in Israel and the Ancient Near East: Proceedings of the Oxford Old Testament Seminar* (JSOT Supplement, 270; Sheffield: JSOT Press, 1998), pp. 434–55, at p. 455.

38. See Amy-Jill Levine, in this volume, pp. 167–84.

was not a prophet, though like Brian some people might have wished to highlight his prophetic characteristics. Perhaps in the end, like Brian in his mother's view, the Teacher was simply 'a very naughty boy' – but that depends upon whom you might have asked or might ask nowadays.[39] John Allegro and André Dupont-Sommer may have juxtaposed the Teacher of Righteousness and Jesus very starkly, too starkly as historical figures, shortly after the discovery of the Dead Sea Scrolls. In this chapter in the end all I have done is to try to make a case that the juxtaposition of the Teacher of Righteousness and Brian is in a not totally dissimilar fashion mutually illuminating, particularly in terms of memory and identity. To paraphrase Philip Davies,[40] Monty Python's *Life of Brian* is 'an indispensable foundation to any student's career' in the study of the Dead Sea Scrolls.

39. Presumably the author of *Pesher Habakkuk* understood that the Wicked Priest considered the Teacher of Righteousness to be 'a very naughty boy' who needed punishing.
40. Davies, '*Life of Brian* Research', p. 400.

Chapter 11

BRIAN AND THE APOCALYPTIC JESUS:
PARODY AS A HISTORICAL METHOD

Bart D. Ehrman

When the *Life of Brian* came out in 1979, I was an earnest and devout 23-year-old student at Princeton Theological Seminary, studying for ministry. Even though Princeton Seminary at the time was not, on the whole, strongly conservative in its theological orientation, I was. I had come to the school from Wheaton, an evangelical Christian liberal arts college; and before that I had studied at Moody Bible Institute, a bastion of fundamentalism in Chicago. By the time I was at Princeton Seminary, I was moving away from my evangelicalism, but I was still a sincere and committed conservative Christian. And even though I knew very little about the *Life of Brian* before seeing it – apart from the ghastly rumours that had been floating around in evangelical circles – I was certain that I would find it offensive to my religious sensibilities.

And sure enough, I was right. As a result, I felt deeply guilty at laughing when I knew that as a committed Christian I was *supposed* to be scowling. But afterward I combatted this moral failing by telling everyone I knew the theological short-comings of the film.

Brian and First-Century Apocalypticism

The one scene that I found particularly offensive at the time is not one that would immediately occur to most viewers as particularly troubling to conservative Christian sensibilities. It is the scene where we find a group of apocalyptic preachers of doom in the midst of Jerusalem. Four wild and crazy men spout dire predictions of coming desolation, in a hilarious caricature of first-century apocalyptic rhetoric.

The reason I found the scene offensive was that I knew full well that Jesus himself was reputed to have delivered some rather graphic apocalyptic discourses (as in Mark 13); moreover, at this transitional stage of my theological thinking, I had already begun to see that the majority of biblical scholars outside the ranks of the conservative evangelicals had good reason to think that Jesus' overarching message was in fact one of coming apocalyptic doom. By suggesting that a Jewish apocalyptic preacher from Galilee was simply regurgitating the kind of fluff and nonsense that could be found on any street corner in Jerusalem, the film – I thought – was completely undercutting the powerful and distinctive message of Jesus himself. The scene was not as obviously offensive as, say, 'Always Look on the Bright Side of Life,' but in many ways for me it was the most subversive scene of them all. In a far more subtle way it undercut the very core of Jesus' message and mission. And it made him, by implication, a complete crazy like these other apocalyptic wackos.

And so I assured everyone I knew – including my three seminary friends who went with me to see it, while we were still in the parking lot – that it wasn't like that at all. Jesus' message was distinct, a revelation from God. He was not simply mouthing typical visionary mumbo-jumbo.

A few years after that, I had calmed down a bit; my views of Jesus had begun to alter significantly, just as my knowledge of first-century Palestinian Judaism had developed significantly. It is not that I came to think that Jesus too was a loony set loose on the curious crowds of Jerusalem, but I had come to see that Jesus' message really was thoroughly apocalyptic, and that it was not entirely unique. It participated much more broadly in the apocalyptic stream of tradition of his day and time.[1]

In Jesus' day this apocalyptic stream of tradition was not *usually* propagated by the likes of those crazies of the *Life of Brian*. The scene is a parody. But as with all good parody, it embodies a kind of historical truth, and by providing a caricature

---

1. The first to popularize the apocalyptic understanding of Jesus was Albert Schweitzer, *The Quest of the Historical Jesus: A Critical Study of its Progress from Reimarus to Wrede* (New York: Macmillan, 1978 [German original: 1906]). This view has remained the broad consensus among critical scholars down to the twenty-first century. Among scholarly representatives of this perspective, see, for example, Dale Allison, *Jesus of Nazareth: Millenarian Prophet* (Philadelphia: Fortress, 1998); Bart Ehrman, *Jesus: Apocalyptic Prophet of the New Millennium* (New York: Oxford University Press, 1999); John Meier, *A Marginal Jew: Rethinking the Historical Jesus*, 4 vols. (New York: Doubleday, 1991–2009); E. P. Sanders, *Jesus and Judaism* (Philadelphia: Fortress, 1985).

of historical reality it highlights a certain aspect of that reality, allowing us to look beyond the incidentals – in this case the spoofed preachers themselves – to the heart of the matter, the apocalyptic fervour of the time. The parody, in other words, has a solid historical basis that is exploited through manipulation of the peripheral matters in order to emphasize a central point.

With the exception of the fourth figure in the scene, who really is an idiot, the reason these apocalyptic preachers seem so funny in the film is not only because of their gloom and doom predictions and physical appearance, but also because of their absurd context. Brian joins them, after all, after taking a *Star Wars*-inspired trip through space, and crash landing in the heart of Jerusalem, only to emerge unscathed. One could argue that this is a particularly appropriate context to introduce our eschatological doomsayers, as what is apocalyptic eschatology if not a kind of ancient science fiction involving greater heavenly powers, bizarre supra-human creatures from space, cosmic battles beyond the ken of mere mortals, fantastic flights of fancy concerning ultimate reality that cannot be experienced, sensed, or even comprehended by the normal person walking through the dusty streets of first-century Jerusalem?[2]

But if you would remove these street preachers from their absurd context in the film and place them instead in known contexts of antiquity, would their preaching really seem all that disjunctive with what we know of that world otherwise?

To answer the question, simply imagine someone from the Monty Python crew mouthing the words of John the Baptist: 'The axe is already laid at the root of the trees; every tree that does not produce fruit will be chopped down and thrown into the fire' (Luke 3.9; translation mine).

Or the words of Jesus the son of Ananias, from Josephus (*War* 6.5.3): 'Woe, woe to Jerusalem ... A voice from the east, a voice from the west, a voice from the four winds, a voice against Jerusalem and the holy house, a voice against the bridegrooms and the brides, and a voice against this whole people!' We should not forget that Josephus tells us that the Jewish rulers thought that this Jesus spoke 'with a kind of divine fury', and that Jesus 'did not leave off his melancholy ditty' until finally the Roman procurator Albinus 'took him to be a mad man'.[3]

Or imagine one of Monty Python's cast intoning the words from the Qumran War Scroll: 'During the remaining thirty-three years of the war the men of renown, those called of the Congregation, and all the heads of the congregation's clans shall choose for themselves men of war for all the lands of the nations (col. 2) ... The

2. A classic study of Jewish apocalypticism is John J. Collins, *The Apocalyptic Imagination: An Introduction to Jewish Apocalyptic Literature*, 2nd ed. (Grand Rapids: Eerdmans, 1998). For a thorough coverage of all relevant topics, see as well John J. Collins (ed.), *Encyclopedia of Apocalypticism*, vol. 1, *The Origins of Apocalypticism in Judaism and Christianity* (London: Bloomsbury Academic, 2000).

3. Translation of William Whiston, *The Works of Josephus*, vol. 1 (Grand Rapids: Baker Book House, 1979).

first division shall heave into the enemy battle line seven battle darts. On the blade of the first dart they shall write, "Flash of a spear for the strength of God". On the second weapon they shall write, "Missiles of blood to fell the slain by the wrath of God" and so on (col 6) . . '[4]

Any of these apocalyptic preachings from roughly the time of Jesus could easily be parodied. To parody them is not necessarily to mock them. It is to concentrate on a key topic by caricaturing the peripherals. The key topic of all these declarations – those of Monty Python's street preachers, of John the Baptist, of Jesus son of Ananias, of the War Scroll, and of Jesus of Nazareth – the key topic is that the end of the current order of things is imminent, disaster is soon to strike, God is soon to intervene, and people need to repent in order to be ready.

Brian as an Eyewitness to the Life of Jesus

One of the most brilliant ways parody works in the *Life of Brian* is by highlighting the complete implausibility of the biblical narratives, or at least the implausibility of widespread and common understandings of the historicity of the events described in the biblical narratives. For some reason, avid Bible readers – at least in my part of the world, the American South – rarely ask commonsensical questions about whether a narrative in scripture actually makes *any* sense if taken literally. The *Life of Brian* manages to ask these questions by parodying the literal sense.

This happens right off the bat in the opening scene, Brian's infancy narrative. The cinematography and music, in case you have never noticed, is not simply a riff on the biblical epics of Hollywood in general; it is a hilarious and virtually plagiaristic replay of the infancy narrative of *Ben-Hur*, and the arrival of the wise men to worship the child Jesus.

Neither biblical account of Jesus' infancy – the one in Matthew or the one in Luke – can be taken as a description of anything like historical reality. One of the many problems with Matthew, on which Brian's infancy is based, involves that implausible star that allegedly leads the wise men to the baby Jesus by stopping over the very house he was in. In order to illustrate the problem, I tell my students to go outside on a clear evening, look up in the sky, and figure out which star is standing over their own house. In Brian's opening parodic scene, the point is made much more convincingly, as the Three Wise Men start out in the wrong house to worship the wrong Capricorn with gold, frankincense, and a balm.

Nowhere are the logistics of the biblical narrative lampooned more famously than in arguably the best known line of the movie, 'Blessed are the cheesemakers'. I take this parody of the Sermon on the Mount to be making a not-so-serious but

4. Translation of Michael Wise, Martin Abegg and Edward Cook, *The Dead Sea Scrolls: A New Translation* (San Francisco: HarperSanFrancisco, 1996).

important point about the implausibility that eyewitnesses could guarantee the historical accuracy of the Gospel narratives.

For a very long time now we have heard a lot from scholars who have wanted to emphasize the existence of eyewitnesses and their value as guarantors of the surviving traditions about Jesus.[5] This perspective is highly problematic, on many levels. The Gospels themselves are not written by eyewitnesses, and don't claim to be written by eyewitnesses. Many of the accounts could not have derived from eyewitnesses: surely if anyone at all other than Pilate and Jesus was present at the so-called trial, they would not have preserved a verbatim transcription for posterity. And after those tragic events, neither Pilate nor Biggus Dickus would have been available for interviews by Christian reporters.

But even if eyewitnesses *were* behind the accounts – for which, in most instances, there is precisely zero evidence – that would not provide some kind of guarantee of historical accuracy. Eyewitnesses are never in the rest of our lives taken to be repositories of historically accurate accounts of the past. If they were, we would not need to have any kind of legal system. If someone saw a crime, we could simply ask them what happened, they would tell us, and we would sentence the culprit accordingly.

The reality is that eye- and earwitnesses cannot be counted on to have perceived an event accurately, to have remembered it accurately, or to have recalled it accurately. These are the stages of memory, for all of us – all of us today and all of those present, at whatever distance, at the Sermon on the Mount (even if Jesus did delivered some such sermon): we experience something, we encode the experience on our memories, we store the memory, and we retrieve the memory. Cognitive scientists have long recognized that things can go very wrong indeed at every one of these stages – and do go wrong, with alarming regularity. Why do so few of the proponents of the eyewitness veracity of our Gospel accounts not read what real experts have told us about eyewitness testimony? Haven't they learned that it is very hard indeed to know whether it is the Greek or the meek who is blessed, even if you ask someone who was there at the time who heard something from a distance?

In the English-speaking world, the leading expert on eyewitness testimony is Elizabeth Loftus, who has studied the phenomenon for both legal and clinical-psychological contexts for well over twenty-five years. In her many publications she is clear and emphatic. Memory is extremely faulty; it not only degenerates with time – which is significant, of course, given the extended time gap between the life of Jesus and the earliest surviving Gospels – it is regularly and consistently subject to distortion. Loftus has demonstrated repeatedly that people – all of us – formulate false memories, remembering clearly things in our past that in fact never happened. It is possible by suggestion to implant false memories; and if one person talks to another about an event, that can shape how the event is remembered – even shifting how the eyewitness herself explicitly recalls it. If enough people tell you

5. For the fullest study, see Richard Bauckham, *Jesus and the Eyewitnesses: The Gospels as Eyewitness Testimony* (Grand Rapids: Eerdmans, 2006).

that what Jesus really said was 'Blessed are the cheesemakers', that is, in fact, how you yourself may well remember it, vividly, even if you were there and distinctly remembered him saying something else, instead, about tea-makers.[6]

Daniel Schachter of Harvard University indicates that about 75,000 criminal cases a year in the United States are decided on the basis of eyewitness testimony. Now that DNA evidence has become available, a number of verdicts have been overturned. This had happened in forty cases in years leading up to the time of his writing in 2001. When DNA decisively revealed the innocence of an alleged criminal, it turned out that in 90 per cent of those cases, the person had been convicted because of eyewitness testimony.[7]

The problem is not simply with face recognition, but with spectacular events, such as, say, walking on the water or making juniper bushes appear in the wilderness, or even everyday spectacular events. There was a horrible disaster in the Netherlands in 1992, when a plane crashed into an apartment building. Ten months later researchers asked a group of people whether they saw the television film of the moment that the crash occurred. 66 per cent of those surveyed said 'Yes'. The problem is that there never was a film of the event.[8]

Even events that we *personally* experience can be misremembered, either because we do not store them in memory accurately or are unable to retrieve them accurately. This is not new knowledge. It has been available for over a century. It is a mystery why this should be obvious to the Monty Python crew but not to New Testament scholars. In 1902, in Berlin, a criminologist named von Liszt staged a dramatic event in his large classroom, which involved two students who had been primed to engage in a shouting match that would lead one of them to pull a revolver and shoot at the other. All the other students in the lecture hall watched, aghast. But they then learned it was an experiment. Some of the students were asked to write up a report of what had just happened; the rest of the students were asked to do the same thing at a later date. The *most* accurate reports were mistaken in 26 per cent of their recollections; some reports were mistaken in 80 per cent of their recollections. And strikingly, the most emotionally charged moments of the staged events were the ones that were remembered most poorly.[9]

The New Testament reports about the sayings, deeds and experiences of Jesus are not the reports of eyewitnesses who wrote down what they had seen and heard the next day. They were written down by authors between forty and sixty-five years later, authors who had not been there themselves, and in most instances did not know anyone who had been there, or anyone who knew anyone who had been there. But even if they were written by someone who had been there, who produced

---

6. Among her many books and articles, see, for example, Elizabeth F. Loftus, *Eyewitness Testimony*, 2nd ed. (Cambridge: Harvard University Press, 1996).

7. See Daniel L. Schacter, *The Seven Sins of Memory: How the Mind Forgets and Remembers* (Boston: Houghton Mifflin, 2001).

8. Schacter, *Seven Sins*, p. 112.

9. See Loftus, *Eyewitness Testimony*, pp. 20–1.

a report twenty minutes later, we *still* may have ended up with eschatological blessings for the cheesemakers and the Greeks.

Brian and the Realities of Crucifixion

One of the most significant parodies of the *Life of Brian* involves his crucifixion, but here I am not principally interested in always looking on the bright side of life or, in fact, any episode explicitly covered in the movie, either for Jesus or for Brian. I am instead interested in the question of whether a Jew crucified outside the walls of Jerusalem would have been given a decent burial.

There is a prescient but fleeting moment early in the movie, right after the famous stoning scene, when Brian and his mother are walking along outside the walls of Jerusalem. As they are shown, in the long shot, to be talking along the path, in the near foreground are crosses on which are the skeletal remains of victims of crucifixion, still hanging on their crosses, obviously long after their death, as they have been left to deteriorate in full public view. I don't know how Terry Jones and his colleagues knew that this in fact was the practice of the Romans, since it does not seem to be known widely among scholars of the New Testament, but it was indeed the norm, as attested in numerous ancient sources. The point of crucifixion was to torture and humiliate a person as fully as possible, and to show any bystanders what happens to someone who is a troublemaker in the face of Roman power. Part of the humiliation and degradation was that the body was left on the cross after death, to be subject to the elements, the ravages of time and scavenging birds and animals.[10]

Dom Crossan may have gone too far in positively asserting that Jesus' body was eaten by dogs, but the reality is that the surviving references to the corpses of crucified criminals do in fact indicate that they were normally left to decompose and feed the scavengers.[11] The Roman author Horace speaks about the carrion crows who feed off of victims; the Roman satirist Juvenal speaks of the vulture who takes off carrion for its young; that Sigmund Freud of antiquity, Artemidorus, writes in his dream book of crucified men serving to sustain many birds; the otherwise hilarious Satyricon of Petronius predicates an entire scene on the widely known practice of leaving the corpse on the cross for days.[12]

The historical question is not whether this was the common practice. It certainly was that. The question is whether an exception was made in the case of Jesus himself. In the Gospels, of course, Jesus *is* an exception. We are not told about the post-mortem fate of the two *lestai* crucified with him, but it is hard to imagine, historically, why an exception would be made in his case but not the others; Pilate

10. See the fuller discussion in Bart D. Ehrman, *How Jesus Became God: The Exaltation of a Jewish Preacher from Galilee* (San Francisco: HarperOne, 2014), pp. 151–79.

11. John Dominic Crossan, 'The Dogs Beneath the Cross', chap. 6 in *Jesus: A Revolutionary Biography* (San Francisco: HarperOne, 1994).

12. References and additional discussion in Ehrman, *How Jesus Became God*, pp. 160–1.

certainly would not have been moved by reverence to allow the Son of God to be given a decent burial, even if Christians have always thought that the Son of God must have been treated differently from everyone else.

In any event, in our accounts, Joseph of Arimathea, a member of the Sanhedrin – that is, one of those who called for Jesus' destruction the night before – takes it upon himself to request his body, and Pilate without a single hesitation cedes to the request (thus Mark 15.42–46).

Could there have been an exception made for Jesus? We have historical record of only *one* kind of exception being made for the Roman policy of humiliating a criminal by disallowing a decent burial and leaving their bodies as a public spectacle to show what happens to those who cross the Roman authorities. It comes in the writings of Philo. Philo indicates that in Alexandria, Egypt, on the birthday of an emperor, and in order to honour the emperor, a local ruler would occasionally allow crucified victims to be given over to their family members for decent burial.[13]

Some conservative Christian scholars have pointed to this passage in order to argue that since exceptions could be made, Jesus could have been an exception. But in my judgment that is completely misreading Philo's account. The *only* reason an exception was made, for Philo, was to honour the emperor's birthday. And then it was an exception made only in certain cases – one would assume that it involved victims related to someone who was highly connected – and it entailed the body being given to family members. There is nothing to suggest that Jesus was executed on the date of an emperor's birthday; he was not well-connected, and his body was not given to his family members. So what relevance does the Philo passage have for the account in the Gospels? So far as I can tell, almost precisely none.

And so more commonly it is argued by Christian apologists that an exception was made not just in the case of Jesus, but for Jews more broadly. And why is that? Because in the Torah it is decreed that a corpse is not to be left unburied after sundown. This was Jewish law. And since it was Jewish law, it must have been practiced. And since it was practiced, Romans must have taken Jews off their crosses and allowed them to have decent burials.[14]

That's the argument that is sometimes made, but in my opinion, it is more romantic than historical, and completely naïve about the brute force exercised by the Romans over their subjects in cowing them into submission and forcing them to realize through graphic realism in public places that the power of Rome was not to be opposed.

The reality is that Jews, who may have wanted to follow Jewish law, did not crucify Jesus. Romans crucified Jesus. Romans did not follow Jewish laws. And

---

13. See the fuller discussion in Ehrman, *How Jesus Became God*, pp. 158–60.

14. See Craig A. Evans, 'Getting the Burial Traditions and Evidences Right', in Michael Bird (ed.), *How God Became Jesus: The Real Origins of Belief in Jesus' Divine Nature* (Grand Rapids: Zondervan, 2014), pp. 71–93; for a lengthy response to Evans, see www.Ehrmanblog. org, posts dating from 1–31 July 2014.

when it came to *sedition* Romans did not have any reason or inclination to rule their subjects in a way that would be inoffensive to local sensibilities, religious or otherwise.

Once more, a parody in the *Life of Brian* highlights the historical reality so well – much better than the conservative apologists intent on vindicating the Gospel accounts of Jesus' decent burial. The scene comes as 'Big Nose' is being crucified and yells at the Roman centurion responsible for the proceeding. The centurion replies by berating him as a Jew. Big Nose responds that he is not a Jew but a Samaritan. Others hanging on their crosses then raise a loud protest: they were to be crucified in a Jewish section, not along with the lowly Samaritans. The centurion caves into their wishes: anyone who does not want to crucified here is to raise his right hand. When no one does so – their hands, of course, are nailed tightly to their crossbeams – the crucifixions continue.

In this case a Jewish sensitivity is invented for the purpose: the Jews do not want to be mingled with the Samaritans in their crucifixions, any more than they would want mixed cemeteries or mixed neighbourhoods. And how much do the Romans care? They don't care a bit. The local sensibilities are mocked and have precisely zero effect on the Romans who are doing what they want to do and are accustomed to doing. After Brian, the Samaritan Big Nose, and everyone else is crucified, they will be left on their crosses for some days, exposed to the elements, the scavengers, and the passing of time as a further humiliation and defilement and as a demonstration of Roman power. Eventually whatever remains of their bodies will be taken from their crosses and tossed into a common grave. To that extent, of course, they will be buried, just as Jesus himself in some sense must have been buried. But they would not be allowed decent burial, let alone immediately upon death.

That an exception would not have been made in the case of Jesus is further supported by what we know about the character of Pontius Pilate, the prefect of Judaea who ordered his crucifixion. Christian readers throughout much of history have seen Pilate in a much milder light than is justified by the historical record. If all one knows is the New Testament Gospels, which increasingly exonerate Pilate over time, or the later Christian legends where Pilate converts to the Christian faith and in some regions comes to be canonized as a Christian saint, the historical Pilate could not have been such a bad fellow. And so it makes sense that he would violate Roman practices of crucifixion, especially in the case of Jesus, for whom he must have harboured a soft spot in his heart.[15]

But, of course, this portrayal of Pilate is completely at odds with what we find in the rest of the written record, whether we read in Luke's Gospel of his mingling of the blood of the Galileans with their sacrifices (Luke 13.1), or in Josephus of his complete insensitivity to Jewish laws and practices, for example in the incident of the standards at the beginning of his reign – when he orders the protesting Jews to accept the images of Caesar in the holy city or be slaughtered; or in the incident of

---

15. For the progressive exoneration of Pilate through the Gospels, see Helen Bond, *Pontius Pilate in History and Interpretation* (Cambridge: Cambridge University Press, 2004).

the riots caused by the building of the Jerusalem aqueduct later – when he commissioned his thugs to quell the crowds by beating them into submission (Josephus, *Antiquities* 18.3.1–2). And so Philo speaks of Pilate's 'venality, his violence, his thefts, his assaults, his abusive behaviour, his frequent executions of untried prisoners, and his endless savage ferocity' (*Embassy to Gaius* 302).

Pilate was not an exception to the brutal expression of Roman power in the face of possible opposition; he was the embodiment of it. As in the crucifixion scene in the *Life of Brian*, so too in reality: when it comes to allowing crucified victims a decent burial, there is little reason to think that Romans would make an exception to their brutal suppression of opposition if someone would just ask nicely.

I conclude with a brief comment on the value of parody as a historical method. Parody is a kind of humorous but insightful caricature. Everyone enjoys the humour of parody, but the insights that it provides should not be overlooked or undervalued. By caricaturing its topic, parody is able to reveal aspects of reality that are otherwise far too easy to miss.

Parody is not the same as mockery, even humorous mockery. Parodic humour is witty, sharp, perceptive, and, most important, generative of ideas. The *Life of Brian* is parody at its best – creative, thoughtful, thought-provoking, and hilarious enough even to make some fundamentalists laugh and, as a result, reflect, at least a bit, on their own tradition. Sometimes shocked discomfiture can be a very good thing indeed.

Chapter 12

'ARE YOU A VIRGIN?' BIBLICAL EXEGESIS AND THE INVENTION OF TRADITION

Paula Fredriksen

Using the Septuagint as a quarry for episodes in the life of the historical Jesus is a little like mining Molière for information on the private life of Bill Clinton. There's the gap in time; there's the gap in languages; there's the gap in subject matter – in the latter case perhaps less than in the former. Nonetheless, this is what the apostle Paul and our four canonical evangelists did, and *Brian* refracts some of their biblically enhanced efforts. I would like to consider here some of the implications, some of the effects, and some of the historical and theological consequences of our early writers' biblical bookishness.

I begin with a truism of historical Jesus research: Jesus' vernacular was Aramaic. Yet the earliest texts that we have from this movement, Paul's letters and the Gospels, are in Greek. This linguistic shift might give us a measure of the movement's rapid diffusion out of Jerusalem into the wider world of the western Diaspora. If Jesus died around 30 CE, if Paul's letters date to the mid-first century, and if Mark were written sometime shortly after the Temple's destruction in 70, then we can trace a trajectory not only linguistic – from Aramaic to Greek – but also geographical – from Judaea to Asia Minor to, possibly, Rome.[1]

Did this linguistic and geographical shift express, as well, an ethnic one, from a Jewish Jesus to a Gentile church? Here this early evidence pulls in two directions. At several places in his letters, mid-first century, Paul gives full-throated expression to his own Jewishness, in tropes that would have made Brian proud. At Philippians 3.6, for example, Paul declares:

'I'm a Kike! A Yid! A Heebie! A Hook-nose! I'm Kosher, Mum! I'm a Red Sea Pedestrian, and I'm proud of it!'

Oh, sorry: that's Brian. Here is Paul, in the RSV translation: '[I am] circumcised on the eighth day, of the people of Israel, of the tribe of Benjamin, a Hebrew born of Hebrews, as to the law a Pharisee, as to righteousness under the Law, blameless.' So too his apostolic competition. 'Are they Hebrews? So am I! Are they Israelites? So am I! Are they descendants of Abraham! So am I!' (2 Cor. 11.22). The apostolic muscle-mass of the movement, circa 50 CE, seems – or still seems – to be predominantly Jewish.

On the evidence of Paul's letters, however, the *hearers* of the new message seem to have been a mixed group of (at least some) Jews together with a majority of

---

1. The association of Mark's Gospel with Rome goes back to the second century CE, when some Christians began to associate its author with Peter: Mark served as Peter's *hermēneutēs* ('interpreter'), writing down the apostle's recollections before his martyrdom there under Nero (thus Papias *apud* Eusebius, *Historia Ecclesiastica* 3.39,14–16; cf. 1 Peter 5.13, where 'Babylon' codes for 'Rome'). More recently, S. G. F. Brandon has speculated about Titus' Roman triumph stimulating the evangelist's imagery, *Jesus and the Zealots* (Manchester: Manchester University Press, 1967), pp. 228–9.

non-Jews.[2] This demography might reflect in turn the mixed populations of Jews together with sympathetic pagans to be found within synagogue communities in the Diaspora.[3]

But the recipients of Paul's letters were pagans with a difference: they were 'ex-pagan' pagans. That is to say that, as a condition of their joining this new movement, these pagans had to repudiate the worship of their own gods and to make a commitment to the exclusive worship of Israel's god.[4] I assume that this deity was familiar to them even before their contact with the apostle. Paul's constant reference to Septuagintal terms and to biblical themes and personages inclines me to think that these pagans, well before any contact with the new messianic movement, would have frequented diaspora synagogues. 'Adam', 'Abraham', 'David', 'Jerusalem', 'Law', 'Messiah', not to mention Paul's regular evocation of *ho theos*, '*the* god', that is, the god of Israel – these terms must have meant something to them already, or Paul could not have used them so freely as the building-blocks of his particular message. Such familiarity as these people would have had with Jewish concepts, traditions and personages would most likely have come orally, from hearing Jewish writings read in Greek during community gatherings, aka 'the synagogue.'

What, then, did they hear? Which Jewish scriptures were read in community? Passages from the first five books of Moses, also known as 'the Law,' surely (cf. Acts 15.21), and passages from 'the prophets;' from the Writings, at least Psalms.[5] If we can infer anything from the frequency of Paul's own citations, as

2. The *ekklesia* in Thessalonica is pagan; ethnicity in the Corinthian community seems to have been mixed (unless the 'ones who are circumcised' are proselytes, 1 Cor. 7.18). Galatians attests to the mixed community in Antioch (2.11–14), though the communities addressed by the epistle are obviously not Jewish (since they were considering circumcision: Jewish men presumably would no longer have had the option; the same argument obtains for Philippians, cf. 3.2–3). The ethnic make-up of the Roman communities seems to have been mixed, though Paul addresses the letter specifically to the *ethnē* there, 1.5–6, though cf. 16 passim.

3. On the presence of non-Jews in diaspora synagogues, well attested in literary and in epigraphical evidence, see, e.g., Lee I. Levine, *The Ancient Synagogue* (New Haven: Yale University Press, 2000); Emil Schürer, *The History of the Jewish People in the Age of Jesus Christ*, ed. Geza Vermes, Fergus Millar, and Martin Goodman, 3 vols. in 4 (Edinburgh, T&T Clark, 1979–87), Vol. 3.1: pp. 1–176; specifically on how this ethnographic fact affected Paul's mission, Paula Fredriksen, 'Judaizing the Nations: The Ritual Demands of Paul's Gospel', *NTS* 56 (2010), pp. 232–52.

4. On the traditions regarding Gentiles turning to Israel's god in the final days, Paula Fredriksen, 'Judaism, the Circumcision of Gentiles, and Apocalyptic Hope: Another Look at Galatians 1 and 2', *JTS* 42 (1991), pp. 532–64; Terence L. Donaldson, *Judaism and the Gentiles: Jewish Patterns of Universalism (to 135 CE)* (Waco, TX: Baylor University Press, 2007). That Paul (and other apostles to Gentiles) made this demand of their pagan hearers gives us the measure of the early Jesus movement's apocalyptic timeframe, when Gentiles-in-Christ were to act as 'eschatological' Gentiles.

5. On synagogues as a type of 'ethnic reading house', Francis M. Young, *Biblical Exegesis and the Formation of Christian Culture* (Cambridge: Cambridge University Press, 1997), p. 13.

well as from a similar distribution of texts that survive from the first-century Judaean library at Qumran, Isaiah in particular would have loomed large.[6] Both Isaiah and Psalms would go on to have a long future in later, specifically Christian scriptures, each source quarried for details to fill in particularly the edges of Jesus' 'biography', the evangelical birth narratives to the one side, and their death narratives – the passion and resurrection stories – to the other. However, I would like to consider these texts from a slightly different angle: How does the LXX in general, and Isaiah in particular, shape our very *earliest* traditions about Jesus' status specifically as 'Messiah'?

We turn again to Paul. As is well known, Paul frequently refers to Jesus as 'Christ', using 'Christos' by itself to indicate Jesus some 150 times in his undisputed letters. As Matthew Novenson has lately demonstrated, the term works not simply as a 'name', as earlier generations of scholars have argued; instead, 'Christ' serves specifically as an honorific, 'a word that can function as a stand-in for a personal name but part of whose function is to retain its supernominal associations'.[7] In other words, 'Christ' functions similarly to 'Your honour', 'Her Highness', and so on.

As will the later evangelists, Paul backlights the few details he has of Jesus' biography with scripture. Occasionally he's only very vague, waving his hand toward the Bible, as at 1 Corinthians 15.3–4: 'Christ died for our sins according to the scriptures; he was buried and was raised on the third day according to the scriptures' and so on. My question is: Why use this term, '*christos*', for Jesus at all? How did the title, and the concept, *initially* attach to him? Paul clearly inherited the designation once he was oriented within the *paradosis* of the new movement; and we can only assume that he explained its appropriateness, and its various meanings, when establishing his own communities. But in his seven undisputed letters, we nonetheless get precious little explanation.[8]

One partial exception comes in Paul's final epistle to the Romans. There, Paul speaks of Jesus specifically as the *Davidic* Messiah, once at the letter's opening and once just toward its close. Jesus, says Paul to the Gentile community in Rome, was 'of the seed of David according to the flesh' (1.3). And at his triumphant eschatological return, Paul concludes, Jesus will appear as 'the shoot of Jesse ... who rises to rule the Gentiles; in him shall the Gentiles hope' (15.12, citing Isa. 11.10 LXX). Within this letter, Jesus' Davidic status functions as a kind of messianic

---

6. See especially J. Ross Wagner's careful study, *Heralds of the Good News: Isaiah and Paul in Concert in the Letter to the Romans* (Leiden: Brill, 2003), and his charts on pp. 342–3 and 349.

7. *Christ among the Messiahs: Christ Language in Paul and Messiah Language in Ancient Judaism* (New York: Oxford University Press, 2012), p. 138. I further think that Paul's use of *kurios* also appeals to this 'royal' aspect of *christos*, and so functions similarly: rulers and social superiors would be addressed as 'Lord,' and the Messiah is a kingly ruler – an association exploited by Mark 12.35–7.

8. This absence of explanation for a long time fuelled the scholarly position that 'Christ' for Paul functioned merely as a 'name', thus without specific messianic content: see Novenson's review (and demolition) of this position in *Christ*, pp. 12–33 and 64–93.

inclusio, binding the epistle's opening lines in chapter 1 to its finale in chapter 15. In short, Paul explicitly links Jesus' Davidic status – a function of fleshly, thus family lineage – to a specifically *post-crucifixion* phenomenon, the *Gentile* mission. This in turn raises the question: To what degree is this ascription of messianic status to Jesus of Nazareth itself a post-crucifixion phenomenon?[9]

Paul's linkage in Romans between a final, Davidic Messiah (Rom. 1), the turning of the nations to Israel's god (Rom. 15), and Jesus' impending *parousia* gives us a fairly precise measure of Paul's own apocalyptic convictions, mid-century; and we'll look at these shortly. But Paul's declaration points us *away* from two things that we know (or at least that I think that we know) about the historical Jesus of Nazareth, some twenty-five to thirty years before Paul composed this letter. These are, first, that Jesus himself seems *not* to have claimed, in any straightforward way, to be 'the' Messiah, Davidic or otherwise; and, second, that Jesus himself did *not* take his message to Gentiles. Let me briefly discuss these assertions in turn.

Did Jesus himself ever claim to be the 'Messiah'? (Did Brian? His mum was not impressed.)

'He's not the Messiah. He's a very naughty boy!'

Each of the evangelists works to portray Jesus in this way, but the vigorous differences in their respective presentations seem to me to undermine their overall efforts. If the historical Jesus had indeed ever claimed to be Messiah, messianic traditions about him should have been more unified, more uniform, or more straightforward: instead, what we find is creative variety. So too with the very bulk

---

9. On this question, see especially Nils Alstrup Dahl's classic essay, 'The Crucified Messiah,' in id. *Jesus the Christ. The Historical Origins of Christological Doctrine* (edited by Donald H. Juel; Minneapolis: Fortress, 1991; orig. pub. 1960), pp. 27–48.

and the vast variety of *scholarly* arguments affirming that Jesus claimed messianic status for himself. (Since the publication of Ed Sanders' *Jesus and Judaism* in 1985, the so-called scene at the Temple is often pressed into service on and at this point, arguments often asserting that flipping over Temple tables at least implicitly equates to or announces a messianic claim.[10]) In brief, I think, not only would Gospel traditions about Jesus' proclaiming himself Messiah during his mission have been less various and ambivalent,[11] but also scholarly wit and creativity perforce less exercised, had Jesus himself during his lifetime proclaimed his own messianic identity.

Yet *someone* during Jesus' lifetime must have thought that he had made such a claim, or Jesus would not have died in the way that he did. The most unambiguously 'messianic' aspect of Jesus' life, in brief, is his death, crucified by Rome as 'King of the Jews'. In the actual historical context of that particular Passover, Roman concerns about sedition must have shaped events.

Still, the Gospels' narrative trajectories leading up *to* that final event fail by and large to explain it. Jesus' teachings, his healings and exorcisms, his arguments about Jewish tradition with his contemporary co–religionists, even his announcing the impending arrival of God's kingdom: No amount of intra-Jewish religious wrangling can adequately explain Jesus' very politically charged, Roman death. And further (as I have argued elsewhere), the solitary nature Jesus' death, Rome's failure or lack of interest in inflicting similar treatment on Jesus' closest followers, complicates our picture in interesting ways. Though Jesus was executed as a political insurrectionist, none of his close followers was. How worried about sedition, then, could Pilate actually have been?[12]

Jesus' public messianic profile in his own lifetime is thus, at best, obscure. How then, whether before or very shortly after his death, did Jesus end up proclaimed not only as Messiah, but specifically as David's descendant? Paul in Romans asserts Jesus' Davidic lineage, as we have seen; but he makes no argument for it. Like Mark and like John, Paul seems unaware of the sort of birth stories that we find in

10. For a review of this position, which represents a surprising consensus, see Paula Fredriksen, 'What You See is What You Get: Context and Content in Current Research on the Historical Jesus,' *Theology Today* 52 (1995), pp. 75-97, surveying the work of Richard Horsley, Dominic Crossan, Marcus Borg, N. T. Wright, and E. P. Sanders. John P. Meier hints that his fifth and final volume of *A Marginal Jew* will also make this association between the scene at the Temple and an [at least implicit] messianic claim on Jesus' part: see, e.g., *A Marginal Jew* 3 (New York: Anchor/Yale University Press, 2001), p. 618; see too, most recently, Dale Allison, *Constructing Jesus* (London: Baker Academic, 2010), pp. 236–8. For the argument that Jesus' overturning the Temple court's tables is a post-destruction story, Paula Fredriksen, *Jesus of Nazareth, King of the Jews* (New York: Random House, 1999), pp. 225–34.

11. For a review of the variety of these traditions, see Paula Fredriksen, *From Jesus to Christ. The Origins of the New Testament Images of Jesus* (New Haven: Yale University Press, 2000).

12. Fredriksen, *Jesus of Nazareth*, p. 9 and passim; cf. Justin Meggitt, 'The Madness of King Jesus', *JSNT* 29.4 (2007), pp. 379–413, who argues that Jesus' solitary death is best explained on the theory that Pilate thought that Jesus was insane.

Matthew and in Luke. Those stories – each in its own way – manage to square the circle of having someone known to have come from Nazareth being born in the correct Davidic village of Bethlehem.[13] By contrast, Mark and John seem at pains to insist on Jesus' *independence* from Davidic tradition. Undomesticated by a preceding Bethlehem birth narrative, Mark 12.35–37 even seems testily *anti*-Davidic. Mark's mysterious Son of Man truly is the Messiah, we have learned from Peter's confession at Caesarea Philippi (8.30), and we will learn again from the high priest, and from Jesus himself, in the Markan trial scene (14.61–62).[14] But in the days before Passover, wittily besting all comers in the Temple precincts, Mark's Jesus seems to disavow any necessary connection between being the Messiah and having Davidic lineage: 'How can the scribes say that the Christ is the son of David?' On the contrary, this passage continues: David himself acknowledges the Messiah as his superior.

John the Evangelist's outsized superhero seems even more independent of Davidic legitimation. John's Jesus hails not from the little town of Bethlehem, but from Above, in the Beginning, with God the Father (John 1.1–4). To think of Jesus as descended from David according to the flesh, implies the fourth evangelist, is to think too small. His characters 'know' that Jesus is from the North, and when some identify Jesus as Christ, others ask, 'Is the Christ to come from Galilee? Has not the scripture said that the Christ is descended from David, and comes from Bethlehem, the village where David was?' (7.41–42). It's a question that the evangelist never again raises: Christologically, he's frying much bigger fish.[15]

Matthew, by contrast, creates a smoother messianic story. As he weaves his opening narrative, Matthew cites scripture ostentatiously, leaving his reader in no doubt as to the authority of his sources, and of the long biblical prequel to his hero's life. Time and again Matthew demonstrates how scripture had foretold Jesus' coming by constructing narrative episodes from biblical testimonies. 'All this took place in order to fulfil what the Lord had spoken by the prophet . . .' Sometimes

---

13. Thus in Matthew, Joseph and Mary both live in Bethlehem; because of Herod's impending massacre of the innocents, they then flee with baby Jesus to Egypt; then, after Herod's death, they return but settle in Nazareth: we have reviewed these details above. Luke, by contrast, situates Mary and Joseph in the Galilee in Nazareth; they travel to Bethlehem on account of a Roman census – just in time for the birth – and then go back home to Nazareth.

14. Neither 'messianic confession' is prepared for in Mark's narrative: Jesus says nothing about his status as Messiah throughout, until he concurs with the high priest's (spontaneous?) identification, 14.62. Scholars have labelled this stylistic reticence of Mark's the 'Messianic Secret'.

15. 'Messiah' see-saws back and forth with 'prophet' as designations for Jesus in the Gospel of John. 'He cannot be the Messiah, can he?' asks the Samaritan woman (John 4.29 NRSV). 'Can it be that the authorities really know that this is the Messiah?' asks a crowd in Jerusalem (John 7.26). Later, some in the crowd pronounce, 'This really is the Prophet', while others claim, 'This is the Messiah' (John 7.40–1). The evangelist prefers the much more elevated title of 'divine Son'.

Matthew uses a non-messianic biblical passage to create an episode in Jesus' life, while the evangelical episode in turn transforms the ancient LXX passage, such as the pregnant 'virgin' of Greek Isaiah 7.14, into a messianic prophecy.[16] Mandy would have understood:

'Are you a virgin?'

'I beg your pardon?'

'Well, if it's not a personal question, are you a virgin?'

'If it's not a personal question'?! How much more personal can you get? Now, piss off!'

We see this sort of double-feedback loop in Matthew's invention of Jesus' childhood 'flight to Egypt' (2.13–15). This is a small piece of the much larger Rube Goldberg of Matthew's nativity story. In Matthew, Joseph and Mary's hometown is Bethlehem; and Matthew opens his book by tracing Jesus' genealogy from Abraham through David to Joseph, himself a 'son of David' (1.18). An angel then effectively vitiates Matthew's genealogical work by letting Joseph know that Mary will give birth even though she is a *parthenos,* a 'virgin', the LXX's rendering of the Hebrew *almah* at Isaiah 7.14. (If Mary's a virgin, then it makes no difference whom Joseph is related to.)

No matter. A bigger problem looms: how will Matthew get his hero from Bethlehem – the messianically correct birthplace – to Nazareth, whence Jesus was known to have come? An angel moves the plot along, warning Joseph of Herod's

16. M. David Litwa explores the ways in which the claim of a god's a 'special' birth is a piece of a common ancient Mediterranean vernacular of deification in *Iesus Deus: The Early Christian Depiction of Jesus as a Mediterranean God* (Minneapolis: Fortress, 2014), pp. 37–67.

plan to slaughter Bethlehem's male children. Off goes the holy family to Egypt. They move back north, this time to Nazareth, only once Herod is safely dead. Their return enables Matthew to mobilize Hosea 11.1, 'Out of Egypt I have called my son'. The 'son' in question, in the original context of Hosea, refers to the people of Israel, escaping Egypt in the Exodus: for Matthew, the 'son' is Jesus. So similarly with Isaiah 7.14: the 'son' in the original Hebrew context, the child of a 'young girl', provides an odd way for the prophet to measure time for King Ahaz. For Matthew, reading Greek, the son of a 'virgin' serves as a way to frame Jesus miraculous birth as *emmanu-el*, 'God with us'. Neither scriptural passage, Hosea or Isaiah, refers to a Messiah. Each becomes a messianic prophecy only through the narrative alchemy of Matthew's birth story.

Paul knows none of this. His *christos* is 'born of woman' (*ek gunaikos*, Gal. 4.4), not of a virgin. And as with the figure in John's Gospel, so too with Paul's: the Pauline 'Christ Jesus' originates from a neighbourhood much more elevated than Bethlehem. Paul's Jesus seems to originate 'up there', being originally 'in the form of [a] god' (no article: *morphos theou*, not *morphos tou theou*)[17] but not grasping at 'equivalence with [a] god' (again, no article). This being then takes on 'the form of a slave', 'the likeness of men' (Phil. 2.5–7), and he is exalted by God (*ho theos*) on account of his humble and obedient crucifixion. Jesus seems here to function as a type of divine mediator. It's a high status, but it does not qualify him in any particular way to be considered a Davidic Messiah. Why then, and how, did Paul make this identification?

Let's go back to the Davidic framing of Romans chapters 1 and 15. Romans 1.3–4 seems to draw a distinction between Jesus as the Davidic Messiah and Jesus as divine Son. The RSV reads:

> Paul, a servant of Jesus Christ, called to be an apostle, set apart for the Gospel of God which he promised beforehand through his prophets in the holy scriptures, the Gospel concerning his Son, who was descended from David according to the flesh, and designated Son of God in power according to the Spirit of holiness by his resurrection from the dead.

Jesus is 'Messiah' is by fleshly descent, but declared or made known as 'divine son' by virtue of his resurrection.[18]

I think that there are several problems with this translation and interpretation. One is that 'son of God' is also a messianic designation, and indicates a human being, albeit a royal human being: 2 Samuel 7, and Psalm 2, are two prime scriptural attestations of this idea. But the other problem is the way to read Paul's statement, *ex anastaseōs nekrōn*, which will come into Latin as *ex resurrectione mortuorum*. The RSV translation, focused as it is on Jesus' own resurrection, seems refracted through the prism of much later church councils.

17. The Greek is miserable to translate, because English can't mark the distinction that the absence of the article gives the Greek. The RSV's capitalization, 'in the form of God', is a post-Nicene piety. In a moment of inspired desperation, Larry Hurtado, in conversation, has suggested 'Jesus' god-ishness' as a plausible rendering. I thank him for his suggestion.

18. This idea fuels the argument in Bart Ehrman's most recent book, *How Jesus Became God* (New York: HarperOne, 2014), see especially pp. 211–30.

The problem of course, is our missing preposition: 'From the dead' requires an *ek* before *nekrōn*; and indeed, a preposition is what we find in those other New Testament passages when an individual resurrection is referred to.[19] Thus Paul's Greek here does not say, 'by [Jesus'] resurrection *from* the dead' but rather 'by *the* resurrection *of* the dead'. Paul evidently has the communal, End-time event is in view – the meaning that Augustine caught in his commentary on Romans, translating this sentence as 'designated Son of God in power ... by the resurrection of *the* dead'.[20] In other words, Romans 1.4 aligns not so much with (for example) Philippians 2 and other passages about divine exaltation; rather, it coheres with (for example) 1 Thessalonians 4 and 1 Corinthians 15 when, at Jesus' second coming, the dead will rise. It is Jesus' role in effecting the End-time *general* resurrection that will announce publicly his powerful status as God's son, that is, as the (Davidic) Messiah.[21]

Paul ties this eschatological event in with another: the End-time turning of the nations to the god of Israel.[22] Here we see the second half of his Davidic messianic *inclusio* in Romans 15.9–12, the Gentiles' rejoicing with God's people, Israel. Paul weaves a cento from Psalms, Deuteronomy and Isaiah. It was precisely to achieve this

19. Thus, Matthew 14.2 gives *apo ton nekrōn*, referring to rumours of John the Baptist's resurrection from the dead; cf. the parallel at Mark 6.14, *ek nekrōn*. When Paul speaks of his own hope of being raised 'from the dead', he also uses *ek nekrōn*, Phil. 3.11. Acts 17.32 and Hebrews 6.2, on the other hand, when referring to the general resurrection, use *anastasis nekrōn*, 'resurrection of dead [persons]' – exactly the same construction that Paul uses here at Romans 1.4.

20. 'And this same one, who 'according to the flesh was born of the seed of David', Paul names 'predestined Son of God in power'; not according to the flesh, but 'according to the Spirit'; and not just any spirit, but 'the Spirit of sanctification by the resurrection of the dead'. For in the [general] resurrection appears the power of Christ who died, so that it might be said, 'predestined in power according to the Spirit of sanctification by the resurrection of the dead' (Rom. 1.4)', *epistolae ad Romanos inchoata expositio* 5.1–2.

21. Jesus already is the divine son (which is the force of the aorist participle *horisthentos*, 'designated,' Latin *praedestinatus*); but he will be manifest as such in power only at his Parousia, which will entail this general resurrection; cf. 1 Thess. 4.16 and 1 Cor. 15.23.

22. Traditions about the fate of Gentiles at the End-time vary, some exclusive (the nations will be destroyed, or will lick the dust at Israel's feet, or be the objects of God's wrath) and some inclusive, e.g., the nations will stream to Jerusalem and worship together with Israel (Isa. 2.2–4//Mic. 4); they will together eat on the Temple mount the feast that God will prepare (Isa. 25.6); Gentiles will accompany Jews at the Ingathering (Zech. 8.23); they will themselves carry exiles back to Jerusalem (Ps. Sol. 7.31–41). At the End, these Gentiles will bury their idols and direct their sight to uprightness (1 Enoch 91.14); many nations will come from afar to the name of the Lord God, bearing gifts (Tobit 13.11); after the Temple is rebuilt, all the nations will turn in fear to the Lord, and bury their idols (Tobit 14.5–6); at the coming of the Great King, the nations will bend knee to God (Sib. Or. 3.616), they will go to the Temple and renounce their idols (3.715–24), and they will come from every land bringing incense and gifts to the Temple of the great god (3.772). See further James M. Scott, *Paul and the Nations* (Tübingen: Mohr Siebeck, 1995), pp. 119–21 for texts from Qumran.

redemption, Paul says, that Christ came: 'For I tell you that Christ became a servant of the circumcision [that is, of the Jews] on account of God's truthfulness, to confirm the promises made to the patriarchs, and for the Gentiles to glorify God for his mercy' (15.8). For Paul, the success of the mission to the Gentiles, mid-century, indexes Jesus' status as God's son, the Davidic Messiah and 'shoot of Jesse' (Isa. 11.10).[23] The coming general resurrection will declare his messianic status as this son of God *in power* (1.4).

Whence this Pauline idea linking the Gentile mission to Jesus' messianic identity? *Not* from Jesus of Nazareth. According to the synoptic Gospels, Jesus spent most of his teaching time in the Jewish villages of the Galilee; according to John, Jesus taught mostly in Jerusalem. Non-Jews were most likely and most often rather thin on the ground in either location; and Jesus, like his mentor John the Baptist, seems to have concentrated on taking the message of God's impending kingdom mostly to fellow Jews. Matthew's Jesus even instructs his disciples *not* to speak to anyone else: 'Go nowhere among the Gentiles' (10.5). In all these Gospel stories, the Gentile mission is pushed off to the period *after* the crucifixion: for Luke, indeed, such a mission gets underway only half-way through volume 2, in the Acts of the Apostles. In Jesus' lifetime there was no 'Gentile mission' as such.

The information in Paul's letters that we have about the movement after Jesus' death confirms this impression: only once the mission that formed around Jesus' memory and message moved out from Jerusalem into mixed cities such as Caesarea, and into the network of synagogue communities in the Diaspora, did it begin to attract not only other Jews but also, and in numbers, interested pagans as well.[24] Surprised by its own successes, the early *ekklesia* seems to have incorporated these people as ex-pagan pagans: not required to convert to Judaism, they nonetheless had to stop worshipping idols and to commit to the sole worship of Israel's god. And by mid-century – as Galatians in particular evinces – its success among pagans was actually fracturing the movement. No one, faced with this evidently unanticipated situation, knew quite what to do.[25]

The arguments internal to the movement caused by its successes among Gentiles, its conflicting 'policy' decisions and its various social improvizations, in other words, make the same point that the Gospels articulate through their narratives: Jesus himself left no teachings on the matter. And yet, from what we can tell, the early post-crucifixion movement also readily accommodated Gentiles, incorporating these people into their communities, thus 'into' Christ. Why?

23. See Wagner, *Heralds*, pp. 219–305 (Rom. 11) and 307–40 (Rom. 15).

24. On the socially destabilizing consequences of this movement's spreading to Gentiles, and the ways that this destabilizing accounts both for Paul's experience as both persecutor and persecuted, see Paula Fredriksen, 'Paul, Practical Pluralism, and the Invention of Religious Persecution in Roman Antiquity', in Peter C. Phan and Jonathan Ray (eds), *Understanding Religious Pluralism: Perspectives from Religious Studies and Theology* (Eugene, OR: Wipf and Stock, 2014), pp. 87–113.

25. Paula Fredriksen, *Augustine and the Jews* (New Haven: Yale University Press, 2010), pp. 20–40, reviews this moment of the movement within the context of the complex religious ecosystem of Graeco-Roman cities.

Here we must consider the larger context of the Jesus movement: Jewish restoration theology. Apocalyptic eschatology is a big and baggy tradition, expressing any number of expectations, predictions and themes: Celestial and terrestrial catastrophes – earthquakes, plagues, falling stars, darkness at noon. A final battle between Good and Evil, the forces of Good led by God himself, or perhaps by a commanding angel, or perhaps by an anointed king. The punishment or destruction of the wicked, who will be the objects of divine wrath: foreign kings, fornicating idol worshippers and apostate Jews, especially those whose views differ from those of the prophetic writer's. The resurrection of the dead, a final judgment and the vindication of the righteous: it's all coming soon. Exiles return to the Land, the tribes are gathered in; they convene at a new or renewed Temple, in Jerusalem. *When* will these things happen? At the approaching End of the Age. *How* can you know what time it is on God's clock? By attending to heavily symbolic, apocalyptic prophecies, thus decoding the signs of the times. The Pythons understood this well:

'For the demon shall bear a nine-bladed sword. Nine-bladed! Not two or five or seven, but nine, which he will wield on all wretched sinners, sinners just like you, sir, there, and the horns shall be on the head, with which he will . . .'

What happens to non-Jews in these Jewish traditions about the Jewish god establishing his kingdom? It depends. Some prophecies are negative, condemning and exclusive: Gentiles are defeated by the forces of good; they are subject to Israel; they lick the dust at Israel's feet. But other prophecies are positive, affirming and inclusive. As an eschatological miracle, at the End of Days, the Gentile nations will destroy their idols, renounce the worship of their native gods, and join with Israel in God's kingdom.[26]

26. See above, n. 22.

Paul, just like his prime biblical source, the LXX's Isaiah, expresses both types of prophecies about Gentiles, the negative ones and the positive ones. In his letters, he warns his readers about the fast-approach Day of the Lord and the Coming Wrath (1 Cor. 1.81; 3.13; 2; 1 Cor. 5.5; 2 Cor. 1.14; Phil. 1.6, 10; 2.16; 1 Thess. 5.2; 2 Thess. 2.2) and also he speaks about the incorporation of Gentiles into the Kingdom – provided that they foreswear their gods (1 Thess. 1.9; Gal. 3.29). How many Gentiles? In some places, he says all of those Gentiles who listen to him. But in his final letter, Romans, he seems to think in terms of bigger numbers: when Christ returns to Zion in glory – an event that Paul expects to live to see – then the *pleroma* of the Gentiles, their 'fullness' or 'full number' will 'come in,' that is, will be saved (11.25).[27]

At that moment not only will these penitent pagans acknowledge Christ and the god whom he represents: so will the pagans' gods. These are the cosmic supernatural forces and personalities to be defeated by Christ at his second coming. A multiplicity of gods 'lower' than the god of Israel was native to ancient Jewish monotheism: they appear not infrequently in the Bible, often in Psalms.[28] 'The gods of the Gentiles are *daimonia*', lower gods, Paul instructs his Gentiles in Corinth, referring to Psalm 95.5 LXX (1 Cor. 10.20). These superhuman forces dwell in the upper air and in the astral spheres: they are *archai* and *exousiai* and *dunameis* (1 Cor. 15.24; cf. Rom. 8.38, and the heavenly knees of Phil. 2.10). The returning Christ will defeat them, in an apocalyptic battle located in what we would now call outer space – a detail nicely caught by the film:

27. On the ways that Paul's phrasing on the 'fullness of the nations and all Israel' recalls the Table of Nations of Genesis 10 and the number of the nations in Deuteronomy 32.8, see especially Scott, *Nations*, pp. 121–49.

28. On the normative polytheism of ancient 'monotheism', see Paula Fredriksen, 'Mandatory Retirement: Ideas in the Study of Christian Origins whose Time Has Come to Go', *Studies in Religion/Sciences Religieuses* 35 (2006), pp. 231–46.

Like their humans, these gods – whether above the earth or below the earth or upon the earth, says Paul in Philippians (2.10), will also at the End of Days acknowledge God and his Messiah.

Allow me to conclude by summing up, this time in historically chronological order, the various points that we have surveyed during our tour through the Jewish Bible, early Christian scriptures, and the invention of tradition. The historical Jesus of Nazareth, a wandering charismatic holy man and an apocalyptic prophet, did not immediately suggest or support traditional ideas of the expected, End-time Davidic Messiah. Presumably his immediate followers knew this. If Mark 12.35–37 preserves an authentic historical reminiscence, Jesus seems to have known this himself. Whether he accepted a messianic designation assigned by other contemporaries is unclear, and the Gospels – their stories of Jesus' crucifixion to one side – are themselves ambiguous. *Brian* well reflects the issue:

'Hail, Messiah!'

'I'm *not* the Messiah! Will you please listen?
I am not the Messiah, do you understand? Honestly!'

'Only the true Messiah denies his divinity!'

'What? Well, what sort of chance does that give me?!
All right, I *am* the Messiah!'

'He is! He is the Messiah!'

'Now fuck off!'

At some point before Jesus' arrest and execution, enough of the crowds in Jerusalem acclaimed Jesus the Messiah for Pilate to act swiftly to disabuse them of the idea. And at some point shortly after this execution, some of his followers became convinced that they had seen Jesus again, raised from the dead (1 Cor.

15.3–4). The significance of these resurrection appearances was eschatological. They affirmed Jesus' original prophecy that the Kingdom was coming soon. As Paul, recounting these events some 20 years after their occurrence, states in 1 Corinthians 15.51–52, Jesus' own resurrection indexed the nearness of the general resurrection, thus the nearness of the End.

This affirmation of Jesus' prophecy mobilized his earliest followers to comb through scripture, to try to understand his message in their new, changed circumstances post-resurrection. Jesus *was* the Messiah, they taught; but now, post-resurrection, he would have to come again. Jesus' first coming had not been particularly messianic, and his followers knew this. Constrained, perhaps, from providing Jesus with a messianic past, these earliest followers instead gave him a messianic future. Leading bands of angels, descending from clouds of glory to the sound of celestial trumpets, defeating evil cosmic forces, raising the dead, and even – especially in Paul's view – turning the nations to the worship of Israel's god: when Jesus came for the second time, said his earliest followers, he was coming the way that a Davidic Messiah *should* come. And he was coming soon.[29]

But Time, of course, did *not* end on time. What we think of as 'Christianity' succeeded precisely as its foundational prophecy failed. And the generations that followed the movement's first generation – which had been convinced that it was history's *last* generation – adopted and adapted to their new circumstances by turning once again to biblical tradition. It was they who now provided Jesus with a messianic past. In the New Testament canon we can trace how Pauline *kerygma* yields to evangelical life story, with the Jewish Bible, in Greek, generating Jesus' new biographical details. A virgin mother, a Davidic genealogy, a birthplace in Bethlehem, a scrum of wise men and shepherds, a star arising from Judah: the tradition was invented, the tropes secured. And the story, finally, can begin.

29. On these apocalyptic pronouncements both in Paul and in the Gospels, Fredriksen, *Jesus of Nazareth*, pp. 78–89; specifically on Jesus as Messiah, pp. 119–54.

Chapter 13

BEARDS FOR SALE: THE UNCUT VERSION OF BRIAN, GENDER AND SEXUALITY

Amy-Jill Levine

The Pythons have not been known as poster-children for feminist causes or, more broadly, their sensitivity to matters of gender/sexuality fronts. Why cast women when men in drag are willing and available? Why worry about a joke about rape (even if 'at first') when the character who experiences it is a man in a dress? And why worry about homophobia when one can count on a sizeable percentage of the audience as finding the stereotypes to be funny? As Susan Aronstein puts it: 'The Pythons' desire to question conventions of narrative, history, and authority does not seem to extend to the conventions of gender and heteronormativity.'[1]

The same queries (that is the right word) apply to the Pythons' treatment of infertility, gender identity disorder and, on the artistic and economic side, women's

---

1. Susan Aronstein, ' "In my own idiom": Social Critique, Campy Gender, and Queer Performance in *Monty Python and the Holy Grail*', in Kathleen Coyne Kelly and Tison Pugh (eds), *Queer Movie Medievalisms* (Farnham: Ashgate, 2009), pp. 115–28, at p. 115.

involvement both behind and in front of the camera. The Pythons are, for the most part, old boys.[2] They will always be so, and there's no reason to belabour the point. As one study of *Life of Brian* stated in a description that could apply to *panta* Python: 'Men act as women, men act as men acting as women, and men even act as men.'[3]

Old boys though they may be, the Pythons do not seek to reinforce hierarchical gender constructions. Rebecca Housel, in a review of *Holy Grail*, notes that they 'use Arthurian legend to speak to the *absurdity* of patriarchy and its reverberations in the twentieth century'.[4] Marcia Landy views the *Flying Circus* as displaying a 'steady erosion of dominant forms of sexuality'.[5] Carl Dyke claims that *Life of Brian* is a 'counter-hegemonic gesture'[6] on various fronts. But generally, this deconstruction works for men only. Women (as defined traditionally) in the Python television universe generally remain girls, and the faux-women portrayed by the men are usually twits (as are the men portrayed by men, but at least they have the alternative of also being the writers and directors). Matters are better in some of the movies, but not substantially so.

For most of the Python productions, stereotypes of femininity and sexuality are reinforced rather than undermined. Masculinity may be skewered, but women, who function primarily as props, derive no benefit from this alternative ethic. Whether in Arthurian times or, for our purposes, late Second Temple Judaism (specifically, 'A.D. 33, around tea time'), whatever good news the film offers regarding the critique of gender constructions becomes attenuated when women actually appear on camera.

Perhaps because viewers are accustomed to the androcentric nature of Python productions, or perhaps because viewers bring their own stereotypes of first-century Judaea and Galilee to the film, the actual roles that *Life of Brian* accords women go unnoted. I suspect Dyke offers the majority view: 'From a feminist standpoint, for example, [*Life of Brian*] is frustratingly uncritical' in that its 'characterizations of women are few, flat and stereotyped'[7] although he suggests

---

2. I have heard that students at British public schools were called 'boys'; those who graduated were therefore 'old boys'. Therefore, the term 'boy' in this context conveys no disrespect (respect for old boys' networks is another matter).

3. Richard C. Stern, Clayton N. Jefford, and Guerric DeBona (eds), *Savior on the Silver Screen* (New York/Mahwah, NJ: Paulist Press, 1999), p. 249. Marcia Landy, *Monty Python's Flying Circus* (TV Milestones; Detroit, MI: Wayne State University Press, 2005), p. 71, points out that the television show, on occasion, had women playing men.

4. Rebecca Housel, '*Monty Python and the Holy Grail*: Philosophy, Gender, and Society', in Gary Hardcastle, George Reisch, and William Irwin (eds), *Monty Python and Philosophy: Nudge Nudge, Think Think!* (Chicago: Open Court, 2006), pp. 83–92, at p. 85.

5. Landy, *Monty Python's Flying Circus*, p. 72.

6. Carl Dyke, 'Learning from *The Life of Brian*: Saviors for Seminars', in George Aichele and Richard G. Walsh (eds), *Screening Scripture: Intertextual Connections between Scripture and Film* (Harrisburg, PA: Trinity Press International, 2002), pp. 229–50, at p. 230.

7. Ibid., p. 240, 241.

that the Pythons sympathetically portray women in the 'limited roles and opportunities available to [them] in biblical times'.[8]

Life of Brian is an opportunity missed. The movie does not indicate 'limited roles' (save for the ability to stone someone) but rather quite numerous and diverse ones: rich and poor; prostitute, lady of leisure, revolutionary, religious leader, spectacle watcher, victim of crucifixion, etc. Indeed, *Life of Brian* may come closer, in several scenes, to an accurate portrayal of gender and sexuality in Judaea in late Second Temple Judaism than do many of today's sermons, popular books and even non-feminist academic literature. The problem is that viewers miss the diversity: the flat female characters and the dominant male presence, coupled with stereotypes of first-century Jewish women that viewers import, thwart any correction.

A quick survey among my feminist friends, on the question, 'What do you remember about women and gender in the movie?' yielded, first, reference to the stoning sequence, and women in beards. As is so often the case with beards, the truth is hidden, and we believe what we want to believe. The second scene cited was Stan's concern for equality, expressed eloquently in his plea, '*I want to be a woman*. From now on, I want you to call me "Loretta"'. Compared to Mrs Cohen and Loretta, Judith – despite her nude scene, and despite her challenge to the stereotypes of first-century Jewish women – is barely memorable.

Life of Brian does, helpfully, open the conversation on what constituted masculinity in antiquity, and so what codes viewers pick up today. It addresses matters of sexual practice: the 'with whom?' (e.g. fellow Jews, Romans, anyone in the neighbourhood), and 'where?' and 'when?' (or, to cite another of the film's memorable lines, 'How shall we fuck off, O Lord?'). And while a fully queer analysis of the film is impossible in the context of this paper, *Life of Brian* gives at least informed viewers a sympathetic gay protagonist. The film can serve to help students think critically about gender and sexuality as well as about colonialism, apocalyptic-eschatological prophesy, relics, messianic expectations, the authority of Scripture, eyewitness reporting, and a host of other subjects appropriate to the study of the Bible. Yet whereas it does correct several negative stereotypes of Jewish women, at the same time it also threatens to reinforce rather than to challenge prevailing negative stereotypes of Brian's (and Jesus') Jewish context.

Mrs Cohen, or The Virgin Mandy

Mrs Cohen's response to Brian about whether she was raped and the later question of her post-partum virginity show the complexity of a woman's sexual identity. Her protecting of Brian and then her reaction to Brian's death show the complexity of the maternal role. Whether intentional or not, *Life of Brian* raises such questions as: How is messianism related to female sexual activity? What constitutes rape and who has the authority to name the act as such? Of what import is paternity? When

8. Ibid, p. 241.

is sexual shame, if ever, appropriate? Where does a woman's loyalty lie: to her parents, her sexual partners, her children, or herself? Is anything stable in her identity? Is it desirable that anything should be?

The Nativity (if we can use this term with Brian, who is *not* Jesus) begins when Mrs Cohen, who has occasional hot flashes of critical awareness, asks the Magi one of the movie's few intelligent questions: 'What are you doing creeping under a couch at two o'clock in the morning?' She then accuses the Magi of 'being led by a bottle, more like' as she shoos them away. Her practicality helps us see, upon turning to the Gospels, just how bizarre, and how funny, Matthew's description of the Magi is.

The Magi should get credit for asking one of the stupidest questions in the Gospels – a laugh-line that Matthew sets up, but which has failed to receive its due response. 'In the time of King Herod, after Jesus was born in Bethlehem of Judaea, Magi from the East came to Jerusalem, asking, "Where is the child who has been born king of the Jews?"' (Matthew 2.1–2a). To ask Herod, the paranoid megalomaniac explicitly identified by the evangelist as 'king' (2.1, and again in 2.3, and a third time in 2.9 just for fun), about the new 'king', is not the best interrogative move in turn-of-the-era Israel. In case readers missed the absurdity of the question, Matthew adds a second laugh line. In 2.10, we learn that the Magi, 'when they saw that the star had stopped, they rejoiced with great joy'. They do not rejoice upon seeing Jesus and his mother; rather they are happy to have arrived.[9]

Were this not enough, these innocents abroad are prepared to return to Herod to provide the baby's location; only a warning dream sends them away. To call them 'wise men' (the label begins with the Venerable Bede) is a misreading of Matthew, who has little fondness for the 'wise and the intelligent' (cf. Matthew 11.25 par.; Luke 10.21).[10] By having the Magi arrive at the wrong crèche, the Pythons become better readers of Matthew than those whose modern-day camels bear the bumper sticker, 'wise men still seek him'.[11]

Upon learning that the Magi have presents, Mrs Cohen changes her mind: 'Well, why didn't you say so? He's over there . . .'. Richard C. Stern, Clayton N. Jefford, and Guerric DeBona see her reaction as 'a look at greed in the suburbs' and so a critique of British society.[12] Then again, Mrs Cohen's neighbourhood doesn't much look like Golders Green or Hampstead. For other viewers, Mrs Cohen may code as Jewish in her attention to income – although I've not found reference to this cultural stereotype in the secondary sources. Or perhaps she is simply being practical.[13]

9. From the back of the camel comes the whine: 'Are we there yet?'

10. Magi are, to this day, Zoroastrian priests. That Matthew may have intended this parody is one thing; that 'we' still find it funny may be another: humour at the expense of another is a tricky thing. For more on various understandings of the Magi, see Mark Allen Powell, *Chasing the Eastern Star: Adventures in Biblical Reader-Response Criticism* (Louisville, KY: Westminster John Knox, 2001).

11. The phrase 'wise men still seek him' got 81,700 results on Google in September 2014.

12. Stern et al., *Savior on the Silver Screen*, p. 259.

13. I have in my office an old *New Yorker* cartoon of the Nativity. The caption reads 'Thank goodness, there's a receipt for the myrrh'.

The Nativity scene begins the correction to the standard tropes found in both popular culture and a few academic circles. Contrary to the view that women in Jesus' environment were repressed and suppressed by Jewish society, and only liberated by Jesus (a view most recently expressed by former US president Jimmy Carter),[14] Mrs Cohen presents an alternative picture. For example, she owns her own home (or at least squats where she wants), as do Martha (Luke 10.38), Mary the mother of John Mark (Acts 12.2), and Lydia (Acts 16.15) who may be Jewish, or perhaps a godfearer. Mrs Cohen has access to her own funds, as do most of the Jewish women encountered in the Gospels: Mary Magdalene, Joanna and Susanna (Luke 8.1–3), the haemorrhaging woman who spends *her funds* on physicians (Mark 5.26; Luke 8.43), the woman who anoints Jesus, whether on his head (Matthew 26.7; Mark 14.3) or on his feet (Luke 7.37–38; John 12.3), the women who anticipate anointing his corpse (Mark 16.1), etc. She has no problem speaking with (very) strange men, and she feels no cultural pressure to withdraw in their presence.

Nor does Mrs Cohen appear to be shunned by anyone in her environs, despite the means by which she earns her daily drachma. No one is hurling stones at her for committing adultery, if that is what in fact she did. I suspect viewers do not notice her independence in part because the stereotypes of women's 'limited roles and opportunities' are already in place, and in part because Mrs Cohen is, for viewers, not really a woman but Terry Jones in drag. Also preventing the impression of independence is Mrs Cohen's lack of any female friends. Unlike the woman who finds her lost coin and calls her (women) friends and neighbours to celebrate (Luke 15.9; the Greek verbs are in the feminine), Mrs Cohen – like the Pythons – lives (on camera) in a male world. The only time she appears among women, she is bearded; there, she is accompanied by her son, not her friends.

Along with depicting Mrs Cohen's independence and so, I suspect unintentionally, tapping into descriptions of women in the Gospels, *Life of Brian* also recognizes the alternatives to the Christian Nativity story (once again, Brian is *not* Jesus, and the film depicts Jesus, from his birth to his Sermon on the Mount, respectfully).

MOTHER: Well, Brian . . . your father isn't Mr Cohen.
BRIAN: I never thought he was.
MOTHER: Now, none of your cheek! He was a Roman, Brian. He was a centurion in the Roman army.
BRIAN: You mean . . . you were raped?
MOTHER: Well, at first, yes.
BRIAN: Who was it?

14. Jimmy Carter, 'Jesus Christ was the greatest liberator of women in a society where they had been considered throughout biblical history to be inferior' (http://www.nytimes.com/2014/06/08/books/review/redeemer-the-life-of-jimmy-carter-and-a-call-to-action.html?_r=1).

MOTHER: Heh. Naughtius Maximus his name was. Hmm. Promised me the known world he did. I was to be taken to Rome. House by the Forum. Slaves. Asses' milk. As much gold as I could eat. Then, he, having his way with me had . . . voom! Like a rat out of an aqueduct.

The missing Mr Cohen is, like Joseph in the Gospels, a marginal figure who disappears quickly after providing his son a name and a genealogy (or two). When Mrs Cohen actually married Mr Cohen is, like the time Mary and Joseph married, indeterminate.

Although claims that Jesus was a *mamzer* and therefore marginalized within his Nazareth neighbourhood, psychologically damaged because of his demeaned status, and/or in search of a father/Father figure,[15] have abated somewhat in the academy, discussion of the claims of his virginal conception remain academic staples.[16] The claim that Jesus was the child of a Roman soldier was already floated by Celsus in the second century. Origen, in *Contra Celsum* 1.32, recounts Celsus' conversation with a 'Jew' who stated of the 'mother of Jesus': 'when she was pregnant she was turned out of doors by the carpenter to whom she had been betrothed, as having been guilty of adultery, and that she bore a child to a certain soldier named Panthera.'

By alluding to Brian's illegitimacy, the film makes several pedagogically opportune moves. It frames such questions as: What do we take literally in the Bible, and why? How have the Gospel narratives been interpreted? What is the role of belief or faith in the study of history? It also opens questions of history, of apologetics and polemics. Finally, it allows discussion of women's sexual identity, including the very difficult questions of rape, so-called illegitimacy, paternity, and ethnic identity.

Pedagogically opportune moments continue as Brian reacts to Mrs Cohen's confession. According to Lloyd Baugh, Brian 'joins a Jewish liberation movement, mainly to get away from his oppressive "Jewish mother" '.[17] Conversely, Stern et al. insist that Brian 'desires to be a good Jewish patriot and to resist Roman domination

---

15. E.g., Bruce Chilton, *Rabbi Jesus: An Intimate Biography* (New York: Doubleday, 2002).

16. Philip R. Davies, 'Life of Brian Research,' in *idem, Whose Bible Is It Anyway?* 2nd ed. (London: T&T Clark International, 2004), pp. 142–55, at p. 146, originally in J. Cheryl Exum and Stephen D. Moore (eds), *Biblical Studies/Cultural Studies: The Third Sheffield Colloquium* (Sheffield: Sheffield Academic Press, 1998), pp. 400–14.

James Crossley, 'Life of Brian or Life of Jesus? Uses of Critical Biblical Scholarship and Non-orthodox Views of Jesus in Monty Python's *Life of Brian*', *Relegere: Studies in Religion and Reception* 1 (2011), pp. 93–114, at p. 102, notes the similar alternative conception narrative in the medieval Jewish *Toledot Yeshu*. See also Adele Reinhartz, 'Jesus in Film: Hollywood Perspectives on the Jewishness of Jesus,' *Journal of Religion and Film* 2.2 (1998): http://avalon.unomaha.edu/jrf/JesusinFilmRein.htm and eadem (ed.), *Bible and Cinema: Fifty Key Films* (London and New York: Routledge, 2013), p. 188, citing the Babylonian Talmud, *Sanhedrin* 104b and 67b.

17. Lloyd Baugh, *Imaging the Divine: Jesus and Christ-Figures in Film* (Kansas City, MO: Sheed and Ward, 1997), p. 49.

in an active way. To this end, he joins a local Jewish zealot group . . .'[18] Stern et al. have the better claim. Brian responds to his mother's revelation of his paternity: 'I'm not a Roman, Mum, and I never will be! I'm a kike! A yid! A hebe! A hook-nose! I'm kosher, Mum! I'm a Red Sea pedestrian, and proud of it!' Brian's motivation is his Jewish identity and not his Jewish mother. The question of 'Who is a Jew?' (or, for a few, a 'Judaean'[19]), including issues of personal choice, maternal vs paternal descent, and community recognition is asked. Brian is, like the New Testament's Timothy (see Acts 16.1), the 'son of a Jewish woman' and a pagan father, and like Timothy when we first meet him, he is also uncircumcised.[20]

The scene ends with Brian leaving to join the revolutionaries, and Mrs Cohen muttering, 'Huh. Sex, sex, sex. That's all they think about, huh? Well, how are you, then, officer?' For this mum, the Romans, and Brian, are motivated by sex. She, however, is not. She has managed to master the Romans: she provides them a service they want, and she takes their money for it; she has knowledge that they lack. Mrs Cohen does what she must to survive. That is what women do. But she shows no sense of wallowing in sin, or even shame about her own situation (it is amusing to set the film against all those biblical studies volumes on 'honour and shame'). She may even be enjoying her chosen profession – which makes her neither the stereotypical Jewish princess[21] nor the British wife who closes her eyes and thinks of England.[22] She is the woman many men want, sort of.

As a mother, she's somewhere in between Mary the mother of Jesus and Sophie Portnoy. When Brian's followers hail him as the messiah, Mrs Cohen responds to

18. Stern et al., *Savior on the Silver Screen*, p. 239.

19. See, most recently, the essays in Timothy Michael Law and Charles Halton (eds), *Jew and Judaean: A Marginalia Forum on Politics and Historiography in the Translation of Ancient Texts*, *The Marginalia Review of Books* (http://marginalia.lareviewofbooks.org/jew-judean-forum [accessed 26 August 2014]).

20. Bob McCabe, *The Life of Graham: The Authorised Biography of Graham Chapman* (London: Orion Books, 2005 [*non vidit*]), states: 'After the first take of the scene where a nude Brian (Graham Chapman) addresses the crowd from his window, Terry Jones pulled Chapman aside and said "I think we can see that you're not Jewish," referring to Chapman being uncircumcised. This was corrected in subsequent takes with the application of a rubber band'. Citation from http://www.circumstitions.com/Famous5a.html, the 'Gallery of Intact Men'. On the details, given the graininess of the tape available at Vanderbilt and my own myopia, also *non vidit*.

21. Jewish foreplay: 'Twenty minutes of begging' (variants run up to four hours). See Alan Dundes, 'The J.A.P. and the J.A.M. in American Folklore', in Joseph Boskin (ed.), *The Humor Prism in 20th-Century America* (Detroit, MI: Wayne State University Press, 1997), pp. 225–49, at p. 235.

22. Origin unknown (but not Queen Victoria); according to http://www.phrases.org.uk/meanings/, the phrase appears in the journal of Lady Hillingdon (1912): 'When I hear his steps outside my door I lie down on my bed, open my legs and think of England'.

their accolades with perhaps her most famous line (at least the one quoted most often on the internet),[23] 'He's not the Messiah – he's a very naughty boy'.[24]

Mrs Cohen's attempt, albeit expressed in a problematic way, to protect her son is consistent with what Mark's Gospel suggests about the relationship between Jesus and his family. Her reaction to claims of Brian's messianic identity once again offers the opportunity for discussion of Jesus' natal family, as they are depicted in the Gospels.

In Mark's account (which Matthew and Luke clean up and which is absent from John), Mary is likely to be among those family members who seek to restrain Jesus – whether to protect him, or to silence him, or both, 'for people were saying, "he has gone out of his mind"' (Mark 3.21). The scene leads to Jesus' rejection of his natal family in favour of his new voluntary association: 'They said to him, "Your mother and your brothers and sisters are outside, asking for you." And he answered, "Who are my mother and my brothers?" And looking at those who sat around him, he said, "Here are my mother and my brothers. Whoever does the will of God is my brother and sister and mother"' (Mark 3.32b–35).

Following the public acclamation of Brian as the messiah, an 'indiscreet man' asks Mrs Cohen, 'Are you a virgin?' Her first reaction is the entirely polite (and so out of character): 'I beg your pardon?' The man presses, 'Well, if it's not a personal question, are you a virgin?' Mrs Cohen responds now more in character: 'If it's not a personal question! How much more personal can you get? Now piss off'.

The scene rejects the old (anti-?)-Jewish joke: We know that Jesus was Jewish, because he thought this mother was a virgin, and she thought her son was God. Perhaps that joke, whose origins I have been unable to trace, developed much like the Panthera slander as a way of responding to claims of the virgin birth.

Only in her final scene does Mrs Cohen morph into Mrs Portnoy; she becomes the stereotypical Jewish mother.[25]

> MRS COHEN: So, there you are! I might have known it would end up like this. Just think of all the love and affection I've wasted on you! Well, if that's how you treat your poor old mother, in the autumn years of her life, all I can say is: Go ahead! Be crucified! See if I care! I might have known . . .
>
> BRIAN: But mum!

23. E.g. http://www.telegraph.co.uk/culture/comedy/comedy-news/10463680/Monty-Pythons-25-funniest-quotes.html?frame=2738922 (quote #4).

24. Jeffrey L. Staley and Richard Walsh, *Jesus, the Gospels, and Cinematic Imagination* (Louisville, KY: Westminster John Knox, 2007), p. 102.

25. Philip Davies ('*Life of Brian*,' p. 149 n. 3) sees in her something quintessentially British: the 'midwinter transvestite pantomime figure' who functions as a parody of the Virgin Mary. Her off-camera identification as the 'Virgin Mandy' is therefore well taken. The designation not only confirms the Marian connection, it moves her name from the Jewish 'Cohen' to the Waspish 'Mandy' (the Jewish name would be Mindy) as well as to the masculine via the encoded 'Man'.

MRS COHEN: Not fine thee ... said ... said ...

BRIAN: Mum! Mum!

MRS COHEN: ... like all young people nowadays, I don't know what the world
is coming to ...

Impossible demands, guilt inducement, choking off responses, universal
indictment, personal suffering ... The Jewish mother stereotype is almost in place
(if it were fully invoked, Mrs Cohen would have threatened to put her head in the
oven at Brian's refusal not to be crucified). There is no subversion of the Jewish
mother stereotype, although perhaps the Pythons should be congratulated for
having restrained themselves until the end.

Conversely, there is a brilliant subversion of attempts to make crucifixion – one
of the most horrible tortures invented – meaningful. The viewer is much more
likely to remember Eric Idle, curls surrounding his angelic face, who sings 'Always
Look on the Bright Side of Life', than to remember anything about Brian's death.
Once again, pedagogical moments open up: for example, do we remember the two
men crucified on either side of Jesus, or are they, like Brian, reduced to background
and then forgotten? Where is hope in the context of death by torture? Have we
made light of Jesus' crucifixion, by turning the cross into an item of jewellery?

Women in Beards

Who knew: the Pythons, in their send-up of women in beards (rather than as
beards; see below on Judith), offer an opportunity for discussion of a major
masculine signifier of the biblical period, and perhaps *the* major signifier in
both the Second Sophistic and rabbinic literature. Although Charles Berg's
psychoanalytic analogy of beards to pubic hair, and so of shaving to castration, has
been rejected by other analysts and anthropologists alike, the connection of
facial hair with masculinity – whether the masculine is the bearded or the clean-
shaven – remains a cross-cultural trope.[26] Beards function as diacritics– they are
marks of difference: for gender, for class, for signalling what is present, or absent.

For ancient Israel, facial hair signified manhood and, more precisely, 'masculine
honour',[27] and to be shaved was to be feminized. This is why, in 2 Samuel 10.4,
'Hanun seized David's envoys, shaved off half the beard of each, cut off their
garments in the middle at their hips, and sent them away'. The cutting of the
garment is a symbolic demasculinization/castration as well. This is also why,

26. Charles Berg, *The Unconscious Significance of Hair* (London: G. Allen and Unwin,
1951). See discussion and sources in Simcha Fishbane, 'Jewish Beards: The Symbolic
Representation of the Rabbinic Beard', Moscow Center for University Teaching of Jewish
Civilization 'Sefer'; *Proceedings of the Seventeenth Annual International Conference on Jewish
Studies* Vol 1, Academic Series 30 (2010), pp. 113–29, at pp. 114–16.

27. Fishbane, 'Jewish Beards', p. 116.

according to the next verse, when David hears what had happened, and that the 'men were greatly ashamed', he advised them to 'Remain at Jericho until your beards have grown, and then return'.

According to Maude Gleason, 'hairiness in general' and especially the beard was a cultural signal for the Romans that would 'announce from afar, "I am a man"'.[28] The symbol was, however, unstable. In his *Second Satire*, Juvenal comments, 'Men's faces are not to be trusted.' So also Martial in his *Epigrams* speaks of 'an ascetic bearded philosopher' who turns out to be a pathetic phallic *pathic*. With beards, across the centuries, what you see is not necessarily what you get.

For *b. Shabbat* 152a, 'The glory of a man's face (*hadrat panim*) is his beard'. But as the saying goes, rabbinic literature is often prescriptive rather than descriptive. Mosaic remains suggest that under Greek and then more so under Roman influence, first-century Jews – especially those assimilated to Roman cultural values – followed their Gentile neighbours in shaving. The Roman emperors did not need beards: their accomplishments, coupled with their musculature (at least in the visual representations), did not need a facial confirmation. Beards come back into fashion under Hadrian, that is, at the time of the Bar Kokhba revolt (ca. 132–35 CE). Later, when beards go out of fashion again, the rabbis adapt. Fishbane notes: 'An exception to the shaving prohibition is suggested in the *b. Bava Kama* 83a where it could be understood that the rabbinical authorities permitted shaving of the beard by persons who had frequent dealings with the Roman authorities.'[29]

Since in the rabbinic worldview, the beard is the pre-eminent sign of masculine performance, the beardless rabbi created questions of gender-identity. In *b. Bava Metzia* 8, Resh Lakish mistakes the beardless Rabbi Yohanan for a woman. The issue of the beard as the male signifier appears in patristic literature as well. Clement of Alexandria (*Paedagogus* 3.3) describes Adam and so male destiny: 'God deemed it right that he should excel, and dispersed hair over a man's body. Whatever smoothness and softness was in him he abstracted from his side when he formed the woman Eve.'

For *Life of Brian*, the beard is both the pre-eminent sign of maleness, and a recognition that the sign is not always in concert with the assumed signified. Of all the members of the People's Front of Judaea, only Brian has a beard, and his violation of certain masculine codes, including his death on the cross, is evident. Also not bearded is the poor fellow who is stoned for uttering the name of God in exclamation over a good piece of halibut, although the women who plan to stone

---

28. Maude W. Gleason, *Making Men: Sophists and Self-Presentation in Ancient Rome* (Princeton: Princeton University Press, 1995), pp. 68–9; see for further references on beards and cultural signification Gleason as well as Patricia Parker, 'Barbers, Infidels, and Renegades: *Antony and Cleopatra*', in Lena Cowen Orin (ed.), *Center or Margin: Revisions of the English Renaissance in Honor of Leeds Barroll* (Cranbury, NJ: Associated University Press, 2006), pp. 54–90.

29. Fishbane, 'Jewish Beards', p. 117.

him, and who eventually stone the priest who proclaimed the death sentence, are. Good for Python: they've achieved semiotic realization of the instability of gender roles.

Even more, they've become the pedagogues of the oppressed by denaturalizing reigning ideologies. The scene offers a critique of patriarchal religious practices whose basis is presumed to be inscribed in ancient and arcane texts – that are nowhere to be found. This is *Life of Brian* read through the lens of Paulo Freire:

> MRS. COHEN: Ohh, I hate wearing these beards.
> BRIAN: Why aren't women allowed to go to stonings, Mum?
> MRS. COHEN: It's written. That's why.

No text is cited, nor is there one to cite. By adducing the non-existent text and then by showing its subversion via a group of bearded, stone-throwing women, the film calls into question religious practice, Scriptural authority, and even, once again, gender roles: Brian, the man, asks his mother to interpret practice for him.

Yet the scene, for all its humour, threatens to reinforce negative stereotypes of Judaism found in some Christian circles. Viewers, already believing that first-century Jewish women are marginalized by ridiculous and repressive laws, will have their stereotypes confirmed rather than challenged. Worse, viewers, already believing that Judaism was legalistic and violent (and therefore that Jesus needed to fix it), again will find confirmation rather than challenge in this scene. Here, the intent of the film is not one of subversion at all; rather, one of the stars confirmed this image of a violent Jewish context. In a *TV Guide* interview about *Life of Brian*,[30] John Cleese stated:

> A lot of people protested. I always get confused about the various Jewish denominations. I think there's Orthodox and Reform and Conservative. Anyway, two out of three of those groups protested. Apparently they were upset at quite an obscure thing. There's a character I play in the stoning scene who's wearing this prayer shawl around his neck and I think there was something sacred about that that we didn't know about. They were also upset about the stoning, but I don't know how they could be, because it happened. Stoning is a documented practice, so they probably should have been upset about the fact that their ancestors stoned people, rather than the fact that we showed a silly stoning on screen.

For the conference at King's College London, Mr Cleese twice repeated the claim that Jews in antiquity were busy stoning people.

The prayer shawl, worn by the priest (played by Mr Cleese), atop an ornate headdress is anachronistic and ahistorical; so is the headdress.[31] In like manner, the

---

30. 27 January, 2008 (http://www.tvguide.com/news/cleese-python-brian-35998.aspx). I thank Scott Gilbert for the reference.

31. See Katie Turner's chapter in this volume.

stoning is also historically questionable. There are no examples of people being stoned for adultery or blasphemy in the Tanakh. The well-known account in John 8 of the 'woman taken in adultery', a passage that found its way into the Gospel several centuries after its initial composition, does not show stoning to be practised. To the contrary, the scene sets up a question designed to entrap Jesus (much as do the questions, 'Should we pay taxes to Caesar?' or 'Whose wife, in the resurrection, is a multiply married woman?'). Jesus is asked if a woman, clearly guilty of adultery, should be stoned. Were he to say, 'yes', he'd be condemned as a brute; were he to say, 'no', he'd be condemned for speaking against Torah. Jesus changes the subject. Those various images readers have of his interlocutors dropping their stones as they walk away come from Hollywood, not John's Gospel (the Temple setting should have been a cue that this is not the place to execute anyone, but again, most viewers would not know this). The stoning of Stephen (Acts 7) is, first, not a legal proceeding; second, it may not have even happened, since Stephen's existence is not otherwise recorded in early Christian sources, since his speech makes no sense in literary context, and since his name ('Stephen' means 'crown' in Greek) sets him up as the archetypal martyr.[32]

In the stoning scene, the joke works because viewers presume Jewish women are fully marginalized and Jewish law is both ridiculous and barbaric. This is not good news.

Loretta

One internet post asserts, 'Monty Python represented the PFJ group as a parody of queer theorists' who are 'manipulating their audience to find humour in the serious issue of reproductive rights whenever it was discussed by feminist activists'; the same post concludes, 'The particular scene where "Stan" admits that he desires to be a woman empowers the idea of heteronormativity'.[33] First, the issue is less heteronormativity than it is the issue of gender construction. Second, to be able to parody something can be a political move in which the importance of the subject is acknowledged. Parody works in this scene as it reflects both occasional pretentiousness of the academic discourse and the shift from practicality into pure theory.

STAN: Women have a perfect right to play a part in our movement, Reg.
FRANCIS: Why are you always on about women, Stan?
STAN: I want to be one.
REG: What?
STAN: *I want to be a woman.* From now on, I want you all to call me 'Loretta'.

32. Discussion in Shelly Matthews, *Perfect Martyr: The Stoning of Stephen and the Construction of Christian Identity* (New York: Oxford University Press, 2010).

33. Erin Kelly, 'A presentation devoted to highlighting the negative influence "Monty Python" has on society, specifically one sketch', 4 December 2012 (http://prezi.com/basr3sk8toza/monty-python-mocks-reality-of-gender-norms/).

The idea of a first-century Jewish man wishing to be a woman should be no surprise to anyone who has kept up with discussions of gender fluidity in the discourse of Second Temple and rabbinic Jewish literature. The co-optation of women's roles, and especially their biological ability to become pregnant and give birth, is something that appears to have been prominent in both cultural and theological discourse.

Regarding gynaecological imagery, two examples from the New Testament demonstrate this fluidity. First, Paul, a first-century Jew and the only Pharisee from whom we have first-person testimony, appropriates maternal and parturition images. In Galatians 4.19 he writes to his congregation, 'My little children, for whom I am again in the pain of childbirth until Christ is formed in you' – he is the mother giving birth to the Christ, who is also the child in the wombs of the Galatians.[34]

Second, according to John 19.34, a centurion pierces Jesus' side with a spear, 'and at once blood and water came out'. The imagery is not only over-determined with concepts of Eucharist and Baptism, it is evocative of parturition as well as, especially in later Christian reception, lactation. The body of Jesus gives birth to those who believe in him, and it nourishes them, as does the body of the mother. That in the Fourth Gospel's opening hymn the incarnate Word bears the characteristics of Sophia/Wisdom confirms the gender-bending aspects of the Johannine Christ.

We can belabour the point. Gender-crossing, with attention more to the male who becomes female, can be seen as a form 'of resistance to a culture that equated power and dominance with maleness and maleness with the "husband's natural position" in coitus. Where Roman culture despised the submissive male, both early Christian and early Jewish cultures valorized him'.[35]

In turn, rabbinic sources depict Rome, often via the image of Esau, as hypermasculine. Again, *Life of Brian* subverts the subversion: Biggus Dickus is, eponymously, hypermasculine, even his lisp puts into question, via stereotype, the correlation of hypermasculinity with heterosexuality.

Stan's desire to transform into something that he is not or, as Reg puts it, a desire that is 'symbolic of his struggle against reality', originally was part of a parody of British trade-union parties, just as Stan's wish to be Loretta can be taken as a subversion of early feminist thought. But the Pythons managed to tap into an actual ancient political, anti-colonial discourse. Stan's 'struggle against reality' may be the only sane response in a chaotic world. Or, he may just be delusional.

Before we leave Loretta, a brief note on biological configuration: the question of where the foetus gestates is posed both by Reg and by the rabbis.

---

34. Daniel Boyarin, 'Jewish Masochism: Couvade, Castration, and Rabbis in Pain', *American Imago* 51.1 (1994), pp. 3–36, suggests similar imagery in rabbinic sources.

35. Daniel Boyarin, 'Homotopia: The Feminized Jewish Male and the Lives of Women in Late Antiquity', *Differences* 7 (1995): 41–81. For additional commentary on the politics of cross-dressing, see the ovarial study by Marjorie B. Garber, *Vested Interests: Cross-Dressing and Cultural Anxiety* (New York: Routledge, 1997).

STAN: Don't you oppress me.

REG: I'm not oppressing you, Stan. You haven't got a womb! Where's the foetus going to gestate?! You going to keep it in a box?!

The same expression occurs in the Babylonian Talmud, *Niddah* 44b, in discussion of a foetus of a mother who has died. Were the mother to die in labour, it is permitted to cut her open even on the Sabbath and remove the foetus, 'because [the foetus] is like [a child] trapped in a box'.[36]

Judith

In Lloyd Baugh's inimitable prose, Judith (whom he does not identify by name) is: 'A radical-chique-feminist-ideologue-terrorist, whose political passion under the unlikely fatal attraction of Brian is converted one night to passion of another kind.'[37] Perhaps Baugh got his women confused: he does introduce his 'radical-chique-feminist' by describing Judith as the leader of the 'group of the gourd'.[38] Judith is a brunette, however, and the woman with the gourd is a blonde.[39]

Generally in the Python universe, a girl is a girl is a girl. Sue Jones-Davies, who played Judith, is quoted as saying, 'They wanted an actress who looked a bit Middle Eastern'.[40] Ms Jones-Davies is from Wales, and Mrs Cohen, in a moment of partial insight that is only half-correct, describes her as a 'Welsh tart'.[41] Ms Jones-Davies continues: 'The members of Monty Python were all of a particular ilk. It was a public-school, male, white, middle-class club. I don't think they have ever written with

36. Gwynn Kessler, *Conceiving Israel: The Fetus in Rabbinic Narrative* (Divinations, Rereading Late Ancient Religion; Philadelphia: University of Pennsylvania Press, 2009).

37. Baugh, *Imaging the Divine*, p. 50.

38. Ibid.

39. The role is uncredited in the cast of characters; Terry Jones, in response to Joan Taylor's query (email of 10 November 2014), responded that the actress is Gwen Taylor. I had originally thought she might be Carol Cleveland the frequent go-to 'girl' in many Python productions. Carol Cleveland instead played the posh lady at the Sermon on the Mount and again in the crucifixion scene, and appears in a brown headscarf on the left of the group following Brian into the wilderness. Marcia Landy is one of few to insist, 'Though not usually designated as such, Carol Cleveland is deserving of recognition as the seventh Python' (*Monty Python*, 4).

40. Emily Hill, 'The amazing Life Of Brian's girlfriend: From her naked film roles and the jailing of her ex-husband to becoming Mayor of Aberystwyth', *Daily Mail* (27 August 2011) at http://www.dailymail.co.uk/femail/article-2030866/The-amazing-Life-Of-Brians-girlfriend-From-naked-film-roles-jailing-ex-husband-Mayor-Aberystwyth.html#ixzz35aVnpqH3.

41. In an interview with *Mail Online* (27 August 2011), Sue Jones-Davies stated, 'My father was a maths teacher and my mother was a housewife. One was from North Wales and the other from South Wales. Here, they call that a mixed marriage' (http://www.dailymail.co.uk/femail/article-2030866/The-amazing-Life-Of-Brians-girlfriend-From-naked-film-roles-jailing-ex-husband-Mayor-Aberystwyth.html#ixzz33gUGmjWP).

women in mind ... There are some very weird things going on in the male psyche. The Pythons seemed to love dressing up as women and putting on funny voices.'[42]

Women serve in most comic films more for titillation than for driving the plot, but there is a difference between late-twentieth century British films and contemporaneous American ones. For Mel Brooks, Madeleine Kahn of *Blazing Saddles* (1974) and Teri Garr of *Young Frankenstein* (also 1974) are more than 'nice knockers' (so Ms Garr): they actually have funny lines and memorable roles. That is not the case with the women in Python productions in general or *Life of Brian* in particular.

Of all the main characters in the movie, Judith is the least interesting, the least funny, the most practical, and also the most noticeably nude. Alongside Brian, who is not particularly funny either, Judith may be the only character in the film who is not a nit.[43] Like Mrs Cohen, she is the one woman in a male universe, but given that the nit is not replaced by wit, she is at best a Jewish (or, well, Welsh) Smurfette.

In discussing Loretta's concerns, Judith is the one who opts for the practical language of compromise:

> JUDITH: I do feel Reg, that any anti-imperialistic group like ours must reflect such a divergence of interest within its powerbase.
> REG: Agreed.
> FRANCIS: Yes, I think Judith's point of view is very valid ...
>
> ...
>
> JUDITH: Here, I've got an idea. Suppose you agree that he can't actually have babies, not having a womb, which is nobody's fault, not even the Romans', but that he can have the right to have babies.
> FRANCIS: Good idea, Judith ...

Good idea indeed. Judith has managed to call attention to the pseudo-universality/ gender neutrality of 'man' in the phrase 'the rights of man' even as she recognizes the disjunction between ideals and actuality.

In discussion of revolution, Judith again emerges as at least having a glimmer of practicality, even as she ignores Brian's non-political infatuation. But then she aborts her initial insight by dropping her egalitarian mode in favour of Brian's leadership. Any chance she had of being a lamp giving light to others is snuffed out.

> JUDITH: We don't need any leaders! You're so right! Reg has been dominating us for too long.
> BRIAN: Well, yes ...
> JUDITH: It needed saying, and you said it, Brian!
> BRIAN: You're very attractive ...

42. Ibid.

43. Crossley, '*Life of Brian* Research,' pp. 99–100, notes, 'With the possible exception of Judith, Brian is the only sane and reasonable figure with any inkling of how to get some kind of result – no mean feat when adrift in a sea of hopeless incompetence'.

JUDITH: It's our revolution! We can all do it together!
BRIAN: Can we? I think . . .
JUDITH: We're all behind you, Brian! The revolution is in your hands!
BRIAN: What? No, that's not what I meant at all!

Yes, Judith has a few bright moments. Upon Brian's arrest, she attempts to rally the troops. She is the only one interested in action rather than discussion. She is absent for the major (stupid) terrorist forays. Even in her conversation with Brian's mother, she is articulate: 'Your son is a born leader. Those people out there are following him because they believe in him, Mrs Cohen. They believe he can give them hope – hope of a new life, a new world, a better future!' The wisely chosen (and overstated) praise of Brian and the respectful 'your son' and 'Mrs Cohen' would go far with any potential mother-in-law.

The image of the wise woman is a staple in the Jewish tradition, from Deborah to the wise women of Tekoa and Abel-bet-maacah to the original Judith. The story of Deborah in Judges 4–5 presents a woman who indicts the general Barak for his cowardice, saves her people from the requisite evil king, and celebrates her victory in song. In much of the *Wirkungsgeschichte*, however, she is recognized as an exceptional woman, who rises up only in cases where all the men around her are too weak to be effectual.[44] A similar trope appears explicitly in the Book of Judith: this heroine arises when her community leaders display a lack of faith in divine protection. 'Brian's' Judith fits, modestly, into this group of exceptional women: she is the only woman among a group of inept men. However, she is not, in any filmic sense, exceptional; she is, rather, flat.

Adele Reinhartz correctly notes that Judith is the feminine form of the name 'Judas', and suggests Judith shares with Judas the role of the protagonist's betrayer: 'In a literal sense, Judith betrays Brian to the Romans, but she does so inadvertently . . . Judith simply fails to intervene when Brian is arrested mistakenly, her judgment clouded by her (false) view of him as an ardent revolutionary and now martyr.'[45] In a later study, Richard Walsh locates the betrayal in Judith's acclamation of Brian's leadership.[46] However, it is Judith who, deliberately, demands that Pilate, 'Release Brian'.

But perhaps Judith is less traitor than she is, finally, protector or, better, beard. She's the girl needed to secure Brian's sexuality and indeed heterosexuality. Viewers who think of Mary Magdalene as having a sexual relationship with Jesus will find a tie-in here; others can assert that Judith's role is one more factor that distinguishes the sexually active Brian from the celibate Jesus.

44. Joy A. Schroeder, *Deborah's Daughters: Gender Politics and Biblical Interpretation* (New York: Oxford, 2014), *passim*.

45. Adele Reinhartz, *Jesus of Hollywood* (New York: Oxford University Press, 2007), p. 168. Richard Walsh, '*Monty Python's Life of Brian*', in Adele Reinhartz (ed.), *Bible and Cinema*, pp. 187–92, at p. 188: 'The revolutionary Judith stands in for Judas'.

46. Walsh, *Bible and Cinema*, p. 188.

Judith also, together with Mrs Cohen, provides the counter to the more puerile aspects of Pythonic sexual humour. Mrs Cohen recognizes that the Romans think only about sex and then manages to use their obsession to her own benefit. Judith too shifts the focus of male-female relationships away from the sexual to the practical.

JUDITH: Brian, you were fantastic!
BRIAN: Well, you weren't so bad yourself.
JUDITH: No no ... what you said just now was quite extraordinary.

Her interest in Brian is more for his politics than his penis.

Although more a question of more recent cultural stereotype than Second Temple Jewish tropes, Judith also opens discussion of what we mean when we speak of 'Jewish women'. Just as Mrs Cohen can be seen as satirizing (either reinforcing or deconstructing, or both) the stereotype of the Jewish mother, so Judith can, at least in the colonies, be seen as correcting the stereotype of the Jewish-American Princess, or JAP. According to this trope, Judith (not Brian) would have been the one to comment, and negatively so, about the size of her nose, would have been wearing designer sandals, and would have longer and redder nails.

Judith's last appearance is at the foot of Brian's cross – a standard scene from the four canonical Gospels. There, she begins the spin on the meaning of Brian's death: 'Terrific! Great! Reg has explained it all to me, and I think it's great what you're doing. Thank you, Brian, I'll ... I'll never forget you.' Brian's crucifixion – absurd in the plotline – is granted meaning by the woman at the foot of the cross. The suggestion that a benighted woman with religious fervour invented the meaning of Jesus' death as well as the claim of his resurrection is also part of antiquity's (and modernity's) response to Christianity. Celsus, who gives us the Jesus-as-Bastard story, also attributes the rise of Christianity to a group of hysterical women. On the other side, Kathleen Corley attributes it to a group of quite sane women.[47]

'I'm Brian, and So's My Wife!' or Ecce Homo

Despite Brian's practicality, which matches even that of Judith, he is ultimately feminized. This was not what we would have expected from the opening credits:

Yes, he grew up to be
A teenager called 'Brian'–
A teenager called 'Brian',
And his face became spotty.
Yes, his face became spotty,
And his voice dropped down low
And things started to grow

47. Kathleen Corley, *Maranatha: Women's Funerary Rites and Christian Origins* (Minneapolis, MN: Fortress Press, 2010).

On young Brian and so
He was certainly no –
No girl named 'Brian',
Not a girl named 'Brian'.
And he started to shave
And have one off the wrist
And want to see girls
And go out and get pissed,
A man called 'Brian'–
This man called 'Brian'–
The man they called 'Brian'– This man called 'Brian'!

He not a man, at least by Roman standards; Schilbrack nails him: 'Brian whimpers. He is pushed around by his mother. As a revolutionary, he is incompetent and he cannot compose a proper sentence in Latin, even one composed of just three words.'[48] At the end, rather than talk himself out of the cross and use Jewish cleverness to live rather than to die,[49] he puts up with the nonsense and so allows his body to become an object on which others act. Even in his death, his is not the image that people remember. He is not the one looking on the bright side. His death is, if not tragic, bathetic. His body, his character, thus become open symbols upon which commentators will continue to express their desires, and ask their questions.

What Has Python Done for Us?

Life of Brian is awash in pedagogical opportunities. Whether that washing will have a cleansing effect is another matter. The movie depicts first-century Jewish women's social freedoms even as it reinforces stereotypes of their oppression. It satirizes Rome's (and any empire's) claim of peace through strength even as it makes fun of people with speech impediments and mental disabilities. It locates gender-bending in the context of colonial rule even as it undermines this concern by parodying trade unionism and the early feminist movement. When parody or satire is done from below or by those who are oppressed it can be hailed. When it is done in order to change systems for the better, it is to be celebrated. When it is done by privileged people and aimed at those with less power, it is not as funny, if it is funny at all. Yes, we should laugh when we watch *Life of Brian*: there are parts that are brilliant. But even as we laugh, perhaps we do well to query at whose expense this laughter comes.

48. Kevin Schilbrack, ' "Life's a Piece of Shit": Heresy, Humanism, and Heroism', in Gary L. Hardcastle and George A. Reisch (eds), *Monty Python and Philosophy: Nudge Nudge, Think Think!* (New York: Open Court, 2006), pp.13–24, at p. 13.

49. Daniel Boyarin, *Dying for God: Martyrdom and the Making of Christianity and Judaism* (Stanford, CA: Stanford University Press, 1999), esp. pp. 55–6.

Chapter 14

'WHAT HAVE THE ROMANS EVER DONE FOR US?' BRIAN AND JOSEPHUS ON ANTI-ROMAN SENTIMENT

Steve Mason

Thoughtful people have long recognized that fiction, like poetry, can crystallize truths more effectively than diligent history. Homer's epics and the tragic plays performed in Athens' theatre brought home powerful emotions of wartime grief, rage, vows and regrets in ways that made historians shudder. One reason that Monty Python's *Life of Brian* is all but required viewing for undergraduates in Classics, aside from the sheer pleasure of watching it, is that it helps us to think about the paradoxes of life under Roman occupation. Pilate and Biggus with their legionary soldiers furnish the stable background, and 'Romans go home!' is the slogan that jumps to everyone's lips.

The Pythons were not the first to assume that anti-Roman sentiment pervaded first-century Judaea. Finding this picture everywhere in their surprisingly careful research, I suppose, they took it as given and turned their hands to drawing out the comedic possibilities. Of many memorable scenes, the one suggested in my title is particularly relevant for our theme. Reg defiantly poses the revolutionary's question, 'What have the Romans ever done for us?', to which the rhetorical answer should be 'Nothing!', only to be forced by his audience to concede 'All right, but apart from the sanitation, the medicine, education, wine, public order ..., what have the Romans ever done for us?' Another scene, shortly before that, portrays the snack-seller Brian's recruitment to the People's Front of Judaea:

> BRIAN: I didn't want to sell this stuff. It's only a job. I hate the Romans as much as anybody ...
> JUDITH: Are you sure?
> BRIAN: Oh, dead sure. I hate the Romans already.
> REG: Listen. If you really wanted to join the PFJ, you'd have to really hate the Romans.
> BRIAN: I do!
> REG: Oh, yeah? How much?
> BRIAN: A lot!
> REG: Right. You're in.

This picture of factions competing in their hatred for Rome only makes vivid an 1893 formulation by the eminent scholar Heinrich Graetz:

> In their native land, and especially in Jerusalem, the yoke of the Romans weighed heavily on the Judaeans, and became daily more oppressive ... The last decades exhibit the nation as a captive who, continually tormented and goaded on by his jailer, tugs at his fetters, with the strength of despair, until he wrenches them asunder.[1]

Since Graetz's time, scholars have deepened and nuanced the picture in many ways, of course, in particular by exploring the spiritual-nationalistic roots of the Judaean 'freedom movement' and the socio-economic issues that may have fuelled it. Whether historians favour ideological or socio-economic reasons or some combination, however, they end up in much the same place: 'From the first imposition of Roman rule in AD 6, Jewish reaction had been adverse ... subjection to Rome affronted the most cherished belief of their religion,' or: 'The lifetime of Jesus and his followers was framed historically by widespread popular revolts against both the Romans and their client rulers.'[2] This accepted picture of pervasive

---

1. Heinrich Graetz, *History of the Jews*. 6 vols. (Philadelphia: Jewish Publication Society of America, 1949 [1893]), Vol. 2, p. 233.

2. Respectively from S. G. F. Brandon, 'The Defeat of Cestius Gallus: A Roman Legate Faced the Problem of the Jewish Revolt', *History Today* 20/1 (Jan. 1970), pp. 38–46, at p. 38, and Richard A. Horsley, 'Jesus and Empire', in Horsley (ed.), *In the Shadow of Empire: Reclaiming the Bible as a History of Faithful Resistance* (Louisville, KY: Westminster John Knox, 2008), pp. 75–96, at p. 81. The fundamental scholarship behind these views includes William R. Farmer, *Maccabees, Zealots, and Josephus* (New York: Columbia University Press, 1956); David M. Rhoads, *Israel in Revolution, 6–74 CE: A Political History based on the*

anti-Roman animus in Judaea provides the backdrop not only for the *Life of Brian* but also for historical dramas from Lew Wallace's *Ben-Hur* (1880) to an episode of the television series *Rome* (2005) via Boris Sagal's *Masada* (1981) and Mel Gibson's *The Passion of the Christ* (2004).

No one should doubt that in 70 CE a legionary force led by the future emperor Titus destroyed Jerusalem and its Temple, after a long and bitter siege. In the decade following the war, Titus and his father Vespasian would tirelessly drive home their achievement, for it was the most politically acceptable basis of their claim to rule: they alone had defeated the Eastern Menace! Given that poorly armed and trained fighters were willing to defy Roman arms in Jerusalem in 70, it might seem almost tautological to conclude that many Judaeans – like Brian – must have really hated the Romans.

But to construe the war's origins from its results would involve fallacious historical reasoning. We know that wars often, perhaps usually, end up in places never imagined by those who initiated them. Issues that trigger a conflict quickly fade to the margins, as one thing leads to another. Two scholars, Martin Goodman and James McLaren, have developed one aspect of this point, standing against the common notion of a steady deterioration in relations between Jerusalem and Rome.[3] Their studies are different in scope and approach, but both stress the absence of such a trajectory of grievance. Both blame Josephus for creating that misleading picture, which they accuse him of being unable to support with evidence. Both nevertheless argue that, when hostilities did erupt, the part of Jerusalem's aristocratic leadership that remained in the city moved decisively to confront Rome – and Josephus obfuscates this too.

I agree with Goodman and McLaren about the lack of evidence for a long-gathering storm, though I suspect that the evidence is lacking because it never crossed Josephus' mind to make such a case. And since Josephus is the one who provides conspicuous evidence for the role of the priestly elite, especially of himself, in the beginnings of the war, it is hard to agree that he tries to conceal this involvement. His role as 'general' is a point of pride, allowing him to illustrate his martial skill and valour. In the following essay, however, we must leave aside the events of 66 and later. I hope to make a modest contribution to a question that my two colleagues, in rightly rejecting the notion of an essential and mounting fury against Rome, have left open. Namely: Where did the energy for eventual Judaean militancy come from?

Writings of Josephus (Philadelphia: Fortress, 1976); and Martin Hengel, *The Zealots: Investigations into the Jewish Freedom Movement in the Period from Herod I until 70 AD*, trans. D. Smith (Edinburgh: T&T Clark, 1989 [German original 1961]).

3. James S. McLaren, *Turbulent Times? Josephus and Scholarship on Judaea in the First Century CE* (Sheffield: Sheffield Academic Press, 1998); idem, 'The Coinage of the First Year as a Point of Reference for the First Jewish Revolt (66–70 CE)', *Scripta Classica Israelica* 22, pp. 135–52; Martin D. Goodman, *Rome and Jerusalem: The Clash of Ancient Civilizations* (London: Penguin, 2007).

In limited space here I shall sketch a case for seeing local hostilities as the engine of conflict, which eventually and predictably brought in Roman medicine even though the Judaeans' quarrel was not with Rome. This case has three parts. First, when Pompey the Great arrived to establish the new Roman province of Syria (64–63 BCE), he found the southern part riven by inter-ethnic hatred, much exacerbated by Jerusalem's domination of the south. Second, Roman rulers from Julius Caesar and Augustus through Claudius found it prudent to maintain Jerusalem's regional hegemony, not with Judaizing Hasmoneans to be sure, but with men they personally trusted as friends and brokers. Third, although this notional alliance benefitted both Rome and Jerusalem, Judaea's neighbours were not happy. Their most effective instrument was the auxiliary army, which was locally recruited. If no one kept it under tight control, the auxiliary could act with local populations against Judaeans under the protection that came from being the law in those parts.

Higher officials normally did keep the auxiliary in check, so that even when hostilities occasionally flared, life remained tolerable for Judaeans. When the checks and balances failed, however, Judaeans turned to self-help and Rome had to intervene. Until Nero's later years, such intervention typically turned in Jerusalem's favour, partly under the influence of Herodians in Rome. The peculiar circumstances of Nero's reign in the mid-60s changed things decisively. Self-help against the auxiliary and 'the new sheriff' Gessius Florus became, in the minds of many, an existential necessity, no matter what the consequences. Although Jerusalem certainly ended up at war with Rome, then, it was local hostility rather than anti-Roman sentiment that fuelled tensions in pre-70 Judaea.

A methodological point before we proceed. I am not suggesting that this reconstruction results from a 'correct' reading of Josephus' *War* or *Antiquities*, or that it can be extruded from these narratives. Josephus had his complex reasons for writing, and we can only be glad that he did. But his interests were not ours, and vice versa. Ancient life, like modern counterparts, was a chaos of thoughts, influences, motives, actions, interactions and reactions. Whoever sets out to write a story about real life can only ever thread a few selected skeins into a meaningful arc, with a beginning, middle, and end. That is what Josephus did; he could not do otherwise. He did not leave us magic powder, to which we can add water to reconstitute the reality.

All we can do is ask our questions and imagine the sorts of past that might answer them, in the process explaining the bits and pieces of evidence that have survived. These include Josephus' accounts, but also material evidence and passages in Tacitus, Suetonius, and Xiphilinus' epitome of the third-century historian Cassius Dio. Lacking the space for a review of all that, I shall simply offer a sketch that differs from the standard anti-Roman scenario and yet explains the evidence economically.[4]

---

4. This sketch reflects the detailed arguments in Steve Mason, *A History of the Jewish War, 66-74* (Cambridge: Cambridge University Press, 2015 forthcoming).

The Regional Situation

The biggest problem we face in thinking about this region originates in our mental maps, for we tend to view the southern part of Syria as a conceptual unity. We may call it the 'Land of Israel' (*Erets-Yisrael*) or 'Palestine' or 'Judaea' in a capacious sense, but maps in biblical or classical atlases conceptualize a unified territory running eastward from the Mediterranean to the Jordan River (plus Peraea) and northward from the Negev to Galilee – a territory matching the modern state of Israel and Palestinian territories (see Figure 14.1). The major adjustments were the divisions were among Herod's three sons after 4 BCE, the replacement of Archelaus' rule with Roman administration from 6 CE, the short-lived kingdom of Agrippa I (41–44 CE), and an enlarged matching Province of Judaea from 44 to 66. One often hears that this Province of Judaea revolted against Rome. That cannot be the case, however, because if such a province had existed, its capital would have been coastal Caesarea. Yet Caesarea, the regional centre of imperial cult and home to both Rome's local agent and the auxiliary, was emphatically non-Judaean and never participated in revolt. The Judaea that found itself in lethal conflict with Rome was not a province, but the ethnic hinterland of Jerusalem up in the hills.

Although a couple of statements in Josephus' *War* suggest that a separate province of Judaea was constituted in 6 CE, they are undercut by other parts of that same narrative, by clearer statements in the *Antiquities*, and by the evidence of writers such as Strabo, Pomponius Mela, Pliny, Tacitus and Cassius Dio.[5] Judaea was the hill country surrounding Jerusalem, a landlocked area that did not include the coastal plain except at Joppa, recognized from Hasmonean times as Judaea's (conquered) outlet to the sea. Along the coast were other cities, at least as ancient, with their own large hinterlands. Inland, just tens of kilometres north and south of Jerusalem, Judaea brushed the frontiers of Samaria and Idumaea, both of which could be competitive and seriously hostile. To the east and northeast lay the proud Syrian-Greek cities of the Decapolis.

When the Persians allowed the Judaeans to rebuild their mother-city in the fifth and sixth centuries, it became a small Temple-centred settlement of a few hundreds or possibly a thousand inhabitants. For the next three or four centuries, it seems, Jerusalem was subordinate to Samaria. Samaria's capital sat about 60 km (37 miles)

---

5. *Ant.* 17.354; 18.2 qualifying *War* 2.117. Werner Eck, *Rom und Judaea: fünf Vorträge zur römischen Herrschaft in Palaestina* (Tübingen: Mohr Siebeck, 2007), pp. 1–54; Gilbert Labbé, *L'affirmation de la puissance romaine en Judée (63 avant J.-C.-136 après J.-C.)* (Paris: Les Belles Lettres, 2012). This was the original view of Emil Schürer, *Lehrbuch der neutestamentlichen Zeitgeschichte* (Leipzig: J. C. Hinrichs, 1874), pp. 249–50, although later editions and especially the current English version – Emil Schürer, *The History of the Jewish People in the Age of Jesus Christ*, ed. Geza Vermes, Fergus Millar and Martin Goodman, 3 vols. in 4 (Edinburgh, T&T Clark, 1979-1987), Vol. 1, pp. 243, 266 – emphasize Judaea's independence.

Figure 14.1 Palestine in the time of Jesus. Map by Charles Foster Kent, 1912.
Wikimedia Commons.

north/northwest of Jerusalem, and there a succession of foreign powers recruited and based their regional military garrison. Samaria famously gave Jerusalem a hard time during the post-Exilic restoration, and its watchful presence continued under Persian rule and that of the successor kingdoms to Alexander the Great. Samaria remained the military-political centre of so-called Coele-Syria into the early second century BCE, as Jerusalem remained a smaller Temple-city, lacking Samaria's geographical benefits as a military centre.

Not far from the Samarians' garrison capital, in the fifth century BCE they had built a Temple on Mt Gerizim for their ancestral cult. This was closely related to the Judaean cult, likewise worshipping the imageless God of Mosaic Law. In the early second century, when the Seleucids finally wrested Coele-Syria from the Ptolemies based in Egypt, their ruler Antiochus III expanded Gerizim's Temple precinct and lavishly endowed it as a major site of piety tourism, just as he rewarded the Judaeans and their priesthood in Jerusalem for their support.

Surrounding the village-culture of Samaria and Idumaea, I have noted, the region was densely populated with the larger centres the ancients called *poleis* with their large dependent territories. A number of these were as old as the Canaanite precursor of Jerusalem, though many had been refounded with superficially Greek forms under Alexander's successors. Whatever their start dates, by the second century they enjoyed distinctive laws, customs, calendars, festivals and in some cases coinage, all now coloured by a common Hellenistic-fusion culture. Gaza, Ascalon, Gerasa, and Gadara, like Tyre and Byblos farther north, had produced world-famous intellectuals. Into this ancient mix, in the late first century BCE, King Herod introduced such impressive new foundations as Panias, Samaria (now Sebaste), and coastal Caesarea (formerly Strato's Tower). These were hybrids comprising older populations with their traditions and cults, military families with their special traditions, and grandiose implementations of the new imperial cult attracted by Augustus.

Although the crow's-fly distances between these places are short, from our perspective in an age of car travel, the succession of empires and changing trade routes, the highly varied terrain, and the many micro-climates of southern Syria had by the first century BCE left a couple of dozen sizeable centres, of quite different character and culture, within 60 km (36 miles) of each other. Most of the time they lived in relative isolation, with traders moving back and forth, and in peace.

In the 160s BCE, however, the usual rivalry among neighbours morphed into something quite different. We have seen that Samaria and Judaea, like other cities in the south, threw their support behind Antiochus III as he took control over Coele-Syria. This was a bright moment in the Seleucids' otherwise imperilled rule, as Parthia encroached from the east, Rome from the west, and internal conflicts abounded. When the great king's usurper son Antiochus IV came to power in 175 BCE, however, he was facing a badly faltering kingdom. Still the Samarian and Judaean elites were keen to maintain his favour. Part of their shared programme, it seems, was to integrate their traditional cults into the general Hellenistic fusion, showing that they were cooperative and trustworthy clients.

Although this appears to have gone smoothly in the case of the Samarian cult, in Jerusalem the elite initiative caused a serious popular backlash. Militant opposition brought harsh reprisals from Antiochus, so much so that he was on the verge of abolishing traditional Judaean ways. Fortunately for Jerusalem, his resources were rapidly dwindling and he could not sustain his retribution. He would soon be dead (164 BCE), on a venture to raid Temple funds elsewhere, and his successors would be plagued by dynastic rivalry.

Seizing the moment in 167, Judaeans led by the rural-priestly Hasmonean family tested their strength and tried to turn the tables on Antiochus. Rather than submitting, they asserted themselves and soon found their capacity increasing. First they reclaimed Jerusalem and its Temple for its traditional cultic sacrifice (164 BCE). By means of shrewd alliances and increasingly with the use of mercenary forces, they managed in the course of the next three generations to massively augment Judaean territory, revenue, and military capability, ensuring that the mother-city would never again find itself vulnerable to another *polis*.

Needless to say, this expansion came at a cost for Jerusalem's neighbours.[6] Jerusalem enlarged its hinterland until it reached far north of Samaria, through Galilee and beyond, as well as east of the Jordan River, west to the Mediterranean and southward through Idumaea. Conquest took many forms, but Judaization was the overriding theme. Newly subject populations were forced either to embrace Judaean law and custom, which brought with it the genital circumcision of all males, or to flee. Those who resisted faced destruction. In Samaria, the Judaeans destroyed both the centuries-old Temple on Gerizim, which would never be rebuilt (ca. 111 BCE), and the garrison capital of Samaria, reducing the survivors to slavery. In Idumaea, much of the elite agreed to Judaize. Those who could not do so fled to Egypt or elsewhere. By these means Jerusalem came to control southern Syria, with the sole exception of Ascalon, a perpetually defiant enemy 70 km (42 miles) to the southwest.

This was roughly the situation that greeted Pompey the Great when he brought Rome to Syria in 64/63. His first step in placing the whole area under Rome's man in Antioch was to remove Jerusalem's vast acquisitions, rebuild the destroyed cities, and restore their populations as far as possible. His rebuilding of Gadara, home to the family of his trusted freedman Demetrius, is the clearest example, for the Gadaranes continued to call themselves 'Pompeian' for centuries. But several cities gave themselves a new civic calendar dating from Pompey's liberation of them from Jerusalem's domination.

Although the massive curtailment of Jerusalem's control served a Roman instinct to keep subject cities in a productive rivalry, that principle competed with a fundamental commitment to government by the smallest possible footprint. The new Syria was a huge province, and the part south of the Lebanon mountains (Coele-Syria) was about three weeks' march from the capital Antioch, also from

---

6. *War* 1.48–106; *Ant.* 13.254–58; Strabo, 16.2.2, 34; Ammonius, *Adfin. voc.* '*Ioudaios/ Idoumaios*'.

the province's legions, which had to be stationed near the Euphrates frontier with Parthia. It was not long before successive Roman officials found the wisdom in taking advantage of Judaea's century-long primacy, especially because bold and capable Judaean leaders who could serve as Rome's brokers presented themselves in the family of Antipater the Idumaean.

Rome's Favour Towards Jerusalem

I am not suggesting that Roman rulers thought in sentimental terms about Zion or Israel or divine chosenness. Far from it: senators and autocrats thought about their interests, seeking maximum return in revenue and renown on minimum risk or cost. Nor is it necessary to imagine that they had a grand strategy for the eastern provinces or any particular interest in local governance. A number of studies have explored Roman provincial governance in terms of values applied by ruling figures to ever-changing problems, without modern conceptions of policy and planning.[7] I would isolate four Roman values relevant for our question.

1. The principle of economy: maximize revenue and incoming benefits with the smallest possible investment of Roman resources, governing apparatus and citizen soldiers (legions). Likewise, expend as little physical force as possible while maintaining maximum power (*imperium*).
2. Cultivate and respect local city aristocracies as the nuclei of each province, letting them handle local affairs as far as possible and to the extent that this poses no danger. Reward and motivate powerful local friends with Roman citizenship, possibly even equestrian status.
3. Endow trusted personal friends as 'allied monarchs' if possible, exploiting their own motivation to succeed as notionally independent potentates. Allowing such grandees kingdoms of their own radically reduces investment. Rome needs only one address, and can hold the monarch personally responsible for peace and various kinds of revenue or other support.
4. Encourage competition for imperial favour among the governed and their leaders, both to accentuate the lines of patronage and to preclude collaboration, grievance-sharing, or conspiracy.

---

7. E.g., Fergus Millar, *The Emperor in the Roman World, 31 BC–AD 337* (Ithaca: Cornell University Press, 1977); Jon E. Lendon, *Empire of Honour: The Art of Government in the Roman World* (Oxford: Clarendon Press, 1997); Susan P. Mattern, *Rome and the Enemy: Imperial Strategy in the Principate* (Berkeley: University of California Press, 1999); Clifford Ando, *Imperial Ideology and Provincial Loyalty in the Roman Empire* (Berkeley: University of California Press, 2000); Eckhard Meyer-Zwiffelhoffer, *Politikōs Archein: zum Regierungsstil der senatorischen Statthalter in den kaiserzeitlichen griechischen Provinzen* (Stuttgart: Franz Steiner, 2002).

In southern Syria these principles gelled marvellously, from Rome's perspective, in the family of Herod the Great. Herod's father, himself an energetic power-player with connections all over the place, shrewdly exploited the diminished Judaean monarchy of Hyrcanus II to groom his sons as Roman favourites. Marc Antony and Augustus recognized loyal talent when they saw it, and gave Antipater's son Herod rapidly expanding control, from Jerusalem, over southern Syria. Herod married his considerable personal ambition with Rome's needs, while firmly re-establishing Jerusalem as regional power.

Herod's children, grandchildren and great-grandchildren grew up in Rome's imperial court circles. Apparently, Augustus and his successors hoped to ride this train as long as possible. When Herod died, and Augustus was faced with the claims of three surviving sons in their early twenties, he gave each of them a share of the father's kingdom to see what they could do, cautiously but decisively leaving the whole under Herodian control, against the appeals of many Jerusalem aristocrats (*War* 2.22, 80–96). Two of the three sons would succeed brilliantly, and remain in place longer even than their father.

If Archelaus had proven as successful and produced an heir to the throne, the conditions that later generated Judaean vigilantism might never have occurred. But he managed to offend both of his main constituents: the Samarian elite and Jerusalem's priestly aristocracy (2.111). Augustus felt he had to remove the man, still only in his early thirties. Augustus' successors tended nevertheless to prefer Herodian governance from Jerusalem whenever possible. When Claudius gave his 51-year-old friend Agrippa I a Jerusalem-based monarchy that included much of modern Lebanon, Syria, and Jordan, he had every reason to expect that it would last a couple of decades, and perhaps that it would continue in perpetuity under Rome-reared Agrippa II and later successors.

To the extent that the Romans had a 'plan' for a southern Syria that was ethnically diverse but formerly dominated by Jerusalem, it seems to have been that: let their friends govern from Jerusalem, with a modest army recruited from across the region. This was the easiest solution: 'Keep the peace, keep in touch, and let us know how you get on!'

Problems arose when no Herodian was available for Jerusalem's throne. This occurred twice: in 6 CE, with young Archelaus' removal, and again in 44 CE, with the sudden death of Agrippa I, as his son Agrippa II was only sixteen. Archelaus was removed after a concerted effort by elites of *both* Jerusalem and Samaria, whose criticisms of the ethnarch had provoked 'savage' responses (*War* 2.111). We have no other information about Samarians' particular complaints, though they are not hard to guess: they did not wish to be under this Jerusalem monarch's thumb. As for Jerusalem's elite, when Herod died they pleaded with Augustus to be annexed to Syria. That would enable them to administer Jerusalem corporately, with no need of a monarch, just as other aristocracies administered their cities (*War* 2.80–91). Loss of regional power was apparently less of a worry for them than their daily humiliation by the autocrat living in the palace on Jerusalem's high western hill.

So the high priest Joazar and his colleagues continued to lobby for Archelaus' removal, possibly scrutinizing his every move and reporting complaints to

Augustus. However it happened, they finally succeeded in 6 CE. Facing predictable unrest from the people, the high priest threw himself into a campaign of reassurance. Everything would be fine: Judaeans had nothing to fear from rejoining the Province of Syria as a normal *polis* (shades of Antiochus IV!). Unfortunately for Joazar, the shift came just in time for Jerusalem to participate in the legate Quirinius' registration of property throughout Syria for the sake of taxation. Perhaps Augustus decided to remove Archelaus just now with the arrival of Quirinius and the census in view. In any case the unavoidably invasive census was salt in the wound, a vivid mark of Jerusalem's radical loss of prestige, and Joazar had to work particularly hard to bring it off peacefully (*Ant.* 18.1–4).

The census aside, this new arrangement brought significant risks for Jerusalem, which may have been more obvious to the common folk and business people than to the land-owning aristocrats, who were so intent on securing their position within Jerusalem. The most obvious risk was that Jerusalem's neighbours would chance their arms, and look to humiliate the city whenever possible in retribution for its long decades at the top of the heap.

In spite of questions about Agrippa's wisdom and his falling out with Tiberius, the emperors Gaius and Claudius gave him the former territories of his uncles Philip and Antipas, then eventually – after he played a crucial role in Claudius' accession – the large kingdom mentioned above. When Agrippa up and died unexpectedly, however, Claudius was forced to return to the stopgap model Augustus had used after Archelaus' removal, this time without a lobbying effort. We have some reason to think that Agrippa I had done a much better job than Archelaus of conciliating the priestly elite.

For simplicity's sake I shall call this alternative model *Plan B*, if I may do so without suggesting that it was an actual plan or strategy. It was simply a response to the failure of Plan A, putting emperors' friends on Jerusalem's throne. Whatever we call it, this alternative arrangement had the following characteristics.

1. Most tellingly, as far as we know Roman emperors never entertained the possibility of appointing an Ascalonite, Gazan, Gadarene, Samarian, Scythopolitan or Idumaean to rule southern Syria from one of *their* cities. Only Jerusalem and Judaeans were ever eligible, and only Herodians.

2. When the friends-and-family arrangement was not feasible, the emperor returned southern Syria to his provincial legate in Antioch. This distinguished senator, a former consul, monitored even the activities of notionally independent kings, standing ready if necessary to send military support – or to confront them over alleged suspect behaviour. So when there was no monarch in the south the legate assumed direct responsibility, and Jerusalem became a high-priority *polis* in his administrative circuit. This meant visiting regularly and staying in close communication with the elite, including any available royals.

3. Because the southern region was so important and yet so far from Antioch, in the absence of a monarch the emperor sent a special representative, with the title of prefect or procurator, to coastal Caesarea. This relatively new city

lacked an ancient stake in the inter-ethnic hostilities; it was no Ascalon, Sebaste or Scythopolis. Built by Herod for the emperor, and being the headquarters of his agent and regional armed forces, it came as close as possible to being neutral in the area's rivalries. Nevertheless, it tended naturally to be an anti-Jerusalem: a city dominated by images, the imperial cult, and Graeco-Roman infrastructure, which bonded with Sebaste, the other main Herodian foundation featuring the imperial cult, which also produced much of the auxiliary army.

4. Although Caesarea was no part of Judaea, the prefect's portfolio could be called 'Judaea', as we see in the famous Pilate inscription (*Praefectus Iudaeae*) found there – because, I would suggest, Judaea's unique position was this man's chief concern.[8] Since it was predictable that Jerusalem's loss of status would encourage its enemies, the Prefect was responsible for ensuring that things did not get out of hand. In a fox-guarding-the-henhouse scenario, he had to ensure that his auxiliary protected Jerusalem and Judaeans, who remained the most widely distributed and influential population, with minorities in most cities including Caesarea.

5. Although Josephus was not concerned to explain any of this, he left substantial evidence of Roman solicitousness toward Jerusalem, which finds support in Philo, the gospels, and the numismatic evidence.

   a. The legate in Antioch frequently, perhaps routinely, visited Jerusalem for Passover. We happen to know, by reconstructing what Josephus does not spell out, that L. Vitellius visited on successive Passovers, to thank Jerusalem's leaders for their cooperation and ask what he could do to help. He brought significant favours. Similarly, the legates Quirinius, Petronius, Marsus, Longinus, Quadratus, and Cestius Gallus all gave Jerusalem a central place in their administration of Syria.[9]

   b. Reciprocally, the Judaean elite turned to the legates in Antioch for redress of any grievances.[10] Usually they found satisfaction, most strikingly in Vitellius' intervention to return control of the high priest's robes to them, in Petronius' delicate moves to stall Gaius' planned installation of one or more statues in the Jerusalem Temple, in Quadratus' dismissal of the equestrian Prefect to Rome (accompanied by regional delegations) to render account, and in Cestius Gallus' repeated efforts to forestall Judaean militancy and his military intervention in 66.

   c. As for the Prefects/Procurators sent to Caesarea, Pontius Pilate governed for at least ten or eleven years, perhaps as many as nineteen. With his coins and otherwise he seems to have gone to considerable lengths to work with

---

8. On the inscription see Schürer (ed. Vermes et al.), *History of the Jewish People*, Vol. 1, p. 358 n. 22.

9. E.g. Philo, *Embassy* 230–31; Josephus, *War* 2.243, 280; *Ant.* 15.405; 18.90; 19.340.

10. Paul McKechnie, 'Judaean Embassies and Cases before Roman Emperors, AD 44–66', *JTS* 56 (2005), pp. 339–61.

Judaean leaders, as his long tenure also suggests. Josephus mentions
two events involving him. One had to do with his effort to build a new
aqueduct (perhaps a new section of one) for Jerusalem. However the
reported unrest over expenses came about, it is hard to doubt that the
project itself was a major boon for Jerusalem. Aqueducts were expensive,
requiring imported technical expertise along with the materials, and a
mark of real prestige for a city. In the other incident, Pilate seems to have
wanted to avoid offending well-known Judaean customs concerning
human images, by having his cohort take theirs into Jerusalem by night
and under covers (*War* 2.169–75).

The partly independent gospels of the New Testament portray
Pilate cooperating closely with Judaean leaders to remove a number
of troublemakers – various robbers and criminals – whom they have
convicted alongside Jesus.[11] According to Philo, Tiberius wrote to
admonish Pilate over an incident that again hardly seems calculated to
cause trouble with Jerusalem. The Prefect had tried to bring *blank* votive
shields – bearing no images – into the auxiliary garrison of Herod's former
palace, perhaps as a compromise on the standards issue. Tiberius told
him off even for that, on the ground that it would offend the Judaeans
(*Embassy* 299–305). We should remember that it was a complaint not
from Judaeans but from the Samarian elite, alleging a history of abuse
and hostility toward *them*, that finally ended Pilate's time in Syria
(*Ant.* 18.89).

d. Of Pilate's successors, after the brief monarchy of Agrippa I, one was
given a clear mandate to keep the Samarians and the auxiliary force in
check. The next hailed from a prominent Judaean family of Alexandria
(Tiberius Julius Alexander, 46–48 CE), and was a nephew of the eminent
Philo. Felix, the next but one, came at the request of Jerusalem's high priest
(*Ant.* 20.162). And soon after arriving, Felix married the daughter of
Agrippa I, Drusilla, the sister of Agrippa II. Claudius and then Nero left
him in place for about seven years, through the fifties. This long tenure
might suggest that young Nero's advisors intended him to hold the
place until his (now) brother-in-law Agrippa II was mature enough to
re-establish the monarchy in Jerusalem. Nero's expansion of Agrippa II's
starter kingdom (from Claudius), with choice Judaean cities nearby on the
Kinneret Lake, also points in this direction (*Ant.* 20.159).

e. Coins issued by the prefects in Caesarea exhibit their great care not to
offend Judaean sensibilities, uncharacteristically (for provincial coinage)
lacking human images. Israeli numismatist Ya'akov Meshorer included
them in his catalogues of *Jewish* coins for just this reason.[12]

---

11. Mark 15; Matthew 27; Luke 23; John 18.28–19.42; Acts 13.28.

12. Ya'akov Meshorer, *A Treasury of Jewish Coins from the Persian Period to Bar Kokhba*
(Jerusalem: Yad ben-Zvi, 2001), pp. 167–72.

f. Back in Rome, Judaean royals remained well positioned and in frequent communication with emperors, to the benefit of Judaea's position. They in turn were closely connected with the Alexandrian-Judaean elite, which had a place in the salon of Claudius' mother Antonia Minor. No other *ethnos* in Syria, as far as we know, enjoyed such privileged and effective access. It is true that we do not know much of what really happened, and that our main information comes from the Judaean Josephus, but some of the incidents he describes preclude the possibility of equivalent Samarian influence, when Samarians lost their emissaries to an emperor's anger. And we have partially independent confirmation in the *Acts of the Alexandrians* of the perception that Judaeans were conspicuously favoured by Claudius' court.[13]

By now the reader might be objecting: 'It's all very well saying that Jerusalem's Romanized elite groups were loyal to Rome, but that served their interests. What about popular Judaean sentiment and the famous rebel groups: Judas the Galilean, the Fourth Philosophy, *Sicarii*, and the others belonging to Martin Hengel's "freedom movement"?' Here I can only make the general remark that while we have plenty of independent evidence of inter-ethnic conflict in the area, that between Judaeans and Samarians being the most famous (in Josephus, the Gospels, and Tacitus), we have little to suggest militant hatred of faraway Rome. Moreover, the regional status of Jerusalem was presumably an issue that mattered to common people, who may have bonded with a Rome-endorsed ruler (Herod or Archelaus) over against the native aristocracy because their city's prominence made them walk taller. Otherwise, I can comment only briefly on the more famous of the players often held to be rabidly anti-Roman.

Judas the Galilean/Gaulanite

Josephus claims that the annexation of Jerusalem and its hinterland to Syria caused popular discontent, which the high priest Joazar temporarily calmed, until Judas and a popular Pharisee whipped it up again. With crushing ridicule, Josephus gives these men a wholly infeasible slogan: 'We accept no ruler except God!' Such an abstract and meaningless platform could hardly have roused the people to fury, however, especially if it was used as a protest against the *removal* of the less than God-like Archelaus. If we put Josephus' hostile characterization to one side and look rather at the circumstances of Judas' revolt, it appears that the people could not have been objecting to Roman rule, to which they had been subject for seventy years already. They were protesting, rather, the changes of 6 CE. If Archelaus had not been removed, presumably they would have had nothing to protest. If that is so, their issue was not Roman rule but Jerusalem's loss of regional primacy, direct

---

13. Andrew Harker, *Loyalty and Dissidence in Roman Egypt: The Case of the Acta Alexandrinorum* (Cambridge: Cambridge University Press, 2008), pp. 10–15, 39–45.

subjection to Antioch, and the dangers this posed for Jerusalem – a concern that the sequel showed to be well founded.

Sicarii

It is remarkable that the name *Sicarii* continues to suggest to many 'Judaean fighters against Rome', though the diverse types that Josephus includes under this label are distinguished by the fact that not a single one fought Romans.[14] Their métier, at least in the main passages, was individual assassination of other Judaeans. We might doubt, indeed, that any group in first-century Judaea answered to the name *sicarius*, a Latin scare-word popular in Rome for individual treacherous killers, not for factions. We must suspect that Josephus' evident enjoyment of this Latin word, something unique in Greek literature, is best explained by the fact that he was writing in Rome, where the term had a particular shock value.

What about the famous episode in which Josephus claims that certain priests halted the sacrifice for the emperor and thus declared war on Rome? As with many famous episodes, this one is often garbled in the retelling. What Josephus actually says – in the context of the Judaeans' growing exasperation at Nero's revenue agent and his heavy handed auxiliary force, while Judaean factions are arming themselves for a move against these Samarians – is that those officiating in the Temple resolved 'to accept no gift or sacrifice from any outsider' (*War* 2.409). It is Josephus as narrator who then explains that this move implied also the stopping of the sacrifice for the emperor's well-being. He could see in retrospect, and allows the elder statesmen of the time to see, the implications for Jerusalem's soon-to-deteriorate relationship with Rome. But within the story itself that is not the motivating issue. The senior priests object to the initiative because it will remove Jerusalem from the community of nations and make them look anti-social, whereas by long tradition they have always been open to foreign visits and pious gifts (*War* 2.412–14).

When it comes to the famed Zealots, finally, we face many problems indeed. It is entirely plausible that some Judaeans modelled themselves on biblical Phineas and the Hasmoneans, who in jealous zeal for divine law (Hebrew: *qana'*) felt free to punish Judaeans they considered insufficiently faithful to the covenant, particularly in relations with neighbouring peoples. But if there were such people, we have little evidence of them. Josephus claims that a priest-affiliated group in the Temple, apparently continuous with Eleazar ben Ananias' faction in severing ties with outsiders (later led by Eleazar ben Simon, then John of Gischala), called themselves Greek *zēlōtai*. But the Greek word has quite different connotations from English Zealots, suggesting not biblical zeal for Torah but emulation of the good – in other persons or foreign legal systems. In Josephus' narrative, which plays only with the Greek meaning, the word suggests that they foolishly made themselves *disciples* or devotees of such unworthy leaders as Menachem or the Eleazars.

14. E.g. *War* 2.254, 425; 4.400, 516; 7.253–62, 410–15; *Ant.* 20.186, 208–10, with Mark Brighton, *The Sicarii in Josephus's Judean War: Rhetorical Analysis and Historical Observations* (Atlanta: Society of Biblical Literature, 2009).

Wherever we press these imagined groups of anti-Roman militants and popular people's fronts, they vaporize. This is not to say that everyone was delighted with Roman administration or taxes. Every government that ever existed has generated some discontent among the governed. The picture that best explains the evidence for militant resistance, however, is of a Judaean *ethnos* and a Jerusalem that were uniquely privileged as far as Rome was concerned, favoured and trusted as their brokers in southern Syria. This situation was not likely to generate massive popular discontent, and it did not as far as we know. Judas of Galilee and his kind led protests when Jerusalem was losing its Rome-enabled primacy. This may have been a simple matter of pride, but it is reasonable to imagine that they felt vulnerable to hostile neighbours.

Inter-Ethnic Hostility

What I have labelled the Romans' 'Plan B', which is to say the stopgap measures taken by Augustus and Claudius in the absence of a monarch, risked precisely this condition. Surrounding peoples were likely to act against Jerusalem whenever they had a chance. Normally they had little chance, because they had no reason to be in Jerusalem and Jerusalem did not visit them. These hostilities were not racial, and Judaean minorities in other cities were apparently tolerated as other foreigners were – unless suspected of conspiracy with Jerusalem, as happened in 66.

The sharp end of regional antagonisms toward Jerusalem was the auxiliary army, which I have mentioned above. This was not a Roman-citizen force, but was recruited mainly from Samaria and Caesarea and officered largely by Roman military professionals. King Herod had commanded a multi-ethnic force of perhaps 18–20,000 as his royal army, with a Judaean majority but several cohorts of Idumaeans and Samarians along with German and Gallic guards.[15] Though this was clearly the Judaean king's army, he had gone out of his way to honour and integrate Samaria in his 'balancing programme'.[16] When Herod died, for various reasons this army began to disintegrate, with the Idumaean contingents apparently returning home. We have few clues about the size or nature of Archelaus' down-sized force, though it seems to have retained key commanders and a strong Judaean contingent.[17] On his removal, however, the Judaean units fade from our evidence. Judaeans were exempt from conscription, a favour granted by Julius

15. Israel Shatzman, *The Armies of the Hasmonaeans and Herod: From Hellenistic to Roman Frameworks* (Tübingen: Mohr Siebeck, 1991); Samuel Rocca, *The Army of Herod the Great* (Oxford: Osprey, 2009).

16. Monika Bernett, *Der Kaiserkult in Judäa unter den Herodiern und Römern* (Tübingen: Mohr Siebeck, 2007), pp. 66–98.

17. Idumaeans: *War* 2.55, 76–79. Archelaus: Herod's loyal 'general' (*War* 1.652) is most likely the man the ethnarch turns to at 2.9. His army is eagerly supportive (2.3), comprising many cohorts of infantry and cavalry, and large enough to dispatch a reported 3,000 (2.11–13).

Caesar (*Ant.* 14.204). Without a monarch in Jerusalem they may simply have been unwilling to move to Caesarea, to live among foreign cults and images under likely uncongenial commanders. The reconfiguration of the military was presumably no small matter, though Josephus does not mention it, and this may have been one of the concerns driving popular protest in 6 CE.

The reconfiguration meant that the force of 3,000 or 3,500 that remained from Herod's allied army to become the auxiliary in southern Syria were chiefly Samarian, from Herod's revived capital and military bastion of Sebaste. Although the military city of Sebaste/Samaria had a different culture and often different cults from the traditional Samarian centre on Gerizim, where Jerusalem's forces had destroyed the great Temple more than a century earlier, several passages in Josephus make clear the bond of blood and community between other Samarians in general and the auxiliary soldiers.

Problems for Jerusalem arose now because this auxiliary was also the authorized police force, responsible for security in Jerusalem and requiring a monopoly of force. One cohort, of 500 or possibly 1,000, would be stationed in Jerusalem on a regular rotation, again highlighting the special importance of this *polis* in southern Syria. They kept guard over the Temple mount, looking down on the Judaeans from the high colonnade around the sacred enclosure. Whatever these soldiers did, every gesture or passing insult, they enjoyed the cover of Roman authority, whereas any action against them – no matter how understandable – was unavoidably an action against Rome's authorized army.

If we now recall some of the incidents between the Judaeans and their neighbours in this light, the notion that Judaeans hated Rome gives way to a very different picture: that Judaeans depended on higher Roman officials to guarantee their security against such antagonistic neighbours.

7/8 CE

Samarians wasted no time in chancing their arm against Jerusalem after it lost regional status. During perhaps the very next Passover, or the one after that, Samarians entered the Temple compound, which was open to all, and scattered human remains around the Temple area (*Ant.* 18.29–31), rendering it instantly unclean and unusable for the festival. The priests were forced to close the entire complex and undertake elaborate purifications. Since the auxiliary cohort failed to protect Jerusalem's interests, we must suspect collusion here. Augustus' removal of his first Prefect, Coponius, may have had something to do with his failure to prevent such a provocation.

20s CE

Pilate reportedly armed his soldiers with sticks rather than swords when controlling a crowd of protestors, presumably to avoid the predictable bloodbath (*War* 2.176), though the other account says that the soldiers 'used much harsher blows than Pilate had ordered' against the Judaeans (*Ant.* 18.61–62).

44 CE

Caesareans and Samarians celebrate the death of Agrippa I so obscenely that they rouse the ire of Claudius (*Ant.* 19.356–58):

> When it became known that Agrippa had departed this life, the Caesareans and Sebastenes . . . took a position of extreme hostility. They hurled slanders at the deceased that would be unseemly to relate. *Those of them who were serving in the military* at that time, and *there were many*, went off to his house and seized the statues of the king's daughters. These they brought en masse into the brothels, and set them up on the roofs, and proceeded to indulge their desires in every possible manner . . . They turned public places into feasting halls and held banquets for everyone: putting crowns on their heads, dousing themselves with perfume, pouring libations to Charon [mythical ferry-master of the dead], and drinking toasts to one another over the king's last breath.

44–46 CE

In a border dispute between Judaeans of Peraea and the Decapolis city of Philadelphia, Judaeans kill some Philadelphians and the Prefect Fadus sternly admonishes them for not trusting him to protect their interests, while punishing the main culprits. Another Judaean harasses villagers on the Idumaean border (*Ant.* 20.2–5).

50–51 CE

Several incidents occur while Ventidius Cumanus is Prefect/Procurator (*War* 2.223–46). An auxiliary soldier makes a rude gesture and noise from the Temple colonnade. Judaean youths below throw rocks, prompting his fellow-soldiers to react with greater force. An auxiliary soldier in Narbatene near Caesarea burns a copy of the Torah. At least one Judaean pilgrim from Galilee is murdered near Jenin while traversing Samaria en route to Jerusalem. Judaeans attack nearby Samarian villages, not Jenin (Ginae), in revenge for the murder. Cumanus takes the side of these Samarian villagers and sends auxiliary units to protect them.

Until this point near the end of Claudius' reign (in 54 CE), the system has apparently worked to protect Judaea's security. But now we suddenly see most of the ingredients of the coming war. Conditions on the ground remain as they ever were: deep animosity between Judaeans and each of their neighbours, which can flare up at any time. It tends to do so on the border areas of the respective hinterlands, between Judaea and Idumaea, Samaria, and the Decapolis. But until the mid-50s at least, 'Plan B' works to protect Judaean interests. Most of the equestrians in Caesarea have been very careful about Jerusalem. Ventidius Cumanus departs from that tradition and illustrates the temptation facing a Procurator to go native and side with his Samarian soldiers. On the other side we see the readiness of some among the Judaeans to resort to armed self-help, if

Roman officials appear unwilling or unable to protect them. They will not wait long, in trust, while being killed.

Yet the arrangement still works here because the emperor Claudius takes a personal interest. He receives advice in Rome from members of the Judaean royal family, Agrippa II and Herod of Chalcis. His legate in Antioch, Quadratus, also takes his responsibility for the south seriously. Although his first instinct is to support the Procurator and punish the Judaeans, he soon adopts a more objective position and sends Cumanus, his tribune, and the leaders of both delegations to Rome. With the Herodians' counsel Claudius exiles the Procurator, summarily executes three Samarian leaders, and returns the tribune Celer to Jerusalem for a violent lynching (*War* 2.245-46).

The regional conditions that we see under Cumanus in the early 50s, I am proposing, also drove the war in 66, which was therefore not anti-Roman. The inter-ethnic hostility involving the auxiliary remained unchanged or likely intensified. What changed dramatically to the Judaeans' detriment was that Nero, after he had turned twenty-one and cast off his senior advisors along with his mother Agrippina (59/60 CE), took a very different approach to governing generally, and to the Judaeans in particular. From that time onward his chief concern in the provinces was revenue collection. This he entrusted to his procurators, while his relations with the Senate and senatorial legates deteriorated.

For Judaea this meant the following. Nero's principal interest was the wealth housed in Jerusalem's world-famous Temple, to which Judaeans from around the world were known to contribute annually. He instructed his Procurators Albinus (62–64) and especially Gessius Florus (64–66) to raid those funds and to crush any resistance they faced. The Procurators' muscle in this was the auxiliary, which took to the task with zeal, exploiting every opportunity to exceed even violent Florus' orders with their own impromptu humiliations, beatings, robbery, and executions of the Judaean populace (*War* 2.277–334). Nero had no Judaean advisors and no interest in Judaean primacy, reportedly looking on the nation with contempt (*War* 6.422). He rejected the Judaeans' bold request to have coastal Caesarea, the crucial centre of the region when there was no monarch in Jerusalem, designated a Judaean *polis* (*War* 2.284).

Most fatefully, Nero's senatorial legate in Antioch, now Cestius Gallus, was neutralized. He himself made every effort to stay in communication with the Judaean elite, as his predecessors had done, visiting Jerusalem at his first Passover in the province (April 66). He worked constantly and closely with Agrippa II. But this was all to no avail because, when Judaeans resisted Florus and his auxiliary, Florus could easily persuade the emperor that they were acting against Rome. Neither Cestius nor Agrippa II could authorize an embassy from Jerusalem to Nero, on his Greek tour, to complain about his man Florus.

When tensions exploded and the exasperated Judaeans armed themselves, besieged the auxiliary cohort in Jerusalem and massacred it, even though Agrippa and Cestius understood the causes of the bloodshed they were powerless to prevent the consequences. Then Caesareans massacred their Judaean minority, and Judaeans upped the ante further by attacking many cities in southern Syria.

Cestius had already begun his march south in the hope of entering Jerusalem to punish the offenders and restore calm, but because the Judaeans were acting violently against authorized Roman forces he had to make an example of some. En route to Jerusalem he burned Judaean villages and ordered his soldiers to destroy Joppa with its inhabitants. These actions finally hardened Judaean anger against Rome itself. Somewhat like the British and the Jewish community in Palestine towards the end of the League of Nations Mandate, the Romans had quickly gone from being the Judaeans' chief protectors to being outright antagonists.

John, Simon and Gamala

Before concluding I would note that three important names in the coming war against Rome were motivated principally by regional conflict. Two were people: John of Gischala and Simon bar Giora. Although they would be the stalwart leaders of Jerusalem during Titus' siege, and face punishment as the war's main culprits, neither man was a Jerusalemite. Both fled to the mother-city from elsewhere, where their fight had been with hostile neighbours. Josephus claims that John fortified Gischala in Galilee because of inveterate hostilities with Tyre and Gadara, just as Tiberias had a history of conflict with Gadara, Hippos and Scythopolis (*Life* 42–45). Simon had spent much of his time overrunning the border areas with Samaria and Idumaea (*War* 2.652–54). Both men fled to Jerusalem for complicated reasons. Once they were there, their situations changed in ways we can no longer track with much clarity and the siege of Jerusalem is another subject. But we have reason to doubt that they were initially or basically motivated by anti-Roman sentiment.

The other famed site of ostensible anti-Roman animus is Gamala in the Golan. Gamala is one of the precious few places outside Jerusalem where material evidence remains of a conflict with Rome. This is most often assimilated to a narrative of general war against Rome, but again we may doubt. Like Tiberias and Taricheae, Gamala was part of Agrippa II's kingdom, not in the Roman province of Syria proper. Many hints in Josephus, though he does not explain the matter, suggest that the issues driving Judaean refugees into this natural fortress-town had to do with inter-ethnic struggles inside Agrippa's kingdom. These were set off by one of the king's lieutenants, a disgruntled nobleman of royal blood from a former local dynasty in Lebanon, which territory the emperor Claudius had given to the Judaean king.[18]

Conclusions

In this foray into a large subject, I have tried to make one negative and one constructive point. Negatively: the near-universal assumption of deep anti-Roman

---

18. *War* 2.481–83; *Life* 48–63.

hostility among Judaeans in the first century CE does not explain our evidence very well. In the complex ethnic environment of southern Syria, Jerusalem was uniquely favoured by Rome. Jerusalem needed Rome and Rome needed Jerusalem. My constructive argument is that war between Jerusalem and Rome finally erupted in 66 because regional conflicts were allowed to explode through an emperor's determined lack of interest and his legate's consequent paralysis.

My proposal draws from what we now call realist analysis of inter-national relations. Realism lowers our gaze from loftier conceptions of freedom to the concrete struggle for survival, as each nation looks constantly to secure itself against immediate threats. Even powerful nations live in perpetual fear of catastrophic loss. Weaker nations form productive security alliances whenever possible, and trust great powers when they must. Some of their leaders will counsel fidelity to the great power even in extreme danger, because of the greater risks of disloyalty. But when their very survival is at stake and that the great power cannot protect their interests, many will see armed self-help as the only option.

Although I doubt that we are supposed to think too much about ancient history while enjoying the *Life of Brian*, in a volume inspired by the film we might indulge a brief reflection. One the one hand, the film assumes a setting that I have argued against: Rome's officials and soldiers are a constant provocation in Jerusalem, and rebel conspiracy lurks in every alleyway as a response. On the other hand, in the famous 'What have the Romans ever done for us?' scene, where Reg's cherished grievances are punctured, a dead-on reference to Pilate's aqueduct project opens the possibility that Jerusalem actually enjoyed Rome's favour. With Pilate's wife as hostage, Reg demands that the Prefect 'dismantle the entire apparatus of the Roman imperialist state' within two days:

REG: They've bled us white, the bastards. They've taken everything we had.
    . . . And what have they ever given us in return?!
XERXES: The aqueduct?

Chapter 15

HOOK-NOSED HEEBIES: BRIAN, JESUS AND JEWISH IDENTITY

Adele Reinhartz

Monty Python's Life of Brian revolves around a case of mistaken identity: from the moment he is born, the ordinary Jew, Brian Cohen, is mistaken for the Messiah while his exact contemporary, Jesus of Nazareth, is almost ignored. In developing a plot based on mistaken identity, the Pythons stand in a long and distinguished comedic line that includes Shakespeare (*Much Ado about Nothing*, *Comedy of Errors* and *Twelfth Night*), Charlie Chaplin (*Modern Times*, 1936), and the Coen Brothers (*The Big Lebowski*, 1998).[1]

By definition, the mistaken identity plot involves a comparison between two individuals. In the Python's film, Jesus and Brian are exactly the same age, having been born on precisely the same day in adjacent mangers. Both are raised by their mothers, and they are of similar height, build and colouring. Both are crucified at the

---

1. For discussion of this theme in Shakespeare's plays, see Wolfgang Clemen, *Shakespeare's Dramatic Art: Collected Essays* (London: Methuen, 1972), pp. 163–88.

order of the Roman governor Pontius Pilate. Finally, both have a large posthumous following – as the history of the Christian church, and the present volume, attest.

Those who accused the film of blasphemy when it was released in 1979 missed the whole point. The humour of Python's *Life of Brian* requires a conventional two-dimensional, dare I say saccharine, depiction of Jesus. The comedy arises from the many ways in which the ordinary Brian differs from the extraordinary Jesus especially as the latter is portrayed by the church, in Jesus epics, and on Hallmark Christmas cards.

And the differences between Brian and Jesus are glaring. Brian is not the Messiah whereas Jesus (for Christians) is. Brian, on the other hand, is a revolutionary, whereas Jesus is not (at least, according to the Gospels). Brian is driven by infatuation; Jesus seems to be immune, or so it is generally thought.[2] Most obviously, Brian is a figment of the Pythons' mighty imagination, whereas Jesus is a historical personage, even if at least some of the stories about him, including the points I have just mentioned, may themselves be the fruit of ancient imaginations as fertile, if less comedic, than those of the Pythons.

This essay will focus on one aspect of Brian and Jesus' identity: their Jewishness. Both Brian and Jesus are undeniably Jewish. But while Brian declares his Jewish identity proudly and loudly, Jesus does not do so, at least not according to the canonical Gospels. In what follows I will suggest some reasons for Jesus' (or, rather, the Gospels') reticence and its implications for Jesus' afterlife in New Testament scholarship.

Brian: A Proud Red Sea Pedestrian

Brian and his mother Mandy return from their afternoon's entertainment – the Sermon on the Mount and a stoning – to find a Roman soldier waiting for Mandy's services. Brian asks, in surprise, 'What's he doing here?' His mother reveals a fact that she has kept hidden since his birth: 'Well, Brian, your father isn't Mr Cohen ... He was a Roman, Brian. He was a centurion in the Roman army.' Brian is shocked: 'You mean ... you were raped?' Mandy hems and haws: 'Well ... at first, yes.' This Roman, Naughtius Maximus, promised her the world, 'had his way' with her, then, 'voom! Like a rat out of an aqueduct!' Brian refuses to accept the horrid news and tantrums loudly: 'I'm not a Roman, mum, and I never will be. I'm a kike, a yid, a heebie, a hook-nose! I'm kosher, mum! I'm a Red Sea pedestrian and proud of it!' He runs up the stairs to his room and slams the door.

We may admire the resilience shown by Brian's mother Mandy, who does not allow her natural resentment of Naughtius Maximus and the disappointment of broken promises to interfere with her professional life. More astonishing is the naivety of her son. Brian seems surprised at the Roman soldier waiting in the

---

2. The question of whether Jesus was married – and if so, to whom – has been asked from at least the second century onwards. For a summary and detailed discussion, see Anthony Le Donne, *The Wife of Jesus: Ancient Texts and Modern Scandals* (London: Oneworld, 2013). See also Karen L. King, 'Jesus Said to Them, "My Wife ...": A New Coptic Papyrus Fragment', *Harvard Theological Review* 107 (2014), pp. 131–59.

apartment, and shocked by Mandy's revelation that his father too was a Roman soldier. He rejects the possibility that this news changes anything about his identity, however. On the contrary, he asserts his Jewishness vigorously, taking on every anti-Semitic epithet and adding one of his own – Red Sea pedestrian.[3]

Underlying this scene is the ancient rumour that Jesus' father was a Roman soldier who had raped or seduced Mary. According to Origen, Celsus, a Greek philosopher, and opponent of Christianity, claimed that Jesus' mother was a poor country-woman who was corrupted or seduced and impregnated by a soldier named Panthera.[4] Rabbinic and medieval Jewish sources refer to Jesus as Yeshu ben Pantera.[5] The legend has no real historical credibility, as it clearly served the purpose of mocking and discrediting the claim that Mary was a virgin whose child was fathered by God. But the film puts it to good use as a springboard for this delightful scene.[6]

Jesus: A Jew but not Proud of it?

Like Brian, Jesus is unquestionably Jewish.[7] Even the most skeptical readers of the Gospels and the most minimalist of historians recognize that Jesus lived within an almost entirely Jewish ethnic, social and cultural milieu.[8] The sabbath disputes

3. For discussion of the use of negative stereotypes to construct positive identity, see Adam D. Galinsky et al., 'The Reappropriation of Stigmatizing Labels', *Psychological Science* 20/10 (2013), pp. 1–10.

4. *Against Celsus*, Book 1:32, 69. http://www.earlychristianwritings.com/text/origen161. html [accessed 29 June, 2014].

5. See t. Hullin 2.22, 23; y. Shabbat, 14d, y. Avodah Zarah 27b. See Jane Schaberg, *The Illegitimacy of Jesus: A Feminist Theological Interpretation of the Infancy Narratives* (San Francisco [etc.]: Harper & Row, 1987), p. 174.

6. The legend is also mentioned in Denys Arcand's 1989 film *Jesus of Montreal*.

7. In referring to Jesus, here and throughout, I do not have in mind the historical Jesus, but rather Jesus as he is presented in the Gospels. While I do believe that the historical Jesus was Jewish, it is impossible to know whether at any point he made a self-declaration similar to Brian's.

8. See, among many others, Geza Vermes, *The Gospel of Jesus the Jew: The Riddell Memorial Lectures Delivered at the University of Newcastle upon Tyne on 17, 18 and 19 March 1981* (Newcastle-upon-Tyne: University of Newcastle-upon-Tyne Press, 1981); E. P. Sanders, *Jesus and Judaism* (Philadelphia: Fortress Press, 1985); James H. Charlesworth, *Jesus' Jewishness: Exploring the Place of Jesus within Early Judaism* (Philadelphia, PA/New York: American Interfaith Institute; Crossroad, 1991); Paula Fredriksen, *Jesus of Nazareth, King of the Jews: A Jewish Life and the Emergence of Christianity* (New York: Knopf, 1999); Amy-Jill Levine, *The Misunderstood Jew: The Church and the Scandal of the Jewish Jesus* (San Francisco: HarperSanFrancisco, 2006). But see also Joel Marcus, 'Jesus the Jew in Recent Western Scholarship', in Chrēstos Karakolēs, Karl-Wilhelm Niebuhr and S. G. Rogalsky (eds), *Gospel Images of Jesus Christ in Church Tradition and in Biblical Scholarship: Fifth International East-West Symposium of New Testament Scholars, Minsk, September 2 to 9, 2010* (Tübingen: Mohr Siebeck, 2012), pp. 235–49, who stresses that what people mean when they talk about Jesus' Jewishness can vary.

(e.g., John 5), the Temple cleansing (e.g., Mark 11.15–19), and various halakhic conflicts with the Pharisees and other interlocutors (e.g., Matt. 15.17–18) do not mask the fact. Arguments about such matters are evidence that they do indeed matter.[9] But we search the scriptures in vain for a proud declaration of Jewish identity of the sort that Brian makes.

This is not to say that Jesus is indifferent to how other people see him. The Gospel of Mark provides the following exchange:

> Jesus went on with his disciples to the villages of Caesarea Philippi; and on the way he asked his disciples, 'Who do people say that I am?' And they answered him, 'John the Baptist; and others, Elijah; and still others, one of the prophets.' He asked them, 'But who do you say that I am?' Peter answered him, 'You are the Messiah.' And he sternly ordered them not to tell anyone about him.
>
> (Mark 8.27–30; cf. Matt. 16.13–20; Luke 9.18–21)

In this exchange Jesus accepts the identification as Messiah but he swears his disciples to secrecy, in keeping with the Gospel of Mark's messianic secret motif.[10] Both the correct and the incorrect answers to the question 'Who am I?' concern not matters of ethnicity but Jesus' role in an unfolding salvation narrative. Nevertheless, all the options – John the Baptist, Elijah, the prophets, and the Messiah – are at home in the context of first-century Judaism.[11]

This chapter will propose three reasons for the absence of any ethnic self-declaration on the part of Jesus as he is presented in the canonical Gospels: sociological, literary, and theological.

Sociology: Differentiation, or Lack Thereof

Everyday experience suggests that declarations of any ethnic identity are needed only when there is a threat to or question about that identity. Brian's outburst illustrates this point, as it was prompted by the astonishing revelation that his father was a Roman, a point that threatens his Jewish identity. Other examples abound.

Joe the Canadian

One self-declaration of identity that is dear to my own heart – as a Canadian who spends considerable time in the United States – is expressed in a 2006 Molson Canadian beer commercial which went viral among Canadians who saw it as a proud and succinct assertion of our national identity in the face of American cultural imperialism and overall ignorance about Canada.

---

9. John P. Meier, *A Marginal Jew: Rethinking the Historical Jesus. Volume 4, Law and Love* (New Haven: Doubleday, 2009).

10. See William Wrede, *The Messianic Secret* (Cambridge: J. Clarke, 1971 [1901]).

11. John J. Collins, *The Scepter and the Star: Messianism in Light of the Dead Sea Scrolls* (Grand Rapids, MI: Eerdmans, 2010).

Hey, I'm not a lumberjack, or a fur trader . . .
I don't live in an igloo or eat blubber, or own a dogsled . . .
and I don't know Jimmy, Sally or Suzy from Canada,
although I'm certain they're really, really nice.
I have a Prime Minister, not a president.
I speak English and French, not American.
And I pronounce it 'about', not 'a boot'.
I can proudly sew my country's flag on my backpack.
I believe in peace keeping, not policing,
diversity, not assimilation,
and that the beaver is a truly proud and noble animal.
A toque is a hat, a chesterfield is a couch,
and it is pronounced 'zed' not 'zee', 'zed' !!!!
Canada is the second largest landmass!
The first nation of hockey!
and the best part of North America.
My name is Joe!!
And I am Canadian!!!

Like Brian, 'Joe' draws upon stereotypes, though, in contrast to Brian's outburst, the stereotypes in Joe's declamation are not hostile or negative, but range from mildly positive (Canadians are nice) to merely ignorant (Canadians live in igloos). The humour derives from the juxtaposition of the true – Canada's hockey prowess, large land mass, distinctive vocabulary and pronunciation – and the ridiculous – the nobility of the beaver, a Canadian symbol. And like Brian, Joe expresses ethnic anxiety, due, in his case, to the encroachment of American culture on Canada, and the difficulty that not only Americans but also many Canadians have in articulating or even perceiving the uniqueness of Canadian identity.[12]

Jesus the Jew

If ethnic self-declarations express difference and differentiation, the Gospels' failure to attribute such declarations to Jesus is not surprising given that he functioned primarily within a Jewish context. The Gospels, however, do portray

12. In other cases, the 'I am' declaration does not express ethnic identity *per se*, but rather affiliation, support or solidarity. One example occurs in a widely reported speech made by John F. Kennedy in Berlin on June 26 1963: 'All free men, wherever they may live, are citizens of Berlin, and therefore, as a free man, I take pride in the words, "Ich bin ein Berliner".' Of course Kennedy himself was not a Berliner but in this speech he threw American support behind West Berlin and West Germany, in their fight against the communism of East Germany and the recently-constructed Berlin Wall. Kennedy's speech, delivered in front of the Schoenberg Rathaus, is considered a turning point in the Cold War because it cut short Soviet aspirations of driving the allies from West Berlin. John F. Kennedy, *Remarks in the Rudolph Wilde Platz 'Ich Bin Ein Berliner'* (Champaign, IL: Project Gutenberg).

other characters who draw attention to such differentiation. Matthew and Mark describe Jesus' encounter with a Syro-Phoenician/Canaanite woman. This woman had a young daughter with an unclean spirit, and learning of Jesus' success in ousting such spirits, she came to him, bowed down at his feet. She then begged him to cast out the demon.

> He said to her, 'Let the children be fed first, for it is not fair to take the children's food and throw it to the dogs'. But she answered him, 'Sir, even the dogs under the table eat the children's crumbs'. Then he said to her, 'For saying that, you may go – the demon has left your daughter'. So she went home, found the child lying on the bed, and the demon gone.
>
> (Mark 7.25–30; cf. Matt. 15.21–28)

Although Jesus acknowledges that the Gentile woman was right, his initial refusal clearly suggests that, at least from Mark and Matthew's perspective, he does not extend his activities to Gentiles, that is, beyond the Jewish community.

In John 4, Jesus is explicitly identified as a Jew (*Ioudaios*) by a Samaritan woman. En route from Jerusalem to the Galilee, Jesus rests at a well in Samaria en route from Judaea to Galilee. There a Samaritan woman has stopped to draw water, and he asks her for a drink. She wonders: 'How is it that you, a Jew, ask a drink of me, a woman of Samaria?' The narrator then explains that 'Jews do not share things in common with Samaritans' (John 4.9). Jesus does not answer the woman's initial question directly. But in the ensuing dialogue he seeks to broaden the conversation beyond the issue of ethnic identity. The Samaritan acknowledges that Jesus is a prophet – he knows that she is living with a man who is not her husband[13] – and then asks him a question that gets to the heart of the longstanding tension between Jews and Samaritans:

> Our ancestors worshiped on this mountain, but you say that the place where people must worship is in Jerusalem.' Jesus said to her, 'Woman, believe me, the hour is coming when you will worship the Father neither on this mountain nor in Jerusalem. You worship what you do not know; we worship what we know, for salvation is from the Jews. But the hour is coming, and is now here, when the true worshipers will worship the Father in spirit and truth, for the Father seeks such as these to worship him.'
>
> (John 4.20–23)

Nowhere does Jesus challenge the Samaritan woman's identification of him as a Jew. Further, Jesus' declaration that 'salvation is from the Jews' – enigmatic as it is – implies the superiority of Jews over Samaritans. At the same time, he broadens the discussion from the topic of ethnicity to cosmology and eschatology: in future true worship will not be localized with either the Jews or the Samaritans, but rather

---

13. Interestingly, she does not take offence at his comment that this is her fifth husband and yet not really her husband, and he does not take her to task for the seeming immorality.

will focus on Jesus as the one who comes from the Father in spirit and truth. This future time is foreshadowed in Chapter 6, when the Jewish crowds remain in the Galilee and gather around Jesus at the Passover, a time when they, and Jesus, would normally be making their way to Jerusalem for the pilgrimage festival.[14]

King of the Jews

If Jesus does not declare his Jewish identity, there are other characters in the Gospels who do. No one wonders whether he is a Jew – that is taken for granted – but they do worry about whether he is also King of the Jews. The Magi of Matthew 2.2 are sure of it, as they seek the whereabouts of 'the child who has been born king of the Jews'. (Presumably the directions they received were more accurate than those of the wise men in *Monty Python's Life of Brian* who arrive at the wrong manger.)

More puzzled is Pilate, who tries – unsuccessfully – to get Jesus to admit that he is King of the Jews. According to Matthew 27.11, 'Jesus stood before the governor; and the governor asked him, 'Are you the King of the Jews?' Jesus said, 'You say so' (see also Mark 15.2; Luke 23.3). In John, Pilate asks the same question but gets a cryptic response: 'Do you ask this on your own, or did others tell you about me?' Pilate persists: 'I am not a Jew, am I? Your own nation and the chief priests have handed you over to me. What have you done?' Jesus does not answer the question, but returns to Pilate's initial question and asserts: 'My kingdom is not from this world. If my kingdom were from this world, my followers would be fighting to keep me from being handed over to the Jews. But as it is, my kingdom is not from here.' Pilate tries to pin him down: 'So you are a king?' but Jesus remains elusive: 'You say that I am a king. For this I was born, and for this I came into the world, to testify to the truth. Everyone who belongs to the truth listens to my voice.' Pilate concludes the exchange by asking: 'What is truth?' apparently giving up on any hope of a straight answer to any question, including this one (John 18.34–38).

Jesus' kingship is mocked by the Roman soldiers, who crown him with thorns and kneel before him, crying out, 'Hail, King of the Jews!' (Matt. 27.29; Mark 15.18; John 19.3; see Luke 23.37). But it is nevertheless the title put on the titulus, as the charge for which Jesus is crucified: 'This is Jesus, the King of Jews' (Matt. 27.37, with variations in Mark 15.26, and Luke 23.38). John has the most detailed description of the controversy surrounding this title:

> Pilate also had an inscription written and put on the cross. It read, 'Jesus of Nazareth, the King of the Jews'. Many of the Jews read this inscription, because the place where Jesus was crucified was near the city; and it was written in Hebrew, in Latin, and in Greek. Then the chief priests of the Jews said to Pilate, 'Do not write, "The King of the Jews", but "This man said, 'I am King of the Jews'"'.
> (John 19.19–21)

---

14. Adele Reinhartz, 'Jesus as Prophet: Predictive Prolepses in the Fourth Gospel', *JSNT* 11, no. 36 (1989), pp. 3–16.

These passages do not tell us whether the historical Jesus 'really' declared himself king or whether others did so on his behalf. They do however provide further evidence that the Gospels portray Jesus as a Jew, who, whether royalty or not, is considered a Jew by the people he encounters within their narratives.

Narrative: The Villains of the Piece

Jesus' supposed kingship is related to the plot of the Gospels' narratives, in which, as we have seen, Jesus is interrogated by Pilate. These scenes suggest that the absence of ethnic self-declaration may pertain to the fundamental hostility between Jesus and the Jews that is at the core of the narrative as the driver of the plot that results in Jesus' condemnation and crucifixion.

Jewish villains and anti-Judaism

In the Gospels, the Jewish Jesus is rejected, persecuted and ultimately executed due to the hostile Jewish authorities. The Gospels of Matthew and John point out the irony of this narrative when citing the proverb that 'a prophet has no honour in the prophet's own country' (John 4.44; cf. Matt. 13.57). The Jews' hostility to Jesus within the Gospels' plot is matched by the Gospels' verbal hostility towards the Jews, most egregiously in Matthew 27.25, the blood curse 'Let his blood be on us and on our children', and John 8.44, in which Jesus tells Jews that they have the devil as their father. In addition, the Gospels associate certain negative characteristics with the Jews or groups among them, most famously in Jesus' diatribe in Matthew 23 which forever brands the Pharisees as hypocrites. It may also be that the greed attributed to Judas reflects an association of Jews and money.

The anti-Jewish element and the deicide charge are absent from the film, in which the conflict is entirely between the Jews and the Romans. Pilate is not a sympathetic seeker of truth but an object of ridicule; the Jewish priests and other authorities are nowhere to be found. Of course, *Life of Brian* pokes fun at Jews as it does at many other groups. This gentle mockery is evident in the crucifixion sequence, in which a posh Jewish couple objects to being crucified in the vicinity of Samaritans. 'This is supposed to be a Jewish section!' the husband cries out. The centurion responds impatiently, 'It doesn't matter! You're all gonna die in a day or two!' The man will not let it go, however, and turns to his wife for confirmation: 'It may not matter to you, Roman, but it certainly matters to us. Doesn't it, darling?' He continues, 'Under the terms of the Roman occupancy we're entitled to be crucified in a purely Jewish area'. Others pipe up, asking not only for separation from non-Jews but from other groups, Jewish or otherwise: 'Pharisees separate from Sadducees!' 'And Swedish separate and Welsh!' The centurion responds, 'All right, all right, all right, we'll soon settle this! 'Ands up, all those who don't want to be crucified here!' Of course, their hands are bound, and the centurion dismisses the entire question.

This scene not only evokes the age-old enmity and tension between Jews and Samaritans, but also mocks the tendency of Jews to dwell among other Jews in life and in death. Nevertheless, this type of teasing parody does not come across as anti-Jewish or anti-Semitic, and it is entirely unconnected to the tension between Jesus and other Jews that is portrayed in some of the Gospel material.

Otto and the suicide squad

More problematic is a scene that was filmed but not included in the final movie.[15] Sometimes referred to as the 'Otto' outtake, the scene features a suicide squad, called the Judaean People's Front, headed by a character named Otto. The squad runs into Brian, and Otto gives him a demonstration of their talents. Otto is pleased with their prompt suicide, until he realizes that they were only pretending. Their excuse: they thought it was a practice; the blood that oozed from their bodies was from sheeps' bladders that they had squeezed as they fell. The questionable elements in this outtake arise from the costuming, accents and the dialogue. The suicide squad is identified by a symbol that combines a Star of David with a swastika. The Nazi connection is reinforced by the German name of their leader, Otto, his thin moustache, and his unmistakably German accent, which is shared by the members of the squad. Finally, the dialogue conflates Jewish and Nazi elements. Otto wants Brian to take them to 'the leader' (English for *der Führer*), and says, 'Oh, I grow so impatient, you know. To see the Leader that has been promised our people for centuries. The Leader who will save Israel by ridding it of the scum of non-Jewish people, making it pure! No foreigners; no riff-raff; no gypsies.' When he addresses them, the members of the Judaean People's Front respond 'Hail, Leader!' and raise their arms in the gesture so firmly associated with 'Heil Hitler'. When he realizes that they have not after all committed suicide, Otto exclaims, 'You are sour! A non-Semitic, mutinous, racially impure, cloth-eared bunch of Roman-lovers!' Brian responds to the entire scene in the only sensible way: 'Silly bugger.'

Eric Idle was instrumental in the decision to cut the scene. He commented: 'It's a funny sketch and if it had happened early on in the film it might have been in, but coming in where it did I felt very strong that it was spoiling the balance and shape of the film.'[16] Idle also recognized that the scene was a 'pretty savage attack on rabid Zionism, suggesting it's rather akin to Nazism, which is a bit strong to take, but certainly a point of view.'[17] Idle's remark implies discomfort with the scene's message, though according to Terry Gilliam, the cut was motivated primarily by fear of offending Jewish film producers in Hollywood.[18] In Gilliam's view, the scene

15. The scene can be viewed at https://www.youtube.com/watch?v=KAGxGp1Bjgs and the transcript at http://www.montypython.net/scripts/LOB-suicide.php. [Accessed 29 June, 2014].

16. Graham Chapman et al., *The Pythons Autobiography by the Phythans* (New York: Thomas Dunne Books, 2003), p. 299. John Cleese has also remarked that the scene just was not funny enough (personal communication, 21 June 2014).

17. Ibid.

18. Ibid., p. 298–9.

was a legitimate comic spoof of Judaism. Gilliam commented: 'Listen, we've alienated the Christians, let's get the Jews now'.[19]

On balance, the decision to cut the Otto scene was a good one; its use of Nazi symbolism is both confusing and offensive, and its main themes are out of line with the rest of the movie. Otto reappears in John Cleese's *A Fish Called Wanda* (1988) as one of a band of hapless burglars. With his small Hitler-like moustache, and repressive leanings, he becomes South Africa's Minister of Justice.

Theology: 'I am'

Perhaps the most important reason for the Gospels' failure to have Jesus declare his Jewish identity is Christology. For the evangelists, the salient aspect of Jesus' identity is not ethnicity but his Messiahship, which, in turn, is integrally related to his role as God's Son (cf. John 20.31). Jesus must be differentiated from others not on account of his ethnicity but on account of his unique nature: what is important is not his human status (which, like his ethnicity, is taken for granted) but his unique relationship to God on the one hand and humankind on the other. Brian declares his Jewish identity when it is threatened by the new knowledge of his Roman *pater*. Joe declares his Canadian identity so that he will not be mistaken for an American. And Jesus declares his Christological identity to those who think he is merely human.

The Jesus of the Gospels is surprisingly reticent to use explicit Christological identifiers about himself. More often it is others who identify Jesus as Christ, the Son of God or the Son of Man, and Jesus is left to ignore, or agree, with these titles. Among those who identify Jesus in this way is the Devil. In Matthew 4.3–10, the Devil challenges Jesus to show that he is the Son of God by commanding stones to become bread, and throwing himself down from the pinnacle of the Temple. Jesus neither accepts nor deflects the identification but he resists the temptations. In the trial before the assembly, Jesus is cross-examined with regard to his identity. Luke's version of the interrogation is as follows:

> They said, 'If you are the Messiah, tell us.' He replied, 'If I tell you, you will not believe; and if I question you, you will not answer. But from now on the Son of Man will be seated at the right hand of the power of God.' All of them asked, 'Are you, then, the Son of God?' He said to them, 'You say that I am'. Then they said, 'What further testimony do we need? We have heard it ourselves from his own lips!'
> (Luke 22.66–71)

Here Jesus does not explicitly claim to be the Son of God and neither does he deny it. Similarly vague is his relationship to the Son of Man title. The context

---

19. Ibid. Julian Doyle, the editor of the film, expressed the same point of view in his remarks at the *Jesus and Brian* conference, Kings College London, 22 June 2014.

implies that he considers himself to be the Son of Man, but the use of the third person instead of the first person creates uncertainty.

The Jesus of John's Gospel is less coy than his synoptic counterpart; he declares 'I am' just as often as Brian does. But nowhere does Jesus declare outright: 'I am the Messiah', 'I am the Son of Man' or 'I am the Son of God'. Rather, 'I am' is followed by a metaphor that gestures towards Jesus' role as saviour. I am, he proclaims, 'the bread of life' (6.35, 41, 48, 51); 'the light of the world' (8.12; 9.5); the sheep's 'gate' (10.7, 9); 'the good shepherd' (10.11, 14); 'the resurrection and life' (11.25); 'the way and the truth and life' (14.6); and the vine (15.1, 5). He also, however, uses 'I am' simply to assert his existence, an assertion most often interpreted as an allusion to God's self-identification in Exodus 3.14: 'I am that I am' (KJV) or, as the New Revised Standard Version put it, 'I am who I am.' This formulation occurs in John 8.58, which Jesus tells the Jews, 'Very truly, I tell you, before Abraham was, I am' (NRSV).[20,21]

Brian has the opposite problem to Jesus'. Whereas Jesus' challenge is that many do not believe him to be the Messiah, Brian's is that many believe that he *is*. In the face of a growing crowd of followers, he denies any Messianic identity as emphatically as he embraces his Jewish one, as the following dialogue illustrates.

ARTHUR (one of the crowd): Hail Messiah!

BRIAN: I am not the Messiah!

ARTHUR: I say you are, Lord, and I should know. I've followed a few.

FOLLOWERS: Hail Messiah!

BRIAN: I am not the Messiah! Will you please listen? I am not the Messiah, do you understand?! Honestly!

GIRL: Only the true Messiah denies His divinity.

BRIAN: What?! Well, what sort of chance does that give me? All right! I am the Messiah!

FOLLOWERS: He is! He is the Messiah!

BRIAN: Now fuck off!

Brian's mother concurs with Brian: her son is not at all the Messiah, just a 'very naughty boy'.

This theme should have made it obvious that those who accused the Pythons of blasphemy missed the mark by overlooking the plot device of mistaken identity which is an important source of the film's humour. What counts about mistaken identity are the differences that underlie the superficial similarities that lead others to confuse one figure for another. What counts in this film is the contrast between someone who is not and does not claim to be the Messiah, and someone for whom

20. For discussion, see David Mark Ball, *'I Am' in John's Gospel: Literary Function, Background, and Theological Implications* (Sheffield: Sheffield Academic Press, 1996); Philip B. Harner, *The 'I Am' of the Fourth Gospel: A Study in Johannine Usage and Thought* (Philadelphia: Fortress Press, 1970).

21. See also John 4.26; 8.23–24, 28; 13.19.

such claims are built into a world religion as well as Western culture. In my view, Brian could have used a bit of Jesus' gravitas; Jesus could have used some of Brian's good nature and Jewish pride. But in this hilarious film of mistaken identity, the differences between them would nevertheless have remained substantial.

Implications

Like Brian, Jesus is undeniably Jewish. But the absence of an explicit, proud, Brian-like declaration in the Gospels created a space for those who ignore or even deny Jesus' Jewish identity altogether. One long-standing element of the historical-methodology used to construct the life and teachings of the historical Jesus is the criterion of dissimilarity. According to this criterion, the authentic words of Jesus are to be found in those sayings that are not paralleled in either Jewish or Christian sources outside the New Testament. The underlying assumption is that, given Jesus' uniqueness, any such parallels could well be the product of invention by his earliest followers (Jews) or by later Christians who adapted and shaped their memories and traditions to suit their needs. This criterion undermines the ascription of Jewish identity to Jesus; if Jesus were 'truly' Jewish, the teachings attributed to him in the Gospels that are paralleled by or similar to those found in other Jewish sources may indeed have been authentic.[22]

The absence of an explicit declaration of Jewish identity also made it possible to deny Jesus' Jewishness altogether, for racial or anti-Semitic reasons. Examples can easily be found on fringe anti-Semitic websites that insist that the claims about Jesus' Jewishness are the consequence of an 'unholy' hoax campaign conducted 'so-called Jews' who are really descendants of the 'pagan Turko-Finn Mongoloid nation' known as the Khazars'.[23]

But the ambivalence about Jesus' Jewish identity is not a recent or even an extremist phenomenon. Halvor Moxnes notes that: 'In the nineteenth century Paul de Lagarde and Houston Stewart Chamberlain especially used racial arguments about Jesus as a Galilean to disassociate him from his Jewish context.'[24] This trend can also be seen in the work of Emil Schürer[25] and was argued forcefully by Ernst

---

22. For detailed discussion, see Gerd Theissen and Dagmar Winter, *The Quest for the Plausible Jesus: The Question of Criteria* (Louisville, KY: Westminster John Knox Press, 2002).

23. http://www.biblebelievers.org.au/jesusjew.htm [accessed 10 June 2014]. This view, however, is not limited to fringe groups but is espoused by at least one scholar, Bruce Malina. See Bruce J. Malina and John J. Pilch, *Social-Science Commentary on the Letters of Paul* (Minneapolis: Fortress Press, 2006), pp. 179–80. See also the cogent critique of Robert J. Myles and James G. Crossley, 'Biblical Scholarship, Jews and Israel: On Bruce Malina, Conspiracy Theories and Ideological Contradictions' http://www.bibleinterp.com/opeds/myl368013.shtml#sdfootnote10sym [accessed 29 June 2014].

24. Halvor Moxnes, *Jesus and the Rise of Nationalism: A New Quest for the Nineteenth-Century Historical Jesus* (London/New York: I. B. Taurus, 2012), p. 118.

Lohmeyer in the 1930s. Lohmeyer argued that Galilee represented a Gentile point of view, in contrast to Judaea, which represented a Jewish perspective. Although Lohmeyer was not an anti-Semite or a Nazi (indeed, he was disciplined in 1935 for supporting Jewish colleagues at the University of Breslau) his work contributed to the separation of Jesus from his Jewish context.[26]

These arguments bore destructive fruit in the Nazi period in the work of the Institute for the Study and Eradication of Jewish Influence on German Church under the leadership of Walter Grundmann, who, along with other Institute members, insisted 'that Jesus was not a Jew, that Galilee was populated by non-Jews, and that Judaism was a violent religion threatening all Christians.'[27]

Always Look on the Bright Side . . .

At the end of their lives, both Brian and Jesus are victims of mistaken identity, mistakes that prove fatal, at least for their earthly existence. Brian nearly escapes his fate when the Romans offer to release someone named Brian. But he misses out due to inattention. Someone else claims to be Brian and is released in his stead. Jesus too is innocent, according to the Gospels, and misses out when the crowd chooses Barabbas for release (Matt. 27.16–17, 20–21, 26; Mark 15.7, 11, 15; Luke 23.18; John 18.40).

Just as Brian is mistaken for the Messiah, so is Jesus – according to the Gospels– mistaken for the King of the Jews. Both their lives end on the cross, with or without cheerful musical accompaniment, but both Brian and Jesus live on thanks to their biographers, and the communities – Python lovers and Christians – who revere them. Brian lives on in the Python's hilarious film as an ordinary man but a proud Jew whose identity and allegiances are plain to all. Jesus lives on in the New Testament, the Christian churches, and in Christian faith, as an extraordinary individual whose identity, both ethnic and messianic, remain contested and ambiguous even two millennia after his death.

25. Schürer, Emil, *The History of the Jewish People in the Age of Jesus Christ*, ed. Geza Vermes, Fergus Millar and Martin Goodman, 3 vols. in 4 (Edinburgh, T&T Clark, 1979–1987), Vol. I, pp. 142, 216–18; vol II, pp. 7–10.

26. Susannah Heschel, *The Aryan Jesus: Christian Theologians and the Bible in Nazi Germany* (Princeton: Princeton University Press, 2008), p. 62.

27. Ibid., 63. For further discussion of the Galilean hypothesis, see Mark A. Chancey, *The Myth of a Gentile Galilee* (Cambridge/New York: Cambridge University Press, 2002). On the Jewishness of the Galilee, and the Jewishness of Jesus, see Seán Freyne, *Jesus, a Jewish Galilean: A New Reading of the Jesus Story* (London: T&T Clark, 2004).

Chapter 16

'THE SHOE IS THE SIGN!' COSTUMING *BRIAN* AND DRESSING THE FIRST CENTURY

Katie Turner

In *Fashioning the Nation: Costume and Identity in British Cinema*, Pam Cook identifies costume, hair and décor as the 'symbolic carriers of period detail'; they provide the film with verisimilitude, and they make the past seem tangible. 'However,' as Cook continues, they are also 'notoriously slippery and anachronistic'. There is a 'tension between truthfulness and infidelity' bound up in costume that, at the same time, informs and subverts historical awareness.[1] This is usually because costume both recreates historical dress and represents contemporary fashions. It is also because costume is used to evoke emotions that enhance a narrative, and thus designers will diverge from accurate recreations in order to achieve this. Walter Plunkett's frothy, voluminous dresses created for *Gone with the Wind* epitomize the successful amalgamation of historical knowledge, contemporary fashion and

---

1. Pam Cook, *Fashioning the Nation: Costume and Identity in British Cinema* (London: BFI Publishing, 1996), p. 67.

emotive appeal (see image 5, plate section). Although skirts in the 1850s were never as large as he presented, and by the early days of the Civil War dresses of that style had already begun to narrow, the costumes Plunkett chose spoke to the over-indulgent decadence of the Southern Plantation owner.[2] They also, perhaps problematically, evoked a sense of nostalgia for a by-gone era. To that point, it is worth remembering that all period dramas, even those that hold the highest regard for the past they are recreating, contain an element of fantasy. The audience is not expecting a documentary, and there should be no responsibility to provide one.

Costume, therefore, communicates much to the audience apart from historical context:

1. As I have already mentioned, it reflects *contemporary fashions*. This is often simply to make it visually appealing to a modern audience as concepts of beauty vary over time,[3] but it can also be a means of better communicating elements of historic fashion that do not translate well by contemporary modes of dress. The fashions we use to express social mores – such as sexuality, morality, gender roles and socio-economic hierarchies – are as fluid as these notions themselves. However, we will often 'read' historic fashion from within our contemporary mindset, with our current understanding of social mores, and therefore 'misread' what the historic fashion was communicating. Costumers can correct this with anachronistic detailing: cutting a dress to communicate modern ideas regarding purity or promiscuity, for example, by altering necklines instead of hemlines.

2. It is one of the key components of *characterization*, providing the audience with visual clues to the character's personality and motivations. The costuming of Judas in Cecil B. DeMille's *King of Kings* (1927) visually indicates his eventual betrayal of Jesus. Judas is extravagantly and flamboyantly dressed, especially when seen in comparison to the other disciples, giving the audience the impression of a materialistic and superficial individual. Costume designer Deborah Nadoolman Landis explains that clothes function as 'social and emotional signposts' for all members of society; in film, they help an audience

2. Edward Maeder provides a good discussion of the costumes in *Gone with the Wind* and the important difference between verisimilitude – what one tends to see – and accurate historical recreation – what one often *thinks* they are seeing – in period film costuming. As regards Plunkett's very admirable attempt, Maeder writes: 'Viewers left the theatre convinced that they had just seen a true reflection of the past; but almost half a century later, a fashion historian cannot help noticing that many aspects of the film's costume styles are rooted more in the 1930s [when *Gone with the Wind* was made] than in the 1860s.' Edward Maeder, 'The Celluloid Image: Historical Dress in Film', in Maeder (ed.), *Hollywood and History: Costume Design in Film* (London: Thames and Hudson, 1987), pp. 9–51.

3. In biblical films, the costuming of Mary Magdalene best illustrates this concept. See especially, *The King of Kings* (1927), *The Last Temptation of Christ* (1988) and *The Bible* (2013).

better understand a character's 'moods, tastes and personality, [their] social and economic aspirations and the time in which [they] live.'[4]

3. *Interpretation* of the period, people, or events is also seen through costume. Mel Gibson's understanding of the New Testament, born from his particular Catholic faith, is clearly evident in his costuming of Mary and Mary Magdalene in a nun-like fashion.[5] In *Jesus Christ Superstar*, Jesus and his followers are presented as hippies (in the film), or as Occupy Wall St. protesters (in the recent stage version). These costumes guide the audience to interpret the message as one that is similar to these politically-motivated groups, thereby presenting Jesus' mission as anti-establishment; part of a counterculture movement.[6]

4. The costuming might also reflect, or magnify, a pre-existing *bias* or *prejudice*. Or, by the same token, it can be used to correct or combat such things by intentionally avoiding stereotyping. In the case of New Testament dramatizations, the biggest concern here is anti-Semitism or anti-Judaism. This can be anything from overt displays of Jewish stereotypes to more subtle displays of religio-cultural difference between Jesus and his followers, and those with whom he came into conflict.[7] This latter type is often accomplished by costuming Jesus and his disciples in an Occidental manner, showing a greater commonality with Western audiences, and the Priests and Pharisees in an Oriental one: demonstrating 'Othering' through costume. Ivan Davidson Kalmar provides an excellent analysis of this in his essay 'Jesus Did Not Wear a Turban'. Kalmar astutely points out that, in art, Orientalist detailing increases in intensity the further away one gets from 'belief in Jesus'.[8] Kalmar's method

---

4. Deborah Nadoolman Landis, *Hollywood Costume* (London: V&A Publishing, 2012), p. 48.

5. When interviewed about designing the costumes for *The Passion of the Christ*, Maurizio Millenotti, said, 'Mel Gibson had a very clear vision of the look of the movie and he guided me while at the same time giving me complete creative freedom.' Landis, *Filmcraft: Costume Design* (Lewes, UK: ILEX, 2012), pp. 114–23.

6. Richard Walsh, *Reading the Gospels in the Dark* (London: SCM, 2003), p. 5.

7. It is very common to find that the costumes of Caiaphas, the other members of the Sanhedrin, and the Pharisees (i.e. those who opposed Jesus) include elements of overt religiosity reminiscent of Orthodox Judaism, such as *payot* (side-curls), long beards, large black hats (or other dark head covering), prayer shawls and *tefillin*, whilst Jesus and his disciples are rarely seen with any of these items. See especially, *Intolerance* (1916), *The King of Kings* (1927), *King of Kings* (1961), *The Last Temptation of Christ* (1988), *The Passion of the Christ* (2004) and *Mesih* (2007), an Iranian film that tells the story of Jesus from the Qu'ranic perspective.

8. Kalmar catalogues the consistent and 'unchanging formal underpinning of Orientalist art with biblical subjects' using two main rules: the first is iterated in the title of Kalmar's essay – Jesus is given exceptional status and thus rarely, if ever, wears a turban (or other form of head-covering). Kalmar dubs this the 'Occidental Jesus rule'. The second rule, the

and analysis can easily be applied to costuming to present similar findings: Even as we better understand Jesus as Jewish, through 'group dress' we are still visually representing Jesus and those who followed him as quite theologically, socially, and culturally removed from those with whom he disagreed, despite their commonalities.

Whatever the end result, all successful period costuming begins the same way: with a strong foundation in history. Creative decisions are made *after* academic research, allowing designers to capture the feel of the period, even if the clothing itself is anachronistic.[9] When it comes to biblical epics, often classed within the broader 'period drama' or 'historical film' genres, however, little research seems to be employed; traditional imagery (itself changing over time) instead seems to provide the framework for costuming the first century. This is not entirely the fault of the filmmakers, however, as academia has little to offer them. Jewish clothing of the first century is quite an understudied topic.

There are a number of reasons for this, the primary one being a supposed lack of source material (which I discuss in this chapter). This can also be attributed to academia's seeming hesitance to give due weight to fashion history, viewing the topic as inferior to other, more 'legitimate' aspects of historical study. However, clothing has always played a central role in how individuals express identity, culture, religion and social position. The idea that what one wore communicated these aspects of one's life was so well understood, that, in the West at least, from the Roman Empire through the Elizabethan period, sumptuary legislation controlled nearly every aspect of textile production and use, and thus what people from different classes could wear. Only citizens of Rome, for example, were permitted to wear the toga. Even aspects of clothing that were not legislated were carefully considered. The voluminosity or restrictive nature of one's clothing spoke to one's

'Implicational Hierarchy of Biblical Orientalism', dictates that representations of the rest of the biblical characters are relative to the first rule. This means, that however Oriental or Occidental Jesus is presented, every other character in the narrative will be presented incrementally more Oriental the further removed they are from belief in him. Thus the disciples will be just slightly more Oriental than Jesus, 'the crowd' (*ho ochlos*, being a character in its own right) will be more Oriental than the disciples, the Pharisees more Oriental than 'the crowd', and so on. Ivan Davidson Kalmar, 'Jesus Did Not Wear a Turban: Orientalism, The Jews, and Christian Art', in Ivan Davidson Kalmar and Derek J. Penslar (eds), *Orientalism and the Jews* (Hanover, NH: University Press of New England), pp. 3–31, at pp. 29–31.

9. 'In the cinema, the actor must fully inhabit the character; the audience's suspension of disbelief is essential ... No matter in what era the story is set, the audience is asked to believe that the people in the movie are real and that they had a life prior to the start of the action.' If a costume *feels* inauthentic (even if it is 'accurate') or if it is too distracting, it will adversely affect the audience's ability to suspend disbelief. Landis, *Hollywood Costume*, p. 48.

wealth, as an individual who needed to farm, cook and clean for themselves would need to be less encumbered by fabric and corsetry. It is short-sighted to ignore such an important aspect of how people from a particular period expressed their own identity and imposed identity on others, how they demonstrated values and hierarchies.

Despite its importance any exploration into Jewish dress is fraught with evidentiary problems. Whilst one should not be deterred by a shortage of materials, a shortage there most definitely is. Anybody attempting to find out how Jewish people of the first century dressed is faced with the same basic problem: Jews did not depict themselves or the human form more generally in art, understanding biblical prohibitions regarding idolatry as restricting such displays (Exod. 20.3–6; Lev. 26.1; Num. 33.52; Deut. 4.16, 27.15). As textiles, especially those made from wool and linen, do not generally preserve well, artistic representations of dress are immensely valuable for the historian, and it is in this form of evidence that the Jewish people of the Roman Empire, particularly those in the Palestinian region, largely remain a mystery. This does not mean, however, that there isn't evidence to be found. There is enough to give us a strong sense of the type of clothing that would have been worn by the people of Judaea.

The most spectacular and convincing evidence comes from an archaeological discovery made more than 50 years ago. In 1960, a group of Israeli archaeologists and volunteers led by Yigael Yadin set out into the Judaean Desert to excavate a number of caves just south of Qumran near Masada. The entrance to one cave in particular, set fifty feet up a steep rocky cliff-side, presented a challenge to Yadin and his team. Once there, however, the rewards for their effort proved monumental. Inside this large, remote cave, now known as the 'Cave of Letters', were dozens of items ranging from common daily objects, such as baskets, dishes and knives, to bronze ritual urns and bowls of Roman origin, as well as numerous human remains. Hidden down a narrow passage, Yadin discovered a treasure-trove of documents and the remains of a woman named Babata and her family. The letters, it was determined, were military orders signed by Simeon Bar Kochba, the leader of the second Jewish revolt against Rome (in 132–136 CE), the first historical evidence of his life. Based on the documents, as well as the discovery of coins minted by Bar Kochba's followers, it was concluded that Babata, her family, and the other members of the cave had been hiding out after the failed revolt. The manufacture of the materials has been dated to between 120 and 135 CE. The climate within the cave and its surrounds had preserved the artefacts very well, and thus Yadin and his team also discovered, what remains to this day, some of the most complete and earliest examples of ancient dress including sandals, jewelry, scarves, blankets, balls of spun and dyed yarn, men's and women's mantels, burial shrouds and a child's tunic.[10]

10. Yigael Yadin, *The Finds from the Bar Kokhba Period in the Cave of Letters* (Jerusalem: Israel Exploration Society, 1963). See also Yigael Yadin, *The Excavation at Masada: Preliminary Report* (Jerusalem: Israel Exploration Society, 1965).

The first thing to note about the clothing discovered is that there is nothing really remarkable about it. It conforms, almost entirely, in shape, colour, design and manufacturing, to wider Graeco-Roman fashion, especially that of the Eastern region of the Roman Empire; the only difference being slight alterations to bring the clothing in line with Jewish law. The two laws of dress – *sha'atnez* and *tzitzit* – set forth in Deuteronomy 22.11–12, as well as the adherence to purity laws, differentiated Jewish dress from its neighbours, though not in a manner immediately noticeable to the passer-by on the street. The law of *sha'atnez*, prohibiting the mixing of fibres, would only have made a difference to the manufacture process.[11] The balls of yarn found in the cave consisted of both wool and linen spun and kept separately from each other; they were not woven together in any of the garments. Adherence to purity laws similarly only seemed to affect clothing construction. In the Graeco-Roman world the *tunic* (Heb. *haluq*, Gk. *chiton*) was the primary article of clothing for men and women alike. It was generally made of one large rectangle of fabric, with the longer dimension wrapped horizontally around the body, pinned at the shoulders, sewn vertically along the short ends of the rectangle, and girded at the waist. Interestingly, the tunics found in the Cave of Letters are not made of a single piece of fabric, but of two (a front and a back), that would have been sewn together at the shoulders and down both sides of the body.[12] Whether unique to Jews or not, it seems that this method aided in the maintenance of purity laws. If a garment became defiled through contact with an impurity, it was to be discarded – a great expense for most people in the first century. However, with two separable pieces of material, 'the ritually unclean half of the tunic could … be removed and replaced without defiling the other half'.[13] Or, as the Mishnah states: 'And so also in the case of the two wings of a shirt, if a leprosy sign appeared on the one, the other remains clean.'[14]

The law of *tzitzit* meanwhile would have been applied to the other staple item of any Graeco-Roman person's wardrobe – the cloak (also referred to as a *mantle*, Gk. *himation*), a large rectangle of fabric wrapped around the body over the tunic.

---

11. As weaving fibres separately was more technically demanding, and dying linen was difficult, the adherence to these prohibitions seemed to have created a specialty cottage industry within Jewish communities of skilled craftsman known for the 'fine quality of [their] cloth'. See Lucille A. Roussin, 'Costume in Roman Palestine: Archaeological Remains and the Evidence from the Mishnah', in Judith Lynn Sebesta and Larissa Bonfante (eds), *The World of Roman Costume* (Madison, WI: University of Wisconsin Press, 2001), pp. 182–90, at pp. 182–3.

12. Yadin, *Finds from the Bar Kokhba Period in the Cave of Letters*, p. 212, Pl. 66. A tunic comprised of two sheets, and decorated with two dark red bands. IAA Number: 1996–9132: http://www.antiquities.org.il/t/item_en.aspx?CurrentPageKey=1&indicator=39&shalemid=515

13. Roussin, 'Costume in Roman Palestine', p. 183. See also: Yadin, *Finds from the Bar Kokhba Period*, pp. 204–5.

14. Mishnah Nega'im 11.9

This law required tassels, or *tzitzit*,[15] to adorn each of the four corners of the cloak (known as a *tallit* – pl. *tallitot* – with this addition). Though the law of *tzitzit* does not specify gender, it has generally been assumed that it only applied to men, thus Jewish women would likely have worn their *himatia* without *tzitzit*. While this is a distinguishing feature of the garment, it is unclear whether this small addition alone would have marked out Jews, *Ioudaioi*, as small drapery weights with tassels or fringes were sometimes added to the usual *himation* to help keep it in place on the body (see image 6, plate section).

In terms of overall appearance, the clothing remains from the Cave of Letters provide a reasonable place to start to build a picture, from which costume design could easily draw. Graeco-Roman tunics of the first century generally fell no longer than the base of the knee for men, and the ankle for women; the tunics Yadin and his team discovered are no exception. They are all adorned with *clavi* – vertical stripes running front and back, from shoulder to hem (see image 7, plate section).[16] *Clavi* (as well as other clothing and accessory detailing) were used to designate rank or social function of the wearer. Based on the varying widths of *clavi* on the found tunics, Yadin theorized that they were used in this community to note age and status in a way similar to the Roman style – the wider the stripe, the older and more senior the individual.[17] The inclusion of *clavi* allows the tunics to be compared to other tunics of the Roman East depicted in mosaics, sculpture, illustration and funerary art, as well as textual references in Talmudic and Gentile literature, thereby broadening the scope of available evidence. Although the *tallitot* discovered were in a poorer condition than the tunics, primarily in small fragments save for one nearly intact cloak, they too are decorated, coloured and woven in such a way as to permit comparison with alternative evidence. Thus whilst Jewish people may not have generally depicted the human form (though there are some exceptions which I discuss below), and therefore the available *direct* evidence is limited, the wealth of non-Jewish illustration from the period and the quality of finds from the

15. The law of *tzitzit* is one of the few that has been explained: the *tzitzit* act as an ever-present reminder to the wearer of God's commandments (Num. 15.39–40). Numbers 15.38 specifies the addition of blue thread in the tassels. It appears that the inhabitants of the Cave of Letters adhered to this proscription. Yadin concluded that a ball of spun and dyed blue wool (with a unique and expensive *kermes* dye) kept 'carefully and separately wrapped' was intended specifically for *tzitzit*, as the dye was not used in any of the other textiles. Yadin, *Finds from the Bar Kokhba Period*, pp. 182–3.

16. See also tunic IAA 1996–9132, see http://www.antiquities.org.il/t/item_en.aspx?CurrentPageKey=17&q=Hever.

17. Though the use of *clavi* as a means to designate rank diminished and eventually disappeared over time (and was certainly already on its way out by the early second century), 'on the basis of the ages of the persons buried within the cave, it may be assumed that the children and youths wore tunics with narrow *clavi*, while the adults, including without doubt the district and town administrators and commanders of high rank, wore tunics with wide clavi'. For a full discussion of *clavi* including a comparison between the finds and Talmudic references see Yadin, *Finds from the Bar Kokhba Period*, pp. 205–11.

Cave allow us to relatively easily find similarities that will aid in determining which Gentile depictions (and later-dated Jewish art) can be used to better illustrate Jewish dress of the early first century. Egyptian funerary art and Roman mosaics are hugely beneficial in this regard. So too are the frescos found in the Dura-Europos synagogue.

The interior of the third-century synagogue at Dura-Europos provides us with the earliest self-depictions of Jewish people – in this case, in the form of murals illustrating biblical scenes. What we see in many of the images is clothing remarkably similar to the textile remains discussed above. The tunics on the male figures all appear to have *clavi* and are draped to just below the knee (see image 8, plate section).[18] This is not all that remarkable however; as has been discussed, this is the standard form of tunic we should expect to see on male inhabitants of the Graeco-Roman world. The resemblance here simply provides further weight to the argument that Jews would not have dressed differently than their neighbours. The similarity between the cloaks drawn and the remains of those in the Cave of Letters is of great interest. Yadin identified two primary types of embroidered decoration on the *tallitot* fragments he discovered: notched bands and, what he called, 'gamma-shaped' patterns – a right-angle design with notched ends (see image 9, plate section). In addition, all of the *tallitot* are dyed in various vibrant colours, though those with the gamma shape are bolder and more colourful than those with the notched band, which are dyed in paler hues. If we look at the figures at Dura that are illustrated in Graeco-Roman dress, we can see the same notched bands (appearing only on the male figures) and gamma-shaped designs (only on the female figures) on the cloaks, as well as the corresponding colour palette of bold and paler colours (see image 10, plate section). Yadin notes that textile fragments with the same decorative patterns were also uncovered at Murabba'at, Palmyra, Karanis in Egypt, and at Dura. He also identified the gamma-shape on a number of first-century female Egyptian mummy-portraits. Consequently, it is fair to reason that this mode of design was, similar to *clavi* on tunics, a common feature of *himatia,* at least in the East. Interestingly, the painted mantles in the Dura murals do not appear to have *tzitzit*. Perhaps this is because they were generally not distinguishing enough to warrant that level of detailed painting, or perhaps the religious proscription was not kept equally across all Jewish communities.[19]

18. The tunics in the illustrations at Dura also have sleeves that reach to the elbow. This feature is not mentioned in any comparison discussion with the textiles from the Cave of Letters that I have come across. It is my assumption that the sleeves and the slightly longer length of the tunics (to below the knee, as opposed to hitting the knee), is due to the time period in which they were painted – the third century – when these modifications to tunics were becoming more fashionable.

19. Dafna Shlezinger-Katsman notes that 'Roman-style clothes worn by Jewish men were not required to have show fringes' (Sifre Deut. 234). It could be that the mantle worn in a Roman way (wrapped over one shoulder so that the *clavi* on the tunic was visible) as

There are of course challenges to using the images at Dura when attempt to reconstruct a picture of Jewish clothing of first-century Judaea. As Bernard Goldman warns,

> ...one must be mindful of the caveat that representations of dress in painting and sculpture need not necessarily reflect current styles. The depersonalized images of gods and heroized figures may be portrayed in the sort of traditional dress deemed appropriate to the figures' statures and roles rather than in the style currently in the streets.[20]

Other challenges specific to these images are, most notably, the synagogue's late dating in relationship to the New Testament narrative, and its more easterly location, in modern-day Syria. In addition, the frescos depict Parthian-Iranian dress as well as the Graeco-Roman styles discussed. Dura was not made part of the Roman Empire until 164 CE, having previously been part of the Parthian empire, and, for a time, serving as the seat of the Parthian provincial governor. It would have experienced a much greater eastern cultural influence (like much of Syro-Mesopotamia) than Judaea. We are therefore looking at evidence quite temporally and culturally removed from Jesus and his contemporaries in order to determine their mode of dress. However, that there is as much of a representation of western-influenced dress as there is, certainly speaks to the prominence of this style across multiple regions and through varying cultures.[21]

I do not believe that the presence of Parthian-Iranian dress, or the fact that the murals were painted in the third century, should diminish the strength of the combined evidence from Dura and the Cave of Letters to argue for Western influence in Jewish clothing of the first century, especially as additional textile remains continue to point towards Occidental modes of dress amongst the Eastern

illustrated at Dura, constituted 'Roman-style clothes', but without clarification on what is meant by 'Roman-style' (and Shlezinger-Katsman makes no attempt in this regard), it is impossible to draw any conclusions. Dafna Shlezinger-Katsman, 'Clothing', in Catherine Hezser (ed.), *The Oxford Handbook of Jewish Daily Life in Roman Palestine* (Oxford: Oxford University Press, 2010), pp. 362–81, at p. 368.

20. Bernard Goldman, 'Graeco-Roman Dress in Syro-Mesopotamia', in Judith Lynn Sebesta and Larissa Bonfante (eds), *The World of Roman Costume* (Madison, WI: University of Wisconsin Press, 2001), pp. 163–81, at pp. 164–5.

21. Goldman argues that in such a small city as Dura, there would not have been sufficient work for a painter to build a local trade and thus it is more likely that the individual who painted the synagogue murals was 'most likely, [a] master painter ... brought in from Palestine'. A number of interesting questions regarding cultural influence would follow such a conclusion such as: Is the dress representative of the painter's experience, or did he fuse his own ideas with that of the synagogue's congregation? The answers to such questions would add a new dynamic to the utilization of the Dura paintings in discussions of Jewish dress. Goldman, 'Graeco-Roman Dress', p. 167.

regions of the Roman Empire. Additionally, that we can see such strong similarities between the decoration painted at Dura and that found on textile remains indicates that the clothing in the paintings do represent clothing of the period.

In addition to the textile remains found in the Cave of Letters, other archaeological digs (at Masada, Qumran, Palmyra, Dura-Europos and Nahal Hever – the location of the Cave of Letters – and Nahal Mishmar; in Wadi Murabba'at and Wadi Daliya; and near Jericho) have uncovered hundreds of textile fragments, remnants of footwear (some more intact than others) and items of jewellery. These remains can further indicate fabric choice, colour and types of dyes used, weaving styles employed, religious regulatory adherence, and the influence of surrounding cultures, especially when fragments allow for a general reconstruction of the shape of the garment. Much of this evidence can be used to support Yadin's conclusions that we have discussed. They also speak to the overall quality of the remains from the Cave of Letters in that nothing has since been discovered as intact or in as good a condition. In fact, they are some of the most complete textile remains of the period from anywhere within the bounds of the Roman Empire. It is easy to see then why Yadin believed they would 'shed new light on the shapes and forms of clothing and other textiles in the Roman period *in general* [emphasis mine], and on Jewish dress in Mishnaic times in particular'.[22] It is a shame that outside a small, interested academic circle, they do not appear to have done so yet.

Apart from the archaeological finds, there are also literary references to clothing and appearance that can be looked at. Those found in biblical texts tend to be regulatory in nature, focusing on issues of appearance (cf. Deut. 22.5; 1 Tim. 2.9; 1 Peter 3.3–4) or brief mentions within an unrelated discussion that can indicate minor details such as the type of garment or colour (most notably, 2 Tim. 4.13; also, Luke 8.44; John 19.2, 23). In addition, there are a few proscriptive passages found in the Hebrew Bible that describe either a particular garment – such as the sacral vestments of the High Priest Aaron, and his sons (Exod. 28, 39; Lev. 8.7-9)[23] – or distinctive elements of Jewish dress applicable to many garments

---

22. Yadin, *Finds from the Bar Kokhba Period*, p. 170.

23. These passages provide the greatest amount of detail of any textual evidence for dress and thus are very interesting to look at in comparison to film portrayals. As is called for in the Tanach, the high priest is often costumed with a breastplate, a turban or large hat, a long tunic and a sash, while the other members of the Sanhedrin are similarly styled (cf. *The King of Kings* (1927), *Jesus Christ Superstar* (1979), *The Last Temptation of Christ* (1988), *The Passion of the Christ* (2004)). However, the text specifies a vibrant colour palette (Exod. 28.6 calls for threads of gold, blue, purple and crimson, for example), and yet we primarily see the high priest in black and grey (as in *The Greatest Story Ever Told*, *The Gospel According to St. Matthew*, *Jesus of Nazareth* and *The Bible* Miniseries). It is also worth noting that throughout Exodus 28 and 39 the text specifies that these garments are only to be worn *whilst officiating*; in other words, in the Temple. Ezekiel 42.14; 44.19 makes this point especially clear, stating that the high priest shall wear his sacral vestments in the inner sanctum of the Temple alone, and remove them before he proceeds into the outer court.

(Deut. 22.11–12 as I have discussed at length). Taken in total, biblical references are minimal; rabbinic discussions of dress found within the Talmud provide our greatest collective resource. Thus Lucille Roussin, building on Yadin's work, provides a good, if brief, comparative analysis between the evidence from the Mishnah, the Cave of Letters remains, and the murals at Dura. In 'Costume in Roman Palestine, Archaeological Remains and the Evidence from the Mishnah', Roussin draws attention to Talmudic passages that discuss what one could carry from a burning home on the Sabbath, or the appropriate method of undressing in a bathhouse, as both provide lists of typical clothing items. Though neither provides descriptions of what the clothing looked like, or how it was worn, by using Hebrew transliterations of Greek and Latin terms, they do 'indicate that the basic items of clothing worn by Jews did not differ significantly from those worn by other inhabitants of the Graeco-Roman world'.[24] If Jewish people wore distinctly different items of dress, Roussin argues, they would have had their own terminology.

The Talmud can also provide more indirect information on clothing and dress through, for example, stories about mistaken identity between Jews and Gentiles (implying a similarity in appearance),[25] or Jews concealing their identity by adopting or neglecting small items of dress such as *tzitzit* or *teffilin* (also called 'phylacteries' – small leather boxes containing passages from the Torah strapped to a man's head and arm for prayer). Similar examples of mistaken identity can be found in other Graeco-Roman texts of the time, or instances of Gentile leaders requiring Jews to wear something distinctive to mark themselves out. If they already looked distinctive, there would be no such need. Shaye Cohen collates a number of such texts highlighting the value not simply of texts that directly discuss clothing but of those whose overall discussions can imply something about dress. For example, Cohen states that in Justin Martyr's *Dialogue with Trypho the Jew*, 'Trypho recognizes Justin immediately as a philosopher (because he is wearing the garb of a philosopher), but Justin has to ask Trypho "who are you"', because he is not identifiable as a 'Hebrew'.[26] In addition, Cohen points out that the absence

Unfortunately, whether the priests had special garments that they wore in public (such as presiding over a trial) is therefore unknown. For clothing worn by the priests in the Temple, see Joan E. Taylor, 'Imagining Judean Priestly Dress: The Berne Josephus and *Judaea Capta* Coinage', in Kristi Upson-Saia, Carly Daniel-Hughes and Alicia J. Batten (eds), *Dressing Judeans and Christians in Antiquity* (Farnham: Ashgate, 2014), pp. 195–212.

24. Roussin, *Costume in Roman Palestine*, p. 183.

25. Shaye Cohen cites a passage from the Babylonian Talmud about a Rabbi fined for mistaking a Gentile woman for a Jew when he criticized her choice of dress (B. Berakhot 20a). Shaye J. D. Cohen, 'Those Who Say They Are Jews and Are Not: How Do You Know a Jew in Antiquity When You See One?' in Shaye J. D. Cohen and Ernest S. Frerichs (eds), *Diasporas in Antiquity* (Atlanta, GA: Scholars Press, 1993), pp. 1–46, at p. 6, reprinted in Shaye Cohen, *The Beginnings of Jewishness* (Berkeley: University of California Press, 1999), pp. 25–68, at p. 33.

26. Cohen also provides examples of a common aspect of later Jewish experience: the requirement in certain times that Jews wear particular items of dress in order to mark them

of texts discussing Jewish clothing at a time when the Greek and Romans liked to
mock difference (and criticize those who adopted the clothing of 'barbarous'
people such as the Celts, Germans, Parthians and Sarmatians) indicates that
there was nothing distinctive about Jewish appearance.[27] 'On the contrary,' he
writes, 'there is much evidence that Jews, whether male or female, were not easily
distinguished from gentiles.'[28]

When looked at collectively, the available evidence for the specific topic of
'dress' directs us to the same conclusions that scholars of the social world of the
New Testament have long since drawn more generally: that the Jewish people of
the Graeco-Roman world were a Hellenized society. As Martin Goodman has
written, 'How and why and to what extent Greek culture was absorbed into the
ancient Jewish world is not always clear. But, that it was is undeniable.'[29] We should
be presenting these conclusions, particularly of Hellenistic dress normativity,
visually in biblical dramas.

Despite the fact that Jesus is most commonly depicted in films wearing a tunic
that descends to the ankles (or longer) and has long sleeves, in the first century
both of these features were considered effeminate and therefore derided. When a
man's tunic of this style—long and with sleeves—was embroidered, it was only
worn by 'Roman dandies'.[30] Wearing a tunic without a belt was punishment for a
Roman soldier, and thought of as immoral in the individual. In fact, even though
Julius Caesar wore a belt, he was criticized for wearing it too loosely. The long,
long-sleeved tunic (sometimes unbelted, sometimes belted loosely) traditionally
associated with Jesus, and thus first-century Jewish men's dress, was not 'accepted'
male fashion within the Roman Empire until the late fourth century or even the

---

out as Jews (linen, in Artapanus, frag. 3 parag. 20; an ivy motif, in 3 Maccabees 2.29),
something that would not be necessary if they were already so marked by their own choice
in appearance; Cohen, 'Those Who Say They Are Jews', p. 6. There is no evidence this was
actually ever actualized, and Cohen notes that non-Jewish women, thought to be Jewish
women, were seized in the Alexandrian riots (Philo, *On Flaccus* 96), because Jewish and
non-Jewish women could not be distinguished.

27. Balsdon gives a long list of occasions where Romans or Greeks wearing the clothing
of an 'other', even each other, were heavily critiqued for doing so. In particular, the male Celts
and Germans wore very thick, generally black cloaks and trousers appropriate for their cold,
wet weather and suitable for riding horses. When Romans who ventured North into these
regions adopted this dress (as it was no doubt practical to do so), they were criticized
(cf. Cicero, *Phil.* 2, 76). It seems unlikely then that Jewish people could have worn thick
black cloaks (cf. the Sanhedrin in *The Passion of the Christ*) with nary a mention by Greeks
or Romans. J. P. V. D. Balsdon, *Romans and Aliens* (London: Duckworth, 1979), pp. 219–22.

28. Cohen, 'Those Who Say They Are Jews', p. 6.

29. Martin Goodman, 'Under the Influence: Hellenism in Ancient Jewish Life', *Biblical
Archaeology Review* 36.1 (Jan/Feb 2010), pp. 60–7, 84, at p. 60.

30. James Laver, *Costume and Fashion: A Concise History*, 5th ed. (London: Thames and
Hudson, 2012), pp. 39–40.

fifth. Even then, this style of dress is found only on ecclesiastics or the wealthy, as in the mosaics of Ravenna.[31]

If the filmmaker's goal is historical accuracy (as often professed), we should be seeing Jesus in a knee-length tunic (with *clavi*) tied at the waist, and a *tallit* that was not much longer than his tunic. Jesus would probably not have been able to afford fine linen, silk or rich dyes. It is more likely that he wore wool or natural linen. Jesus should not be in a fourth-century ankle-length, long-sleeved tunic. His *tallit* should not be long and voluminous, as he spent his days travelling and labouring, and this would have been highly impractical.[32]

As for Caiaphas, a wealthy and powerful member of society, the Cave of Letters remains prove illuminating. Like Jesus, Caiaphas' tunic should reach his knees and no longer. His *tallit* on the other hand, would demonstrate his wealth, and thus would likely be made from a very large piece of fine wool that would reach his ankles (the more cumbersome, the more it impeded one's movement, the greater the show of status).[33] It would have been richly coloured, and decorated with notched bands. He probably wrapped it in such a manner as to display the broad *clavi* on his tunic.[34] And this, at long last, brings us to *Brian*.

31. For a good overview on Roman attitudes to impropriety in dress see Balsdon, *Romans and Aliens*, pp. 2, 220–1. Also, Jonathan Edmondson, 'Public Dress and Social Control in Late Republican and Early Imperial Rome', in Jonathan Edmondson and Alison Keith (eds), *Roman Dress and the Fabrics of Roman Culture* (Toronto: University of Toronto Press, 2008), pp. 21–46, at pp. 35–6.

32. For further detail on Jesus' clothing, see Joan E. Taylor, 'What Did Jesus Look Like?' in *The Life of Jesus of Nazareth* (i5 Magazine special issue, 2014), pp.10–15.

33. For much of human history, even as fashions changed, impracticality in dress denoted a member of the 'leisure class', those who did not need to move much throughout the day, while an abundance of fabric was an overt display of wealth. In 1899, Thorstein Veblen wrote, 'If, in addition to showing that the wearer can afford to consume freely and uneconomically, it can also be shown in the same stroke that he or she is not under the necessity of earning a livelihood … Our dress, therefore, in order to serve its purpose effectually, should not only he expensive, but it should also make plain to all observers that the wearer is not engaged in any kind of productive labor': *The Theory of the Leisure Class* (London: Macmillan, 1899). Over time, the toga, in following this principal, became so unwieldy that it fell out of favour entirely. Shelley Stone, 'The Toga: From National to Ceremonial Costume', in Judith Lynn Sebesta and Larissa Bonfante (eds), *The World of Roman Costume* (Madison, WI: University of Wisconsin Press, 2001), pp. 13–45, at p. 17. Similarly, the draping of a large *himation* to expose the shoulder made movement difficult and thus would likely *have been avoided by labourers*. Robin Osborne, *The History Written on the Classical Greek Body* (Cambridge: Cambridge University Press, 2011), pp. 61–2. See also Malcolm Barnard, *Fashion as Communication* (New York: Routledge, 2002); Christopher Breward, *The Culture of Fashion* (Manchester: Manchester University Press, 1995).

34. It is quite probable that Caiaphas and the other priests would have worn something that identified them to the public, such as a particular hat, white garments or specially

Figure 16.1 A crowd has come to worship Brian. *Monty Python's Life of Brian* (1979).

I've often said in conversation that the *Life of Brian* (1979) has the most historically accurate costumes of any Jesus film. Hazel Petheg, veteran Monty Python costume designer, clearly knew her craft. Nevertheless, it is entirely anachronistic to depict the crowds as a sea of beige-wearing Bedouin displaced into first-century Judaea that we see in nearly every biblical epic (Figure 16.1).[35]

There is no evidence to suggest, for example, that anybody in the ancient world, Jew or not, wore a *kaffiyeh* (a traditional Arabic head covering made from a square of cloth often held in place with rope).[36] However, there are a few specific points on

tailored garments, as other priests in the ancient world were known to have done so. For example, Egyptian priests of the Osiris cult were only permitted to wear linen (Plutarch, *On Isis and Osiris* 352c–d). If this held true for priests of the Temple in Jerusalem, then it is less likely that their mantles bore decoration or were colourful. The picture I have drawn is one based on social status, wealth and degree of Hellenization therefore, and not on Caiaphas' role as high priest, as we are unsure as to how this would have impacted his choice in clothing. However, it should not be assumed that priestly sacred vestments worn in the Temple precincts were worn outside it; see above n. 20.

35. Although Bedouin generally wear clothing dyed a multitude of colours, their style of clothing, including the *kaffiyah*, are what costume designers mistakenly tend to emulate. The fact that costumes veer towards beige and other 'natural' colours does not represent Bedouin-styling, but instead, other impressions of first-century Judaean clothing.

36. Exploration and conquest of the East in the eighteenth and nineteenth centuries brought the West into greater contact with Bedouin tribes – often remarked upon as being true conservationists to an ancient way of life in contrast to the 'degenerate' city dwellers who represented the failing Ottoman Empire. The Arab and the Bedouin specifically became seen almost as a 'living fossil'. In the newly developed field of race science, the Bedouin were

which *Life of Brian* favourably differs from standard depictions that are worth highlighting.

Individuality

Costume is used to great effect both to group people together and to tell them apart. While this can be a useful tool for the audience, it can prevent us from seeing people within a group as individuals. It also contributes to a more heightened sense of division between groups and like-mindedness within groups, than what might be indicated by narrative alone. In New Testament dramatizations, the traditional costuming of Pharisees and Temple priests in the same manner gives the impression that historically these two groups were one and the same; however, while some Pharisees might have been priests, most priests were not Pharisees; the Sadducees and Pharisees too were quite different groups, with their own distinctive concerns about Jesus' teaching.[37] The Pythons, on the other hand, managed to imbue a personality on many of the characters, even those in self-elected groups who chose to dress similarly. If dramatizations were to costume its characters with a greater variability, as in *Brian*, perhaps based on *social status* rather than on belief or disbelief in Jesus, we might be presented with a better picture of the social world of the New Testament.

Social class

In the ancient world, as in much of human history, clothing styles, fabrics and dyes 'helped to underline the key hierarchical status layers into which [society] was divided'.[38] That first-century Judaeans were no different is evidenced by the use of *clavi* of varying widths in the Cave of Letters remains, as well as certain colours of dye that are used more or less frequently than others. Jerusalem was a city with an aristocracy; the Sadducees; and an educated class as many of the Pharisees were, as

seen as the most racially and culturally 'pure' Semites. And just as Hebrew and Aramaic were scientifically grouped together, so too were Jews and Arabs – the standard bearers for the Semitic peoples. The Jew was now no longer simply a theological or religious 'other' but a 'racial' other as well. At the same time, the Jewishness of Jesus, which was becoming an academic topic in its own right, could not be denied and thus he and his followers also took on a Bedouin look, and thus the *kaffiyeh* made its way into biblical dramatizations. Kalmar, 'Jesus Did Not Wear a Turban', p. 17.

37. By depicting them so differently to Jesus, it appears as if the Pharisees and Sadducees are in complete agreement and in total opposition to Jesus. Josephus makes it repeatedly clear in his writings that these two groups (a third being the Essenes) are distinctly different groups (*Antiquities* 13.171; *War* 2.119; *Vita* 7): The Sadducees appear to be from an aristocratic class (2 Chron. 31; Ezek. 40.46), while the Pharisees had 'the multitude on their side' (*Antiquities* 13.293).

38. Edmondson and Keith, *Roman Dress*, p. 6.

Figure 16.2 Brian at the Sermon on the Mount with others.
Monty Python's Life of Brian (1979).

well as many people of lower, labour-based classes. In the Sermon on the Mount
scene in *Life of Brian*, one does not need to hear the characters' English accents to
know that we are looking at people from different social classes (Figure 16.2). Like
Ben-Hur, the *Life of Brian* is one of the few New Testament films that alludes to the
existence of a differentiated social hierarchy.

Hellenization

Not only does the Jerusalem of the Monty Python universe have social classes,
but it is a world clearly touched by the Hellenistic and Roman Empires. Many
of the characters wear knee-length tunics appropriate to the time, Brian wears a
petasos (a Hellenistic sun hat known to have been worn by Jews, 2 Macc. 4.12)
in the coliseum, and its wealthiest couple, adorned in jewellery, fine cloth and
long garments, appears the most Hellenized (even whilst being crucified!).
As we have seen from the historical evidence, this is how first-century Jews *should*
appear.

Pontius Pilate

When a film about the life of Jesus claims historical accuracy, there is one simple
litmus test that can be used: what does Pontius Pilate wear? By the late Republican/
early Imperial period of Rome, fashion had become an incredibly important
mechanism of social interactions. 'The sheer comprehensiveness of the ancient
scholarly literature on dress illustrates how deeply significant it was to the Roman

mentality.[39] What one wore and how it was worn was dictated by legislation, part of which included the requirement that all male citizens must wear the toga in any civic context, such as presiding over a trial as a representative of Rome. If Monty Python can get this right, so should any other film of this period, especially those that ask audiences to take them seriously.[40]

So, does it matter if anachronistic costuming taints the audience's knowledge or understanding of a particular period? I would imagine that many historians like myself would assert the importance of an accurate public awareness of the past, even if they have differing reasons for doing so. As to whether the responsibility for educating the public falls, even in part, on the film industry, is a question much more open to debate. We might begin to answer this question by asking another: When it comes to biblical epics, are audience expectations the same? Do they watch *The Passion of the Christ* with the same mindset as *Gone with the Wind*? Based on the public response to Mel Gibson's film in particular, from church screenings, to educational information distributed, a more likely answer would be that for many people, they are not simply seeing the past on screen for the purpose of entertainment, they are seeing a representation of a deeply held truth. Conversely, when a film does not appear to recognize this different standard, as in the case of the *Life of Brian*, some religious groups protest or censor it. Does this then change the film industry's level of responsibility? This, I believe, is a complex question best answered in another book.

For the purposes of this chapter, however, I will briefly argue for responsibility on the part of the film industry, though the degree depends on what it is that they are presenting and what message is coming across. I would not argue for, and I think one should never expect, a true facsimile of the clothing of the first century, or any period, on screen. However, it is important that the costuming accurately, or as accurately as possible, represents the historical context: The sense of the past, the feeling of the time should be presented appropriately, even if the clothing itself is not. It is here that the *Life of Brian* succeeds. Even though there were many inaccuracies in the costuming, visually the film presented a Jerusalem that was hot, crowded, lively, colourful (in some of its clothing and in its people), cosmopolitan and culturally influenced by having been part of both the Hellenistic and Roman empires.

39. Ibid., p. 13.

40. It was quite reasonably suggested to me at the *Jesus and Brian* conference (20–22 June 2014), that since Pilate's position in Judaea was a military one, military garb would be appropriate. However, 'given its emblematic force ... male citizens were ... required to wear the toga for all civic occasions – political, judicial, and religious', Edmondson, 'Public Dress', p. 22. Or as Shelley Stone puts it: 'throughout the Empire ... [the toga] was always considered the garment to be worn by the Roman man conducting public business', Stone, *The World of Roman Costume*, p. 13. If Pilate was indeed presiding over a public trial, surely a civic occasion, then he would have been required by Roman law to wear a toga whilst doing so.

COMPOSITE BIBLIOGRAPHY

Monty Python's Life of Brian *and the Bible in Film*

Altman, Rick, 'The Semantic/Syntactic Approach to Film Genre', in Barry Grant (ed.), *Film Genre Reader* (Austin: University of Texas Press, 1986).

Altman, Rick, *Film/Genre* (London: British Film Institute, 1999).

Apostolos-Cappadona, Diane, 'Iconography', in John Lyden (ed.), *The Routledge Companion to Religion and Film* (London and New York: Routledge, 2011), pp. 440–64.

Babington, Bruce and Evans, Peter W., *Biblical Epics: Sacred Narrative in the Hollywood Cinema* (Manchester: Manchester University Press, 1993).

Batson, C. Daniel and Ventis, W. Larry, *The Religious Experience: A Social-Psychological Perspective* (New York: Oxford University Press, 1982).

Baugh, Lloyd, *Imaging the Divine: Jesus and Christ-Figures in Film* (Kansas City, MO: Sheed and Ward, 1997).

Benko, Stephen, 'Ironic Faith in Monty Python's *Life of Brian*', *Journal of Religion and Film [digital]*, 16, 1 (2012), Article 6, available at http://digitalcommons.unomaha.edu/jrf/vol16/iss1/6

Campbell, Richard H. and Pitts, Michael R., *The Bible on Film: A Checklist, 1897–1980* (Metuchen, NJ: Scarecrow, 1981).

Chapman, Graham, Cleese, John, Gilliam, Terry, Idle, Eric, Jones, Terry and Palin, Michael, *Monty Python's Life of Brian (of Nazareth)* (New York City: Ace Books/London: Methuen, 1979).

Chapman, Graham, Cleese, John, Gilliam, Terry, Idle, Eric, Jones, Terry, Palin, Michael, with McCabe, Bob, *The Pythons Autobiography by The Pythons* (London: Orion Publishing Group, 2003; new ed. 2005).

Christianson, Eric, Francis, Peter and Telford, William R. (eds), *Cinéma Divinité: Religion, Theology and the Bible in Film* (London: SCM-Canterbury, 2005).

Christie, Ian and Thompson, David (eds), *Scorsese on Scorsese* (London: Faber & Faber, 1989).

Crossley, James G., 'Life of Brian or Life of Jesus? Uses of Critical Biblical Scholarship and Non-orthodox Views of Jesus in Monty Python's *Life of Brian*', in *Relegere: Studies in Religion and Reception* 1 (2011), pp. 93–114.

Crossley, James G., *Harnessing Chaos: The Bible in English Political Discourse since 1968* (London: T&T Clark Bloomsbury, 2014), pp. 129–52.

Davies, Philip R., '*Life of Brian* Research', in J. Cheryl Exum and Stephen D. Moore (eds), *Biblical Studies/Cultural Studies: The Third Sheffield Colloquium* (London: Sheffield Academic Press/Continuum Books, 1998), pp. 400–14.

Davies, Philip R., '*Life of Brian* Research', in id. *Whose Bible is it Anyway?* (2nd ed.), London: T&T Clark International, 2004), pp. 142–55.

Deacy, Christopher, *Screen Christologies: Redemption and the Medium of Film* (Religion, Culture and Society; Cardiff: University of Wales Press, 2001).

Detweiler, Craig, 'Christianity', in John Lyden (ed.), *The Routledge Companion to Religion and Film* (London and New York: Routledge, 2011), pp. 109–30.

Doyle, Julian, *The Life of Brian/Jesus* (Leicester: Matador, 2011).

Dyke, Carl, 'Learning from *The Life of Brian*: Saviors for Seminars', in George Aichele and Richard G. Walsh (eds), *Screening Scripture: Intertextual Connections Between Scripture and Film* (Harrisburg, PA: Trinity Press International, 2002), pp. 229–50.

Harries, Dan, *Film Parody* (London: British Film Institute, 2000).

Hasenberg, Peter, 'The "Religious" in Film: From *King of Kings* to *The Fisher King*', in J. R. May (ed.), *New Image of Religious Film* (Kansas City, MO: Sheed & Ward, 1997), pp. 41–56.

Hewison, Robert, *Monty Python: The Case Against* (New York: Grove/London: Eyre Methuen, 1981).

Housel, Rebecca, '*Monty Python and the Holy Grail*: Philosophy, Gender, and Society', in Gary Hardcastle, George Reisch and William Irwin (eds), *Monty Python and Philosophy: Nudge Nudge, Think Think!* (Chicago: Open Court, 2006), pp. 83–92.

Jasper, David, *Readings in the Canon of Scripture: Written for Our Learning* (Studies in Literature and Religion; New York: St. Martin's, 1995).

Katz, Ephraim (ed.), *The Macmillan International Film Encyclopedia* (2nd ed.), (London: HarperCollins, 1994), 'Monty Python', p. 963.

Kinnard, Roy and Davis, Tim, *Divine Images: A History of Jesus on the Screen* (New York: Citadel Press, 1992), pp. 192–5.

Landy, Marcia, *Monty Python's Flying Circus* (TV Milestones; Detroit, MI: Wayne State University Press, 2005).

Malone, Peter, *Movie Christs and Antichrists* (New York: Crossroad, 1990).

Malone, Peter, 'Jesus on Our Screens', in John R. May (ed.), *New Image of Religious Film* (Franklin, WI: Sheed and Ward, 2000), pp. 57–71.

Malone, Peter, 'The Roman Catholic Church and Cinema (1967 to the Present)', in John Lyden (ed.), *The Routledge Companion to Religion and Film* (London and New York: Routledge, 2011), pp. 52–71.

Marsh, Clive and Ortiz, Gaye (eds), *Explorations in Theology and Film: Movies and Meaning* (Oxford: Blackwell, 1997).

McCabe, Bob, *The Life of Graham: The Authorised Biography of Graham Chapman* (London: Orion Books, 2005).

Meldrum, John C., '*Star Wars*' Saving Return', *Journal of Religion and Film* 13 (1) (2009) http://www.unomaha.edu/jrf/vol13.no1/StarWars.htm.

Morgan, David, *Monty Python Speaks!* (New York: Spike/Avon/London: Ted Smart, 1999).

Nash, David, *Blasphemy in the Christian World: A History* (Oxford: Oxford University Press, 2007).

Nowell-Smith, Geoffrey (ed.), *The Oxford History of World Cinema* (Oxford: Oxford University Press, 1996).

Ortiz, Gaye, 'Jesus at the Movies: Cinematic Representation of the Christ-Figure', *The Month* (December, 1994), pp. 491–7.

Palin, Michael, *Diaries 1969–1979: The Python Years* (London: Phoenix/Orion, 2007).

Palin, Michael, *Diaries 1980–1988: Halfway to Hollywood* (London: Phoenix, 2009).

Perry, George, *The Life of Python* (London: BCA Pavilion, 1994).

Phillips, Kendall R., *Controversial Cinema: The Films That Outraged America* (Westport, CT: Greenwood, 2008).

Python, Monty, *The Life of Brian Screenplay* (London: Methuen, 2004).

Pythons, the, with Bob McCabe, *The Pythons: Autobiography* (London: Orion, 2003).

Reinhartz, Adele, 'Jesus in Film: Hollywood Perspectives on the Jewishness of Jesus', *Journal of Religion and Film* 2.2 (1998): http://avalon.unomaha.edu/jrf/JesusinFilmRein.htm.

Reinhartz, Adele, *Jesus of Hollywood* (Oxford: Oxford University Press, 2007).

Reinhartz, Adele, 'Jesus and Christ-Figures', in John Lyden (ed.), *The Routledge Companion to Religion and Film* (London and New York: Routledge, 2011), pp. 420–39.

Reinhartz, Adele, *Bible and Cinema: An Introduction* (Abingdon and New York: Routledge, 2013).

Reinhartz, Adele (ed.), *Bible and Cinema: Fifty Key Films* (London and New York: Routledge, 2013).

Schilbrack, Kevin, ' "Life's a Piece of Shit": Heresy, Humanism, and Heroism in Monty Python's *Life of Brian*', in Gary L. Hardcastle and George A. Reisch (eds), *Monty Python and Philosophy: Nudge Nudge, Think Think!* (New York: Open Court, 2006), pp. 13–24.

Schneider, Stephen Jay, *1001 Movies You Must See before You Die* (9th ed.; London: Quintessence, 2013).

Sellers, Robert, *Always Look on the Bright Side of Life: The Inside Story of HandMade Films* (London: John Blake/Metro Publishing, 2003).

Shepherd, David, *The Bible on Silent Film: Spectacle, Story and Scripture in the Early Cinema* (Cambridge: Cambridge University Press, 2013).

Staley, Jeffrey L. and Walsh, Richard, *Jesus, the Gospels, and Cinematic Imagination: A Handbook to Jesus on DVD* (Louisville, KY and London: Westminster John Knox, 2007).

Stern, Richard C., Jefford, Clayton N. and DeBona, Guerric, *Savior on the Silver Screen* (New York and Mahwah, NJ: Paulist Press, 1999).

Stockwood, Mervyn, *Chanctonbury Ring: An Autobiography* (London: Hodder & Stoughton, 1982).

Tatum, W. Barnes, *Jesus at the Movies: A Guide to the First Hundred Years* (Santa Rosa, CA: Polebridge, 1997¹, 2004², 2013³).

Telford, William R., 'Jesus Christ Movie-Star: The Depiction of Jesus in the Cinema', in Clive Marsh and Gaye Ortiz (eds), *Explorations in Theology and Film: Movies and Meaning* (Oxford: Blackwell, 1997), pp. 115–39.

Telford, William R., 'Appendix 2: Christ-Figures in Film', in Eric Christianson, Peter Francis and William R. Telford (eds), *Cinéma Divinité: Religion, Theology and the Bible in Film* (London: SCM-Canterbury, 2005), pp. 351–3.

Thompson, John O., *Monty Python: Complete and Utter Theory of the Grotesque* (London: British Film Institute, 1982).

Vintaloro, Giordano. ' "Non sono il Messia, lo giuro su Dio!" Messianismo e modernità', in Life of Brian *dei Monty Python* (Trieste: Battello Stampatore, 2008).

Walker, John (ed.), *Halliwell's Filmgoer's Companion* (London: HarperCollins, 1995), 'Monty Python', p. 430.

Walker, John, *Halliwell's Film and Video Guide 2003* (18th ed.; London: HarperCollins, 2003), '*Monty Python's Life of Brian*', p. 565.

Walsh, Richard, '*Monty Python's Life of Brian* (1979)', in Adele Reinhartz (ed.), *Bible and Cinema: Fifty Key Films* (London and New York: Routledge, 2013), pp. 187–92.

Wiersma, Hans, 'Redeeming *Life of Brian*: How Monty Python (Ironically) Proclaims Christ Sub Contrario', *Word and World*, 32 (2012), pp. 166–77.

Williams, Tony, *Body and Soul: The Cinematic Work of Robert Aldrich* (Lanham: Scarecrow Press, 2004), pp. 335–47.

Reception Exegesis and Critical Methodologies

Exum, J. Cheryl, 'Toward a Genuine Dialogue between the Bible and Art', in *Congress Volume Helsinki 2010*, ed. M. Nissinen (VTSupp, 148; Leiden: Brill, 2012), pp. 473–503.

Gadamer, Hans-Georg, *Truth and Method*, trans. Joel Weinsheimer and Donald G. Marshall of *Wahrheit und Methode* (2nd ed.), (New York: Crossroad, 1992).

Joyce, Paul M., 'King's College London, Samuel Davidson, and the Scope of Biblical Studies', *JTS* New Series, 65/2 (2014), pp. 407–24.

Joyce, Paul and Lipton, Diana, *Lamentations through the Centuries* (Wiley-Blackwell Bible Commentaries; Oxford: Wiley-Blackwell, 2013).

Klint, Stefan, 'After Story – A Return to History: Introducing Reception Criticism as an Exegetical Approach', *Studia Theologica – Nordic Journal of Theology* 54/2 (2000), pp. 87–106.

Knight, Mark, '*Wirkungsgeschichte*, Reception History, Reception Theory', *JSNT* 33 (2010), pp. 137–46.

Kreitzer, Larry J., *The New Testament in Fiction and Film: On Reversing the Hermeneutical Flow* (Sheffield: Sheffield Academic Press/London: Continuum, 1993).

Kreitzer, Larry, *The Old Testament in Fiction and Film: On Reversing the Hermeneutical Flow* (Sheffield: Sheffield Academic Press, 1994).

Kreitzer, Larry J., 'The Journey of the Magi: Intimations of Passion in the Birth Narratives', *Gospel Images in Fiction and Film: On Reversing the Hermeneutical Flow* (Sheffield: Sheffield Academic Press, 2002), pp. 24–44.

Riches, John, 'Reception Exegesis of Lamentations', *Expository Times* (4 March 2014), pp. 383–7.

Saroglou, Vassilis, 'Religiousness, Religious Fundamentalism, and Quest as Predictors of Humor Creation', *International Journal for the Psychology of Religion* 12 (2002), pp. 177–88.

Sawyer, John F. A., *A Concise Dictionary of the Bible and its Reception* (Louisville, KY: Westminster John Knox, 2009).

Sawyer, John F. A., 'Ezekiel in the History of Christianity', in Andrew Mein and Paul M. Joyce (eds), *After Ezekiel: Essays on the Reception of a Difficult Prophet* (Library of Hebrew Bible/Old Testament Studies, 535; New York and London: T&T Clark/Continuum, 2011), pp. 1–10.

Tollerton, David C., *The Book of Job in Post-Holocaust Thought* (Bible in the Modern World, 44; Sheffield: Sheffield Phoenix Press, 2012).

Additional Resources on Life of Brian *(with thanks to William R. Telford)*

Websites

Full online version

Featured: Monty Python's Life of Brian-1979-full movie <http://www.bmetv.net/video/2122/monty-python-s-life-of-brian-1979-full-movie> [accessed 4 September 2014].

Watch Life of Brian Online <http://putlocker.bz/watch-life-of-brian-online-free-putlocker.html> [accessed 4 September 2014].

Trailer

Life of Brian (1979) Trailer <https://www.youtube.com/watch?v=vVHhg67RVd4&feature=kp> [accessed 4 September 2014].

Monty Python's Life of Brian (1979) <http://www.rottentomatoes.com/m/monty_pythons_life_of_brian/> [accessed 4 September 2014].

Clips (YouTube)

Monty Python's Life of Brian (stoning) <https://www.youtube.com/watch?v=ZNeq2Utm0nU (Scene 4, The Stoning) > [accessed 4 September 2014].

Funniest bit of 'life of brian' <https://www.youtube.com/watch?v=krb2OdQksMc (Scene 18, Hail the Messiah) > [accessed 4 September 2014].

He's Not The Messiah – *Monty Python's Life of Brian* <https://www.youtube.com/watch?v=Zjz16xjeBAA (Scene 19, He's not the Messiah . . .)> [accessed 4 September 2014].

He's Not The Messiah – He's a VERY Naughty Boy <https://www.youtube.com/watch?v=LhGqsqW_Wtg (Oratorio) > [accessed 4 September 2014].

Apps

Monty Python stars reunite to launch app <http://www.telegraph.co.uk/culture/culturenews/9246736/Monty-Python-stars-reunite-to-launch-app.html> [accessed 4 September 2014].

MontyPython.net (Script)

Monty Python's 'Life of Brian' Script Part 1 <http://www.montypython.net/brianmm1.php> [accessed 4 September 2014].

Monty Python's 'Life of Brian' Script Part 2 <http://www.montypython.net/brianmm2.php> [accessed 4 September 2014].

Monty Python's 'Life of Brian' Script Part 3 <http://www.montypython.net/brianmm3.php> [accessed 4 September 2014].

Monty Python's Life of Brian Script <http://montypython.50webs.com/Life_of_Brian.htm> [accessed 4 September 2014].

Wikipedia

Monty Python <http://en.wikipedia.org/wiki/Monty_Python> [accessed 4 September 2014].

Monty Python's *Life of Brian* (album) <http://en.wikipedia.org/wiki/Monty_Python%27s_Life_of_Brian#Album> [accessed 4 September 2014].

Life of Brian <http://en.wikiquote.org/wiki/Life_of_Brian> (Quotes) [accessed 4 September 2014].

Not the Messiah (He's a Very Naughty Boy) <http://en.wikipedia.org/wiki/Not_the_Messiah_(He's_a_Very_Naughty_Boy)> (Oratorio) [accessed 4 September 2014].

Imdb

Life of Brian (1979) <http://www.imdb.com/title/tt0079470/?ref_=nv_sr_1> [accessed 4 September 2014].

Life of Brian (1979) Quotes <http://www.imdb.com/title/tt0079470/quotes> [accessed 4 September 2014].

Newspaper articles, reviews and television debate

The Telegraph

Bingham, J., '*Monty Python's Life of Brian* "extraordinary tribute to Jesus", says theologian decorated by Pope Francis' <http://www.telegraph.co.uk/news/religion/10543149/ Monty-Pythons-Life-of-Brian-extraordinary-tribute-to-Jesus-says-theologian- decorated-by-Pope-Francis.html> [accessed 4 September 2014].

Rainey, S., '*Life of Brian*: facts and figures' <http://www.telegraph.co.uk/culture/8818328/ Life-of-Brian-facts-and-figures.html> [accessed 4 September 2014].

Roche, T., 'The *Life of Brian*: When Monty Python took on God' <http://www.telegraph. co.uk/culture/tvandradio/8833320/The-Life-of-Brian-When-Monty-Python-took-on- God.html> [accessed 4 September 2014].

Singh, A., 'Monty Python star: we'd think twice about making *Life of Brian* today' <http://www.telegraph.co.uk/culture/culturenews/8818056/Monty-Python-star- wed-think-twice-about-making-Life-of-Brian-today.html> [accessed 4 September 2014].

The Guardian

Campbell, D., 'Reid cites *Life of Brian* over Rushdie award' <http://www.theguardian.com/ politics/2007/jun/21/religion.immigrationpolicy> [accessed 4 September 2014].

Dee, J., 'Monty Python, everything you need to know – infographic' <http://www. theguardian.com/culture/interactive/2013/feb/08/monty-python-infographic> [accessed 4 September 2014].

Dowell, B., 'BBC to dramatise unholy row over *Monty Python's Life of Brian*' <http://www. theguardian.com/media/2011/jun/21/bbc-monty-python-life-of-brian> [accessed 4 September 2014].

Glaister, D., '*Life of Brian* comes back to bait Mel' <http://www.theguardian.com/ world/2004/mar/24/filmnews.religion> [accessed 4 September 2014].

Kermode, M., 'Why the *Life of Brian* beats *The Passion of The Christ*' <http://www. theguardian.com/film/2006/dec/24/religion> [accessed 4 September 2014].

Monty Python's Life of Brian <http://www.theguardian.com/film/monty-python-s-life-of- brian> [accessed 9 September 2014].

Sellers, R., 'Welease Bwian' <http://www.theguardian.com/culture/2003/mar/28/ artsfeatures1> [accessed 4 September 2014].

Thorpe, V., '*Monty Python's Life of Brian* recreated for BBC comic drama' <http://www. theguardian.com/film/2011/aug/13/monty-python-life-brian-bbc> [accessed 4 September 2014].

Tunzelmann, Alex von, '*Life of Brian*: birth, blessings and blasphemy', 25 December 2008 <http://www.theguardian.com/film/2008/dec/25/life-of-brian-monty-python-reel- history> [accessed 10 October 2014].

Other newspapers

Hill, Emily, 'The amazing *Life Of Brian*'s girlfriend: From her naked film roles and the jailing of her ex-husband to becoming Mayor of Aberystwyth,' *Daily Mail* (27 August 2011) at <http://www.dailymail.co.uk/femail/article-2030866/The-amazing-Life-Of- Brians-girlfriend-From-naked-film-roles-jailing-ex-husband-Mayor-Aberystwyth. html#ixzz35aVnpqH3>

Reviews

Ebert, R., LIFE OF BRIAN <http://www.rogerebert.com/reviews/life-of-brian-1979> [accessed 4 September 2014].

Ebert, R., MONTY PYTHON'S LIFE OF BRIAN (2004), <http://www.rogerebert.com/reviews/monty-pythons-life-of-brian-2004> [accessed 4 September 2014].

Ferguson, J., *Monty Python's Life of Brian* <http://www.radiotimes.com/film/9rfx/monty-pythons-life-of-brian> [accessed 4 September 2014].

Life of Brian (re-release) <http://www.metacritic.com/movie/life-of-brian> [accessed 4 September 2014].

Monty Python's Life of Brian <http://www.timeout.com/london/film/monty-pythons-life-of-brian> [accessed 4 September 2014].

Monty Python's Life of Brian (1979) <http://www.rottentomatoes.com/m/monty_pythons_life_of_brian/> [accessed 4 September 2014].

Monty Python's Life of Brian <https://www.commonsensemedia.org/movie-reviews/monty-pythons-life-of-brian> [accessed 4 September 2014].

TV debate (1979)

Antitheist, 'The Life of Brian defended by Monty Python's John Cleese and Michael Palin. COMPLETE DEBATE', <https://www.youtube.com/watch?v=tl8acXl3qVs> [accessed 4 September 2014].

Atheist Media Blog, 'The Full "Life of Brian" Debate (1979)', <http://www.atheistmedia.com/2012/05/life-of-brian-debate-1979.html> [accessed 4 September 2014].

'Cleese and Palin relive the 1979 Life of Brian debate' <http://www.bbc.co.uk/news/entertainment-arts-25464820> [accessed 4 September 2014].

Dangerous Minds <http://dangerousminds.net/comments/monty_python_vs._god1> [accessed 4 September 2014].

nir0bateman, 'Life Of Brian- 1979 Debate (1/4)', <https://www.youtube.com/watch?v=1ni559bHXDg> [accessed 4 September 2014].

Wikipedia, 'Friday Night, Saturday Morning', <http://en.wikipedia.org/wiki/Friday_Night,_Saturday_Morning> [accessed 4 September 2014].

https://www.youtube.com/watch?v=CeKWVuye1YE [accessed 6 September 2014].

https://www.youtube.com/watch?v=oM46jRJnHM [accessed 6 September 2014] ten-minute compilation of clips with a commentary.

Not the Nine O'Clock News Sketch: <https://www.youtube.com/watch?v=asUyK6JWt9U; https://www.youtube.com/watch?v=Ku9lt_TvR1k>

Holy Flying Circus (2011)

Dangerous Minds <http://dangerousminds.net/comments/monty_python_vs._god1> [accessed 4 September 2014].

Dowell, B., 'BBC to dramatise unholy row over *Monty Python's Life of Brian*' <http://www.theguardian.com/media/2011/jun/21/bbc-monty-python-life-of-brian> [accessed 4 September 2014].

Roche, T., 'The *Life of Brian*: When Monty Python took on God' <http://www.telegraph.co.uk/culture/tvandradio/8833320/The-Life-of-Brian-When-Monty-Python-took-on-God.html> [accessed 4 September 2014].

Sharp, R., 'Pythons annoyed by "inaccurate" ' portrayal of debate in BBC drama' <http://www.independent.co.uk/arts-entertainment/tv/news/pythons-annoyed-by-inaccurate-portrayal-of-debate-in-bbc-drama-2368104.html> [accessed 4 September 2014].

Thorpe, V., '*Monty Python's Life of Brian* recreated for BBC comic drama' <http://www.theguardian.com/film/2011/aug/13/monty-python-life-brian-bbc> [accessed 4 September 2014].

Wilson, B., 'One unholy Hullabaloo! It's regularly voted the greatest comedy film ever, but *Monty Python's Life Of Brian* caused uproar on its release, as a new BBC comedy drama reveals' <http://www.dailymail.co.uk/femail/article-2046493/Monty-Pythons-Life-Of-Brian-caused-uproar-release-BBC-drama-reveals.html> [accessed 4 September 2014].

Documentaries

BBC Radio 2, aired 22 December 2009, 22.30: Comedian Sanjeev Bhaskar celebrates this anarchic British classic, looking at the film's origins, the shoot in Tunisia, and its controversial afterlife <http://www.bbc.co.uk/programmes/b00p1njn>

Rev. Canon Prof. Richard Burridge on The Today Programme, *31 December 2013 and further reports*

https://www.youtube.com/watch?v=Od2ni3okcww [accessed 6 September 2014].

John Bingham, '*Monty Python's Life of Brian* "extraordinary tribute to Jesus", says theologian decorated by Pope Francis', *Telegraph* (December 31, 2013), available at http://www.telegraph.co.uk/news/religion/10543149/Monty-Pythons-Life-of-Brian-extraordinary-tribute-to-Jesus-says-theologian-decorated-by-Pope-Francis.html [accessed 6 September 2014].

http://www.dailymail.co.uk/news/article-2532171/A-U-turn-Biblical-proportions-34-years-release-senior-churchman-calls-Life-Brian-extraordinary-tribute-Jesus.html [accessed 6 September 2014].

http://www.independent.ie/world-news/life-of-brian-was-true-theologian-swears-on-bible-29876229.html [accessed 6 September 2014].

http://www.thesun.co.uk/sol/homepage/suncolumnists/jeremyclarkson/5356133/more-iron-man-films-and-explosions-suit-jeremy-clarkson.html [accessed 6 September 2014].

http://sheffieldbiblicalstudies.wordpress.com/2014/01/05/life-of-brian-richard-burridge-and-the-media/ [accessed 6 September 2014].

http://www.dagbladet.no/2014/01/03/kultur/komedie/monty_python/life_of_brian/religion/31094614/ [accessed 6 September 2014].

Richard Burridge, 'Is he more than a "naughty boy"?', *Church Times* (13 June 2004), available at http://www.churchtimes.co.uk/articles/2014/13-june/comment/opinion/is-he-more-than-a-naughty-boy [accessed 6 September 2014].

Further impact

Prime Minister's Questions, 3 May 2006, <http://www.publications.parliament.uk/pa/cm200506/cmhansrd/vo060503/debtext/60503-03.htm#60503-03_spmin17> [accessed 10 August 2014].

Ian Garland, 'Feeling sad about the end of the Games? Eric Idle leads 80,000 crowd in rendition of "Always Look on the Bright Side of Life"', *The Daily Mail*, 12 August 2012, <http://www.dailymail.co.uk/news/article-2187413/London-2012-Closing-Ceremony-Eric-Idle-leads-crowd-rendition-Always-Look-Bright-Side-Life.html> [accessed 10 August 2014].

Jesus and Brian conference, *King's College London, June 2014*

https://www.youtube.com/watch?v=CspatcnNWSg – Richard Burridge interviews John Cleese and Terry Jones.

http://www.kcl.ac.uk/artshums/depts/trs/events/jandb/about.aspx.

http://marginalia.lareviewofbooks.org/now-something-completely-different-brianology-comes-age-pythons-done-us/.

General Bibliography

Allegro, John M., *The Dead Sea Scrolls (2)*, pp. 6–7 (unpublished script for broadcast on the North of England Home Service, 23 January 1956).

Allegro, John M., *The Dead Sea Scrolls (3)*, p. 1 (unpublished script for broadcast on the North of England Home Service, 30 January 1956).

Allison, Dale, *Jesus of Nazareth: Millenarian Prophet* (Philadelphia: Fortress, 1998).

Allison, Dale, *Constructing Jesus* (London: Baker Academic, 2010).

Ando, Clifford, *Imperial Ideology and Provincial Loyalty in the Roman Empire* (Berkeley: University of California Press, 2000).

Arnal, William, *The Symbolic Jesus: Historical Scholarship, Judaism and the Construction of Contemporary Identity* (London and Oakville: Equinox, 2005).

Aronstein, Susan, ' "In my own idiom": Social Critique, Campy Gender, and Queer Performance in *Monty Python and the Holy Grail*', in Kathleen Coyne Kelly and Tison Pugh (eds), *Queer Movie Medievalisms* (Farnham: Ashgate, 2009), pp. 115–28.

Ball, David Mark, *'I Am' in John's Gospel Literary Function, Background, and Theological Implications* (Sheffield: Sheffield Academic Press, 1996).

Balsdon, J. P. V. D., *Romans and Aliens* (London: Duckworth, 1979).

Barnard, Malcolm, *Fashion as Communication* (New York: Routledge, 2002).

Bauckham, Richard, *Jesus and the Eyewitnesses: The Gospels as Eyewitness Testimony* (Grand Rapids, MI: Eerdmans, 2006).

Berg, Charles, *The Unconscious Significance of Hair* (London: G. Allen and Unwin, 1951).

Bernett, Monika, *Der Kaiserkult in Judäa unter den Herodiern und Römern* (Tübingen: Mohr Siebeck, 2007).

Bird, Michael F., 'Biblica Hipsteria', http://www.youtube.com/watch?v=6K9N3vYM4vc.

Bird, Michael F., 'The Peril of Modernizing Jesus and the Crisis of Not Contemporizing the Christ', *Evangelical Quarterly* 78 (2006), pp. 291–312.

Bird, Michael F., *Evangelical Theology: A Biblical and Systematic Introduction* (Grand Rapids, MI: Zondervan, 2013).

Bird, Michael F. et al., *How God Became Jesus: The Real Origins of Belief in Jesus' Divine Nature – A Response to Bart Ehrman* (Grand Rapids, MI: Zondervan, 2014).

Bishop, M. C. and Coulston, J. C. N., *Roman Military Equipment, From the Punic Wars to the Fall of Rome* (2nd ed.), (Oxford: Oxbow, 2006).

Bond, Helen K., *Pontius Pilate in History and Interpretation* (Cambridge: Cambridge University Press, 1998).

Bond, Helen K., *Historical Jesus: A Guide for the Perplexed* (London: Bloomsbury, 2012).

Boyarin, Daniel, 'Jewish Masochism: Couvade, Castration, and Rabbis in Pain', *American Imago* 51.1 (1994), pp. 3–36.

Boyarin, Daniel, 'Homotopia: The Feminized Jewish Male and the Lives of Women in Late Antiquity', *Differences* 7 (1995), 41–81.

Boyarin, Daniel, *Dying for God: Martyrdom and the Making of Christianity and Judaism* (Stanford, CA: Stanford University Press, 1999).

Brandon, S. G. F., *Jesus and the Zealots* (Manchester: Manchester University Press, 1967).

Brandon, S. G. F., 'The Defeat of Cestius Gallus: A Roman Legate Faced the Problem of the Jewish Revolt', *History Today* 20/1(Jan. 1970), pp. 38–46.

Brecht, Bertold, with introduction by Steve Giles, *Rise and Fall of the City of Mahagonny* (London: Methuen Drama, 2007).

Breward, Christopher, *The Culture of Fashion* (Manchester: Manchester University Press, 1995).

Brighton, Mark, *The Sicarii in Josephus's Judean War: Rhetorical Analysis and Historical Observations* (Atlanta: Society of Biblical Literature, 2009).

Brooke, George J., 'The Pesharim and the Origin of the Dead Sea Scrolls', in Michael O. Wise, Norman Golb, John J. Collins and Dennis G. Pardee (eds), *Methods of Investigation of the Dead Sea Scrolls and the Khirbet Qumran Site: Present Realities and Future Prospects* (Annals of the New York Academy of Sciences 722; New York: New York Academy of Sciences, 1994), pp. 339–54.

Brooke, George J., 'Kingship and Messianism in the Dead Sea Scrolls', in John Day (ed.), *King and Messiah in Israel and the Ancient Near East: Proceedings of the Oxford Old Testament Seminar* (JSOT Supplement, 270; Sheffield: JSOT Press, 1998), pp. 434–55.

Brooke, George J., 'Was the Teacher of Righteousness Considered to be a Prophet?', in Kristin De Troyer and Armin Lange (eds), *Prophecy after the Prophets? The Contribution of the Dead Sea Scrolls to the Understanding of Biblical and Extra-Biblical Prophecy* (Contributions to Biblical Exegesis 52; Leuven: Peeters, 2009), pp. 77–97.

Brown, Raymond E., *The Death of the Messiah: From Gethsemane to the Grave*, 2 vols (London: Geoffrey Chapman, 1994), I: 875.

Chancey, Mark A., *The Myth of a Gentile Galilee* (Cambridge/New York: Cambridge University Press, 2002).

Chapman, David W., *Perceptions of Crucifixion among Jews and Christians in the Ancient World* (Tübingen: Mohr Siebeck, 2008).

Charlesworth, James H., *Jesus' Jewishness: Exploring the Place of Jesus within Early Judaism* (Philadelphia, PA/New York: American Interfaith Institute; Crossroad, 1991).

Charlesworth, James H., 'The Historical Jesus in the Fourth Gospel: A Paradigm Shift?', *JSHJ* 8 (2010), pp. 3–46.

Chilton, Bruce, *Rabbi Jesus: An Intimate Biography* (New York: Doubleday, 2002).

Clemen, Wolfgang, *Shakespeare's Dramatic Art: Collected Essays* (London: Methuen, 1972).

Cohen, Shaye J. D., 'Those Who Say They Are Jews and Are Not: How Do You Know a Jew in Antiquity When You See One?' in Shaye J. D. Cohen and Ernest S. Frerichs (eds), *Diasporas in Antiquity* (Atlanta, GA: Scholars Press, 1993), pp. 1–46, reprinted in Shaye Cohen, *The Beginnings of Jewishness* (Berkeley: University of California Press, 1999), pp. 25–68.

Coleman, Kathleen M., 'Fatale Charades: Roman Executions Staged as Mythological Enactments', *JRS* 80 (1990), pp. 44–73.

Collins, Adela Yarbro, 'The Charge of Blasphemy in Mark 14.64', *JSNT* 26 (2004), pp. 379–401.

Collins, John J., *The Apocalyptic Imagination: An Introduction to Jewish Apocalyptic Literature* (2nd ed.), (Grand Rapids, MI: Eerdmans, 1998).

Collins, John J. (ed.), *Encyclopedia of Apocalypticism*, vol. 1, *The Origins of Apocalypticism in Judaism and Christianity* (London: Bloomsbury Academic, 2000).

Collins, John J., *The Scepter and the Star: Messianism in Light of the Dead Sea Scrolls* (Grand Rapids, MI: Eerdmans, 2010).

Cook, John G., 'Envisioning Crucifixion: Light from Several Inscriptions and the Palatine Graffito', *NT* 50 (2008), pp. 262–85.

Cook, John G., 'Crucifixion as Spectacle in Roman Campania', *NT* 54 (2012), pp. 68–100.

Cook, John G., 'Roman Crucifixions: From the Second Punic War to Constantine', *ZNW* 104 (2013), pp. 1–32.

Cook, Pam, *Fashioning the Nation: Costume and Identity in British Cinema* (London: BFI Publishing, 1996).

Corley, Kathleen, *Maranatha. Women's Funerary Rites and Christian Origins* (Minneapolis, MN: Fortress Press, 2010).

Crossan, John Dominic, *Jesus: A Revolutionary Biography* (San Francisco: HarperOne, 1994).

Crossley, James G., *Jesus in an Age of Terror: Projects for a New American Century* (London & Oakville: Equinox, 2008).

Crossley, James G., *Jesus in an Age of Neoliberalism: Quests, Scholarship and Ideology* (Durham: Acumen, 2012).

Crossley, James G., 'A "Very Jewish" Jesus: Perpetuating the Myth of Superiority', *JSHJ* 11 (2013), pp. 109–29.

Dacey, Austin, *The Future of Blasphemy: Speaking of the Sacred in an Age of Human Rights* (London: Continuum, 2012).

Dahl, Nils Alstrup, *Jesus the Christ: The Historical Origins of Christological Doctrine* (edited by Donald H. Juel; Minneapolis: Fortress, 1991; orig. pub. 1960), pp. 27–48.

Danby, Herbert (trans.), *The Mishnah* (Oxford: Oxford University Press, 1933).

Dänekin, Erich von, *Erinnerungen an die Zukunft: Ungelöste Rätsel der Vergangenheit* (Düsseldorf: Econ Verlag, 1968).

Dänekin, Erich von, *Chariots of the Gods: Unsolved Mysteries of the Past* (New York: Putnam, 1970).

Davies, Philip R., *The Damascus Covenant: An Interpretation of the 'Damascus Document'* (JSOT Supplement 25; Sheffield: JSOT Press, 1982).

Donaldson, Terence L., *Judaism and the Gentiles: Jewish Patterns of Universalism (to 135 CE)* (Waco, TX: Baylor University Press, 2007).

Donne, Anthony Le, *The Wife of Jesus: Ancient Texts and Modern Scandals* (London: Oneworld, 2013).

Dundes, Alan, 'The J.A.P. and the J.A.M. in American Folklore', in Joseph Boskin (ed.), *The Humor Prism in 20th-Century America* (Detroit, MI: Wayne State University Press, 1997), pp. 225–49.

Dupont-Sommer, André, *The Dead Sea Scrolls: A Preliminary Survey* (Oxford: Basil Blackwell, 1952).

Durkheim, Emile, *On Morality and Society*, Robert Bellah (ed.) (London and Chicago: University of Chicago Press, 1973).

Eck, Werner, *Rom und Judaea: fünf Vorträge zur römischen Herrschaft in Palaestina* (Tübingen: Mohr Siebeck, 2007).

Edmondson, Jonathan, 'Public Dress and Social Control in Late Republican and Early Imperial Rome', in Jonathan Edmondson and Alison Keith (eds), *Roman Dress and the Fabrics of Roman Culture* (Toronto: University of Toronto Press, 2008), pp. 21–46.

Ehrman, Bart, *Jesus: Apocalyptic Prophet of the New Millennium* (New York: Oxford University Press, 1999).

Ehrman, Bart D., *How Jesus Became God: The Exaltation of a Jewish Preacher from Galilee* (San Francisco: HarperOne, 2014), pp. 151–79.

Epplett, Chris, 'Spectacular Executions in the Roman World', in Paul Christesen and Donald G. Kyle (eds), *A Companion to Sport and Spectacle in Greek and Roman Antiquity* (Oxford: Wiley-Blackwell, 2013), pp. 520–32.

Evans, Craig A., 'Getting the Burial Traditions and Evidences Right', in Michael Bird (ed.), *How God Became Jesus: The Real Origins of Belief in Jesus' Divine Nature* (Grand Rapids, MI: Zondervan, 2014), pp. 71–93.

Farmer, William R., *Maccabees, Zealots, and Josephus* (New York: Columbia University Press, 1956).

Feugère, Michel, *Les armes des Romains, de la République à l'Antiquité tardive* (Paris: Errance, 1993).

Fiorenza, Elisabeth Schüssler, *But She Said: Feminist Practices of Biblical Interpretation* (Boston: Beacon Press, 1992).

Fischer, Thomas, *Die Armee der Caesaren, Archäologie und Geschichte* (Regensburg: Friedrich Pustet Verlag, 2012).

Fishbane, Simcha, 'Jewish Beards: The Symbolic Representation of the Rabbinic Beard', Moscow Center for University Teaching of Jewish Civilization 'Sefer', *Proceedings of the Seventeenth Annual International Conference on Jewish Studies* Vol 1, Academic Series 30 (2010), pp. 113–29.

Forsdyke, Sara, *Slaves Tell Tales: And Other Episodes in the Politics of Popular Culture in Ancient Greece* (Princeton: Princeton University Press, 2012).

Franck, Thomas M., *The Empowered Self: Law and Society in an Age of Individualism* (Oxford: Oxford University Press, 1999).

Fredriksen, Paula, 'Judaism, the Circumcision of Gentiles, and Apocalyptic Hope: Another Look at Galatians 1 and 2', *JTS* 42 (1991), pp. 532–64.

Fredriksen, Paula, 'What You See is What You Get: Context and Content in Current Research on the Historical Jesus', *Theology Today* 52 (1995), pp. 75–97.

Fredriksen, Paula, *Jesus of Nazareth, King of the Jews: A Jewish Life and the Emergence of Christianity* (New York: Random House, 1999).

Fredriksen, Paula, *From Jesus to Christ: The Origins of the New Testament Images of Jesus* (New Haven: Yale University Press, 2000).

Fredriksen, Paula, 'Mandatory Retirement: Ideas in the Study of Christian Origins whose Time Has Come to Go', *Studies in Religion/Sciences Religieuses* 35 (2006), pp. 231–46.

Fredriksen, Paula, *Augustine and the Jews* (New Haven: Yale University Press, 2010).

Fredriksen, Paula, 'Judaizing the Nations: The Ritual Demands of Paul's Gospel', *NTS* 56 (2010), pp. 232–52.

Fredriksen, Paula, 'Paul, Practical Pluralism, and the Invention of Religious Persecution in Roman Antiquity', in Peter C. Phan and Jonathan Ray (eds), *Understanding Religious Pluralism: Perspectives from Religious Studies and Theology* (Eugene, OR: Wipf and Stock, 2014), pp. 87–113.

Freyne, Seán, *Galilee and Gospel* (Boston: Brill, 2002).

Freyne, Seán, *Jesus, a Jewish Galilean: A New Reading of the Jesus Story* (London: T&T Clark, 2004).

Galinsky, Adam D. et al., 'The Reappropriation of Stigmatizing Labels', *Psychological Science* 20/10 (2013), pp. 1–10.

Garber, Marjorie B., *Vested Interests: Cross-Dressing and Cultural Anxiety* (New York: Routledge, 1997).

Genette, Gerard, *Palimpsestes* (Paris: Seuil, 1982).

Gleason, Maude W., *Making Men: Sophists and Self-Presentation in Ancient Rome* (Princeton: Princeton University Press, 1995).

Goldberg, David T., *The Threat of Race: Reflections on Racial Neoliberalism* (Oxford: Wiley-Blackwell, 2009).

Goldman, Bernard, 'Graeco-Roman Dress in Syro-Mesopotamia', in Judith Lynn Sebesta and Larissa Bonfante (eds), *The World of Roman Costume* (Madison, WI: University of Wisconsin Press, 2001), pp. 163–81.

Goodman, Martin D., *Rome and Jerusalem: The Clash of Ancient Civilizations* (London: Penguin, 2007).

Goodman, Martin, 'Under the Influence: Hellenism in Ancient Jewish Life', *Biblical Archaeology Review* 36.1 (Jan/Feb 2010), pp. 60–7, 84.

Graetz, Heinrich, *History of the Jews*. 6 vols. (Philadelphia: Jewish Publication Society of America, 1949 [1893]).

Gray, Rebecca, *Prophetic Figures in Late Second Temple Jewish Palestine: The Evidence from Josephus* (Oxford: Oxford University Press, 1993).

Hare, Ivan, 'Blasphemy and Incitement to Religious Hatred: Free Speech Dogma and Doctrine', in Ivan Hare and James Weistein (eds), *Extreme Speech and Democracy* (Oxford: Oxford University Press, 2009), pp. 289–310.

Harker, Andrew, *Loyalty and Dissidence in Roman Egypt: The Case of the Acta Alexandrinorum* (Cambridge: Cambridge University Press, 2008).

Harner, Philip B., *The 'I Am' of the Fourth Gospel: A Study in Johannine Usage and Thought* (Philadelphia: Fortress Press, 1970).

Hart, Marjolein 't and Dennis Bos (eds), *Humour and Social Protest* (Cambridge: Cambridge University Press, 2007).

Harvey, David, *The Condition of Postmodernity* (Oxford: Blackwell, 1989).

Harvey, David, *A Brief History of Neoliberalism* (Oxford: Oxford University Press, 2005).

Heelas, Paul and Woodhead, Linda, *The Spiritual Revolution: Why Religion is Giving Way to Spirituality* (Oxford: Blackwell, 2005).

Heim, David, 'A Joking Matter: And Jesus Laughed', *Christian Century* 120 (2003), pp. 27, 29–30.

Hengel, Martin, *Crucifixion: In the Ancient World and the Folly of the Cross* (London: SCM, 1977).

Hengel, Martin, *The Zealots: Investigations into the Jewish Freedom Movement in the Period from Herod I until 70 AD*, trans. D. Smith (Edinburgh: T&T Clark, 1989 [German original 1961]).

Heschel, Susannah, *The Aryan Jesus: Christian Theologians and the Bible in Nazi Germany* (Princeton: Princeton University Press, 2008).

Hope, Valerie M., *Death in Ancient Rome: A Sourcebook* (London/New York: Routledge, 2007), pp. 39–45.

Horsley, Richard A., 'Jesus and Empire', in Horsley (ed.), *In the Shadow of Empire: Reclaiming the Bible as a History of Faithful Resistance* (Louisville, KY: Westminster John Knox, 2008), pp. 75–96.

Hutcheon, Linda, *A Theory of Parody: The Teachings of Twentieth Century Art Forms* (New York and London: Methuen, 1985).

Ilan, Tal, *Lexicon of Jewish Names in Late Antiquity, Part 1, 330 BCE–200 CE* (Tübingen: Mohr Siebeck, 2002).

James, Simon T., *The Arms and Armour and other Military Equipment: The Excavations at Dura-Europos conducted by Yale University and the French Academy of Inscriptions and Letters 1928 to 1937, Final Report VII* (London: Oxbow, 2004).

Jameson, Frederic, 'Postmodernism, or the Cultural Logic of Late Capitalism', *New Left Review* 146 (1984), pp. 53–92.

Jameson, Fredric, *Postmodernism, or, The Cultural Logic of Late Capitalism* (London and New York: Verso, 1991).

Jasper, David, *Readings in the Canon of Scripture: Written for Our Learning* (Studies in Literature and Religion; New York: St Martin's, 1995).

Jobling, David, ' "David on the Brain": Bertolt Brecht's Projected Play "David" ', in Tod Linafelt, Claudia V. Camp and Timothy Beal (eds) *The Fate of King David: The Past and Present of a Biblical Icon* (LHBOTS, 500; London: T&T Clark, 2010), pp. 229–40.

Jokiranta, Jutta, 'Qumran – The Prototypical Teacher in the Qumran Pesharim: A Social-Identity Approach', in Philip Esler (ed.), *Ancient Israel: The Old Testament in Its Social Context* (London: SCM, 2005), pp. 254–63.

Kalmar, Ivan Davidson, 'Jesus Did Not Wear a Turban: Orientalism, The Jews, and Christian Art', in Ivan Davidson Kalmar and Derek J. Penslar (eds), *Orientalism and the Jews* (Hanover, NH: University Press of New England), pp. 3–31.

Kennedy, John F., *Remarks in the Rudolph Wilde Platz 'Ich Bin Ein Berliner'* (Champaign, IL: Project Gutenberg).

Kessler, Gwynn, *Conceiving Israel: The Fetus in Rabbinic Narrative* (Divinations, Rereading Late Ancient Religion; Philadelphia: University of Pennsylvania Press, 2009).

Khamaisi, Rassem, et al., *Jerusalem: The Old City: Urban Fabric and Geopolitical Implications* (Jerusalem: International Peace and Cooperation Center; Publication XVII, 2009).

King, Karen L., 'Jesus Said to Them, "My Wife . . .": A New Coptic Papyrus Fragment', *Harvard Theological Review* 107 (2014), pp. 131–59.

Kirk, J. R. Daniel, 'How God Became Jesus: Part 1, In Review of the Evangelical Response to Ehrman', *Storied Theology* (24 April, 2014), http://www.jrdkirk.com/2014/04/24/god-became-jesus-part-1-review-evangelical-response-ehrman/

Klausen, Jytte, *The Cartoons That Shook the World* (New Haven: Yale University Press, 2009).

Knibb, Michael A., 'The Teacher of Righteousness – A Messianic Title?', in Philip R. Davies and Richard T. White (eds), *A Tribute to Geza Vermes: Essays on Jewish and Christian Literature and History* (JSOT Supplement 100; Sheffield: JSOT Press, 1990), pp. 51–65.

Knibb, Michael A., 'Teacher of Righteousness', in Lawrence H. Schiffman and James C. VanderKam (eds), *Encyclopedia of the Dead Sea Scrolls* (New York: Oxford University Press, 2000), pp. 918–21.

Labbé, Gilbert, *L'affirmation de la puissance romaine en Judée (63 avant J.-C.–136 après J.-C.)* (Paris: Les Belles Lettres, 2012).

Landis, Deborah Nadoolman, *Filmcraft: Costume Design* (Lewes: ILEX, 2012).

Landis, Deborah Nadoolman, *Hollywood Costume* (London: V&A Publishing, 2012).

Laver, James, *Costume and Fashion: A Concise History* (5th ed.) (London: Thames and Hudson, 2012).

Law, Timothy Michael, *When God Spoke Greek: The Septuagint and the Making of the Christian Bible* (Oxford: Oxford University Press, 2013).

Law, Timothy Michael and Halton, Charles (eds), *Jew and Judaean: A Marginalia Forum on Politics and Historiography in the Translation of Ancient Texts, The Marginalia Review of Books* (http://marginalia.lareviewofbooks.org/jew-judean-forum [accessed 26 August 2014]).

Lendon, Jon E., *Empire of Honour: The Art of Government in the Roman World* (Oxford: Clarendon Press, 1997).

Lentin, Alana and Titley, Gavin, *The Crises of Multiculturalism: Racism in a Neoliberal Age* (London: Zed Books, 2011).

Levine, Amy-Jill, 'Women's Humor and Other Creative Juices,' in Athalya Brenner (ed.), *Are We Amused? Humour About Women in the Biblical Worlds* (London: T&T Clark, 2003), pp. 120–6.

Levine, Amy-Jill, *The Misunderstood Jew: The Church and the Scandal of the Jewish Jesus* (San Francisco: HarperSanFrancisco, 2006).

Levine, Amy Jill, 'The Many Faces of the Good Samaritan—Most Wrong,' *Biblical Archaeology Review* 38:01 (Jan/Feb 2012).

Levine, Amy Jill, *Short Stories by Jesus* (New York: Harper Collins, 2014).

Levine, Lee I., *The Ancient Synagogue* (New Haven: Yale University Press, 2000).

Levy, Leonard W., *Treason Against God: A History of the Offense of Blasphemy* (New York: Schocken, 1981).

Litwa, M. David, *Iesus Deus: The Early Christian Depiction of Jesus as a Mediterranean God* (Minneapolis: Fortress, 2014).

Loffreda, Stanislao, *Capharnaum, the Town of Jesus* (Jerusalem: Franciscan Printing Press, 1985).

Loftus, Elizabeth F., *Eyewitness Testimony* (2nd ed.) (Cambridge: Harvard University Press, 1996).

Maeder, Edward, 'The Celluloid Image: Historical Dress in Film', in Maeder (ed.), *Hollywood and History: Costume Design in Film* (London: Thames and Hudson, 1987), pp. 9–51.

Magness, Jodi, 'Masada – Arms and the Man', *Biblical Archaeology Review* 18 (1992), pp. 58–67.

Malina, Bruce J. and Pilch, John J., *Social-Science Commentary on the Letters of Paul* (Minneapolis: Fortress Press, 2006).

Marcus, Joel, 'Crucifixion as Parodic Exaltation', *JBL* 125 (2006), pp. 73–8.

Marcus, Joel, 'Jesus the Jew in Recent Western Scholarship,' in Chrēstos Karakolēs, Karl-Wilhelm Niebuhr and S. G. Rogal'sky (eds), *Gospel Images of Jesus Christ in Church Tradition and in Biblical Scholarship: Fifth International East-West Symposium of New Testament Scholars, Minsk, September 2 to 9, 2010* (Tübingen: Mohr Siebeck, 2012), pp. 235–49.

Martínez, Florentino García, 'Beyond the Sectarian Divide: The "Voice of the Teacher" as an Authority-Conferring Strategy in Some Qumran Texts', in Sarianna Metso, Hindy Najman and Eileen Schuller (eds), *The Dead Sea Scrolls: Transmission of Traditions and Production of Texts* (STDJ 92; Leiden: Brill, 2010), pp. 227–44.

Mason, Steve, *Josephus, Judea and Christian Origins: Methods and Categories* (Peabody: Hendrickson, 2009).

Mason, Steve, *The Jewish-Roman War of 66–74: A Historical Inquiry* (Cambridge: Cambridge University Press, 2015).

Mattern, Susan P., *Rome and the Enemy: Imperial Strategy in the Principate* (Berkeley: University of California Press, 1999).

Matthews, Shelly, *Perfect Martyr: The Stoning of Stephen and the Construction of Christian Identity* (New York: Oxford University Press, 2010).

McKechnie, Paul, 'Judaean Embassies and Cases before Roman Emperors, AD 44–66', *JTS* 56 (2005), pp. 339–61.

McLaren, James S., 'The Coinage of the First Year as a Point of Reference for the First Jewish Revolt (66–70 CE)', *Scripta Classica Israelica* 22, pp. 135–52.

McLaren, James S., *Turbulent Times? Josephus and Scholarship on Judaea in the First Century CE* (Sheffield: Sheffield Academic Press, 1998).

Meggitt, Justin, 'Laughing and Dreaming at the Foot of the Cross: Context and Reception of a Religious Symbol', *Journal for the Critical Study of Religion, Ethics, and Society* 1 (1996), pp. 9–14.

Meggitt, Justin, 'The Madness of King Jesus', *JSNT* 29 (2007), pp. 379–413.

Meier, John P., 'Did the Historical Jesus Prohibit All Oaths? Part 1', *JSHJ* 5 (2007), pp. 175–204.

Meier, John P., 'Did the Historical Jesus Prohibit All Oaths? Part 2', *JSHJ* 6 (2008), pp. 3–24.

Meier, John P., *A Marginal Jew: Rethinking the Historical Jesus*, 4 vols. (New York: Doubleday, 1991–2009).

Meshorer, Ya'akov, *A Treasury of Jewish Coins from the Persian Period to Bar Kokhba* (Jerusalem: Yad ben-Zvi, 2001).

Meyer-Zwiffelhoffer, Eckhard, *Politikōs Archein: zum Regierungsstil der senatorischen Statthalter in den kaiserzeitlichen griechischen Provinzen* (Stuttgart: Franz Steiner, 2002).

Millar, Fergus, *The Emperor in the Roman World, 31 BC–AD 337* (Ithaca: Cornell University Press, 1977).

Mirowski, Philip and Plehwe, Dieter (eds), *The Road from Mont Pelerin: The Making of the Neoliberal Thought Collective* (Cambridge, MA: Harvard University Press, 2009).

Moxnes, Halvor, *Jesus and the Rise of Nationalism: A New Quest for the Nineteenth-Century Historical Jesus* (London/New York: I.B. Taurus, 2012).

Murphy, Ronald, *Brecht and the Bible: A Study of Religious Nihilism and Human Weakness in Brecht's Drama* Mortality and the City (Chapel Hill, NC: University of North Carolina Press, 1980).

Murphy-O'Connor, Jerome, 'The Damascus Document Revisited', *Revue Biblique* 92 (1985), pp. 223–46.

Myles, Robert J., *The Homeless Jesus in the Gospel of Matthew* (Sheffield: Sheffield Phoenix Press, 2014).

Myles, Robert J. and Crossley, James G., 'Biblical Scholarship, Jews and Israel: On Bruce Malina, Conspiracy Theories and Ideological Contradictions' http://www.bibleinterp. com/opeds/myl368013.shtml#sdfootnote10sym [accessed 29 June, 2014].

Netzer, Ehud, *The Buildings, Stratigraphy and Architecture: Masada III, The Yigael Yadin Excavations 1963–1965, Final Reports* (Jerusalem: Israel Exploration Society and the Hebrew University of Jerusalem, 1991).

Novenson, Matthew, *Christ Among the Messiahs: Christ Language in Paul and Messiah Language in Ancient Judaism* (New York: Oxford University Press, 2012).

Osborne, Robin, *The History Written on the Classical Greek Body* (Cambridge: Cambridge University Press, 2011).

Parker, Patricia, 'Barbers, Infidels, and Renegades: *Antony and Cleopatra*', in Lena Cowen Orin (ed.), *Center or Margin: Revisions of the English Renaissance in Honor of Leeds Barroll* (Cranbury, NJ: Associated University Press, 2006), pp. 54–90.

Pederson, Bertel, 'The Theory and Practice of Parody in the Modern Novel: Mann, Joyce and Nabokov', unpublished PhD dissertation, University of Illinois, Urbana-Champaign, 1972.

Plehwe, Dieter, Walpen, Bernhard J. A. and Neunhoffer, Gisela (eds), *Neoliberal Hegemony: A Global Critique* (London: Routledge, 2007).

Popović, Mladen (ed.), *De Dode Zeerollen: Nieuw licht op de schatten van Qumran* (Zwolle: WBooks, 2013).

Popović, Mladen and Ziv-Esudri, Adi, *De Dode Zeerollen: De tentoonstelling* (Assen: Drents Museum, 2013).

Powell, Mark Allen, *Chasing the Eastern Star: Adventures in Biblical Reader-Response Criticism* (Louisville, KY: Westminster John Knox, 2001).

Priest, J., 'Testament of Moses', in James H. Charlesworth (ed.), *The Old Testament Pseudepigrapha* (London: Darton, Longman and Todd, 1983), pp. 919–34.

Pullman, Philip, *The Good Man Jesus and the Scoundrel Christ* (Edinburgh: Canongate, 2010).

Qimron, Elisha and Strugnell, John, 'An Unpublished Halakhic Letter from Qumran', *Israel Museum Journal* 4 (1985), pp. 9–15.

Reed, Jonathan, 'Instability in Jesus' Galilee: A Demographic Perspective', *JBL* 129 (2010), pp. 343–65.

Reinhartz, Adele, 'Jesus as Prophet: Predictive Prolepses in the Fourth Gospel', *JSNT* 11 (1989), pp. 3–16.

Rhoads, David M., *Israel in Revolution, 6–74 CE.: A Political History based on the Writings of Josephus* (Philadelphia, PA: Fortress, 1976).

Robertson, Geoffrey, *Obscene: An Account of Censorship Laws and their Enforcement in England and Wales* (London: Weidenfeld and Nicolson, 1979).

Robilliard, St John A., *Religion and the Law: Religious Liberty in Modern English Law* (Manchester: Manchester University Press, 1984).

Rocca, Samuel, *The Army of Herod the Great* (Oxford: Osprey, 2009).

Roussin, Lucille A., 'Costume in Roman Palestine: Archaeological Remains and the Evidence from the Mishnah', in Judith Lynn Sebesta and Larissa Bonfante (eds), *The World of Roman Costume* (Madison, WI: University of Wisconsin Press, 2001), pp. 182–90.

Safrai, Shmuel and Stern, Menahem (eds), in co-operation with David Flusser and Willem C. van Unnik, *The Jewish People in the First Century: Historical Geography, Political History, Social, Cultural and Religious Life and Institutions* Vol. 2 (Compendia Rerum Iudaicarum ad Novum Testamentum; Assen: Van Gorcum, 1976).

Sanders, E. P., *Jesus and Judaism* (London/Philadelphia: SCM/Fortress, 1985).

Sandford, Michael J., *Poverty, Wealth, and Empire: Jesus and Postcolonial Criticism* (Sheffield: Sheffield Phoenix Press, 2014).

Schaberg, Jane, *The Illegitimacy of Jesus: A Feminist Theological Interpretation of the Infancy Narratives* (San Francisco [etc.]: Harper & Row, 1987).

Schacter, Daniel L., *The Seven Sins of Memory: How the Mind Forgets and Remembers* (Boston: Houghton Mifflin, 2001).

Schroeder, Joy A., *Deborah's Daughters: Gender Politics and Biblical Interpretation* (New York: Oxford, 2014).

Schürer, Emil, *Lehrbuch der neutestamentlichen Zeitgeschichte* (Leipzig: J.C. Hinrichs, 1874).

Schürer, Emil, *The History of the Jewish People in the Age of Jesus Christ*, Geza Vermes, Fergus Millar and Martin Goodman (eds), 3 vols. in 4 (Edinburgh: T&T Clark, 1979–1987).

Schwartz, Seth, 'Josephus in Galilee: Rural Patronage and Social Breakdown', in Fausto Parente and Joseph Sievers (eds), *Josephus and the History of the Greco-Roman Period: Essays in Memory of Morton Smith* (Studia Post-Biblica 41; Leiden, The Netherlands: Brill, 1994), pp. 290–306.

Schweitzer, Albert, *The Quest of the Historical Jesus: A Critical Study of its Progress from Reimarus to Wrede* (New York: Macmillan, 1978 [German original: 1906]).

Scott, James C., *Domination and the Arts of Resistance: Hidden Transcripts* (New Haven: Yale University Press, 1990).

Scott, James C., *Weapons of the Weak: Everyday forms of Peasant Resistance* (New Haven: Yale University Press, 1985).

Scott, James M., *Paul and the Nations* (Tübingen: Mohr Siebeck, 1995).

Segal, Erich, *Roman Laughter: The Comedy of Plautus* (Cambridge: Harvard University Press, 1968).

Seltzer, Robert M., *Jewish People, Jewish Thought: The Jewish Experience of History* (London and New York: Macmillan, 1980).

Shatzman, Israel, *The Armies of the Hasmonaeans and Herod: From Hellenistic to Roman Frameworks* (Tübingen: Mohr Siebeck, 1991).

Shepherd, David, *The Bible on Silent Film: Spectacle, Story and Scripture in the Early Cinema* (Cambridge: Cambridge University Press, 2013).

Shlezinger-Katsman, Dafna, 'Clothing', in Catherine Hezser (ed.), *The Oxford Handbook of Jewish Daily Life in Roman Palestine* (Oxford: Oxford University Press, 2010), pp. 362–81.

Speirs, Ronald, *Brecht's Early Plays* (London and Basingstoke: Macmillan Press, 1982).

Stegemann, Hartmut, *Die Entstehung der Qumrangemeinde* (Bonn: Privately published 1971).

Stiebel, Guy D., ' "Dust to dust, ashes to ashes" – Military Equipment from Destruction Layers in Palestine,' *Carnuntum Jahrbuch* (2005), pp. 99–108.

Stiebel, Guy D., '*Armis et litteris* – The Military Equipment of Early Roman Palestine in Light of the Archaeological and Historical Sources', Ph.D. dissertation submitted and approved at University College London, University of London, 2007.

Stiebel, Guy D. ' "*Miles Gloriosus*"? – The Image of the Roman Legionary', in Ofra Rimon (ed.), *The Great Revolt in the Galilee* (Haifa: Hecht Museum and the University of Haifa, 2007), pp. 111–18 (Hebrew).

Stiebel, Guy D., 'Military equipment from the Jericho and Cypros', in Rachel Bar-Nathan and Judit Gärtner (eds), *Hasmonean and Herodian Palaces at Jericho, Volume IV, Final Reports of the 1973–1987 Excavations, The Finds from Jericho and Cypros* (Jerusalem: Israel Exploration Society and the Hebrew University of Jerusalem, 2013), pp. 290–8.

Stiebel, Guy D., 'Dressed to Kill – Military Dress as an Ideological Marker in Roman Palestine', in Shoshana-Rose Marzel and Guy D. Stiebel (eds), *Dress and Ideology: Fashioning Identity from Antiquity to the Present* (London: Bloomsbury, 2014), pp. 153–67.

Stiebel, Guy D. and Jodi Magness, 'The Military Equipment from Masada', in Joseph Aviram, Gideon Foerster, Ehud Netzer and Guy D. Stiebel (eds), *Masada VIII: The Yigael Yadin excavations 1963–1965, Final reports* (Jerusalem: Israel Exploration Society, 2007), pp. 1–65.

Stone, Shelley, 'The Toga: From National to Ceremonial Costume', in Judith Lynn Sebesta and Larissa Bonfante (eds), *The World of Roman Costume* (Madison, WI: University of Wisconsin Press, 2001), pp. 13–45.

Strugnell, John, 'MMT: Second Thoughts on a Forthcoming Edition', in Eugene Ulrich and James VanderKam (eds), *The Community of the Renewed Covenant: The Notre Dame Symposium on the Dead Sea Scrolls* (Notre Dame: University of Notre Dame Press, 1994), pp. 70–3.

Stuckenbruck, Loren T., 'The Teacher of Righteousness Remembered: From Fragmentary Sources to Collective Memory in the Dead Sea Scrolls', in Stephen C. Barton, Loren T. Stuckenbruck and Benjamin G. Wold (eds), *Memory in the Bible and Antiquity: The Fifth Durham–Tübingen Research Symposium (Durham, September 2004)* (WUNT 212; Tübingen: Mohr Siebeck, 2007).

Taylor, Joan E., *The Essenes, the Scrolls, and the Dead Sea* (Oxford: Oxford University Press, 2012).

Taylor, Joan E., 'Imagining Judean Priestly Dress: The Berne Josephus and *Judaea Capta* Coinage', in Kristi Upson-Saia, Carly Daniel-Hughes and Alicia J. Batten (eds), *Dressing Judeans and Christians in Antiquity* (Farnham: Ashgate, 2014), pp. 195–212.

Taylor, Joan E., 'What Did Jesus Look Like?' in *The Life of Jesus of Nazareth* (i5 Magazine special issue, 2014), pp. 10–15: http://asorblog.org/2015/04/17/ what-did-jesus-look-like/.

Theissen, Gerd and Winter, Dagmar, *The Quest for the Plausible Jesus: The Question of Criteria* (Louisville, KY: Westminster John Knox Press, 2002).

Tollerton, David C., 'Two Jewish-American Interpretations of the Book of Job in the Aftermath of the Holocaust: A Short Discussion of the Relationship between Job's Modern Reception and Its Ancient Production', in Lidia D. Matassa and Jason M. Silverman (eds), *Text, Theology, and Trowel: New Investigations in the Biblical World* (Eugene, OR: Pickwick, 2011), pp. 59–74.

Tzaferis, Vassilios, *Excavations at Capernaum I, 1978–1982* (Winona Lake, Indiana: Eisenbrauns, 1989).

VanderKam, James C. and Flint, Peter W. (eds), *The Dead Sea Scrolls After Fifty Years: A Comprehensive Assessment* (Leiden: Brill, 1998–1999).

Veblen, Thorstein, *The Theory of the Leisure Class* (London: Macmillan, 1899).

Vermes, Geza, *Jesus the Jew: A Historian's Reading of the Gospels* (London: SCM, 1973).

Vermes, Geza, *The Gospel of Jesus the Jew: The Riddell Memorial Lectures Delivered at the University of Newcastle upon Tyne on 17, 18 and 19 March 1981* (Newcastle-upon-Tyne: University of Newcastle-upon-Tyne Press, 1981).

Vermes, Geza (trans.), *The Complete Dead Sea Scrolls in English* (London: Penguin, 1997).

Vermes, Geza, 'Was Crucifixion a Jewish Penalty?', *Standpoint*, April 2013, pp. 66–9.

Wagner, J. Ross, *Heralds of the Good News: Isaiah and Paul in Concert in the Letter to the Romans* (Leiden: Brill, 2003).

Welborn, Laurence L., *Paul the Fool of Christ: A Study of 1 Corinthians 1–4 in the Comic-Philosophic Tradition*. JSNT Supplement Series 293 (London/New York: T&T Clark, 2005).

Whipple, Amy C., 'Speaking for Whom? The 1971 Festival of Light and the Search for the "Silent Majority"', *Contemporary British History*, 24, 3 (2010), pp. 319–39.

Whiston, William, *The Works of Josephus*, vol. 1 (Grand Rapids, MI: Baker Book House, 1979).

Whitehouse, Mary, *Quite Contrary: An Autobiography* (London, Sydney and Auckland: Pan Books, 1993).

Wise, Michael, Abegg, Martin, and Cook, Edward, *The Dead Sea Scrolls: A New Translation* (San Francisco: HarperSanFrancisco, 1996).

Witherington, Ben, *Women in the Ministry of Jesus: A Study of Jesus' Attitude to Women and Their Roles as Reflected in His Earthly Life* (Cambridge: Cambridge University Press, 1984).

Wrede, William, *The Messianic Secret* (Cambridge: J. Clarke, 1971 [1901]).

Wright, N. T., *Jesus and the Victory of God* (London: SPCK, 1996).

Yadin, Yigael, *The Finds from the Bar Kokhba Period in the Cave of Letters* (Jerusalem: Israel Exploration Society, 1963).

Yadin, Yigael, *The Excavation at Masada: Preliminary Report* (Jerusalem: Israel Exploration Society, 1965).

Yadin, Yigael, 'Epigraphy and Crucifixion', *IEJ* 23 (1973), pp. 18–22.

Young, Francis M., *Biblical Exegesis and the Formation of Christian Culture* (Cambridge: Cambridge University Press, 1997).

Žižek, Slavoj, 'Multiculturalism, or, the Cultural Logic of Multinational Capitalism', *New Left Review* (1997), pp. 28–51.

Žižek, Slavoj, *Welcome to the Desert of the Real! Five Essays on September 11 and Related Dates* (London & New York: Verso, 2002).

Žižek, Slavoj, *The Puppet and the Dwarf: The Perverse Core of Christianity* (Boston: MIT Press, 2003).

Žižek, Slavoj, 'Liberal Multiculturalism Masks an Old Barbarism with a Human Face', *Guardian* (3 October, 2010), http://www.theguardian.com/commentisfree/2010/oct/03/immigration-policy-roma-rightwing-europe

Žižek, Slavoj, *Living in the End Times* (revised ed.) London and New York: Verso, 2011).

INDEX OF ANCIENT SOURCES

Biblical Literature

Old Testament/Hebrew Bible

Exodus 159
2.3	45
3.4	47
3.14	217
4	49 n.18
20.3–6	225
20.17	72
22.18	xxvi
22.28	57
28.6	230
38	230

Leviticus
8.7–9	230
21.7; 13–14	100
24.16	56
26.1	225

Numbers
15.38	105, 227 n.15
15.39	227 n.15
33.52	225

Deuteronomy 160
4.16	225
5.21	72
18.11–12	xxvi
21.22–23	86
22.5	230
22.11–12	226, 231
27.15	225

Judges 4–5   182

2 Samuel
7	159
10.4	175

2 Chronicles 31 235 n.37

Tobit
13.11	160 n.22
14.5	160 n.22

Judith 182

2 Maccabees 4.12   236

Job 34
1.21	122

Psalms 154, 160
2	159

Isaiah 154, 160
2.2–4	160 n.22
7.14	158, 159
11.10	161
25.6	160

Lamentations 96

Ezekiel
40.46	235 n.37
42.14	230 n.23
44.19	230 n.23

Hosea 11.1   159

Joel 2.23   133–4

Micah 134
4	160 n.22

Zechariah 8:23 160 n.22

Extra-Canonical Jewish Literature

1 Enoch 91.14 160 n.22

Ps. Sol. 7.13   160 n.22

Sib. Or. 3.616   160 n.22

3 Maccabees
2.29	232 n.26

The Dead Sea Scrolls and Other Judaean Cave Manuscripts

1QH (Hodayot) 136

1QM (War Scroll)
2, 6	143–4

1QpHab (Pesher Habakkuk) 135, 137
1:5	135
7.4–5	135

1QS (Community Rule)
6.27–7.2	56

4QpIsaᵉfrgs
1–2, l. 3	134

4QMMT (*Miqsat Ma'aśeh ha-Torah*) 129–30

Damascus Document 130, 134, 136

pesharim 130, 134, 136, 138

Psalms (*Pesher*) 134
37.23–24	135

New Testament

Matthew 57, 144, 157–9, 161, 170, 174
1.18	158

2.1–2a	170, 213	6.25–34	71	8.44	230
2.10	170	6.34–52	9	9.18–21	210
2.13–15	158	7.25	212	9.59–60	79
4.3–10	216	8.1–9	9	10.21	170
5	38	8.27–30	210	10.25–37	101
5.1–10	97	8.31	125	10.38	178
5.1–12	72	8.38	98	11.3	102
5.3	102	9	98	12.22	102
5.9	8, 30, 97	9.2–8	97	12.22–31	9
6.11	102	9.3	97, 125	13.1	149
6.25	102	10.33	125	13.5–6	9
6.25–34	71	10.37	98	15.2	104
7.1–2	9	11.1–10	125	16.1–8	71
7.3–5	105	11.12–18	125	17	52
8.21–22	79	11.15–19	210	18.10	104
10.5	161	12.35–37	157, 164	19.11–27	71
11.5	102	12.40	105	19.12–27	9
11.19	104	13	142	22.66–71	216
11.25	170	13.9–13	xxvi	23.3	213
13.57	214	13.26–27	98	23.18	219
14.2	160 n.19	14.32–42	125	23.37–38	213
15.17–18	210	14.61–62	98, 157	24.19	98
15.21–28	212	14.63–64	xxvi	26.44–53	98
16.13–20	210	14.64	57		
18.23-3-5	72	14.65	117	John 159, 217	
21.28–32	72	15.2	213	1.1–4	157
21.31	104	15.6–14	9	1.46	100
23	214	15.7	219	4	212
23.5	105	15.11	219	4.44	214
25.14–30	9, 72	15.15	219	4.9	212
26.7	171	15.16–20	117	4.20–23	212
27.11	213	15.18	213	5	210
27.16–17	219	15.21	9	6.35	217
27.20–21	219	15.26	213	6.41	217
27.25	214	15.29–32	117	6.48	217
27.26	219	15.36	126	6.51	217
27.29	213	15.39	22	7.41–42	157
27.37	213	15.42–46	148	8	178
				8.12	217
Mark 57, 117, 152		Luke 95, 144, 161		8.44	214
2.13–17	100	1.53	102	8.58	217
2.15–16	100	3.9	143	9.5	217
2.15–17	103	6.20	102	10.7	217
3.21	174	6.20–26	72	10.9	217
3.22–30	xxvi	6.21	102	10.11	217
3.32b–35	174	6.37–38	9	10.14	217
5.9	8	6.42	105	10.18	125
6.7	xxvi	7.22	102	10.30–33	xxvi
6.25–33	9	7.34	104	11.25	217

11.35	104	Galatians 161		*Antiquities* 188, 189, 199	
14.6	217	2.11–14	153 n.2	13.171	235 n.37
15.1	217	3.13	86	13.293	235 n.37
15.5	217	3.29	163	14.204	201
18.20	219	4.4	159	15.405	196 n.9
18.34–38	213	4.19	179	17.354	189 n.5
19.2	230			18.1–4	195
19.23	230	Philippians		18.29–31	201
19.3	213	1.6	163	18.3.1–2	150
19.19	213	2	160	18.61–62	201
19.30	125	2.5–7	159	18.89	197
19.34	179	2.10	164	19.356–58	202
20.21–29	86	2.16	163	20.2–5	202
20.31	216	3.2–3	153 n.2	20.49–53	103
		3.6	152	20.101	103
The Acts of the Apostles		3.11	160	20.159	197
95, 161		10	163	20.162	197
7	178			20.185–186	108
11. 27–28	103	1 Thessalonians			
12.2	171	4	160	*Life of Josephus*	
15.21	153	5.2	163	7	235 n.37
16.1	173			42–45	204
16.15	171	2 Thessalonians		76	117
17.32	160 n.19	2.2	163	235	102
Romans		1 Timothy		*The Judaean War*	
1.3	154, 155	2.9	230	1.429–430	110
1.3–4	159	6.7	34,	2.22	194
1.4	160		122–3	2.80–96	194
1.9	163			2.111	194
8.38	163	2 Timothy 4.13	230	2.117	189 n.5
15.8	161			2.119	235 n.37
15.9–12	160	Hebrews 6.2	160	2.169–75	197
15.12	154, 155			2.176	201
		1 Peter 3.3–4	230	2.223–46	202
1 Corinthians				2.243	196 n.9
1.81	163	**Classical and Early**		2.245–46	203
2	163	**Christian Literature**		2.258	99
3.13	163			2.277–334	203
7.18	153	Cicero *Philippics*		2.280	196 n.9
10.20	163	2, 76	232 n.27	2.284	203
15.3–4	154, 165			2.409	199
15.23	160	Clement of		2.412	199
15.24	163	Alexandria		2.576	109
15.51–52	165	(*Paedagogus*)		2.649	108, 109
		3.3	176	2.652–54	204
2 Corinthians				3.43	102
1.14	163	Josephus 187, 188, 196, 198,		3.321	121
11.22	152	199ff., 235 n.37		5.51	115

6.301	143	96	232 n.26	Tacitus 188, 189	
6.422	203				
7.299	109	Pliny (Gaius Plinius		**Rabbinic Literature**	
		Secundus 111, 189			
Juvenal *Second Satire* 147,		*Natural History*		Mishnah 231	
176		*(Historia Naturalis)*		Sanhedrin	
		28.39	111	7.5	56, 57
Martial *Epigrams* 176					
		Seneca			
Origen*Contra Celsum*		*Dialogue 6* 20.3	115	Babylonian	
1.32	209	*On the Happy*		Talmud	
1.69	15, 209	*Life 19.3*	121	Bava Kama	
1.32	172			83a	176
		Suetonius 188		Bava Metzia	
Philo of Alexandria 57, 148,		*Galba* 9.1	116	8	176
196, 197				Niddah	
Embassy to		Silius Italicus *Punica*		44b	180
Gaius 302	150	179–181	121	Sanhedrin	
230–3	196 n.9			67b	15
299–305	197	Strabo 189		104b	15
On Flaccus		*Geographica*		Shabbat	
73–85	116	3.4.18	121	152a	176

GENERAL INDEX

Adams, Douglas 74
Adams, Edward xxvii
Allegro, John M. 127, 140
Altman, Rick 50
'Always Look on the Bright Side of Life' 9,
    10, 26, 33, 34, 35, 62, 72, 86, 122–3,
    142, 175
apocalyptic tradition 142–4, 155, 162–4
Aronstein, Susan 167
ascension 94–5
Atkinson, Rowan 21–2, 27–8, 32, 105

Bar Kokhba revolt (132–35 CE) 176, 225
Barabbas 7, 9, 118, 219
Baugh, Lloyd 13, 172, 180
Ben-Hur 96, 144, 187
Berg, Charles 175
Beuselinck, Oscar 22
biblical films 43–54, 96, 131
    use of *doppelgänger* in 45, 46, 49, 85
    see also Jesus, films about; *Life of Brian*
Bird, Michael 77–8, 79
blasphemy xv, xxi, xxvi, 22–4, 28, 55–67, 70
    and censorship 65
    historical ideas of 55–60, 67
    idea of 63–6
    and Islamic community 62–3
    in *Life of Brian* 22–4, 32, 55–67, 72, 208,
    217–18
Bond, Helen 33
Brecht, Bertolt 53–4
Brian Cohen (character in *Life of Brian*)
    6–7, 14, 15–16, 29–30, 40, 47, 51, 69,
    70–81, 85, 88–9, 94, 95, 98–106, 119,
    136–7, 171–7, 182–4, 207–8
    absurdity/futility of life in 84, 95, 104,
    106, 119
    comparison/parallels with Jesus xv, 6,
    15–16, 17–18, 30, 31–2, 40, 70, 71, 73,
    81, 85, 89, 98, 131, 134
    and the crucifixion scene 119, 120,
    121–2, 124, 183, 184

father of and identity questions 135–6,
    171–3, 208–9, 210
individualism of 64–5, 71, 74, 75, 76,
    139
infancy, portrayal of 144
Jewishness of xv, 46, 71, 76–7, 135, 173,
    208–9, 210, 216, 217–18, 219
as a Messiah 7, 46, 139, 155, 164–5, 174,
    207, 217–18, 219
and mistaken identity 207–8, 217–18,
    219
as 'ordinary man' 96, 98–9, 104, 106
as a prophet 136–7, 140
Burridge, Richard A. xxii, xxiii, 5, 29, 70–1,
    72

Carey, George 61
Cassius Dio 188, 189
Chapman, Graham 22, 31, 64 n.40
Chariots of the Gods 94, 95
Charlesworth, James 77
Chesterton, G. K. 114
Cleese, John xv, xvii, xxi–xxiv, 3, 11, 12, 14,
    20, 20, 24, 26–8, 29, 30, 31, 33, 34, 36,
    76, 104, 108, 118, 177–8
Cohen, Shaye 231–2
Colley, Ken 29
Collins, Adela Yarbro 57
Cook, Pam 221
Corley, Kathleen 183
costume and clothing 221–37
    1st century Judaism, depiction of 224,
    225, 234, 237
    and historical accuracy 221, 224–5, 233,
    236–7
    Jesus, depiction of 223–4, 229, 232,
    233–4
    in *Life of Brian* 234–7
    Orientalism in 223–4
Crossan, Dom 147
Crossley, James xxv, 21, 31–2, 34, 98
crucifixion 8, 9, 86, 113–26, 147, 164, 214

Gospels, presentation of 114, 117, 123–4, 125, 164, 165
and humour/parody, use in 114–26, 147, 149
Life of Brian presentation of 9, 33–6, 72, 86, 113, 114, 117–26, 147, 149, 150, 164–5, 175, 214
Roman use of 115–16, 147, 148, 150
use of nails, question in 86–7

Dacey, Austin 65
Dänekin, Erich von 94, 95
Davies, Philip xxi, xxv, xxvii, 10, 31–2, 35, 134, 137, 140
Dead Sea Scrolls 31, 40, 76, 127, 128–32, 133–40
Drents Museum exhibition (2013–14) 131–3
see also Teacher of Righteousness
Delfont, Bernard 22, 26
DeMille, Cecil B. 46, 222
Denning, Alfred 58
Doyle, Julian xxiv, xxv, 35
dress *see* costume and clothing
Dunn, James 102
Dupont-Sommer, André 128, 140
Durkheim, Emile 63, 64, 65
Dyke, Carl 12, 168–9

Eco, Umberto 84
Eichelberger, Alyce F. 26
Essenes 57, 133
see also Dead Sea Scrolls
exegesis xviii, xxvi, 83
see also reception exegesis
eyewitness testimony 145–6

Festival of Light 23–4, 37, 58–9
Fiorenza, Elisabeth Schüssler 99
Fletcher, Michelle xxii
Forsdyke, Sara 99, 102, 105
Franck, Thomas 64
Freire, Paulo 177

Gamala 204
excavations in 110, 111
Gay News 22, 23, 58–60
gender and sexuality
beards, ancient significance of 175–6

gender-crossing 178–9
in Judaea 171, 178, 179, 181, 183, 184
in *Life of Brian* 167–84
see also women
Genette, Gerard 50
Gibbons, Gillian 61
Gibson, Mel 117 n.11, 121, 187, 223, 237
Gilliam, Terry 12, 30, 35, 39, 47, 62, 73, 215–16
Gleason, Maude 176
Goldman, Bernard 229
Good Samaritan parable 100
Goodman, Martin 187, 232
Goulbourne, Russell xxii
Graetz, Heinrich 186
Grundmann, Walter 219
Gutmann, Shemaryahu 110

Hadrian 111, 176
HandMade Films 26
Harrison, George 8, 26
Harvey, David 75, 80
Hasenberg, Peter 12
Heelas, Paul 65
Hengel, Martin 115, 198
hermeneutics
reversing flow of xxvi–xxvii, 66, 95–6
Herod Antipas 101
Herod the Great 109–10, 170, 194
Housel, Rebecca 168

Idle, Eric 26, 30, 31, 33, 34, 35, 39, 44, 60, 128, 175, 215
Ilan, Tal 99
individualism 64–6, 74, 75, 76
neo-liberal values of 75, 80
and religiosity 65
in Thatcherism 75

Jameson, Frederic 80
Jannaeus, Alexander 127
Jasper, David 8, 10, 13 n.47, 17 n.70
Jesus, films about 4–5, 7, 9–11, 15, 16–17, 43, 96–8, 187
costuming effects in 222–4, 230 n.23, 232–7, 234–7
crucifixion, depiction in 114, 117–18
and the Hollywood Christ 96–7, 98, 106

Jesus Christ Superstar 223
The Last Temptation of Christ 7, 8, 11, 13, 126, 230 n.23
The Passion of the Christ (2004) 187, 237
see also Life of Brian
Jesus (historical/biblical) xv, 32, 40, 41, 76–81, 96, 103–4, 105, 136–7, 151
'Christ', use of for xv, 154, 159, 161, 216
and crucifixion narratives 124–6, 147–9, 156, 164, 165
as David's descendant 155, 156–7
and father identity questions 172, 209
in the Gospels 85, 123, 125–6, 172
and historical context 86–7, 123, 124–5, 151–2
infancy/nativity, account of 144, 158–9, 166, 170, 171
Jewish identity of xv, 76, 77–81, 174, 208, 209–10, 211–13, 216–19
as Messiah 154–6, 157, 159–61, 164–6, 210, 216, 217, 219
resurrection of 159–60, 165
scholarly reconstructions of 76, 78–81
as Son of God/Man 216–17
and 'wrong-doers', relations with 103–4, 105, 106, 125
as Yeshua bar Yosef 99
Jesus (character in *Life of Brian*) xv, 6, 15, 29, 69, 71, 74–5, 81, 89, 98, 123
Brian, relationship with 6, 24, 29, 30, 69, 71, 89, 98, 123, 207–8
contemporary values in 74–5, 80–1
as quest for 'real' Jesus 69, 123
serious presentation of 74
see also Brian (*Life of Brian*)
Jesus and Brian conference (2014) xxi–xxiv, xxvii, 5, 17, 19, 21, 29, 33, 34, 36, 38–41, 66, 177–8
Jewish Revolt (First) (66–70 CE) 107, 109, 111, 131, 187, 205
John the Baptist 143, 144
Johnston, Raymond 23, 37
Jokiranta, Jutta 138
Jones, Terry xv, xvii, xxi, xxii, xxiii–xxiv, 12, 24, 27, 29, 31, 36, 75, 147, 171
Jones-Davies, Sue 24, 180–1
Joseph 158–9, 172
Joseph of Arimathea 148

Josephus 57, 99, 102–3, 108, 115, 121, 137, 187, 188, 194–8, 199, 235 n.37
historical veracity of 187, 188, 196, 198
Joyce, Paul xxii, xxvii, 96
Judaea 189–205
'Cave of Letters' excavations 225–6, 227–8, 233, 235
dress in 225–33, 235–6
Life of Brian portrayal of 107–8, 111, 184
military artefacts, discovery of 108–10
rebel groups in 186, 198–200
Roman occupation *see* Romans
Second Temple period 57, 58, 108, 168–9
social class in 235–6
see also Roman army; Romans
Judaism 77, 162–3
beard, significance in 175–6
burial practices in 148–9
and cultural interpretation 77–81, 177
Gentile prophecies in 162–3
and Jesus' Jewishness 76, 77–81
midrash 96
stoning practice in 177–8
see also Judaea
Judas 7, 16, 87, 182, 214
Judas the Galilean 198–9, 200
Judith (character in *Life of Brian*) 7, 16, 33, 34, 35, 71, 121, 124, 169, 181–3
as Mary Magdalene 7, 34, 182
Justin Martyr 231

Kalmar, Ivan Davidson 223–4
King of Kings 7, 8, 10, 15, 47, 96–7, 98, 222–3
Kirk, J. R. Daniel 77
Kirkup, James 22, 58, 61
Klint, Stefan 96
Kreitzer, Larry xxvi–xxvii, 66, 95
Kubrick, Stanley 122

Landis, Deborah Nadoolman 222–3
Landy, Marcia 168
Last Temptation of Christ 7, 8, 11, 13, 126, 223 n.7, 230 n.23
Lemon, Denis 22
Levine, Amy-Jill 101
Levites 100

Levy, Leonard 57
Life of Brian
  alien abduction scene 94–5, 98, *163*
  apocalyptic preachers, scene in 142–3,
    144
  audience of 12
  banning attempts of 24
  beards, significance of, in 176–7
  blasphemy in *see under* blasphemy
  Brian *see under* Brian (character)
  costuming in xv, 221, 233–7
  critique of xv, xxvi, 6, 12, 13–15, 20, 70,
    75, 141–2
  crucifixion scene *see under* crucifixion
  as cultural change marker 129, 131
  cultural/social context of 12, 74–5, 94,
    95, 179
  deleted scenes 35–6, 39, 60, 215–16
  film intentions (Pythons') 25, 27, 28, 30,
    31, 64, 76, 128
  film success 4–7, 8, 13, 25–6, 43 n.2
  funding of 26
  gender and sexuality in 167–84
  generic dimension of 12, 13–14, 16–17,
    18
  Gospels, use in 9, 31, 76
  Jesus *see under* Jesus (character)
  Judaism, depiction of, in 177–8, 214–15
  Judith see under Judith (character)
  leper scene in 49, 52
  Mandy *see under* Mandy (character)
  mistaken identity plot in 207–8, 217–18,
    219
  nativity scene 15, 30, 45, 72, 89, 97,
    170–1
  'Otto' outtake in 35–6, 215–16
  People's Front of Judaea (PFJ) 33, 37,
    52, 107, 108, 121, 137, 176, 186, 215
  Pontius Pilate *see under* Pontius Pilate
    (character)
  religiosity, portrayal in 85–6
  Romans, portrayal of 107, 108, 117–19,
    185–6, 205, 214, 236–7
  satire/parody in 36, 43, 45, 49, 50, 51–4,
    118–19, 143, 144, 147, 149, 150
  Sermon on the Mount scene 8, 30, 38,
    47, 51, 83–4, 96, 97, 119, 144–5, 146,
    147, 236
  Transfiguration scene 97–8

  women in beards in 55, 59, 81, 103, 119,
    169, 171, 175–8
  see also blasphemy; Muggeridge/
    Stockwood interview
Lipton, Diana xxvii, 96
Loftus, Elizabeth 145
Lohmeyer, Ernst 218–19

McKellen, Ian 61
McLaren, James 187
Maeder, Edward 222 n.2
Magi 169–70, 213
Mandy (character in *Life of Brian*) 7, 14, 29,
  33, 35, 49, 71, 99, 100, 135, 139, 158,
  169–75, 181, 182, 183, 208–9, 217
  'historical' 99, 103, 105, 170, 171, 173
  Jewish mother stereotype in 174–5, 183
  and Mary 7, 71
  sexual identity in 169–70, 171
  virgin query of 174
Martha 171
Mary, mother of Jesus 7, 158–9, 171, 172,
  173, 174, 209
  as a virgin 158, 159, 166, 172, 174, 209
Mary Magdalene 7, 171, 182
Masada, Siege of (73–74 CE) 35, 109, 111,
  137, 225, 230
Mason, Steve 38
Meaning of Life, The 30, 34
Meier, John 79
Middleton, Kate 63
Milligan, Spike 8
Monty Python and the Holy Grail 5, 6, 14,
  20, 27, 30, 73, 168
  and *Spamalot* 27
Monty Python's Flying Circus 168
Mortimer, John 22
Moses 44, 45, 97, 153
  blasphemy against 57
  and *Wholly Moses* 43–53
Moxnes, Halvor 218
Muggeridge, Malcolm xv, 3–4, 5, 20–39, 72,
  75, 76, 84, 105
Muggeridge/Stockwood interview xv, 3, 20,
  21–2, 23, 24–39, 72, 75, 76, 84, 105
  criticisms of 22, 24–36, 72
  parody 21, 27–8
  establishment power, use in 37, 41
multiculturalism 80–1

Nash, David 60
neoliberalism 75, 80
Nero 125, 188, 197, 203
New Testament scholarship 85–8
    gender in 179
    and iconopoeic religiosity 85
    religious agenda in 88
    tradition and historical fact in 87–8,
        151–66
Nicene Creed 96
Not the Nine O'Clock News parody 21, 27–8,
    32, 105
Novenson, Matthew 154

O'Brien, Denis 26
Otto (Python) 8, 35, 39, 60, 80, 215–16

Palin, Michael xv, xxii, 3, 20–4, 25, 27, 28,
    29, 30, 32, 49, 76, 120, 128
    Diaries 22, 23, 37, 26, 59–60, 64
    Radio 4 interview 29, 37, 39, 105
parodic inversion, concept of 32
parody xv, 45, 50, 142, 150, 178
    and biblical films 43–54
    and historical truth 142–3, 149, 150
    in *Life of Brian* 38, 43, 45, 49, 50, 51–4,
        118–19, 143, 144, 149, 150
    and pastiche 45–6
    and satire 51, 52–3
    see also Wholly Moses
Paul, St. 151–66, 179
    apocalyptic tradition in 155, 164
    Gentiles and Judaism 162–4
    Jesus as Christ/Messiah in 154–62
    Letters xv, 151–3
Petheg, Hazel 234
Pharisees 103, 104, 105, 122, 210, 214, 223,
    224 n.8, 235
Plautus 120
Plunkett, Walter 221–2
Pontius Pilate 145, 147–8, 149–50, 156, 165,
    196–7, 201, 213, 214
Pontius Pilate (character in *Life of Brian*) 7,
    16, 33, 88, 113, 118, 122, 185, 205,
    208, 214, 236–7
Popović, Mladen 131
Pullman, Philip 75
Putin, Vladimir 110, 111
Pythagoras 136

reception criticism xix
reception exegesis xviii, xix, xxvii, 66–7, 93,
    94, 96, 106
reception history xvii–xix, xxvi, 94, 95,
    129
redaction xviii
Reed, Jonathan 101
Reinhartz, Adele 14, 36, 182
resurrection 89, 95
Rice, Tim 20, 23, 26, 27, 29, 32
Roman army 108, 109–11, 188
    and Gamala excavations 110
Romans xv, 107, 108, 109–10, 111, 118,
    148–9, 176, 179, 185–206
    Judaean hatred, question of xv, 187, 201,
        204–5
    militancy against 187, 199–200, 201
    occupation of Judaea 108, 131–2, 137,
        185, 186, 188, 189, 192–205, 214
Rosen, A. xxv
Roussin, Lucille 231

Saroglou, Vassilis 84
Satyricon of Petronius 147
Saunders, Ed 87
Schachter, Daniel 146
Schilbrack, Kevin 64, 184
Schneider, Stephen 25
Schürer, Emil 218
Sicarii 108, 109, 198, 199
Scorsese, Martin 7, 11, 13, 126
Scott, James C. 118
Sermon on the Mount 8, 40, 171
    see also under *Life of Brian*
Shepherd, David 32, 131
Sherlock, David 31
Simon of Cyrene 9
Smith, Mel 21, 27
Spartacus 10, 33, 47, 122
Spikings, B. 22
Staley, G. 11
Stephenson, Pamela 21
Stern, Richard C. 172–3
Stockwood, Mervyn xv, 3, 20–2, 23, 24–41,
    72, 75, 76, 84, 85, 105, 113, 126
    see also Muggeridge/Stockwood
        interview
Stuckenbruck, Loren 134, 135, 136
synoptic Gospels 98, 103

Tatum, W. Barnes 16
Taylor, Joan E. 20–1
Teacher of Righteousness xv, 127, 128,
    129–31, 133–40
  conflict times, use in 137
  discursive construction of 137–8
  identity, scholarship of 128, 129–30,
    133–40
  and *Life of Brian* insights 133, 134,
    135–6, 137, 138–40
  and life of Jesus 128, 136, 140
  use of sobriquet 133–4, 135
Telford, William xv, xxv, 47
Ten Commandments 46, 47–8
Thatcher, Margaret 74–5
Timothy 173
Tollerton, David 93
Transfiguration 97–8
  see also ascension
Turner, K. xxii

Veblen, Thorstein 233 n.33
Vermes, Geza 57, 77, 87

Walker, Alexander 21
Walsh, Richard 11, 73, 182
Weis, Gary 44, 49
Whitehouse, Mary 22, 58–9, 75
Wholly Moses 43–53
Williams, Rowan 28
Witherington, Ben 79
women
  1st century Jewish 101, 109, 171, 175,
    183, 184
  Life of Brian characterisation 167–75,
    178–84
  and wisdom 182
  see also characters Judith; Mandy; Mary,
    mother of Jesus
Woodhead, Linda 65
Wright, N. T. 79, 81, 87

Yadin, Yigael 225, 227, 228, 230, 231

Zealots 199
Žižek, Slavoj 80–1